VOLUME TW

SACRED PLACES

NEW YORK AND PENNSYLVANIA

A Comprehensive Guide to Early LDS Historical Sites

Series Titles

NEW ENGLAND AND EASTERN CANADA
NEW YORK AND PENNSYLVANIA

Other Titles Planned for the Series

OHIO AND ILLINOIS
MISSOURI
IOWA AND NEBRASKA
WYOMING AND UTAH

VOLUME TWO

SACRED PLACES

NEW YORK AND PENNSYLVANIA

A Comprehensive Guide to Early LDS Historical Sites

LaMar C. Berrett,
General Editor

Larry C. Porter

DESERET BOOK

Library of Congress Catalog Card Number 99-72525

ISBN 1-57008-667-2 (hardback)

ISBN 1-57008-668-0 (paperback)

Printed in the United States of America   72082-6596

10   9   8   7   6   5   4   3   2   1

CONTENTS

PREFACE

When the Prophet Moses came to the mountain of God and the burning bush, the Lord said unto him, "Put off thy shoes from off thy feet, for the place whereon thou standest is holy ground" (Ex. 3:5).

Through the ages, the locations at which sacred historical events occurred have traditionally become holy. How holy or sacred a site is depends on the understanding of those beholding it. Elizabeth Barrett Browning wrote that "Earth's crammed with heaven, / And every common bush afire with god; / But only he who sees, takes off his shoes— / The rest sit round it and pluck blackberries" (*Aurora Leigh*, Book 7, 820–23).

The Church has a long tradition of recognizing and recording sacred places and events. In 1838 the Lord said to Joseph Smith, "Let the city, Far West, be a holy and consecrated land unto me; and it shall be called most holy, for the ground upon which thou standest is holy" (D&C 115:7). Even earlier, when the Church was organized on April 6, 1830, the Prophet was told that "there shall be a record kept among you" (D&C 21:1). Since those early times, places and events central to the Church's struggles and successes have been sanctified and recorded. *Sacred Places* was written to bring the history and geography of the early period of the Church to life.

Following the history and movement of the Saints from their early days in New York through to their settlement in the valley of the Great Salt Lake, this series will function as a valuable resource for academic historians and amateur Church history enthusiasts alike. *Sacred Places* provides detailed maps, interesting narratives, and numerous photographs in its effort to document the many places made sacred by the faith and testimonies of past generations of Saints. The comprehensive nature of the guide encourages readers to follow in the footsteps of Joseph Smith, Brigham Young, and other Church leaders, or to seek out the paths of their own ancestors. The series also enables armchair tourists to vicariously visit the many magnificent places relevant to Church history.

Sacred Places is the culmination of over 25 years of research and study. Its authors, all university professors, have devoted much of their lives to this work—to the work of preserving and documenting the legacy of our literal and spiritual ancestors. By purchasing and preserving many of these sacred sites, modern prophets have encouraged member and nonmember alike to visit locations important to our history. Visiting sites such as the Sacred Grove, the Hill Cumorah, Adam-ondi-Ahman, or Carthage Jail enables us to understand the history of the Church in terms of the real places and real people who witnessed the very real and sacred events of the Restoration.

ACKNOWLEDGMENTS

So many individuals have contributed to the completion of *Sacred Places* that it is impractical, even impossible, to give personal credit to all those who deserve it. A blanket "thank you" is given to all who have helped in any way.

Brigham Young University's College of Religious Education, Department of Church History and Doctrine, and Religious Studies Center have been instrumental in the realization of *Sacred Places*. Through various means—time, student assistants, secretarial help, research grants, and various other forms of financial aid—these organizations and the people associated with them have been indispensable.

Gratitude is expressed to past and present General Authorities of The Church of Jesus Christ of Latter-day Saints who have ensured that significant Church history sites have been purchased and preserved for the edification and enjoyment of future generations. General editor LaMar C. Berrett is particularly grateful to President Spencer W. Kimball, who told him that "we need to know and tell the truth about our Church history sites." President Kimball also related a fable concerning the Joseph Smith home in Palmyra, NY. "Some used to say that when the angel Moroni appeared to Joseph Smith the first time, it occurred in the Joseph Smith frame home," he stated, adding "but we know that this is not true." This statement has impressed upon the editor the great responsibility he has in providing correct information regarding our tremendous heritage and its relation to these sacred sites. *Sacred Places* has been significantly impacted by this great prophet's interest and encouragement. Special thanks are also given to those writers, researchers, journal keepers, Church historians, and others who laid the groundwork upon which *Sacred Places* has been constructed.

We are grateful to the staffs and administrators of the many repositories who have been so helpful in our research. Especially gracious were the staffs of the Brigham Young University Harold B. Lee Library and the LDS Church Archives. We are also grateful for the efforts of archaeologists Dale Berge, Ray T. Matheny, and Virginia Harrington in conducting archaeological digs at various Church history sites.

A special thanks is given to Wilford C. Wood who spent much of his life purchasing and preserving sites and objects pertaining to the life of the Prophet Joseph Smith.

The authors also acknowledge and thank Thomas Child for his help in fine-tuning the maps that LaMar C. Berrett created for the various volumes.

We are grateful to the personnel at Deseret Book Company, who have helped bring this series to publication. We especially acknowledge Cory H. Maxwell, Jana Erickson, Richard Erickson, Laurie Cook, Preston Draper, and Peter B. Gardner for their efforts in editing and publishing this important information.

Finally we thank our wives and children for their patience and support over the past 25 years as we have labored to bring about this monumental work.

INFORMATION CONTAINED
IN *SACRED PLACES*

Several symbols have been employed in *Sacred Places*. These symbols include small black squares ■ (both in text and on maps) indicating sites with direct ties to LDS history. Small black circles ● indicate important sites not directly related to LDS Church history.

Because of the voluminous nature of the information sources used by the authors, abbreviations were used in the text to identify various sources. Along with noting the sources used in preparing the book, the authors have also included many references for the reader who is interested in learning more about a particular event or Church history site. A complete bibliography with an alphabetic listing of abbreviations is included in the back of the volume. Also included is a list of abbreviations used to identify sources of photographs and other illustrations.

Many maps and other illustrations, including photographs, have been included in an effort to help the reader to locate, visualize, and more fully appreciate the numerous sites identified in *Sacred Places*.

NEW YORK

Larry C. Porter
LaMar C. Berrett

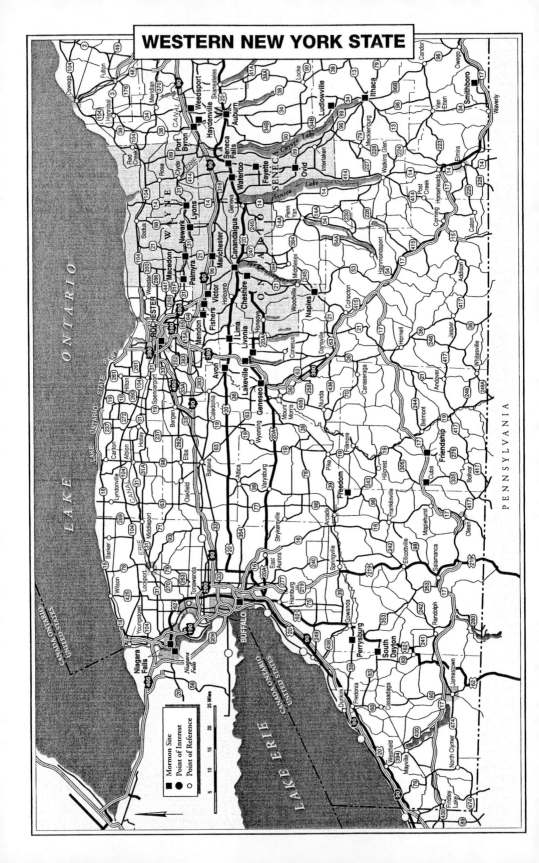

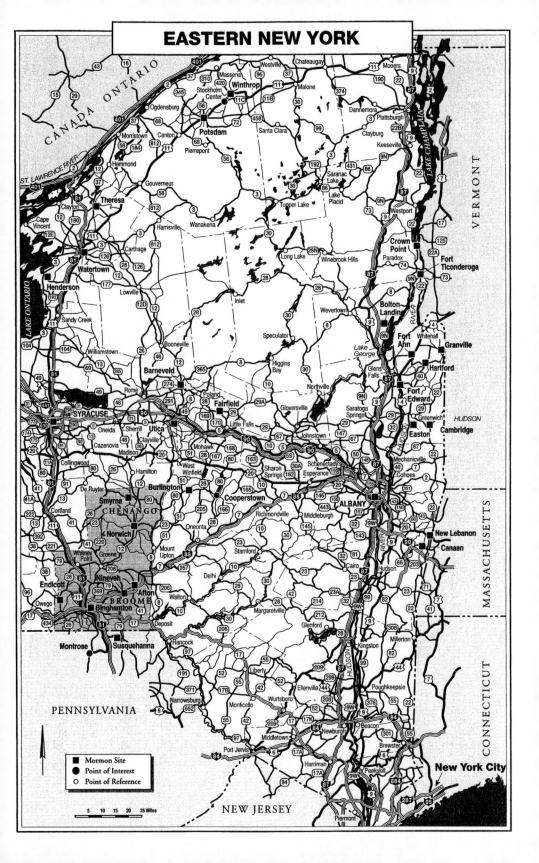

EASTERN NEW YORK

INTRODUCTION TO NEW YORK

Heavily populated New York State is located on the east coast of the United States, mostly west of the New England states. Lakes Erie and Ontario form its western boundary, and the Hudson River flows south near its eastern boundary. New York State takes its name from its original settlement, New York City, and it was the eleventh of the original thirteen states. Because of its economic and political influence, it became known as the "Empire State."

Although skyscrapers are apt symbols of New York, the state also has vast native forests and wild beauty. It is a region of great physical contrasts, along with many varieties of urban and rural life.

Tribes of Indians, such as the six nations of the Iroquois Confederacy—the Oneidas, Mohawks, Cayugas, Senecas, Onondagas, and Tuscaroras—inhabited the area. Apparently **Giovanni da Verrazano,** an Italian in the service of the French king Francis I, was the first European to explore the area. While searching for a northwest passage to the Orient in 1524, he discovered the island of Manhattan. **Henry Hudson,** an Englishman, was the first European to actually land on Manhattan. He also was trying to find a passage to the Orient while working for the Dutch East India Company. Hudson later explored the Albany area in 1609 by sailing up the river that now bears his name.

In 1613 Dutch explorer **Adriaen Block** was the first European to live on Manhattan Island. The area was initially called New Netherland and later New Amsterdam. In 1624, 30 Dutch families settled in the province, eight of them in Manhattan. For 114 years, 1669–1783, Great Britain controlled the area, and it was renamed New York after the Duke of York.

One-third of the battles of the **American Revolution** took place in New York. George Washington fought in the Manhattan area, which fell to the British. However, in 1783, after the British surrendered at Yorktown and a peace treaty was signed, Washington returned to Manhattan in triumph. New York City was the nation's capital from 1785 to 1790, and Washington became the first president of the United States of America when he took his oath of office on the balcony of Federal Hall at the corner of Nassau and Wall Streets in 1789.

New York is a leading state in manufacturing, shipping, theater, music, television, publishing, and finance. Its largest city, New York City, is one of the most renowned cities of the world.

Latter-day Saints in New York State

Sometimes referred to as the "Cradle of Mormonism," New York State was indeed the birthplace of the restored gospel of Jesus Christ in the latter days. The family of the **Prophet Joseph Smith** moved from Vermont into the Palmyra, NY, area in 1816, and it was there that young Joseph was directed by the Savior to organize His Church once again on the earth. Heavenly visitations, visions, and manifestations led to the formal organization of The Church of Jesus Christ of Latter-day Saints in Fayette, NY, on Apr. 6, 1830. (Within a year of the Church's organization, the followers of Joseph Smith moved to Kirtland, OH, then to Independence, MO, Nauvoo, IL, and finally to Salt Lake City, UT, in 1847.) From that small group of six men who first met to do the will of God and to incorporate a religious society according to law, the Church has seen very rapid growth. In a mere 168 years the Church that was organized in a small log house in western New York has expanded manyfold into a worldwide Church of over 11 million members.

NEW YORK CITY

LaMar C. Berrett

Immediately after the Church was organized in 1830, missionaries began preaching in New York City. Joseph Smith visited the city in 1832 and 1836 and was one of the first missionaries to preach here.

Thomas B. Marsh from 1814 to 1818 and Orson Pratt in the 1820s both lived in New York City before they joined the Church, but it was not until 1837 that an enduring Mormon presence in New York City became a reality.

Elijah Fordham was one of the **first Mormons** in New York City. He was living here when the first **American and Canadian missionaries** bound for Great Britain arrived in June of 1837. He was the only known Latter-day Saint in the city. Fordham rendered assistance to the seven missionaries (HC 2:494–95) and a month later became a successful missionary companion to Parley P. Pratt. As the missionaries called to Great Britain in 1837 assembled in New York City, they did missionary work and published a broadside titled "Timely Warnings," which they distributed on the street and sent to all of the 180 ministers in the city.

Elder Parley P. Pratt arrived in New York City in July 1837 to do missionary work and to preside over the Church in New York. He published the book *A Voice of Warning* here the same year. Parley P. Pratt and Elijah Fordham labored together as missionaries and participated in many of the first baptisms in the area, including those of three local New Yorkers: **David Rogers, Wandle Mace,** and **Joshua Parker.** These men and their families became pillars of the Church in New York City. In Apr. 1838, Parley P. Pratt led a small group of Saints from New York City to Missouri, and his brother Orson Pratt presided over the Church in the East in Parley's stead. Before Parley left in April, he selected Wandle Mace to be the first president of the New York City Branch (JWMa 21–22). In May

1839, Joseph Smith appointed John P. Greene to replace Orson Pratt. Lucian R. Foster, a photographer, was president of the New York Branch from 1841 to 1843, after which George T. Leach was branch president (HC 5:549–52).

In the fall of 1839, members of the Quorum of the Twelve gathered in New York City before sailing together to Great Britain on Mar. 9, 1840. They preached the gospel to the New Yorkers while waiting for the remaining Apostles to arrive.

Successful missionary work in Great Britain led to the first immigration of Saints to the United States in 1840. During the 19th century thousands of converts came through the customshouse in New York City as they traveled toward the Salt Lake Valley. Church emigration agents were assigned to work in the city, and Church meetings were held with small numbers of Saints. In 1843, Elder Parley P. Pratt presided over the Church in the eastern states, and in 1844 he served as the Church emigration agent and the editor[1] of an LDS periodical, *The Prophet,* which began publication May 18, 1844. The *New York Messenger,* a continuation of *The Prophet,* was first published July 5, 1845. Parley and Orson Pratt were editors of the first issue, and then Samuel Brannan continued as editor until printing was terminated Nov. 15, 1845. The press and printing materials were then taken aboard the *Brooklyn* with Samuel Brannan and later used to publish the *California Star,* San Francisco's first newspaper.

By June 1845, Parley P. Pratt was discouraged with the prospects of the Church's growth in New York. He wrote to the Twelve in Nauvoo that after working hard for six months, he felt as if he were done with the city (HC 7:425–26).

In July 1845, Elder Orson Pratt of the Twelve again succeeded his brother Parley as the president of the Eastern States Mission of the Church. He edited the *Prophetic Almanac,* which was published at the office of the *New York Messenger.*

In Sept. 1845, Elder Orson Hyde, an Apostle, shipped 4,000 yards of canvas from New York City to Nauvoo to be used for a temporary tabernacle. In Dec. 1845, Orson Pratt purchased 42 Allen revolving six-shooters to use in the pioneer trek west and transported them to Nauvoo. (The "pepperboxes" were like the one Joseph Smith had in Carthage Jail.)

---

[1] Other editors were G. T. Leach, William Smith, and Samuel Brannan.

On Feb. 4, 1846, **Elder Samuel Brannan** left New York Harbor with about 235 Saints aboard the ship *Brooklyn.* From 1846 to 1848 Jesse C. Little and Wm. I. Appleby had charge of the Saints in the eastern states.

In 1854, **Elder John Taylor** of the Twelve was appointed to preside over the Saints in the Eastern States Mission and to publish a weekly newspaper for the Church. The first issue of *The Mormon,* with Taylor as editor, was printed Feb. 17, 1855. It ran until Sept. 19, 1857, when it was discontinued because of the Utah War.

Very little missionary work was done in New York City for the next 30 years. In the 1880s New York State was a part of the Northern States Mission. In 1893, Elder Job Pingree reopened the Eastern States Mission, with headquarters in Brooklyn. The **New York Stake** was organized by President Heber J. Grant on Sept. 9, 1934, and was the first stake of the Church organized east of the Mississippi River. Membership of the stake at the time of organization was 1,548. The stake included New York City, Long Island, Westchester Co., and parts of Connecticut and New Jersey (CN Dec. 23, 1984, 5).

Well-known mission presidents of the Eastern States Mission headquartered in Brooklyn include Ben E. Rich (1908–13), B. H. Roberts (1922–27), and James H. Moyle (1928–30). The mission headquarters were later moved to Fifth Avenue near Central Park.

The first LDS-owned chapel had been a synagogue owned by the Central Christian Church. It was located at 142 W. 81st St., $\frac{1}{2}$ block away from Central Park. It was purchased in 1945 and was used for 30 years before a new chapel was dedicated at 2 Lincoln Square. A Baptist congregation purchased the old chapel from the Church (CN Dec. 23, 1984, 5).

Although **Manhattan** is the most famous part of New York City, there are also four other boroughs located on three sides of Manhattan Island. The **Bronx,** immediately north of Manhattan, is the only part of New York City attached to the mainland. **Queens** and **Brooklyn** are both located on the west end of Long Island, and **Staten Island** is located to the SW of Manhattan. Brooklyn is the most populous borough with 2.25 million residents. Trade, business, finance, and the cultural arts blend together to make New York City one of the most influential of all cities.

Geographically, New York City was relatively small in the first part of the 19th century. When Joseph Smith visited the city in 1832, it consisted mainly of that portion of Manhattan Island from

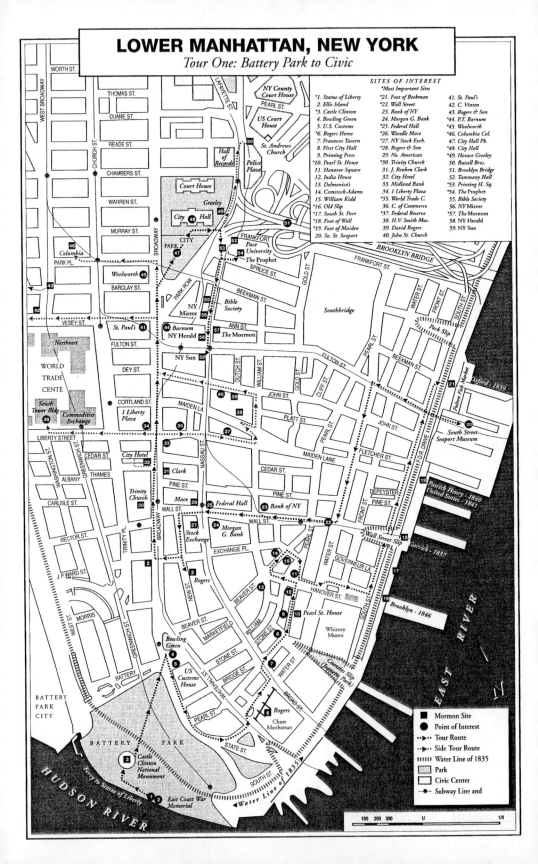

LOWER MANHATTAN, NEW YORK
Tour One: Battery Park to Civic

SITES OF INTEREST
Most Important Sites

*1. Statue of Liberty
2. Ellis Island
*3. Castle Clinton
4. Bowling Green
5. U.S. Customs
*6. Rogers Home
7. Fraunces Tavern
8. First City Hall
9. Printing Press
*10. Pearl St. House
11. Hanover Square
12. India House
13. Delmonico's
14. Comstock-Adams
15. William Kidd
*16. Old Slip
*17. South St. Port
*18. Foot of Wall
*19. Foot of Maiden
20. So. St. Seaport

*21. Foot of Beekman
*22. Wall Street
23. Bank of NY
24. Morgan G. Bank
*25. Federal Hall
*26. Wandle Mace
*27. NY Stock Exch.
*28. Rogers & Son
29. No. American
*30. Trinity Church
31. J. Reuben Clark
32. City Hotel
33. Midland Bank
34. 1 Liberty Plaza
*35. World Trade C.
36. C. of Commerce
*37. Federal Reserve
38. H.V. Smith Mus.
39. David Rogers
40. John St. Church

41. St. Paul's
42. C. Vinten
43. Rogers & Son
*44. P.T. Barnum
*45. Woolworth
*46. Columbia Col.
47. City Hall Pk.
*48. City Hall
*49. Horace Greeley
50. Russell Bros.
51. Brooklyn Bridge
52. Tammany Hall
*53. Printing H. Sq.
*54. The Prophet
55. Bible Society
56. NY Mirror
*57. The Mormon
58. NY Herald
59. NY Sun

Legend:
- ■ Mormon Site
- ● Point of Interest
- ···▶··· Tour Route
- –·–·– Side Tour Route
- ‖‖‖‖ Water Line of 1835
- ▨ Park
- ▢ Civic Center
- ●–●– Subway Line and

21st St. south to Battery Park. This is an area about three miles long and two miles wide between the Hudson and East Rivers. Farmland was located north of this small area.

In 1800 the population of New York City was only 60,000, but phenomenal growth followed. By 1852 the population was 630,000, and by 1900 it had reached 3,437,200, spread over five boroughs. By 1991 the population of New York City and nearby areas was 18.1 million, the largest urban center in the United States.

Early population increase caused the city to expand north on Manhattan Island. By 1902 the whole of Manhattan was filled with buildings, and the era of skyscrapers began. For half a century the Empire State Building was the tallest building in the world and the main feature of the Manhattan skyline. Built in 1931, it had a grace, elegance, and strength that made it famous worldwide.

This magnificent city has been very important in the lives of thousands of Latter-day Saints. Identifying LDS historical sites should serve the visitor by marking the setting of important events in the early history of the restored Church.

The offices and chapel of the New York New York Stake are located at 2 Lincoln Square, directly across the street from the Lincoln Center at Broadway and 65th Street. This building was built between 1972 and 1975 and serves as headquarters for the stake, meetinghouse for all of the Manhattan area wards and branches, and home of the Church's New York public affairs office. It also houses an extensive family history library. Visitors are welcome.

Lower Manhattan Walking or Auto Tours

Tour One: Battery Park to Civic Center

The best starting point for a Lower Manhattan Mormon Walking Tour is **Battery Park** on the southern tip of Manhattan Island. The walk is 2.7 miles, and with an hour-long lunch stop at South Street Seaport and an hour's visit to the New York Stock Exchange or the Federal Reserve Bank, the tour requires approximately five hours. If you include the Statue of Liberty and Ellis Island, another two to three hours are necessary. If you take the first boat of the day to the Statue of Liberty, then the following tour can be easily done within an eight-hour day.

● **1. THE STATUE OF LIBERTY.** The Statue of Liberty has greeted generations of immigrants and others to America. It is the work of sculptor **Frederic-Auguste Bartholdi** and the great structural engineer **Alexander Gustave Eiffel.** The statue was presented to the people of the United States as a gift from France and was dedicated by President Grover Cleveland in 1886. The statue was refurbished for her one hundredth birthday in 1986.

The 151-foot-tall copper-plate statue, the tallest structure built in its day, stands on a 154-foot-high pedestal and weighs 225 tons. The index finger is eight feet long. The pedestal stands on the walls of Fort Wood, completed before 1812. Liberty is represented by a crowned woman trampling beneath her feet the broken shackles of tyranny. Her right hand holds the symbolic torch of liberty 305 feet above sea level.

A bronze plaque on the statue bears lines by the American poet Emma Lazarus:

> Give me your tired, your poor,
> Your huddled masses yearning to breathe free,
> The wretched refuse of your teeming shore,
> Send these, the homeless, tempest-tost to me,
> I lift my lamp beside the golden door.

An elevator will take visitors up the first 10 stories; then there is a 168-step (12-story) climb to the crown of the statue for a bird's-eye view. Tickets for the Liberty Island Ferry are purchased at the Castle Clinton in Battery Park. If you plan on climbing to the top of the statue, it is wise to be one of the first off the first ferry of the day and the first to the base of the statue for the climb. The museum at the base of the statue is excellent.

● **2. ELLIS ISLAND NATIONAL MUSEUM OF IMMIGRATION.** This museum is located in the original main building (1897) of Ellis Island. It traces the history of immigration to America. The 27-acre Ellis Island took the place of Castle Garden as a processing center for immigrants from 1892 to 1954. Approximately 12 million immigrants were processed here. Access to the island is by the Liberty Island Ferry (CN May 14, 1988, 11).

■ **3. CASTLE CLINTON NATIONAL MONUMENT AND CASTLE GARDEN.** Castle Clinton is located in the 21-acre Battery Park at the south end of Broadway, and at the confluence of the Hudson and East Rivers. From 1807 to 1811, Fort Clinton was built on a small island just off Manhattan's southern shoreline. In 1824 it was transformed into **Castle Garden** and used for opera and entertainment.

Between 1855 and 1892 the buildings were used as an immigrant landing depot. Many Latter-day Saints passed through Castle Garden as they entered America. The first LDS immigrant ship, ***Britannia***, left Liverpool June 6, 1840, and landed in New York City on July 17, 1840. There were 41 Saints on board, with John Moon as their leader. Two other LDS immigrant ships landed in New York in 1840 and 1841 with a total of 330 passengers.

Between 1841 and 1855, nearly all (81) LDS immigrant ships went to New Orleans. After 1855, when Castle Garden became the

Latter-day Saint immigrants at Castle Garden, the New York Custom House (1878)

principal immigrant landing depot, nearly all LDS immigrant ships came into the port of New York after their six-week transatlantic journey. Between 1855 and 1900, 232 LDS immigrant ships docked in eastern ports: 214 in New York, 10 in Boston, and 8 in Philadelphia. An average of about seven LDS immigrant ships came into NYC every year. Those members who would form the Willie Handcart Company in 1856 came through the New York harbor. In addition to LDS immigrants, there were many LDS missionaries and General Authorities of the Church who passed through Castle Garden.

In 1870, land was filled in between the tiny island and Manhattan, resulting in Battery Park. Fort Clinton has been restored as a national monument and is named after DeWitt Clinton, mayor of New York City, governor of the state of New York, and the person most responsible for the completion of the Erie Canal. After **Ellis Island** opened in 1892, Castle Garden housed the New York Aquarium until 1941. Note the display in a small museum at Castle Clinton.

The **Staten Island Ferry Terminal** is located on the SE corner of Battery Park, and statues of Emma Lazarus, Giovanni da Verrazano (the first European to discover Manhattan), and Peter Minuit are located in the park (see site no. 5 below).

- **4. Bowling Green and Kennedy House.** An egg-shaped lawn area directly north of the statue of Peter Minuit was the **Bowling Green,** the city's first park. Its 1771 fence is still intact. This area is where the first Dutch settlers lived. In 1776 citizens tore down a gilded lead statue of King George III here and melted it to make bullets for use in the Revolution. This was five days after the Declaration of Independence was read in City Hall Park.

  Across the street west of Bowling Green is No. 1 Broadway, the site of the **Captain Archibald Kennedy House** (1771–1882). It was once the Revolutionary War headquarters of George Washington (1776).

- **5. U.S. Customshouse.** The U.S. Customshouse, located on the east side of State Street across from Battery Park, is built on the site of the **Old Fort of New Amsterdam.** This is near the site where, according to tradition, Peter Minuit of the Dutch West India Company bought Manhattan Island from the Algonquian Indians in 1626 for 24 dollars' worth of goods. The building was finished in 1907 with a monumental facade of white Tennessee marble and walls of Maine granite.

- **6. David White Rogers Home Site.** The second David White Rogers home site in New York City (1833–35) was at No. 1 Water Street near the Battery. That address is now No. 1 New York Plaza, where Chase Manhattan Bank is located. Part of the front yard of the Rogerses' lot is now part of Water Street (PEM), and the house was located just south of the front of the Chase Manhattan Bank building (PEM; LCD 1833–35).

  David White Rogers was a carpenter-joiner with a shop at nearby 34 New Street and was one of four residents who were pillars of the early Church in New York City. The other three were

Elijah Fordham, Wandle Mace, and **Joshua Parker.**

David and Martha Rogers moved to New York City in 1830, where David was the owner of **Rogers and Son, House Carpenters and Joiners,** located at 34 New Street, close to the New York Stock Exchange building. In 1835 David moved his family to 515 Greenwich Street in NYC and contin-

David White Rogers home site at #1 Water St. His house and lot were at the right side in this photo. (1990)

ued his cabinet business. After David saw Joseph Smith during a special spiritual experience and Martha had a dream in which she saw **Elijah Fordham** and **Parley P. Pratt,** the couple accepted missionaries, Elder Pratt and Fordham, into their home in 1837. The David Rogers family was baptized Dec. 19, 1837, in the East River, as a part of the first NYC converts to the LDS Church. Latter-day Saint Sabbath meetings were held in the Rogerses' home. The Rogers family moved to Nauvoo, then to Salt Lake City, and finally to Provo, UT.

Hannah Caroline, the eighth child of David and Martha, married Aaron Eugene Daniels, then, after Daniels apostatized and they divorced, in 1886 she became a plural wife of Abraham O. Smoot, Salt Lake City's first mayor. Hannah Caroline bore 11 children, and one of her great-grandchildren was **Barbara Bradshaw Smith,** general president of the Relief Society from 1974 to 1984 (APH 467–500; APPP 169–72).

● **7. Fraunces Tavern Museum.** At 54 Pearl Street, on the SE corner of Pearl and Broad Streets, is the Fraunces Tavern Museum, probably the oldest existing structure in NYC. Dating to 1719, it was originally a Neo-Georgian brick home owned by Stephen Delancey. It became Samuel Fraunces Tavern in 1762, and was restored in 1907. After the British evacuated New York in 1783, **General George Washington** resided here for 10 days and gave a farewell speech to his officers in the "Long Room" above the tavern on Dec. 4, 1783. The two top floors of the building currently house a museum with exhibits of early New York and the American Revolution. A restaurant is located on the bottom floor.

Pearl Street follows the original (1624) bank of the East River before it was filled in to make room for more buildings. **Broad Street** follows the line of the old canal and was once the main street of NYC.

- **8. FIRST CITY HALL SITE.** The First City Hall (*Stadt Huys,* New Amsterdam's first city hall) was built in 1642 as a tavern, but was

being used as the city hall by 1653. It was located at the head of Coenties Slip at 71–73 Pearl Street. It is believed that once a copper weather vane shaped like a rooster graced the top of the building. The rooster was a symbol of the Apostle Peter's denial (see Mark 14:66–72) and served as a reminder to residents of

New Amsterdam's first city hall, 1653, at 71–73 Pearl St. The crowing cock weather vane warned of the spiritual pitfalls that come to those who deny Christ (see Mark 14:68, 72).

the spiritual pitfalls that could result from any denial of Christ (AYP 18).

In 1836 the weather vane was presented to Washington Irving by a prominent Manhattan resident. It is now preserved at the New York Historical Society.

Archaeological excavations to the left of the city hall site have uncovered **Governor Lovelace's Tavern.** It is outlined with colored bricks.

- **9. FIRST PRINTING PRESS SITE.** The first printing press in NYC was located at 81 Pearl Street (west side) and is marked by a **plaque** erected in 1893 which reads: "On this site, William Bradford Jr., appointed public printer Apr. 10, 1693, established the first printing press in the colony of New York." The Cotton Exchange Building now stands on the site.

■ **10. PEARL STREET HOUSE SITE.** The Pearl Street House site, across the street from the first printing press site, was located at 88 Pearl Street on the east side of the street about halfway between Coenties Slip and Hanover Square. The left half of the front of the Pearl Street House was located where there currently is a truck dock at the back of a building, which faces Water Street at No. 7 Hanover Square (PEM; LCD 1837–38:413).

Pearl Street House, 1841. Nos. 88 and 89 were located at the center section of the building in 1832.

The Pearl Street House was a large boardinghouse (50' wide, about 100' long, and six stories high) for males and was one of the principal hotels in New York City when **Joseph Smith** stayed here on his first visit in the fall of 1832. He was accompanied by **Newel K. Whitney,** who was directed to negotiate a $15,000 loan to ensure the stability of the United Order Firm in Kirtland. Joseph Smith was

Pearl Street House site. The right side of this photo has two truck delivery doors separated by a white pillar. The right delivery door was No. 88 and the left delivery door was No. 89. This 50-foot span was the front of Pearl Street House. (1988)

also told by revelation from the Lord to warn the people in the East of the desolation that would come upon those who rejected the gospel (D&C 84:112–16; HC 1:270; CHC 1:284–85). They are the first known LDS missionaries to labor in New York City.

The dry goods merchants had their warehouses on Pearl Street, so the Pearl Street House was a convenient hotel for Whitney as he purchased goods for the Church stores. One writer indicated that on Pearl Street "the conveyance of merchandise to the different warehouses employs two thousand carts. Their passing and repassing produces a continual noise" (PWJS 671). While Whitney was

purchasing the dry goods, Joseph stayed part of the time in the
Pearl Street House and wrote a prophetic letter to his wife, Emma:

Oct 13 1832
Pearl Street House NY

My Dear Wife
     This day I have been walking through the most splendid part
of the City of New Y— the buildings are truly great and wonderful
to the astonishing of eve[r]y beholder and the language of my
heart is like this[.] can the great God of all the Earth maker of all
thing[s] magnificent and splendid be displeased with man for all
these great inventions saught out by them[?] my answer is no[.] it
can not be[,] seeing these works are calculated to mak[e] men
comfortable wise and happy[.] therefore not for the works can
the Lord be displeased[,] only aga[i]nst man is the anger of the
Lord Kindled because they Give him not the Glory[.] therefore
their iniquities shall be visited upon their heads and *their works
shall be burned up with unquenchable fire* [emphasis added]. . . . my
breast is filld with all the feelings and tenderness of a parent
and a Husband and could I be with you I would tell you many
things[.] yet when I reflect upon this great city like Ninev[a]h
not desearning their right hand from their left[,] yea more
then two hundred thousand souls[,] my bowels is filled with
compasion towards them and I am determined to lift up my
voice in this City and leave the Event with God who holdeth all
things in his hands and will not suffer an hair of our heads
unnoticed to fall to the ground[.] . . . I feel for you for I know
you[r] state[1] and that others do not but you must cumfort yourself knowing that God is your friend in heaven and that you
hav[e] one true and living friend on Earth your Husband[2]

Joseph Smith Jr

PS . . . Brother Whitney is received with great kindness by all
his old acquaintance[s.] he is faithful in prayr and fervant in

---

[1] Emma was expecting her fourth child, Joseph III.

[2] While Newel K. Whitney was purchasing goods for the Church mercantile business,
Joseph prayed and meditated in his hotel room; he then went onto the streets where he
met a young man from Jersey. Joseph taught him, and their conversation went on till late
at night. They became good friends, and Joseph did his missionary work.

spirit and we take great comfort together[.] there is about one hundred boarders and sometimes more in this house every day from one to two from all parts of the world[.] I remain your affectionate Husband until Death

Joseph Smith Junior

Emma Smith
Kirtland Geauga Co
Ohio. (PWJS 251–57, 671 [original letter in the RLDS Church Archives]; ENS [Dec. 1984]: 29–31)

Three years after this prophetic statement came the great New York City fire of Dec. 16, 1835. It burned the most prominent business area of the city, a quarter of a mile square, including about 600 stores. Many of the buildings had four to five stories and were filled with dry goods and hardware. The area from Broad Street to the East River and from Wall Street to the Coenties Slip was devastated. The fire started a block away from Pearl Street House where Joseph recorded the prophecy of the "unquenchable fire." The 17-degrees-below-zero temperature of Dec. 16 froze the water in the fire hydrants, and the fire was indeed "unquenchable." Philip Hone, mayor of NYC, said the fire was "the most awful calamity which has ever visited these United States" (AYP 58–62). Property loss was valued at 20 to 40 million dollars.

Because of the building of the Kirtland Temple and other economic forces, the Church was in financial distress in 1836. To get relief from New York creditors, Joseph Smith, Hyrum Smith, Oliver Cowdery, and Sidney Rigdon left Kirtland, July 25, 1836, and traveled by steamer and train to New York City, where they stayed for four days and took care of business matters, which included inquiry into printing notes for a Church bank in Kirtland (HC 2:463–64; SIS 1:432–33). Of this second visit to New York City, Joseph Smith recorded: "While in New York I visited the burnt district—the part of the city where it was estimated fifteen millions of property was consumed by fire on the 16th of December, 1835, according to the prediction of the ancient Prophets, that there should be 'fire and vapor of smoke' in the last days" (HC 2:464).

Joseph's letter of Oct. 13, 1832, and his statement after visiting the burned district of NYC in 1836 seem to indicate that Joseph felt the great fire of 1835 was a fulfillment of not only ancient prophecy

Monument commemorating the Great Fire of 1835, erected on the center of the front of Pearl St. House.

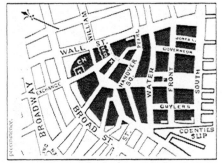

Map of Lower Manhattan showing the section of New York City destroyed by the Great Fire of 1835.

but also of his own prophecy three years before: "Their works shall be burned up with unquenchable fire."

Perhaps it is more than strange coincidence that when a monument consisting of a statue and tablet was made to commemorate the catastrophic New York City fire of 1835, it was erected on the Pearl Street House, wherein three years earlier, Joseph had written down his "unquenchable fire" prophecy in a letter (AYP 60). The monument is now located in the Harold V. Smith Museum of fire-fighting relics (see site no. 38). The Pearl Street House was saved from complete devastation and was in full operation after the fire.

- **11. HANOVER SQUARE.** Hanover Square was once called Printing House Square because **William Bradford Jr.** established the first printing press in the Colonies at 81 Pearl Street. The square is a small park located a half block north of Pearl Street House on Pearl Street. It was the principal business center of NYC in the 1830s, and the city's first newspaper, the *New York Mercury*, was published here starting in 1752. The East River once flowed into Old Slip and lapped the foundations of the SE side of the square.

- **12. INDIA HOUSE.** Located in the SW corner of the square between Stone and Pearl Streets is the India House. It was built in 1851 and housed the Hanover Bank from 1851 to 1854, the New York Cotton Exchange from 1870 to 1885, and at the time of this writing was a private club.

- **13. DELMONICO'S RESTAURANT.** Delmonico's Restaurant, established in the 1830s, has been famous for over 150 years. It is located NW of the India House on the corner of South William and Beaver Streets (56 Beaver St.).

- **14. COMSTOCK AND ADAMS STORE.** Located on the SW corner of Hanover and Beaver Streets, a half block north of Hanover Square, was the Comstock and Adams Store. This is where the Great New York Fire of 1835 started, as prophesied by Joseph Smith (PWJS 251–57, 691; AYP 53, 59–62).

- **15. CAPTAIN WILLIAM KIDD'S HOME SITE.** Scottish Captain William Kidd lived on the north side of the square on Beaver St. from 1691 to 1696. His home site is across the street from the Comstock and Adams Store site where the NYC fire of 1835 started. In 1701 Kidd was hanged in England for piracy and murder, and legends soon grew concerning Kidd's buried treasure and bloody deeds. Perhaps the most famous writing about Captain Kidd is Robert Louis Stevenson's *Treasure Island* (AYP 51).

- **16. "OLD SLIP" AND THE SHIP *BROOKLYN*.** "Old Slip" in the South Street Seaport was where the ship *Brooklyn* docked in 1846. It was a protected dock or wharf made by a finger of water as wide as two streets that protruded into the land from the East River to Pearl Street in 1624. The Old Slip area was filled in after the 1835 fire, and a "new" Franklin Market was built on the site where the water had been (between South and Front Streets). At the time of this writing this was the location of the 1st Precinct police station. The street located where sailing vessels once docked is named Old Slip (AYP 47, 52).

Old Slip St., Franklin Market, and 1836 dock.

It was in front of (east of) the "new" Franklin Market at the "foot" of Old Slip that the ship *Brooklyn* was docked in 1846 to load Mormon pioneers and ship crew who were sailing to California

(SCL Jan. 3, 21, 28; Feb. 4, 1846:1; NYCA Feb. 5, 1846; EvM Feb 5, 1846; NYP Feb 5., 1846; NYTr Feb. 6, 1846; NYH Feb. 5, 1846; PEM; DIA 21, no. 3:47–72). On Feb. 4, 1846, 230 Latter-day Saints (70 men, 60 women, 100 children), a crew of 16, plus 4 others, boarded the *Brooklyn* to begin the longest point-to-point voyage in the world, in time and distance. Their six-month, 15,000-mile voyage took them from New York City around the Cape Horn of South America, to Hawaii to deliver supplies, and finally to San Francisco (then Yerba Buena). Like the Saints who were leaving their homes in Nauvoo on this very same day, the *Brooklyn* Saints longed to find a home in the Rocky Mountains where they could worship God without persecution.

Orson Pratt, an Apostle and president of the Eastern States Mission, encouraged the Saints to "flee out of Babylon, either by land or by sea" (HC 7:516). Young **Samuel Brannan,**[3] age 27, was chosen to direct the Saints from New York and neighboring states who were to go by sea (T&S 6:1042–44).

The Saints leased the old ship *Brooklyn* for an inexpensive $1,200 a month plus expenses. Passengers paid a fare of $75 each, plus half that for children. The 11-year-old *Brooklyn* was 125' long, 25' wide, and weighed 445 tons. The Saints remodeled the ship for their journey by adding 32 small staterooms with bunks. The ship's captain was Abel W. Richardson, who was very capable and well-liked by the Saints.

In addition to passengers and crew, the boat took on a consignment of paying freight to be delivered to Hawaii. The Saints took ploughs, forks, nails, tools, a printing press, books, muskets, water, chickens, 40–50 pigs, two milk cows, and many other items needed for colonization.

Saints, relatives, and curious onlookers packed the wharves on Wed., Feb. 4, 1846, to bid farewell. The Saints on the pier sang hymns and a song about going to California. Three lusty cheers from the crowd on the wharf were echoed by the Saints on the *Brooklyn* as the sailing vessel swung around the pier into the East River at 2:00 P.M. As the sails were raised, the breeze was engaged

---

[3] Brannan was born in Saco, ME, in 1819 and was converted to the LDS Church in 1833 by Heber C. Kimball and Orson Hyde. In 1844 he helped to found a Church-sponsored newspaper, *The Prophet*, in NYC. Brannan was disfellowshipped for marrying a plural wife, but was reinstated in 1845 and was sent to NYC to assist Parley P. Pratt in publishing the *New York Messenger*. After directing the Saints to California he fell away from the Church, died in 1899, and is buried in the Mt. Hope Cemetery in San Diego, CA (ABM 19–23).

Old Slip St. and old police station, New York City. The ship Brooklyn *docked in the East River directly east of (behind) this old police station. (1990)*

and the *Brooklyn* disappeared into the choppy, frigid waters of the Atlantic to begin its six-month journey, which was five times longer than the voyage of the *Mayflower* (VOB 52; T&S 6:1126–27; HC 7:515–22; CHC 3:28–30; DIA 21, no. 3:46–72).[4]

The pioneers aboard the

The Brooklyn. *Painting by Arnold Friberg. (Courtesy of LDSCA)*

Brooklyn experienced many hardships during their voyage. They encountered storms so vicious that a cow died and the pioneers had to lash themselves to their bunks. Two babies were born, John Atlantic Burr and Georgiana Pacific Robbins. Twelve people died, including Laura Goodwin, the mother of seven children under 14 years of age. These travelers experienced dictatorial leadership, slimy water, rats, cockroaches, vermin in the provisions, a stop at the island of Juan Fernandez (of *Robinson Crusoe* fame), the long, out-of-the-way journey to Hawaii, military drills, and four excommunications. Finally, on July 31, 1846, they landed in the San Francisco Bay (Yerba Buena) after an impressive and memorable journey.

---

[4] The author is indebted to Lorin Hansen for his excellent research on the voyage of the *Brooklyn*, and his willingness to share information before his work went to the press. (See DIA 21, no. 3:47–72).

■ **17. SOUTH STREET SEAPORT (PACKET ROW).** South Street Seaport or Packet Row is located along the west side of the East River and

south of the Brooklyn Bridge. It was the heart of the port of New York and the center of its worldwide shipping activities in the 19th century. South Street Seaport served many missionaries and Saints during that time. During a 10-year period (1837–46), five sailing vessels departed South Street Seaport with important Mormons aboard: the

South Street Port or Packet Row (Courtesy of the New York Public Library)

Garrick (1837), the *Oxford* (1839), and the *Patrick Henry* (1840), carrying Apostles and other missionaries to England; the *United States* (1841), with Orson Hyde traveling to England en route to the Holy Land; and the *Brooklyn* (1846), with Samuel Brannan and 230 Saints journeying to the west coast of California.[5]

At the time, there were man-made docks called "slips" that were finger-like extensions of water that reached inland from the East River. There were also piers built out from the Manhattan mainland into the East River. The East River was deep enough for early sailboats and steamboats, but with the introduction of larger ships, the main port area of NYC was changed to the deeper waters of the Hudson River on the west side of Manhattan.

■ **18. "COFFEE HOUSE SLIP" AT THE "FOOT" OF WALL STREET AND THE SHIP *GARRICK*.** The "foot" of Wall Street is where Wall Street meets South Street on the west bank of the East River and is where the ship *Garrick* was docked when **the first missionaries to England** boarded to go to their fields of labor as predicted by Parley P. Pratt (APPP 130–31).

The year 1837 was distressful for the Saints in Kirtland because of apostasy and economic turmoil. When the powers of darkness

---

[5] The author is deeply indebted to Albert W. Hoffmann, who spent several days in the New York Historical Society Library researching and gathering information about the five ships that sailed from South Street Seaport with prominent Mormons aboard. His careful research makes this information available to the LDS audience for the first time.

combined to try to overthrow the Church, Joseph Smith said that God revealed to him what must be done "for the salvation of His Church" —missionaries had to be sent to England (HC 2:489). Elder **Heber C. Kimball** was set apart about June 1, 1837, to be the president of the first mission established in England. Elders **Orson Hyde** and **Willard Richards** joined

The Garrick *transported the first seven LDS missionaries to England (1837). (Courtesy of the Marines Museum, Newport News, VA)*

Heber. Four Canadian missionaries, **Joseph Fielding, John Goodson, Isaac Russell,** and **John Snider,** also joined the Apostles. By June 22, 1837, all seven missionaries had arrived in NYC, where **Elijah Fordham,** the only Latter-day Saint in New York City, was very helpful to them.

Elijah Fordham was born in New York City in 1798, but was living in Pontiac, MI, when he was converted to the Church in 1833. Fordham marched in Hyrum Smith's division of Zion's Camp and acted as camp historian. He later went to NYC where his father lived, and was the only Latter-day Saint there when the first seven missionaries to England arrived in June 1837. Elijah was a missionary and faithful member of the Church in New York City during the 1830s.

In July 1839, Elijah was raised from his deathbed by Joseph Smith in Montrose, IA (HC 4:4). He served on the high council of the Zarahemla Stake in 1839, carved the oxen and ornamental molding on the baptismal font of the Nauvoo Temple (HC 4:446), and on Apr. 8, 1845, he returned again from New York with $1,263 for the Nauvoo Temple (HC 7:394–95). He later went to Salt Lake City and lived on South Temple Street.

The missionaries rented a room in an unfinished storehouse belonging to Elijah Fordham's father, George. They slept on the floor and worked for their rent (six cents for the week) (HC 2:495). Elijah Fordham gave the missionaries $10 to help them on their way. On June 29, the missionaries mailed a copy of Orson Hyde's tract, "Timely Warnings," to each of the 180 ministers in New York, and handed out more copies to the people on the streets.

Heber C. Kimball said the tracts had opened the doors for Parley and Orson Pratt to introduce the gospel there. Many persons who later came into the Church had read Hyde's tract (ORH 90). When the missionaries left NYC to go to England, Elijah wanted to go with them, but the Brethren thought it wise for him to stay in NYC to help build the Church there. This he did until 1838 when he moved to Quincy, IL. Elijah was a great help to Parley P. Pratt and others who came to NYC in the 1830s.

On June 29, 1837, the seven missionaries boarded the ship *Garrick*. Their fare was $25 each and they supplied their own provisions and cooking utensils. The *Garrick* moved away from the dock into the East River and laid at anchor for two nights. Then on July 1, its sails were raised and the first LDS missionaries to England sailed for 19 days across the Atlantic to Liverpool. Missionary labors in England proved to be very successful—the seven missionaries baptized 2,000 converts, and the Church was saved (HC 2:489, 498; 4:313–14; TWP 3–43; ERA 63:720–21, 744–46; NYT June 29, 1837; July 1, 1837; NYTCA Dec. 17, 1839).

■   **19. PIER 19 AT THE "FOOT" OF MAIDEN LANE AND THE SHIPS *PATRICK HENRY* AND *UNITED STATES*.** Pier 19 at the "foot" of Maiden Lane, where Maiden Lane meets South Street, is where the Apostles going to England in 1840 boarded the ship **Patrick Henry**. Here also, the ship **United States** was boarded by **Orson Hyde** as he traveled to the Holy Land in 1841.

Seven Apostles left the temple site in Far West, MO, on Apr. 26, 1839, to start on missions to England, just as Joseph Smith had prophesied (D&C 118:1, 4–5). From Nauvoo they traveled separately, regrouping in New York City, where they stayed at Parley P. Pratt's home at 58 Mott Street. From NYC they departed for England in two groups on two different dates. Apostles **John Taylor** and **Wilford Woodruff,** along with Elder **Theodore Turley,** departed from the foot of Beekman Street on the South Street Seaport Dec. 18, 1839, on the packet ship *Oxford* (T&S 1:61; WW 113).

Elders **Brigham Young, Heber C. Kimball, Parley P. Pratt, Orson Pratt,** and **George A. Smith** of the Twelve (plus Elder Reuben Hedlock, a missionary) boarded the *Patrick Henry* at Pier 19 at the foot of Maiden Lane (APPP 300–301; SCL Mar. 4, 1840:1; NYCA Mar. 6, 1840; HC 4:94) and left NYC on Mar. 9, 1840. As they left the pier, the New York Saints bid them "Godspeed," sang "The Gallant Ship Is Under Way," and rejoiced for the Apostles' mission to England. (For the other Apostles' departure see site no 21.)

The missionaries had steerage passage for $18 plus $1 to pay the cook, and they provided their own provisions. They landed 28 days later in Liverpool, England, on Apr. 6, 1840 (ThC 4:122; BE 1:10). Their missions were extremely successful, resulting in 7,000 to 8,000 baptisms.

In a special revelation given to **Orson Hyde** through Joseph Smith in 1831, the Lord indicated that Orson would "proclaim the everlasting gospel, by the Spirit of the living God, from people to people, and from land to land, in the congregations of the wicked, in their synagogues, reasoning with and expounding all scriptures unto them" (D&C 68:1). After many spiritual manifestations, on Apr. 15, 1840, Elder Orson Hyde left Nauvoo, IL, for Jerusalem on his ninth mission. He and his companion, **John E. Page,** first preached in Dayton, OH, then Cincinnati, OH, where Page and Hyde parted company. Hyde continued alone on his mission toward New York, preaching on the way.

When he arrived in NYC in 1841, he met a new convert, **George J. Adams,** a very eloquent preacher in the area. They became friends, and Adams joined Hyde as a missionary companion. On Feb. 13, 1841, Hyde and Adams boarded the packet ship *United States* at the foot of Maiden Lane and spent 18 days crossing the Atlantic before landing at Liverpool on Mar. 3, 1841 (HC 4:298; SCL Feb. 13, 1841; NYCA Feb. 12–13, 1841). After laboring together in England for four months, Hyde left Adams to labor in England and proceeded on toward the Holy Land alone.

Orson Hyde was the first missionary to preach the gospel on the European continent and in far-off Asia Minor. From London he traveled to Holland, Prussia (Germany), Romania, Turkey, and Lebanon before reaching Palestine, where, on Oct. 24, 1841, he dedicated the land for the return of the Jews. After visiting Egypt, Germany, and England, he returned to the United States, arriving at his Nauvoo home in Dec. 1842. He had traveled 20,000 miles alone, completing a very exciting, successful, and purposeful mission (T&S 2:482–83; HC 4:298; ORH 109–41). Although George J. Adams did not go with Hyde to Palestine in 1841, he still maintained an interest in that land, and led a colony of settlers there in 1866 (TF).

● **20. SOUTH STREET SEAPORT, HISTORIC DEVELOPMENT.** On the East River, south of the Brooklyn Bridge and at the "foot" of Fulton Street, is the South Street Seaport. This 11-block district was, in the 19th century, the heart of the New York Harbor for sail and steamboats. A development program of the 1980s revitalized the South Street Seaport with the new three-story Fulton Market building as its center-piece. The area bounded by Fulton, John, South, Water, and Beekman Streets is now a complex of pedestrian malls, restaurants, shops, waterfront piers, excursion sailboats, and historical ships reminiscent of 19th century seaport days. **The South Street Seaport Museum,** located at 12 Fulton Street, offers tours of its galleries and large collection of ships. The **Seaport Experience,** located at 210 Front Street, provides a multimedia presentation of the story of South Street Seaport. The **Fulton Fish Market** is located on the NE part of this newly revived historic seaport. The present building is the fourth market to be built on this site since 1822. **Sailboat Cruises** of the harbor are available on the *Pioneer.*

■ **21. "FOOT" OF BEEKMAN STREET AND THE SHIP *OXFORD*. John Taylor** and **Wilford Woodruff** arrived in New York to depart for their two-year missions to England (1839–41) much earlier than the other members of the Twelve. They decided to leave as soon as possible, so they and **Theodore Turley** boarded the ship *Oxford* at the "foot" of Beekman Street, where the current Fulton Fish Market is located. They sailed on Dec. 18, 1839 (HC 4:46; SCL Dec. 18, 1839; NYCA Dec. 17, 1839; NYTC Dec. 17, 1839). (For the other Apostles' departure see site no. 19.)

● **22. WALL STREET AND TONTINE COFFEE HOUSE SITE.** In 1653 the Dutch built a wooden palisade (plank wall) across Manhattan from the Hudson to the East River to protect themselves from the Indians. The wall marked the northern limits of the city. After the British took over the area in 1699, they dismantled the wall. They made a street (Wall Street) where the palisade had been and built a new city hall on the corner of Broad and Wall Streets (where the Federal Hall is now located). Wall Street became an administrative and residential street for the wealthy.

Financiers such as Jay Gould, Cornelius Vanderbilt, and J. P. Morgan were at the forefront in helping Wall Street replace London as the financial capital of the world in the 1920s. The tall skyscrapers on both sides of Wall Street hide the sunlight for much of the day from the busy crowds.

The first formally organized **New York Stock Exchange** was located in the Tontine Coffeehouse built in 1792 at the NW corner of Wall and Water Streets, a block west of Coffeehouse Slip. The stock exchange was organized because there was a need to create a formal marketplace to handle the $80 million of stock that was issued by the Congress of 1789–90 to pay Revolutionary War debts.

- **23. BANK OF NEW YORK.** The Bank of New York at 48 Wall Street was established in 1784 and is the oldest bank in NYC. Alexander Hamilton drafted the bank's charter, which served as a precedent for future banking rules in the country. The present building, built in 1927 and 1928, is the third building on the site since 1798. This is one of 12 banks that were located within a two-block area on the north side of Wall Street in 1832.

  Joseph Smith and **Newel K. Whitney** visited NYC in 1832 to arrange for a loan of $15,000 to ensure the stability of the Church. The Bank of New York may have been one of the banks they visited (PWJS 251–52).

- **24. MORGAN GUARANTY BANK.** The Morgan Guaranty Bank at 31 Wall Street still has holes in its granite walls made when a wagon filled with dynamite mysteriously exploded. This happened as the Trinity Church clock struck noon on Sept. 16, 1920.

- **25. FEDERAL HALL NATIONAL MEMORIAL AND GEORGE WASHINGTON STATUE.** The second city hall (first English city hall) was built on this site, 26 Wall Street, between 1699 and 1703 to replace the Dutch *Stadt Huys*. In front of the city hall was the "pillory" where minor offenders were exposed to public derision and the "stake" where they were flogged. The hall also served as the courthouse and debtors' prison. Thirty years after the city hall was built, the Stamp Act Congress met here to oppose English colonial policy.

  In 1788 and 1789 the city hall was remodeled under the supervision of French engineer and architect Major Charles Pierre L'Enfant, who also designed the master plan of Washington, D.C. The building became Federal Hall, **the first capitol of the United States** and the seat of Congress. President **George Washington** and Vice President **John Adams** took their oaths of office as the first president and vice president of the United States on the balcony of Federal Hall on Apr. 30, 1789. Washington's statue,[6] on the front steps of the building, was sculpted by George Q. A. Ward and commemorates that event. Here the first Congress adopted the Bill of Rights.

After one year in New York, the federal government and the United States capitol were transferred to Philadelphia, PA, and the Federal Hall building was used for state and city offices. The building was sold for salvage in 1812 for $425.

The present building, the third on this site, was built in Greek Doric style with Westchester marble in 1842. It served as the NYC Customshouse until 1862, then as the United States Subtreasury, and finally as government offices until 1955 when it became a national monument. Today it houses mementos of John Peter Zenger (a pioneer in freedom of the press) and Washington, an exhibit of the Bill of Rights and freedom of expression, and dioramas portraying the history of the three buildings that have stood on this site. The balcony galleries contain art exhibits.

■ **26. MACHINE SHOP OF WANDLE MACE.** Wandle Mace was one of the first converts to the LDS Church in New York City and the first branch president of the New York City Branch of the Church. He is listed in the 1830 city directory as a machinist at 20 Wall Street, just east of a Presbyterian church and on the NW corner of Wall and Nassau Streets. Across the street to the east is the Federal Hall, and across the street to the south is the New York Stock Exchange. The Bankers Trust Company building at 14 Wall Street sits over the site today (LCD 413; PEM; AYP 44–45; ERA 45:522). Besides his portable mill shop at 20 Wall St., Mace had the following shops at different times during his residence in New York City: a grocery store at 44 Bayard St. (1831–32); a coach maker's shop at 161 W. Broadway (1833–34); a coach maker's shop at 249 Elizabeth St. (1836–37); and a machinists's shop at 264 Elizabeth St. (1838).

Wandle Mace was born Feb. 19, 1809, in Johnstown, NY, and at age seven moved to New York City. At age 13 he apprenticed as a wheelwright and worked in a blacksmith shop making wheels and coaches. He became a prominent businessman and artisan. In 1828

---

[6] The temple work for many prominent figures in American history including George Washington, Benjamin Franklin, and Christopher Columbus was performed in the St. George Temple in Aug. 1877 (JWW 7:369).

Engraving looking east from Trinity Church down Wall St. in about 1837. The First Presbyterian Church is on the left. Just east (right) of the church, outlined in black, is the machine shop of Wandle Mace (1837–38) at 20 Wall St. The New York Stock Exchange is directly across the street (south).

he married Margaret Merkbe and, with his brother John, opened two grocery stores in NYC. When banks failed in 1830, the two brothers lost their grocery businesses and Wandle farmed for two years on Long Island. In the fall of 1833 he returned to NYC and worked as a coach maker. He patented two machines for post mortising and rail sharpening. He sold the patents and with his profits he paid off his debts. With extra money he purchased land in Quincy, IL, for $3,200. Little did he realize that within two years, because of his conversion to the LDS Church, he would move to Quincy, IL, only to find out that he had been swindled and owned no property there.

A Mr. Kidder of NYC planned and designed a machine for sweeping the streets of NYC, and hired Wandle Mace to build it. This Wandle did, and the machine worked. Of this machine, Wandle said, "This was the first street sweeping machine ever made and used in New York City" (JWMa 4).

In 1837 Wandle Mace was in the business of making portable mills called conical grinders at his shop at 20 Wall Street. Of this invention he said, "I . . . turned my attention to making Portable

Engraving looking west up Wall St. toward Trinity Church during the panic of 1884. The Federal Hall National Memorial and George Washington Statue is on the right, and the Wandle Mace machine shop site (1837–38), outlined in black, is immediately west (left) of Federal Hall.

Mills. I bought the Patent right with the 'title,' 'interest,' etc. in what was called a Conical Grinder with improvements in Thrashing Machine and Horse Power, for which I paid fifteen hundred dollars in company with Mr. William Shay. We done a good business. I was engaged in this business when Elder Parley P. Pratt came along preaching the gospel" (JWMa 12; APPP 168–72).

Mace had been a member of the New School Presbyterian Church, but he did not believe some of the Presbyterian doctrines and was excommunicated. He then met privately with groups of truth-seeking friends who discussed the scriptures. Each Sunday he fasted and prayed and went from house to house preaching the gospel as he understood it. After preaching for two years, he decided that he had no authority to preach, so he stopped. He saw nothing in all the churches and sects in NYC that resembled his concept of Christianity.

It was in one of the group meetings held in NYC that Elijah Fordham introduced Wandle Mace to Parley P. Pratt, who had arrived in NYC in late July 1837. When Wandle told Parley that he was looking for "gifts of the Spirit" and "authority" (JWMa15) Pratt told him about Joseph Smith and the Church. After Parley P. Pratt healed Mace's one-year-old son, Charles, and a Mrs. Dexter and her daughter at Mace's home at 13 Bedford Street (see site no. 89), Mace and his family and others were baptized in the icy East River in Dec. 1837.

Mace was appointed by Orson Pratt, the mission president, to be the **first local branch president** of the Church in New York City, and his home was the Church meeting place until he moved to Quincy, IL, with David W. Rogers's family in Sept. 1838. In Quincy, Mace served on the committee to select land for the settling of the Saints in Commerce (later renamed Nauvoo). Soon after Joseph Smith was released from prison in Liberty, MO, he spoke to the Saints from the stairs of Mace's Quincy home. Mace said of Joseph Smith after hearing his address: "He was a fine looking man, tall and well proportioned, strong and active, light complexion, blue eyes, and light hair, and very little beard. He had a free and easy manner, not the least affection, yet bold and independent, and very interesting and eloquent in speech" (JWMa 37).

Wandle Mace remained true to the faith and died Aug. 10, 1890, in Kanab, UT (EXWM, BWM). Wandle Mace was certainly one of the solid pillars of the Church in New York City during the 1830s.

■ **27. NEW YORK STOCK EXCHANGE.** Diagonally across the street from the Federal Hall is the New York Stock Exchange, the nation's largest organized market for stocks and bonds. The ground floor is a beehive of activity as Exchange members trade shares of the leading companies of American industry. Visitors may enter at 20 Broad Street, and from the visitors gallery see what appears to be chaos on the trading floor below.

Florence Elliot Doyle, the first woman stockbroker in New York City, worked for 44 years as a stockbroker on Wall Street and retired in 1971. In the early 1920s she was convinced that a new invention called the radio was going to catch on. She bought 500 shares of RCA stock at $2.00 a share and ultimately made $37,000 on that investment. Although dealing in stock was considered a man's job in the 1920s, she was hired in 1927 to help women customers. Her office was near Trinity Church and Wall Street.

At the New York World's Fair of 1964–65, Florence met Mormon missionaries and was later baptized into the LDS Church. She said it was the patience, kindness, and humility of the 19-year-old elders that impressed her and piqued her interest in the LDS Church. Sister Doyle, a very active Latter-day Saint, died Jan. 31, 1986, at age 94 (MWN 1, no. 7 [Nov. 1971]; NYT Feb. 3, 1986; SmS Oct. 1971).

■ **28. ROGERS & SON, HOUSE CARPENTERS & JOINERS—BUSINESS SITE.**
David White Rogers, one of the first Latter-day Saint converts in
NYC and a strength to the Church in NYC during the 1830s, had a

shop at 34 New
Street, about a
block south (SW)
of the New York
Stock Exchange
and on the east
side of New Street
from   1831   to
1834. A sign on
the building read:
"Rogers & Son,
House Carpenters

Rogers & Son, House Carpenters & Joiners site at
34 New St. The building was located at the exact center
of this photo and was 30' wide.

& Joiners." The
shop was 30' wide,
and the north

side of the shop was 70' south of Exchange Place (Street) (LCD
1831–34; PEM).

David White Rogers was born Oct. 4, 1787, at Lincoln, Grafton
Co., NH. He married Martha Collins on Dec. 5, 1811, and they
were the parents of 11 children, born between 1813 and 1833.

After their marriage, David and Martha Rogers moved from
Montreal, Canada, to various places in New York. From
Chautauqua, in western New York, David moved to NYC in 1830.
His wife and children followed him later the same year and his
nine-year-old son, Ramson, later wrote of this arrival, "We had
landed at the foot of Water Street [perhaps at or near Coenties
Slip], passed up that throughafare to the battery up Washington
Street to Courtland Street, up Broadway Street to Exchange Street
to New York Street [actually New Street as he later states] to num-
ber 34, and then my brother pointed to my father['s] sign, 'Rogers
& Son House Carpenters and Joiners'" (APH 496).

Later the Rogerses lived in a large house with an address of
"the Battery at #1 Water Street and Castle Gardens." Daughter
Carolyn said, "My sister and I used to take great pleasure in walking around the Battery Park and sitting on the benches under the
trees and also looking at the ships land" (APH 474).

David closed his shop at 34 New Street in about 1832 and

moved to Caldwell's Landing, a town north of NYC. He returned to NYC in 1833, and then moved again in 1835 to 515 Greenwich (Spring and Greenwich Streets), where he made his home and his cabinet- and furniture-making shop (APH 496–97) (see site no. 83).

Martha Rogers, David's wife, had a dream in 1835. In it, two men came to her house with a book they said was of great importance. Because of her dream, she was ready to accept Parley P. Pratt and Elijah Fordham into her home in 1837, two years later. Parley had arrived in NYC in July and had met little success after laboring for six months. He later said in his autobiography, "From July to January we preached, advertised, printed, published, testified, visited, talked, prayed, and wept in vain. . . . We had baptized about six members, and organized a little branch, who were accustomed to meet in a small upper room in Goerck street; sometimes two or three others met with us" (APPP 169).

Parley was discouraged and ready to take leave for New Orleans when, he writes:

> The Lord said that He had heard our prayers, beheld our labors, diligence, and long suffering towards that city; and that He had seen our tears. Our prayers were heard, and our labors and sacrifices were accepted. We should tarry in the city, and go not thence as yet; for the Lord had many people in that city, and He had now come by the power of His Holy Spirit to gather them into His fold. . . .
>
> Now there was in this little meeting a man named David Rogers, whose heart was touched. He, being a chairmaker, fitted up a large room, and seated it with the chairs of his ware house, and invited us to preach in the same. This room was crowded. He then joined with one of our members, who was a joiner, and rented a small place, and seated it for a regular place of meeting; this was generally crowded. (APPP 170–71)

Within three weeks of the prophecies being given, the missionaries had 15 preaching places in the city, all of which were filled to capacity. They preached about 11 times a week, besides visiting from house to house, and commenced baptizing almost daily during the winter and spring. They blessed a lady with a crippled leg and her leg was instantly restored whole. They blessed a lady who had been in bed four years with dumb palsy, and she arose and walked. A child of Wandle Mace was healed, and Mrs. Dexter's daughter and granddaughter were healed. The promises of the Lord were fulfilled as prophesied (APPP 171–72).

David Rogers received a spiritual witness in his home on Greenwich Street, and on Dec. 19, 1837, he, his wife, Martha, and their children Susannah, Charles, Amelia Ann, Ross, Hester Ann, and Hannah Caroline were baptized in the East River.

David Rogers and Wandle Mace (see site no. 26) were stalwarts in the New York City Branch of the Church until they both left NYC together on Sept. 14, 1838, to go to Missouri to be with the Saints. They eventually emigrated to Utah, and both David and Martha Rogers died in Provo in 1881 (APH 500).

David and Martha's child **Hannah Caroline** married **Aaron Eugene Daniels** at Nauvoo in Dec. 14, 1845. Hannah and Aaron were pioneers to Utah in 1850, and settled at Wanship in 1859. Aaron named the village and built a stagecoach station there. Daniels Canyon, near Heber, UT, was named after him. Like her mother, Caroline bore 11 children, and one of her great-grand-children was **Barbara Bradshaw Smith,** general president of the Relief Society (1974–84). After Aaron apostatized and they divorced in 1886, Caroline married **Abraham O. Smoot** in 1886 as one of his plural wives. Smoot had been Salt Lake City's first mayor, and was then president of the Provo Stake (see sites no. 6 and 83).

■ **29. NORTH AMERICAN EXCHANGE COMPANY, LTD., SITE.** John Willard Young's North American Exchange Company Ltd., was located at 57 Broadway Street, a block south of Trinity Church on the west side of the street, on the SW corner of Broadway and Exchange Place (PEM: LCD 1887–90). The company was run by **John Willard Young** (1844–1924), son of Brigham Young (not to be confused with Brigham Young's son Willard, the first Mormon graduate from West Point).

John Willard Young was born in Nauvoo on Oct. 1, 1844, to **Brigham Young** and **Mary Ann Angell.** John Willard had a flamboyant personality, expensive tastes, and an unexcelled drive and determination. He was the president of the Salt Lake Stake (1868–74), First Counselor in the First Presidency (1876–77), and a counselor to the Twelve Apostles (1877–91). In 1869 he entered the railroad business and became a railroad magnate, building in Utah and Arizona.

In the 1880s John Willard spent time in the East assisting in efforts to gain political independence for Utah and freedom from anti-polygamy legislation. He operated behind the doors of his **North American Exchange Company Ltd.** (1887–90), and through the pages of his newspaper, the *Saturday Evening Globe.* John wielded an influence with important men in government, finance, and newspapers that had an ameliorating effect on hostile legislation and sentiment against the Church.

By 1900, despite nominal business success, John's course had led to financial ruin and tarnished dreams. He died in an obscure apartment house overlooking Broadway, NYC, on Feb. 11, 1924.

■ **30. TRINITY CHURCH.** Located on the west side of Broadway where Wall Street begins, and in full view as one walks west on Wall Street, is Trinity Church. Although now dwarfed by surrounding skyscrapers, it was the tallest building in NYC for nearly 50 years after its construction in 1846. The third church built on this site, the Trinity Church received additions in 1913 and 1966.

The cemetery near the church was used as early as 1681 and is the final resting place of several prominent people. The grave of **Frances Lewis**[7] (1713–1802), the only signer of the Declaration of Independence buried on Manhattan Island, is near the NE corner of the church. Frances Lewis, a prosperous merchant and government contractor was appointed as a delegate to the Continental Congress where he served from 1775 to 1779.

Publisher **Williams Bradford's** grave is about 25 feet south of Lewis's grave and has the oldest carved gravestone in NYC, dated 1681. Artist, engineer, and steamboat inventor **Robert Fulton** (1765–1815) is buried along the west side of the cemetery between the church and the north fence. **Alexander Hamilton** (1757–1804), statesman, first U.S. Secretary of the Treasury, member of George Washington's first cabinet, and vigorous promoter of the U.S. Constitution, is buried in the south side of the cemetery along

---

[7] Frances Lewis was one of the men who appeared to President Wilford Woodruff in the St. George Temple in 1877. Of that occasion, Woodruff said: "Every one of those men that signed the Declaration of Independence with General Washington called upon me, as an Apostle of the Lord Jesus Christ, in the Temple at St. George two consecutive nights, and demanded at my hands that I should go forth and attend to the ordinances of the house of God for them. . . . Brother [J.D.T.] McAllister baptized me for all these men" (TMH 90). Baptisms for all the Founding Fathers were performed Aug. 21, 1877, and they were endowed the next day.

Rector Street. In a political dispute with U.S. Vice President Aaron Burr, Hamilton was challenged by Burr to a duel. Hamilton was wounded and died the next day, July 12, 1804. Hamilton's son, Philip, was also killed in a duel by the same set of pistols that killed his father.

■ **31. LAW OFFICES OF J. REUBEN CLARK JR.** Located at 120 Broadway, on the east side of the street, between Cedar and Pine Streets, were the law offices of **President J. Reuben Clark Jr.,** who served as a counselor to three prophets of the Church, Heber J. Grant, George Albert Smith, and David O. McKay, over a period of 28 years (1933–61).

J. Reuben Clark Jr. (1871–1961), from Grantsville, UT, was 32 years old when he entered law school at Columbia University in NYC. His abilities were soon recognized, and he helped edit the *Columbia Law Review.* After two years of law school, he was hired in 1906 as assistant solicitor for the Department of State. After seven years of work in government circles in Washington, D.C., he entered a private law practice.

On Jan. 1, 1916, he announced the opening of his new law offices on the 26th floor of the new Equitable Life Assurance Society Building. He represented the newly organized American International Corporation (AIC) that had been formed to promote world trade.

After about five-and-a-half years in NYC, Clark closed his office on June 1, 1922, and moved to Salt Lake City, UT. He soon was appointed undersecretary of state (1928–29) and then ambassador to Mexico (1930–33) (JRC 339–65; YR 135–38).

■ **32. CITY HOTEL SITE.** New York's City Hotel was built on the site of the Tontine City Tavern in 1794 between Thames and Cedar Streets (Nos. 113–19). It had a 100-foot facade and an entrance facing Broadway; the back of the building was on Trinity Place (PEM; LCD). The four-story brick building occupied the entire city block and was one of the most impressive buildings in the city. It was New York's first full-facility hotel and the greatest hostelry in the United States. After 55 years of service, the hotel was demolished in 1849 (IOM 3:688–89).

Thomas B. Marsh (1800–68) was a teenage employee at the City Hotel for four years between 1815 and 1820. By 1830 he was in

Palmyra where he met Martin Harris in Egbert B. Grandin's printing office. Marsh was baptized in Sept. 1830, and a special revelation was given through Joseph Smith to Marsh, indicating that he would be a "physician unto the church" (D&C 31:10). Marsh became the senior member of the

City Hotel site, 1794–1849, at 113–19 Broadway, between Thames and Cedar Streets.

Quorum of the Twelve Apostles in 1835 and was temporarily appointed president of the Church in Missouri on Feb. 10, 1838. In Aug. 1838, he became disaffected and turned against the leadership of the Church. He was excommunicated in 1839 and was out of the Church for 18 years. In 1857 he was rebaptized in Florence, NE. The once-distinguished Apostle eventually moved to Springville, UT, where he taught history and geography (JD 5:206–10; BE 74–76; IGA).

- **33. MARINE MIDLAND BANK.** On the east side of Broadway, at No. 140, is the Marine Midland Bank, a tall, dark-colored, glass-curtained tower 55 stories high. Its smooth, unbroken exterior is typical of buildings constructed in the 1960s and later.

- **34. ONE LIBERTY PLAZA.** The 53-story skyscraper on the NW corner of Broadway and Liberty Street is the headquarters of **Merrill Lynch,** one of the world's largest securities companies.

    At this intersection, it is possible to take one or two extended side tours west and east of Broadway.

Extended Side Tours

From the intersection of Liberty and Broadway it is a short two blocks to the west (left) on Liberty Street to the **World Trade Center** (site no. 35) with its beautiful Twin Towers. A turn to the east on Liberty Street will lead to other interesting sites including the **Federal Reserve Bank** with its stockpile of gold bars (see sites no. 36–40).

The extended side tours include sites 35–40, but if you continue up Broadway on the original Mormon walking tour, the next site will be no. 41, **St. Paul's Church.**

● **35. WORLD TRADE CENTER.** The World Trade Center is on a 16-acre site near the Hudson River and is bounded by Church, Vesey, West, and Liberty Streets. The purpose of the Center is to promote international business services. Exporters, importers, manufacturers, freight forwards, customshouse brokers, international banks, federal and state trade agencies, transportation lines, etc., make this a very busy international trade center. Twenty-two restaurants and Manhattan's largest mall are also found in the Center.

The Center is graced by the **Twin Towers,** two monolithic buildings that have 110 stories each and are 1,350' tall. In the United States, only the Sears Roebuck Building in Chicago (110 stories and 1,454') is taller. Both the gallery on the 107th floor and the observation deck on the 110th floor are open daily from 9:30 A.M. to 9:30 P.M. On a clear day, one can see 55 miles from this position $^1/_4$ mile above the streets. This was the world's highest outdoor observation platform when it was built. Each floor is nearly one square acre in size.

Offices first opened in the Twin Towers in late 1970. Approximately 50,000 people work here. It is estimated that an additional 80,000 businesspeople and visitors go to the center daily. To avoid crowds, visit the Center before 10 A.M. or after 7 P.M.

Immediately west of the World Trade Center is Battery Park City, with its 1.2-mile-long Esplanade and World Financial Center.

● **36. CHAMBER OF COMMERCE.** The Chamber of Commerce of the State of New York is located at 65 Liberty Street (north side). This building was built in 1901 and its dominant interior feature is the Great Hall (90' x 60') with its elaborately decorated ceiling rising 38 feet above the floor.

● **37. FEDERAL RESERVE BANK OF NEW YORK.** Surrounded by Nassau and Liberty Streets and Maiden Lane is the Federal Reserve Bank of New York at 33 Liberty Street. The 14-story masonry building is designed after Italian Renaissance palaces that housed wealthy Florentine bankers. It was built in 1924.

The Federal Reserve Bank is a "bank of banks"; one of 12 regional banks that (1) help to regulate credit and cash flow; (2) collect and clear checks; (3) distribute coins and currency; (4) market and redeem government securities; and (5) store gold reserves. Eighty feet below street level is a chamber half the length of a football field that houses about 350 million troy ounces of gold reserves belonging to 80 nations. Tours of the bank are by appointment only.

■ **38. H. V. SMITH MUSEUM.** While at the helm of the largest fire insurance organization in the world, Harold V. Smith was responsible for collecting and preserving the nation's most complete collection of equipment, art, and history of fire fighting and fire insurance. The museum is located on the 12th floor of the Home Insurance Company building at 59 Maiden Lane. In this museum is the tablet commemorating the 1835 New York City fire. The tablet had been placed on the **Pearl Street House** where **Joseph Smith** stayed while in NYC (see site no. 10; AYP 101).

■ **39. DAVID W. ROGERS CARPENTER AND JOINER BUSINESS SITE.** One of David W. Rogers's two last carpenter and joiner business sites in NYC was at 64 John Street, which was on the south side of the street where the east end of John Street Church is now located (LCD 1838–39) (see sites no. 6, 28, 83).

● **40. JOHN STREET CHURCH (UNITED METHODIST).** At 44 John Street, between William and Nassau Streets, is the John Street Church— "the Mother Church of American Methodism." The present church, the third on this site, was built in 1841 and was restored in 1967. It is the oldest Methodist chapel in America.[8]

● **41. ST. PAUL'S CHAPEL (EPISCOPAL).** Located on Broadway between Fulton and Vesey Streets is St. Paul's Chapel, the **oldest church and public building in continuous use in Manhattan.** This 1766 Georgian-style building was constructed of New York stone. The tower and steeple were added in 1796. It is a chapel of the Episcopal Church, the pre-American Revolution "established church" because of its strong ties with the Anglican Church in England. Even though the Episcopal Church still had ties with England, George Washington worshipped here regularly after his inauguration (1789–91). His pew is in the north aisle with the Great Seal of the United States above it.

---

[8] John Wesley, founder of the Methodist Church, was one of five great religious leaders who had their temple work done and who were vicariously ordained high priests in the St. George Temple in Aug. 1877 (JWW 2:369; ETB 446).

Extended Side Tours

Sites 42, 43, and 46 are included as possible side tours.

■ **42. C. VINTEN, PRINTER OF LDS SACRED HYMNS.** C. Vinten Printers
was located on the north side of Vesey Street at no. 63, about where
Greenwich Street crosses Vesey Street today (PEM; LCD 1838).
C. Vinten Printers produced the hymnal, *A Collection of Sacred
Hymns for the Church of the Latter-day Saints.* These were selected and
published by David W. Rogers in 1838. There were 90 hymns in the
hymnal, the same number as was in the **Emma Smith hymnbook**
published in Kirtland in 1835.

■ **43. ROGERS & SON, HOUSE CARPENTERS & JOINERS BUSINESS SITE.**
David W. Rogers and his son had their first carpenter and joiners
shop at 214 Washington Street from 1829 to 1831. Their shop was
at this site again from 1837 to 1838. In 1831 they moved their business from here to 34 New Street (site no. 28) near the New York
Stock Exchange (LCD 1837–38) (see sites no. 6, 28, 83).

● **44. P. T. BARNUM MUSEUM SITE.** At the SE corner of the intersection
of Ann and Broadway Streets (222 Broadway) was P. T. Barnum's
famous museum. Barnum (1810–91) was a great showman and
circus operator, and his museum was at the center of the amusement
world. Barnum purchased the American Museum in 1841 and the
show began. **"General" Tom Thumb** made his appearance here in

*An engraving of the P.T. Barnum Museum site (1850) at 222 Broadway (the SE
corner of Broadway and Ann Streets).*

1842. Tom Thumb and his wife, Lavinia Warren, were later entertained by **Brigham Young** at a dinner in the Beehive House in Salt Lake City. The story is told that Tom Thumb looked up at President Young and said, "There is one thing that I can't understand and that is this belief in polygamy." Brigham Young smiled and answered, "I couldn't understand it either when I was your size" (BYAH 208). The Siamese Twins, animals, snakes, displays, Jumbo the Elephant, and other attractions, made Barnum's name famous (AYP 126–27).

● **45. WOOLWORTH BUILDING.** Located at 233 Broadway at Barclay Street is the famous, Gothic-style Woolworth Building. It was built in 1913 as the tallest building in the world (792') and remained so for 17 years until the Chrysler Building was completed in 1930. Frank W. Woolworth, founder of the five-and-ten-cent store, paid $13.5 million in cash for the building. The grand opening of the building was a gala affair—U.S. President Woodrow Wilson (1913–21) pressed a button in Washington, D.C., that lit up 80,000 light bulbs in the building. An ornate entrance leads to New York's most elegant lobby, three stories high with a vaulted ceiling and Byzantine-style mosaics and frescoes.

■ **46. OLD COLUMBIA COLLEGE SITE.** One and one-half blocks NW of the Woolworth Building is the Old Columbia College site. In the 1820s Columbia College faced north toward Murray Street, with the present Park Place on the south, Chapel Street (now known as West

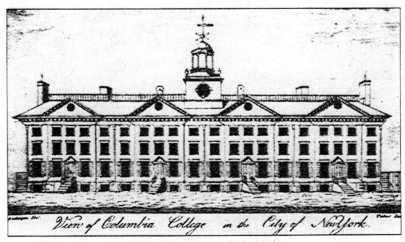

Columbia College, 1755–1897

Broadway) on the west, and Church Street on the east. A plaque located on the Dodge Building at 53 Park Place (SW corner of the campus), tells about Columbia College.

In 1897 the college was moved to its present location between Riverside Drive and Morningside Drive on the east and west, and 114th and 121st Streets on the north and south.

Now known as Columbia University, the school boasts a world-renowned reputation as one of the oldest, largest, and wealthiest private universities in the United States.

Martin Harris, witness to the Book of Mormon plates

Martin Harris (see site no. 77), a witness of the Book of Mormon plates and a scribe for Joseph Smith, had an experience involving Columbia College. In Feb. 1828 Harris left his wife and farm in Palmyra, NY, and traveled to Harmony, PA, where he helped as a scribe while the Prophet Joseph translated the Book of Mormon into English from the "Reformed Egyptian" characters engraved upon the golden plates. Soon after his arrival in Harmony, Harris went to NYC to show "learned men" some of the Book of Mormon characters copied from the golden plates. Harris hoped to receive verification of the genuineness of the characters.

Harris presented the Book of Mormon characters ("Anthon Transcript") to professors of ancient languages **Charles Anthon** and **Dr. Samuel L. Mitchill.** Professor Anthon (1797–1867) of Columbia College (1820–67), was a professor of Greek and Latin.

When Anthon examined the characters, he said that "the translation was correct, more so than any he had before seen translated from the Egyptian" (HC 1:20). Anthon told

Charles Anthon (Courtesy of Paul Cheesman)

Harris that if he would bring the golden plates to him, he would translate them. Harris informed Anthon that part of the plates were sealed, and Anthon replied, "I cannot read a sealed book" (HC 1:20). By so stating, Anthon fulfilled a prophecy given by Isaiah the prophet, over 2,000 years earlier (see Isa. 29:9–14; HC 1:19–20; CHC 1:99–109; 2 Ne. 27). Anthon apparently gave Harris a statement concerning the genuineness of the characters, which statement Anthon ripped up when Harris told him that an angel had delivered the plates to Joseph Smith. Harris was convinced that the characters were genuine and he returned immediately to Harmony, PA, and resumed acting as a scribe to Joseph Smith (HC 1:20–21; CHC 1:108–10; BE 1:271–76).

Dr. Mitchill (see site no. 75) was called the "Magnus Apollo." He was brilliant and knew several languages. He had an M.D. degree and was a physician in NYC for 20 years. He was a professor at Columbia College (1792–1801) and was the vice president of Queen's Medical College (now Rutgers) when Martin Harris contacted him.

- **47. CITY HALL PARK.** The City Hall Park area was a pasture and parade ground (called The Commons) during the Dutch period. In July 1776, the **Declaration of Independence** was read here in the presence of **George Washington,** his troops, and other patriots. When the British returned to NYC a few weeks later, they converted the park's apple trees into gallows. A **statue of Nathan Hale,** located on the Broadway side of the park (west of City Hall), commemorates the American hero who was hanged here by the British for espionage. Hale's famous last words were, "I regret that I have but one life to lose for my country."

- **48. CITY HALL.** Facing Murray Street between Broadway and Park Row is the third and current city hall (built 1803–12) (see sites no. 8 and 25). The building contains the mayor's offices and the city council chamber.

New York City Hall, 1826 (Drawn by W.G. Wall; engraved by L. Hill)

The "Governor's Office" has a notable collection of portraits and furniture.

City Hall, with its Georgian interior and French Renaissance facade, was restored in 1956 at a cost of $2 million and is among New York City's most elegant buildings. It is the focus of welcoming ceremonies for visiting dignitaries and is the starting point of ticker tape parades.

Several state funerals have been held in City Hall, including those of Presidents **Abraham Lincoln** (1865) and **Ulysses S. Grant** (1885).

■ **49. HORACE GREELEY STATUE.** On the east (right) side of City Hall is a large statue of Horace Greeley. He was the founder and editor of the *New York Tribune* and was a noted antislavery leader. His editorials played an important part in molding public opinion in pre-Civil War years. He advocated prohibition and popularized the phrase "Go West, young man," as advice to the unemployed of New York City. Greeley founded other newspapers including: the *New Yorker,* the *Log Cabin,* the *Tribune,* and *Weekly Tribune.*

In June 1859, Greeley traveled to Salt Lake City by stagecoach. After spending 10 days with the Mormons, Greeley claimed he knew "all about" Mormons and printed articles about them. On July 13, 1859, he had a two-hour interview with **Brigham Young,** chiefly about Mormonism and such topics as infant baptism, a personal devil, and polygamy. In Greeley's book, *Overland Journey,* he described Brigham Young as a "very plainly dressed" man with "no air of sanctimony or fanaticism." He said, "In appearance, he is a portly, frank, good-natured, rather thick-set man of fifty-five, seeming to enjoy life" (AOJ 216; CHC 4:523). Greeley attended meetings in the "Old" Tabernacle, and he felt that the Saints were sincere in their religious beliefs. He also said they had a very good appearance.

On taking his leave of Salt Lake City, he said: "I bid *adieu* to Salt Lake City, the great mass of whose people, I am sure, have an unfeigned 'zeal for God,' though I must deem it 'not according to knowledge.' Long may they live to unlearn their errors, and enjoy the rich fruits of their industry, frugality, and sincere, though misguided piety" (CHC 4:533; AOJ 242).

John Taylor, who knew Greeley personally, said of him, "I believe him to be as dishonest a man as is in existence . . . a mean, contemptible cur. . . . He is a poor, miserable curse" (JD 5:119).

A statue of Horace Greeley and a plaque to Joseph Pulitzer are reminders that this was once the center of newspaper publishing in New York.

■ **50. CIVIC CENTER AND "RUSSELL BROS., PRINTERS" SITE.** In a two- to three-block-wide area immediately north and a little east of City Hall is the Civic Center with its federal and city courthouses and office buildings. The New York City 40-story **Municipal Office Building** was built in 1914 and 1915. It straddles Chambers Street and is crowned by a statue titled *Civic Fame.*

At the north end of the Municipal Office Building (perhaps entirely or partially under the north end of the building), at what was 28 and 30 Center Street in 1869–70, was Russell Bros., Printers (LCD 1870).

In 1852, **Brigham Young** asked the Board of Regents of the University of Deseret to "cast out from their system of education, the present orthography and written form of our language, that when my children are taught the graphic sign for A, it may always represent that individual sound only" (JD 1:70).

By inventing a new alphabet, foreign converts could learn to read English with less difficulty, and clear and distinct enunciation would be assured. In 1853 an alphabet of 38 characters was adopted by a committee, and it was called the **Deseret Alphabet** (CHC 5:78–80). **George D. Watt,** the first person baptized in England, was its principal designer.

After **Orson Pratt** transcribed two primers for school children, the type for the new alphabet was cast in St. Louis and the Deseret News Printing Company printed 10,000 copies in Salt Lake City in 1868.

In 1869 Orson Pratt finished transcribing the entire **Book of Mormon** into the Deseret Alphabet and followed through with its publication the same year. Russell Bros., Printers, of NYC, printed and bound 8,000 copies of the translation of the small plates of Nephi (1 Nephi–Words of Mormon), and 500 copies of the complete Book of Mormon (DA).

● **51. BROOKLYN BRIDGE.** Located less than a block east of City Hall is

The Brooklyn Bridge, with footpath (1877).

the west entrance to the Brooklyn Bridge. It can be reached from Frankfort Street or Park Row.

The Brooklyn Bridge over the East River was the first bridge linking Manhattan and Brooklyn. It was the longest suspension bridge in the world for 20 years and was one of the great engineering feats of the 19th century. The bridge was completed in 1883, after 13 years of construction, at a cost of $25 million. Twenty construction workers were killed working on the project. The total length of the bridge including approaches is 6,775'. The four cables holding the bridge are nearly 16" in diameter. For a spectacular view of Manhattan's skyline and an exciting walk across the bridge, cross Park Row from City Hall Park, or from the Brooklyn Bridge—Worth Street subway station, to reach the pedestrian walkway.

■ **52. TAMMANY HALL.** Tammany Hall, built in 1811, was located on Printing House Square, SE of City Hall on the SE corner of Nassau and Frankfort Streets. It was just north of Horace Greeley's *Tribune* building (built later) and was about where the *Sunday Times* building later stood. The building was used for meetings by LDS missionaries in 1838 (AYP 133, 141, 183; APPP 171).

When **Parley P. Pratt** arrived in New York City as a missionary in 1837, he wrote a book of about 200 pages entitled ***A Voice of Warning***. He published 4,000 copies of the first edition.

Parley P. Pratt wrote:

> . . . I was invited by the Free Thinkers to preach, or give a course of lectures, in Tammany Hall. In short, it was not three weeks from the delivery of the prophecies in the upper room till we had fifteen preaching places in the city, all of which were filled to overflowing. We preached about eleven times a week, besides visiting from house to house. We soon commenced baptizing, and continued doing so almost daily during the winter and spring. (APPP 171)

■ **53. PRINTING HOUSE SQUARE AND BENJAMIN FRANKLIN STATUE.** Formed by the intersection of Nassau Street, Park Row, Spruce Street, and Frankfort Street is a small triangle island that marks the site of Printing House Square. It was once called City Hall Square, but by 1861 it had become the undisputed **center of the newspaper publishing district in NYC.** Thirteen different newspapers were published between 1830 and 1860 within four blocks of Printing House Square.

Printing House Square, (1857–58), showing (left to right) the buildings of the Sunday Times, *the* Tribune, *and the* New York Times. *The Latter-day Saints published* The Prophet *and the* New York Messenger *at #7 Spruce Street, which was right behind the* Tribune *building.*

The LDS Church, although it had only a very small membership in NYC, published three newspapers in this district: *The Prophet,* the *New York Messenger,* and *The Mormon.*

The statue of **Benjamin Franklin**[8] (1706–90) stands in Printing House Square today. Franklin was a statesman, philosopher, patriot,

---

[8] Benjamin Franklin and other significant figures in American History appeared to President Wilford Woodruff in 1877 and demanded that their temple work be done. President Woodruff was baptized for Benjamin Franklin Aug. 21, 1877, and his endowments was given the next day. Franklin was also vicariously ordained a high priest on Aug. 23, 1877 (JWW 7:369; JD 19:229; TMH 84–93).

soapmaker, book printer, writer, and inventor. He was one of the signers of the Constitution of the United States.

■   **54. *THE PROPHET* AND *NEW YORK MESSENGER* SITE.** Next door to (behind) Horace Greeley's *New York Tribune* building (154–60

The Pace College building on Spruce St. The 25-foot-wide building at #7 Spruce St., where The Prophet *and* New York Messenger *were published, was located in the center of this photo, left of the tree above the first car on the left, 45 feet from the corner of the Pace College building. The tree is nearly centered on the building where* The Prophet *was published. The* Tribune *was published in a building just left of* The Prophet *building. The Pace College building covers the sites of both of these newspapers. (1988)*

Nassau), is #7 Spruce Street, where *The Prophet* was published and printed. This was the first Mormon newspaper outside of a Mormon community in the United States. At the time of this writing Pace University buildings covered the site of both the *New York Tribune* building and 7 Spruce Street. Number 7 was on the north side of Spruce Street. The building was 25' wide, and the west side of the building was 75' from the east curb of Nassau Street or 70' feet from the SW corner of the Pace University building (PEM; LCD 1837; ThP).

The Prophet was a four-page, five-column-per-page newspaper published each Saturday from May 18, 1844, to May 22, 1845 (52 issues). The paper's motto was "We contend for the truth." The editors, in chronological order, were Elder G. T. Leach (May 18, 1844), William Smith (June 29, 1844), Samuel Brannan (July 20, 1844), and Parley P. Pratt.

When Orson Pratt succeeded his brother Parley as president of the Eastern States Mission in July 1845, *The Prophet* was renamed the *New York Messenger.* Twenty issues of the *New York Messenger* were printed from July 5, 1845, to Nov. 15, 1845. Editors of the *New York Messenger* were Parley P. Pratt, Orson Pratt, and Samuel Brannan. The last issue of the *New York Messenger* contained a plea to the Eastern Saints to "flee out of Babylon."

The **printing press** used to publish *The Prophet* and the *New York Messenger* was taken aboard the ***Brooklyn*** when it set sail from New York City on Feb. 4, 1846, with 230 Saints bound for California. The press was used in California to print the *California Star,* the first regular English language newspaper printed on the Pacific Coast.

The **Prophetic Almanac** was also published at the office of *The Prophet* at 7 Spruce Street. This was an annual magazine published from 1845 to 1865 in NYC by editor Orson Pratt.

■ **55. AMERICAN BIBLE SOCIETY SITE.** During the 1850s the American Bible Society was located at 119–121 Nassau Street (west side) in the heart of the newspaper publishing district, a half of a short block north of Ann Street and the publishing house of *The Mormon* (1855–57). A 10-story building built in 1919 marks the site of the 1850s American Bible Society (LJT 258–59; PEM; LCD 1857). (Learn about the American Bible Society, site no. 55, while standing at the NE corner of Nassau and Ann Streets and reading about site no. 57, *The Mormon.*)

American Bible Society building site. In 1850 the building had a 100-foot-wide front along the west side of Nassau St. and centered on the arches just left of the center of this photo. (1988)

■ **56.** *NEW YORK MIRROR* **SITE.** On the NW corner of Nassau and Ann Streets was the publishing house of the *New York Mirror* from 1855 to 1857. The address was 40 Ann Street or 113–115 Nassau Street. This newspaper published anti-Mormon sentiments while *The Mormon* was being published in a building diagonally across the street. (LJT 249–50; LCD; PEM; AYP 144). (Learn about the *New York Mirror,* site no. 56 while standing at the NE corner of Nassau and Ann Streets and reading about site no. 57, *The Mormon.*)

Looking north, the New York Mirror *building was on the NW corner of Nassau and Ann Streets. It was located diagonally (NW) across Nassau from* The Mormon *publishing house.*

■ **57.** *THE MORMON* **SITE.** From the NE corner of Nassau and Ann Streets, one can easily see four related sites, nos. 55, 56, 58, 59, that are mentioned along with this site.

Masthead of The Mormon, *Feb. 7, 1857*

After Orson Pratt announced publicly in 1852 that the Latter-day Saints believed in the practice of polygamy, the Saints decided that they should tell their own story rather than be maligned by "gentile" editors. Four Apostles and George Q. Cannon were sent as editors to different parts of the United States where they published supportive newspapers.[9]

John Taylor was sent to New York City, where he published *The Mormon* at 102 Nassau Street (on the SE corner of Ann and Nassau Streets, where the business "Optic Masters" was located in 1996). This location was in the middle of the newspaper publishing district of NYC and right by three large newspapers: the *Sun,* one short block south, on the SW corner of Fulton and Nassau Streets; the *New York Herald,* a short half block south on the NW corner of Nassau and Fulton Streets; and the *New York Mirror,* NW across the street, on the NW corner of Ann and Nassau Streets. The *New York Tribune* and the *New York Times* were located one block north of *The Mormon.* At least seven newspaper publishers were nearby (NYD 801; AYP 141–44; LJT 245–62).

The Mormon was a weekly newspaper published from Feb. 17, 1855, to Sept. 19, 1857. The editor, John Taylor, was assisted by

The Mormon *was published in a building on the SE corner of Ann and Nassau Streets with the front at 102 Nassau.*

---

[9] Orson Pratt, in Washington, D.C., published the *Seer* (1853–54); Erastus Snow, in St. Louis, published the *St. Louis Luminary* (1854–55); John Taylor, in New York City, published *The Mormon* (1855–57); George Q. Cannon, in San Francisco, published the *Western Standard* (1856–57); Augustus Farnham published *Zion's Watchman* (1853–55) in Sydney, Australia, and Orson Hyde was already publishing the *Frontier Guardian* (1849–52) in Kanesville, Iowa (DLP LJT:243–45).

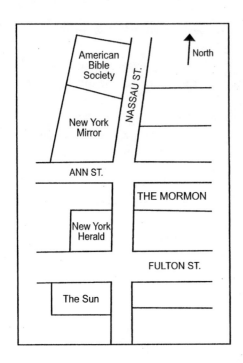

Thomas B. H. Stenhouse. It was a handsome, well-printed newspaper, and several columns of each issue were printed in French. The paper was suspended in 1857 after 135 issues because of the so-called "Utah War" (DLP 30–31).

Although John Taylor had been elected a member of the Utah Territorial Legislature, he resigned his position to accept a mission call in the fall of 1854. This time he was called to preside over the branches in the eastern states, supervise the immigration of the Saints, and publish a paper in the interest of the Church. The paper was to instruct the eastern Saints about emigration and to correct false reports about the Church (ThM 1, no. 2:2) Money to publish was scarce, but John Taylor borrowed a few hundred dollars and sold the teams and wagons that brought him and five others from Utah to NYC. The first issue of the paper was dated Feb. 17, 1855. Elder Taylor reported to President Brigham Young, saying, "We commenced our publication. . . . How long we shall be able to continue, I don't know. We are doing as well as we can, and shall continue to do so; but I find it one thing to preach the gospel without purse or scrip, and another thing to publish a paper on the same terms" (LJT 245–46).

B. H. Roberts described *The Mormon* with these words:

It had a very striking and significant heading, filling up at least one fourth of the first page. It represented an immense American eagle with out-stretched wings poised defiant above a bee-hive, and two American flags. Above the eagle was an all-seeing eye surrounded by a blaze of glory, and the words: "Let there be light; and there was light." On the stripes of the flag on the left was written:"Truth, Intelligence, Virtue and Faith;" signed, "John Taylor;" upon those on the right; "Truth will prevail;" signed, "H. C. Kimball;" while in the blue fields of one of the flags, the star of Utah shone resplendently. . . . Two scrolls on either side of the eagle bore the following inscriptions: "Mormon creed—mind your own business," Brigham Young; and "Constitution of the United States, given by inspiration of God," Joseph Smith.

On the inside, at the head of the editorial column was the American eagle standing on a bee-hive. . . . On one side, leaned the Doctrine and Covenants, Book of Mormon and Bible; on the other a tablet on which was written: "Peace and good will to man." The eagle held in its beak a scroll on which was written: "Holiness to the Lord." (LJT 246–47)

B. H. Roberts continued, writing:

The very name, Mormon—which they had derided and made the synonym for all that was absurd in religion, impure in social life, or disloyal to government, [Taylor] took up and made the title of his paper—wrote it in bold letters and surrounded it with the symbols of liberty, intelligence and truth, and defied its slanderers to pluck from it the emblems in which he enshrined it.

"We are Mormon," he writes in the first number, "inside and outside; at home or abroad, in public and private—everywhere. We are so, however, from principle. We are such, not because we believe it to be the most popular, lucrative, or honorable (as the world has it); but because we believe it to be true, and more reasonable and scriptural, moral and philosophic; because we conscientiously believe it is more calculated to promote the happiness and well-being of humanity, in time and throughout all eternity, than any other system which we have met with. (LJT 249)

Roberts also described the method of distribution:

It was the custom at the time to distribute the first issue of newspapers free to the news boys, and let them sell them for what they pleased. Accordingly, on the first day of its publication hundreds of news boys filled the lower offices and thronged the stairway leading to the upper rooms, clamoring for *The Mormon*. As they were promptly supplied, the paper with its conspicuous heading was waved in the face of the public and all through the principal thoroughfares the cry of "*Mormon*," "*Mormon*"—"Here's yer *Mormon*," was heard ringing and echoing on every side. (LJT 247–48)

In one of the earlier issues, Elder Taylor printed the following challenge:

> We have said before and say now, that we defy all the editors and writers in the United States to prove that Mormonism is less moral, scriptural, philosophical; or that there is less patriotism in Utah than in any other part of the United States. We call for proof; bring on your reasons, gentlemen, if you have any; we shrink not from the investigation, and dare you to the encounter. If you don't do it, and you publish any more of your stuff, we shall brand you as poor, mean, cowardly liars; as men publishing falsehoods knowing them to be so, and shrinking from the light of truth and investigation. (LJT 249)

The *New York Mirror*, located on the corner opposite of *The Mormon* (NW corner of Ann and Nassau Streets), made the following statement about the rise of Mormonism:

> While our public moralists and reformers are making war upon the hotels and taverns and private property of our citizens, a hideous system—an immoral excrescence—is allowed to spring up and overtop the Constitution itself. Why are there no public meetings convened in the tabernacle to denounce Mormonism? The evil has become a notorious fact—its existence cannot be any longer ignored—and it is not therefore prudent that the eyes of the public should be closed to its effects. (LJT 250)

Both the *New York Herald* and the *New York Sun* published their slander. Elder Taylor said to them:

Your malicious slanders only excite contempt for those base enough to utter them. Your contemptible falsehoods fail to ruffle a feather in our caps. . . . The God of Jacob in whom the Mormons trust—He who brought up Israel out of Egypt— He it is who sustained the Mormons in their tedious journeyings over the barren deserts and wild mountain passes of this continent. In the dark hour of trial, amid all their distresses, without friends or home—God upheld and sustained them; He sustains them still, and will cause them to shine forth with the bright radiance of eternal truth over the wide world, long after their malicious slanderers shall have sunk to oblivion in the filth of their own corruptions. (LJT 252)

While John Taylor was in NYC, a number of plans were suggested for the overthrow of Mormonism. Roberts said, "the [*New York*] *Sun*, seized with a sudden spasm of confidence that Christianity could overwhelm Mormonisn, [sic] called upon the churches of New York to send ministers to convert the Mormons from the error of their ways" (LJT 259). Others said, let the grasshoppers take care of them. Others wanted to send "woman's rights" advocates to incite a revolution among the wives of the Apostles. Perhaps one of the most humorous suggestions was proposed by the American Bible Society. It suggested flooding the settlements of Utah with Bibles. When John Taylor heard of this, he called at the office of the society, which was a short half block away (north), and offered his assistance in the enterprise, urging them to send well-bound books because the Mormons would read them. Taylor approved of the undertaking of sending the ministers to Utah, but expressed his doubts as to their going. He later referred to the failure of the Bible Society, saying: "The Bible Society got up a report about two months ago, that they were going to send a Bible agent to Utah. We then hastened to offer them our co-operation, but as we advanced to receive the precious gifts, they vanished into their original element—gas!" (LJT 259).

The *New York Herald*, whose manager and proprietor was James Gordon Bennett, wrote that Mormon women were ripe for rebellion, and that good-looking soldiers could be sent to Salt Lake City to prostitute and debauch the plural wives and lead them away from their husbands. Taylor questioned the character of James Gordon Bennett who openly proposed "the introduction of debased characters into a Territory for the avowed purpose of seduction, prostitution and infamy, for the purpose of corrupting the Mormons" (LJT 261–62).

John Taylor helped to change the attitude of the Easterners through the pages of *The Mormon,* took care of emigration, and oversaw the missionary work in the eastern states. He reported that there were large and flourishing branches of the Church in the different parts of the state, that the Spirit of the Lord rested among the assemblies of the Saints, and that the light of eternal truth was bursting forth with resplendence and glory (LJT 266). Taylor left *The Mormon* in the hands of Judge William I. Appleby and T. B. H. Stenhouse, and in May 1857, left for Utah. Stenhouse's name was removed from the paper after two issues and Appleby served as assistant editor in Taylor's absence until the end of the publication, Sept. 19, 1857 (BE 1:14–19; HiR 5:59–62).

Site 57, where sites 55, 56, 58, and 59 are also discussed, is the last site of the lower Manhattan walking tour. A very short block south of site 57 are sites 58 and 59, at the corner of Nassau and Fulton Streets. There is a subway station nearby for easy transportation. Approximately ½ mile east is the South Street Seaport, a lively place for a meal, shopping, or entertainment. One block south is Broadway and another subway station.

■ **58. *NEW YORK HERALD* SITE.** Offices of the *New York Herald* newspaper were at 125 Fulton Street, on the NW corner of Nassau and Fulton Streets, one short block south of *The Mormon* office at 102 Nassau. In 1996 the business in the existing corner building was Kid's Time, and the address was 93–105 Nassau or 125–131 Fulton (PEM 1852; NYD). While *The Mormon* was being published (1855–57), the *New York Herald* printed many bitter anti-Mormon articles (LJT 250–51). James Gordon Bennett was the manager and proprietor at the time. (Read about the *New York Herald,* site no. 58, while standing at the NE corner of Nassau and Ann Streets and while reading about site no. 57.)

■ **59. *NEW YORK SUN* SITE.** The *New York Sun* newspaper offices were located across the street from the *New York Herald* offices, on the SW corner of Nassau and Fulton Streets, one block south of *The Mormon* offices (PEM; NYD). In 1996 the business in the existing building was "Moshells." The address was 87–91 Nassau or

124–136 Fulton (LJT 251–52). (Learn about the *New York Sun,* site no. 59, while standing at the NE corner of Nassau and Ann Streets and reading about site no. 57)

Tour Two: Chinatown to Greenwich Village

The starting point for the Chinatown to Greenwich Village walking or auto tour will be the east end of Delancy Street at the East River Park along the west bank of the East River near the Williamsburg Bridge. The tour will proceed from the **East River** and go basically west to the Hudson River, then north to Greenwich Village. The distance is approximately five miles.

Sites no. 63, 64, 67, 68, 70, 73, 76, 80, 82, 84–86, 88, and 90 are not as important, and by skipping them, tour two will be shorter and more practical.

■ **60. EAST RIVER BAPTISM SITE AND WILLIAMSBURG BRIDGE.** Parley P. Pratt and Elijah Fordham did missionary work in New York City from about June 1837 until Apr. 1838. During this time there were many converts to the Church, and many baptisms took place in the East River near its west bank, close to the west end of Williamsburg Bridge, and probably on the north side of the bridge near Houston Street. The Williamsburg Bridge, located north of the Brooklyn Bridge, spans the East River to connect Manhattan with Brooklyn. On the Manhattan side, the entrance to the bridge is from Delancy and Clinton Streets. The bridge was built in 1903 and is supported by truss and pier, rather than pendant cable.

Elijah Fordham, missionary companion to Parley P. Pratt, in NYC, 1837–38

The first six known baptisms were performed by Elijah Fordham on about Dec. 19, 1837. Those baptized were Margaret Merkbe Mace (wife of Wandle), Theodore Curtis (1815–1903) and his wife, Margaret Morgan, a Mrs. Dexter and her daughter (whose baby had been

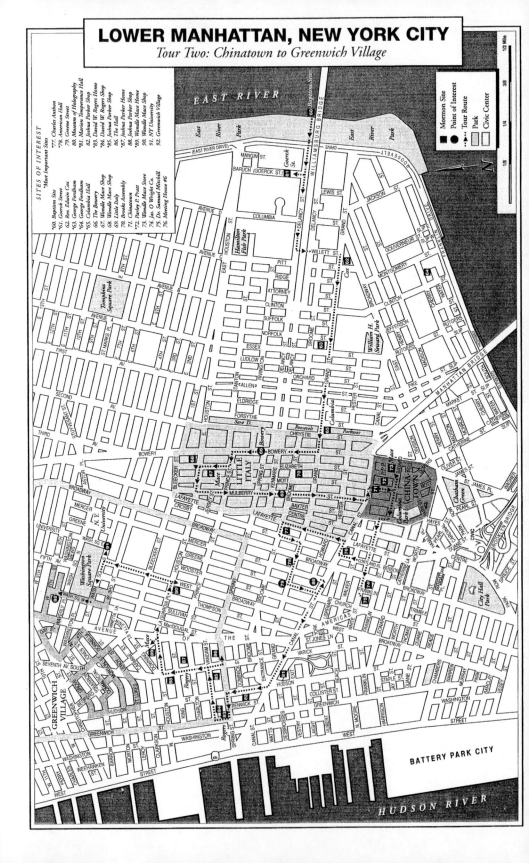

LOWER MANHATTAN, NEW YORK CITY
Tour Two: Chinatown to Greenwich Village

SITES OF INTEREST
Most Important Sites

*60. Baptism Site
*61. Goerck Street
62. Rev. Edwin Cox
63. George Fordham
64. George Fordham
*65. Columbia Hall
66. The Bowery
67. Wandle Mace Shop
68. Wandle Mace Shop
69. Little Italy
70. Brooks Assembly
71. Chinatown
*72. Parley P. Pratt
73. Wandle Mace Store
74. Jas. O Wright Co.
75. Dr. Samuel Mitchill
76. Meeting House #6

*77. Charles Anthon
*78. American Hall
79. Greene Street
80. Museum of Holography
*81. Marion Temperance Hall
82. Joshua Parker Shop
*83. David W. Rogers Home
*84. David W. Rogers Shop
*85. Joshua Parker Shop
86. The Hall
*87. Joshua Parker Home
88. Joshua Parker Shop
*89. Wandle Mace Home
90. Wandle Mace Shop
91. NY University
92. Greenwich Village

Legend:
- Mormon Site
- Point of Interest
- Tour Route
- Park
- Civic Center

EAST RIVER

HUDSON RIVER

BATTERY PARK CITY

GREENWICH VILLAGE

LITTLE ITALY

CHINA TOWN

1/2 Mile

healed), and Miss Ann Shaffer, who was later married to Elijah Fordham. The Curtis family, like the Mace family, remained faithful and moved with the Saints to Utah.

Of that day of baptisms Wandle Mace said:

> It was a very wet disagreeable day, with snow and rain, the side-walks was shoe deep with snow and mud. . . . I stood upon a block of ice and witnessed the baptisms, all retired to the house of brother [Edwin] Cox [see site no. 62], who live nearby [probably at 465 Division St.], where those who had been baptized, changed their clothing and we then returned home. . . .
>
> All wondered why I was not then baptized. My reasons for this was, that I wanted to see them act on their own volition, not because I set them the example. A few days after this, I was baptized in the same place, by Elder Parley P. Pratt. (JWMa 21; APPP 168–72)

Parley P. Pratt said, "We soon commenced baptizing, and continued doing so almost daily during the winter and spring" (APPP 171). The families of Wandle Mace, Edwin Cox, David Rogers, Addison Everett, and Joshua Parker were some of the earliest baptized in New York City.

■ **61. GOERCK STREET LDS MEETINGHOUSE SITE NO. 1.** Goerck Street, now Baruch Place, runs through a housing development and is about five blocks long. It runs approximately north and south and goes between Houston and Delancy Streets at a point about three blocks west of the East River near the Williamsburg Bridge. The address of the upper room, on Goerck Street, which was the **first LDS meeting place** in New York City, is unknown.

When Elder Parley P. Pratt arrived at NYC in late July 1837 as one of the first LDS missionaries to NYC, Elijah Fordham, an elder, was the only member here. Fordham helped Parley P. Pratt in his missionary labors. After baptizing about six members, Parley said they "organized a little branch who were accustomed to meet in a small upper room in Goerck street; sometimes two or three others met with us" (APPP 169). Although Parley calls this small group a "branch" of the Church, it appears that it operated with Parley as the religious leader. There was not a formal branch president until Apr. 1838, when Wandle Mace was set apart as the first president of the New York Branch. Mace served until Sept. 1838, when he gathered with the Saints in Nauvoo.

After Parley P. Pratt, with the assistance of Elijah Fordham (EJ Oct. 1837, 9), published 4,000 copies of his *Voice of Warning* in Oct. 1837, and after working for six months in NYC with little success, he was ready to leave the city. Discouraged, he wrote:

> Of all the places in which the English language is spoken, I found the City of New York to be the most difficult as to access to the minds or attention of the people. From July to January we preached, advertised, printed, published, testified, visited, talked, prayed, and wept in vain. To all appearance there was no interest or impression on the minds of the people in regard to the fulness of the gospel. . . .
>
> We had retired to our private room up stairs [on Goerck Street] with the few members we had, to hold a last prayer meeting, as I was about taking leave for New Orleans. We had prayed all round in turn, when, on a sudden, the room was filled with the Holy Spirit, and so was each one present. We began to speak in tongues and prophesy. Many marvelous things were manifested which I cannot write; but the principal burthen of the prophesyings was concerning New York City, and our mission there.
>
> The Lord said that He had heard our prayers, beheld our labors, diligence, and long suffering towards that city; and that He had seen our tears. Our prayers were heard, and our labors and sacrifices were accepted. We should tarry in that city, and go not thence as yet; for the Lord had many people in that city, and He had now come by the power of His Holy Spirit to gather them into His fold. (APPP 169–70)

They did tarry in NYC, and they found much success.

In that very special meeting was David Rogers, an investigator whose heart was touched. He invited Parley to hold meetings in his home at 515 Greenwich Street, which would be the second meeting place of the Saints in NYC.

■ **62. ELDER EDWIN COX HOME SITE.** Through information gleaned from New York City directories (LCD 1837:178) and Perris Maps of 1852 (PEM), it is concluded that Elder Edwin Cox (spelled "Coxe"

LDS Meeting Sites in New York City (1837–57)		
Date	**Site #**	**Location**
1. 1837	61	Small upper room, Goerck Street (Baruch Place)
2. 1837	83	David White Rogers's home, 515 Greenwich Street
3. 1837–38	83	"A small place," location unknown (perhaps 245 Spring Street)
4. 1839–41	65	Columbia Hall, 263 Grand Street
5. 1840–42	86	"The Hall," 245 Spring Street (next to Rogers' shop at 247 Spring Street)
6. 1841–43	76	29 and 31 Canal Street
7. 1843–44	65	Columbia Hall, 263 Grand Street
8. 1844	81	Marion Temperance Hall, 183 Canal Street
9. 1844–45	78	American Hall, corner of Grand Street and Broadway
10. 1856	78	Broadway House, 116 Grand Street
11. 1856–57	70	Brooks Assembly Rooms, 361 Broome Street

These are the main locations, but not necessarily all locations. Parley P. Pratt preached in Tammany Hall at Printing House Square in 1837–38 (site no. 52). Meeting sites 4 and 7 and meeting sites 9 and 10 are in the same location.

in the directory), a Methodist minister before converting to Mormonism, lived at 465 Grand Street (PEM; NYD). Parley P. Pratt wrote about Rev. Cox: "A Methodist clergyman came to hear me [apparently at David Rogers's house at 515 Greenwich Street, site no. 83], whose name was Cox. He invited me to his house to preach [465 Grand St.], near East River; he and household were obedient to the faith, with many of the members of his society"(APPP 171).

■ **63. GEORGE FORDHAM HOME SITE NO. 1.** George Fordham, father of Elijah Fordham, lived at 51 Norfolk Street during 1837 and 1838.

■ **64. GEORGE FORDHAM HOME SITE NO. 2.** George Fordham also lived at 327 Cherry Street between 1837 and 1838 (HC 2:495, 4:314; NYD; PEM).

■ **65. COLUMBIA HALL, LDS MEETING SITE NO. 4.** Columbia Hall, also called "Columbian Hall," was located on the south side of Grand Street "a few doors east of the Bowery" at no. 263, between Chrystie and Forsythe Streets (HC 4:22; PEM 1852; NYD).

When the Quorum of the Twelve stopped in NYC in the winter of 1839–40 on their way to serve missions in England, they baptized nearly 40 persons and held a conference in Columbia Hall, for which Parley P. Pratt wrote a special hymn (APPP 299–300). Parley said there were 150 to 200 members of the Church in New York City and Brooklyn, and that three meetings were held each Sunday in Columbia Hall on Grand Street, a few doors east of the Bowery. Pratt said that Columbia Hall "is very central, and one of the best places in the city; it will hold nearly a thousand people." He said that, at the November conference, the hall was "well filled with attentive hearers" (HC 4:22).

In 1840, conferences were held in Columbia Hall on Feb. 2, Mar. 8, and Dec. 4 (HC 4:77, 94, 237). The Twelve conducted meetings in February prior to their departure for England. George A. Smith and Brigham Young preached at these meetings. Brigham Young preached every evening during the week, three times in Columbia Hall. As a result, he exhausted himself so much that he was not able to dress himself for four or five days (HC 4:77). By Feb. 23, Brigham Young was able to attend sermons given by Parley P. Pratt in Columbia Hall (CHC 4:87).

At the Mar. 8, 1840, meeting, the day before the Twelve boarded the *Patrick Henry* for England, Brigham Young presided and preached in Columbia Hall (HC 4:94).

Orson Hyde presided at the Dec. 4, 1840, conference, and during the conference revelations claimed to have been received from God by Sidney Roberts were rejected. The revelations concerned a gold watch, a suit of clothes, and saluting the sisters with a holy kiss. Roberts refused to receive counsel and was subsequently excommunicated (HC 4:237).

Many other important meetings and conferences were held at Columbia Hall between 1839 and 1844, including a meeting Aug. 27, 1843, when the Quorum of the Twelve met with the Saints. Brigham Young, George A. Smith, Wilford Woodruff, Heber C. Kimball, John E. Page, and Orson Pratt were speakers. Elder George T. Leach was appointed to preside over the Church in New York, in place of L. R. Foster, who was about to move to Nauvoo (HC 5:393, 549–53).

● **66. THE BOWERY.** The Bowery is a street about 12 blocks long that runs north and south through Little Italy and Chinatown, but the part of the street between East Houston and Delancy Streets in particular is called "the Bowery." Although Vaudeville made the Bowery an important place of entertainment in the early 20th century, it is now a hangout for derelicts.

■ **67. WANDLE MACE COACH MAKER'S BUSINESS SITE.** Wandle Mace's coachmaking shop was located at 249 Elizabeth Street. Mace operated this business between 1836 and 1837 (PEM; NYD). (See sites no. 26 and 89 for related information.)

■ **68. WANDLE MACE MACHINIST'S SHOP SITE.** Wandle Mace maintained a machinist's shop at 264 Elizabeth Street in 1838 (PEM; NYD). (See sites no. 26 and 89 for related information.)

● **69. LITTLE ITALY AND MULBERRY STREET.** In the center of East Houston Street on the north, Canal Street on the south, Lafayette on the west, and Second Avenue on the east is the most important area of the Old Italian center of NYC. **Mulberry Street** is a lively street to walk down, and during festival time it becomes very colorful.

The most exciting **bazaar** in NYC is located in the area in SE Little Italy. Between Grand and Canal Streets are Lower Eldridge, Allen, and Orchard Streets; these are especially spirited on weekends. **Orchard Street** has clothing for sale and is one of the most hectic, but exciting bazaar streets in New York City.

■ **70. BROOKS ASSEMBLY ROOMS, LDS MEETING PLACE SITE NO. 11.** Used from 1856 to 1857, the Brooks Assembly Rooms were one of the last meeting sites in New York City before the Saints were urged to "flee out of Babylon." The assembly rooms were located at 361 Broome Street (ThM 3, no. 5:3; NYD; PEM).

■ **71. CHINATOWN.** Although Chinatown is rapidly encroaching on Little Italy, the heart of Chinatown is on **Mott, Bayard,** and **Pell Streets.** These three streets are located about three blocks east of Broadway in Lower Manhattan, near the exit of the Manhattan Bridge.

Chinese restaurants, tiny streets, and oriental shops make a visit to Chinatown an exciting cultural experience. About 125,000 people of Asian descent live in the area surrounding the main streets of Chinatown. The first Asian settlers in Chinatown came from the California gold fields in the 1850s and from the transcontinental railroad work force after the railroad was completed in 1869.

- **72. PARLEY P. PRATT HOME SITE.** Parley P. Pratt (1807–57) left Nauvoo on Aug. 29, 1839, for an Apostolic mission to England. He

traveled to New York City with his wife and three children. Parley wanted to do more missionary work in New York City where he had labored as a missionary in 1837–38 (see site no. 61).

When the Pratts arrived in NYC they rented a house at 58 Mott Street. Parley lived in this house with his family for six months while he did missionary work in New York City and environs. Elder Pratt boarded the ship *Patrick Henry* with others of the Twelve and left for England on Mar. 9, 1840. He had to leave his wife, Mary Ann, and their children in their rented home on Mott Street in New York City (HC 4:80).

The Parley P. Pratt home site (1839–40) at 58 Mott Street in Chinatown. The 25-foot-wide front of the five-story red brick building was the location of the front of Pratt's home.

The Pratt home at 58 Mott Street was located in the very center of what is now **Chinatown;** but there was no Chinatown when the Pratts lived here. But Chinatown did not have its beginnings as an ethnic community until the 1850s, after the Pratts left NYC. Parley's rented home was located on the east side of Mott Street, about halfway between Canal Street on the north and Bayard Street on the south. In 1996 the building covering

Parley P. Pratt

the site of 58 Mott housed a business named "Wah Kue Inc., Hobbies, Toys, Stationery," and the whole building was numbered 56. The home that Parley rented was 25' wide and 50' deep, a typical size of a home or business building in NYC during the mid-1800s (PEM 1853; NYD; HC 4:80).

Brigham Young, John Taylor, and **Wilford Woodruff,** all three of whom became Presidents of the Church, stayed in Parley P. Pratts' home as they waited to go by ship to England. George A. Smith also stayed at the Pratt's and it is assumed that all of the England-bound missionaries including Orson Pratt and Rueben Hedlock stayed at the Pratt home at some time during the winter of 1839–40.

While staying at Parley P. Pratt's home at 58 Mott in Dec. 1839, **Wilford Woodruff** saw his wife twice in a dream, who told him of the future death of his two daughters. Matthias F. Cowley wrote: "The second time she was weeping, and both times was in great affliction. Upon his inquiring after their little daughter, Sister Woodruff answered, 'She is dead.' This warning in this dream received fulfilment on the 17th of the following July, the child dying on that date, while he was in England" (WW 113).

Elder Parley P. Pratt lived in New York City as a missionary at least three different times: (1) July 1837 to Apr. 1838, (2) Aug. 1839 to Mar. 1840, (3) Dec. 1844 to July 1845 (as mission president). In June 1845 Parley was ready to leave New York City, feeling that he could do no more good here. He wrote to the Quorum of the Twelve:

> I have become convinced that I can do no good here. The public are entirely indifferent, and will neither come to meeting, hear, nor read the truth. The saints are few, about fifty of them attended a Sunday meeting in a large hall, and perhaps half a dozen strangers come in and out to gaze and gape and wonder and perish.
>
> I have labored hard for six months without an idle moment, and have used economy in living, traveling and clothing. I feel as if I was now done with this city, and nearly so with the nation. My garments are clear, if they all perish. (HC 7:425–26)

Parley left NYC and arrived in Nauvoo in Aug. 1845. Twice more he visited NYC—once in 1846 on his way to England, and again in 1857, for his last time. He was assassinated in Arkansas on May 13, 1857, while returning to Utah from New York City (APPP 436–61).

■ **73. WANDLE MACE GROCERY BUSINESS SITE.** Wandle Mace and his brother John operated two grocery stores in New York City. One store was located here at 44 Bayard Street (PEM; NYD). This store was in business from 1831 to 1832. (See sites no. 26 and 89 for related information.)

■ **74. JAS. O. WRIGHT & COMPANY, PUBLISHERS SITE.** The Jas. O. Wright & Company, publishers, was located between Franklin and White Streets at 377 Broadway. The company was on the west side of the street, with just one business (no. 379) between their building and White Street. Wright's business front was the second building from the corner of White and Broadway Streets (PEM; NYD).

Two editions of the **Book of Mormon** were published at Jas. O. Wright & Company as reprints of the third American edition of 1842 (Nauvoo). The first, known as the "Wright Edition," was the first unauthorized edition of the Book of Mormon. It was printed in 1858, apparently as a business venture.

The second unauthorized edition of the Book of Mormon, also printed in 1858, was the same as the first, except it had an "Introduction" written by **Zadok Brooks.** Brooks, an elder in the Church of Christ, was a leader of dissidents from the original Church of Jesus Christ of Latter-day Saints, and his group is sometimes known as the "Brooksites." Brooks apparently affiliated with Granville Hedrick and the Whitmer family in Richmond, MO; but he later became a follower of Alexander Campbell. Brooks's "Introduction" indicated that he believed the Book of Mormon was true, but that he was opposed to the principle of polygamy. The later Brooks-Hundley Edition of the Book of Mormon (ca. 1861) was, according to its title, an impression of the 1858 edition but was actually from the 1852 Liverpool edition and was used by most RLDS members between 1862 and 1874 (AMB 48). The edition was also the source for the 1874 RLDS edition of the Book of Mormon.

■ **75. DR. SAMUEL MITCHILL HOME SITE.** When Martin Harris visited Dr. Samuel Mitchill in 1828 to show him the characters from the Book of Mormon gold plates, Mitchill lived at 47 White Street. The

Dr. Samuel L. Mitchill

house was about halfway between Franklin Place and Church Street on the south side of the street and about a block west of Broadway (PEM 1828; NYD). The home was located a short block west of where the "Wright Edition" of the Book of Mormon was published (see site no. 74). This was Mitchill's home from 1822 until his death in 1831.

A modern Jewish synagogue now covers the site. The Mitchill home, with a 25-foot front, was on the left half of the site where the synagogue sits as one faces the synagogue (see site no. 46 for details on Mitchill; CHC 1:99–109).

■ **76. LDS MEETING PLACE SITE NO. 6.** From 1841 to 1843 the Saints in New York City met in a building at 29 and 31 Canal Street (NYD; PEM).

■ **77. CHARLES ANTHON HOME SITE.** Charles Anthon, of the "Anthon Book of Mormon Manuscript" fame, lived on the south side of Broome Street at no. 417. This address was between Lafayette (Elm Street in Anthon's day) and Crosby Streets. His 25-foot-wide home facade started at a point 50 feet west of the NE corner of the current building on the SW corner of Broome and Lafayette Streets. The 1828 and 1830 NYC directories listed Anthon's business address as 7 Columbia College; no home address was listed (NYD; PEM 1828, 1830; see also site no. 46).

■ **78. AMERICAN HALL, MEETING SITE NO. 9, AND BROADWAY HOUSE, MEETING SITE NO. 10.** Between 1839 and 1856, the Saints held their meetings at two different sites on Grand Street, with the addresses of 263 and 116 (corner of Grand Street and Broadway).

The ninth and tenth meeting places were located at the same site but had different names at different times.

During 1844 and 1845, the meeting place was called the **American Hall** or **American Republican Hall.** It was located on the NW corner of Grand Street and Broadway with the entrance on Broadway (NYD; PEM 1853).

During 1856 the meeting place was called **Broadway House,** and like the American Hall, it was also located at 116 Grand Street, which was still on the NW corner of Grand Street and Broadway, with an entrance, probably number 116, on the Grand Street side of the building. In 1996, the same NW corner was a parking lot (NYD; PEM 1853).

Every Sunday between Aug. 31 and Oct. 5, 1844, **Samuel Brannan** gave lectures at the American Hall.

At a conference held in the American Hall on Nov. 12, 1845, **Orson Pratt,** president of the Eastern States Mission, and **Samuel Brannan,** who was to preside over the Saints on the ship *Brooklyn,* were the main speakers. Orson Pratt explained the necessity for all Saints to move to the West. Elder Brannan called upon all who wanted to accompany him to the West on the ship *Brooklyn,* to come forward at the close of the meeting and put down their names (CHC 3:25–26). The conference also sanctioned the excommunication of William Smith (HC 7:520–22).

Apparently, the American Hall was the last place the Saints met in New York City until about 1856. Little is known about the Saints in NYC between 1845 and 1856 because most of the Saints had emigrated to the West.

In Mar. 1856, the Saints held meetings at 1:30 P.M., 3:00 P.M., and 7:00 P.M. each Sabbath day in the **Broadway House.** In June 1856, the meeting place was changed to the "large hall of **Brooks' Assembly Rooms,**" at 361 Broome Street (ThM 2, no. 5:3, and 18:2).

● **79. GREENE STREET.** Cast iron facades were fashionable in the 1850s and 1860s. Cast iron was much less expensive than stone decorative columns and was used to embellish NYC homes and buildings.

The 26-block area around Greene Street includes many buildings that are decorated with cast iron. A walk on Greene Street between Grand and Canal Streets is a unique architectural adventure.

● **80. MUSEUM OF HOLOGRAPHY—NO. 11 MERCER ST.**

■ **81. MARION TEMPERANCE HALL SITE.** The Marion Temperance Hall was located at 183 Canal Street, immediately SE of Hudson Street. A description indicates that the hall was on the corner (it was actually 175 feet from the corner) of Canal and Hudson Streets (PEM 1853). This is now the location of the exit to the Holland Tunnel

Marion Temperance Hall site, meeting site no. 8 (1844) at 183 Canal Street. The black lines on this photo show where the hall was located. Traffic exiting the Holland Tunnel passes under the Marion Temperance Hall Site. The center of the Temperance Hall was 177 feet past the tunnel exit.

which runs under the Hudson River. The retaining wall along the south side of the exit is approximately where the 25-foot facade of the Marion Temperance Hall was located. Canal, Hudson, and Vestry Streets form a triangle here. The center of the front of the hall was 50 feet NW of the center of the long side of the triangle, which was the south side of Canal Street. The Hudson Tunnel exit is under the site of the Marion Temperance Hall (PEM 1853).

A **conference** was held in the Marion Temperance Hall on Sept. 4 and 5, 1844. William Smith presided, and he suggested that the members "uphold the authorities of the church of God." George J. Adams spoke "in his usual bold, pointed, and forcible manner" (T&S 5, no. 19:680–82).

■ **82. JOSHUA PARKER CABINET SHOP SITE.** (See sites no. 87 and 88).

■ **83. DAVID WHITE ROGERS HOME SITE.** The David White Rogers home site in 1836–38 was on the NE corner of Greenwich and Spring Streets. It faced Greenwich (west) and was numbered 515. An office building with white columns against black walls is now

David White Rogers home site (1836–38), 515 Greenwich Street, meetinghouse site No. 2 (1837).

located on the site. It was numbered 315 (NYD 1836–39; PEM 1836–37; APH 497).

In 1830 David White Rogers (1787–1880) moved to NYC and opened a carpenter's and joiner's shop at 214 Washington Street; then in 1831 he moved his shop to 34 New Street, near the New York Stock Exchange. David and his family lived near the Battery at 1 Water Street, and then on May 1, 1835, they moved to 515 Greenwich, on the corner of Greenwich and Spring Streets. He had his cabinet shops nearby at 247 Spring St. (1835–36) and 90 Vandam St. (1836–37) (NYD; PEM 1836–38).

The original bank of the Hudson River was located immediately west of Greenwich Street, but by the 1830s, the bank was moved west, and Greenwich Street was lined with handsome private homes occupied by many of the city's foremost merchants, including many cabinet makers. The first elevated railway was constructed on Greenwich Street in 1869–70 from Battery Place to 30th Street. It was built on iron supports and the cars were pulled by cable until locomotive power was added in 1871 (AYP 80).

It was through the missionary efforts of Elijah Fordham and Elder **Parley P. Pratt** that David White Rogers and his family became converted to The Church of Jesus Christ of Latter-day Saints. After laboring as a missionary in New York City from July 1837 to Jan. 1838, Parley P. Pratt was very discouraged. As he prepared to leave for New Orleans, a last prayer meeting was held in the upper room on Goerck Street (site no. 61). After a very spiritual experience the missionaries attending the prayer meeting spoke in tongues, prophesied, and were inspired by the Lord to stay in New York City. Parley P. Pratt recorded his thoughts concerning this meeting: "Now there was in this little meeting [on Goerck St.] a man named David Rogers, whose heart was touched. He, being a chairmaker, fitted up a large room, and seated it with the chairs of his ware house, and invited us to preach in the same. [This was in the parlor of his house.] This room was crowded. He then joined with one of our members who was a joiner [probably Joshua Parker], and rented a small place, and seated it for a regular place of meeting" (APPP 170–71).

David White Rogers was a class leader in the Methodist Church, so he was cautious about becoming a Mormon. David's daughter, **Caroline,** recorded the following memory of her father's efforts to gain a testimony of Joseph Smith:

> I remember when my father did not come to his breakfast one morning. To find the reason, I went to his bedroom. There I saw my father by the side of the bed on his knees, so I shut the door carefully and went away. Every little while I returned to look through the door to see if father was still there. My father stayed there for four days and nights seeking a testimony of the truth of the restored gospel as told by the prophet Joseph Smith.
>
> During that time, he said, "The room was a blaze of light as the noon day sun. I saw Joseph Smith sitting at a stand in the corner of the room with the Book of Mormon in his hand." Father described the man he saw in his room to Parley P. Pratt who said he could not have described the prophet any better himself, and he knowing the prophet where my father had never seen him.
>
> My mother also had a testimony to the truth of the gospel. About two years before Parley P. Pratt came to New York City with the gospel, my mother dreamed that two men came to our house. They had a book with them, which they told her was of great importance. The men she recognized as Parley P. Pratt and Elijah Fordham, who came to our house together and brought the Book of Mormon with them. (APH 476)

It was in David Rogers's house at 515 Greenwich, where meetings were held after Parley P. Pratt prayed so fervently in the upper room on Goerck Street. David Rogers was an investigator to the LDS Church when he offered to allow Parley P. Pratt use of his home as a meetinghouse.

David and Martha Rogers were baptized in the East River on Dec. 19, 1837, along with six of their 11 children. In Sept. 1838 David Rogers and his family joined with Wandle Mace and his family and journeyed toward Far West, MO. When they arrived at Quincy, IL, they found that the Saints had been driven out of Missouri, so they stayed in Quincy. They eventually moved to Commerce, IL (Nauvoo), then Montrose, IA, before emigrating to the West. David and Martha both died in Provo, UT, in 1881 (see sites no. 6 and 28).

■   **84. DAVID WHITE ROGERS CARPENTER SHOP SITE.** David White Rogers located his carpenter's shop at 90 Vandam Street from 1836 to 1837 (PEM 1836–37). The shop was the fourth 25-foot building front east of the corner of Greenwich and Vandam Streets (see also sites no. 6, 28, and 83).

■   **85. JOSHUA PARKER CABINET SHOP SITE.** Joshua Parker made his cabinet shop at 48 Vandam Street from 1831 to 1832 (PEM; LCD 1831). The building the shop was originally in no longer exists, but the site is occupied by a brown building with dark windowsills. (See also site no. 87.)

■   **86. "THE HALL," LDS MEETING SITE NO. 5.** The fifth site where the Latter-day Saints met in New York City was in the building at 245 Spring Street. It is the eighth building from the corner of Spring and Varick Streets. This site served as the branch's meeting place from 1840 until 1842 (HC 5:12; PEM; LCD 1842).

■   **87. JOSHUA PARKER HOME SITE.** The house at 29 Charlton Street, where **Joshua Parker** lived in New York City, was still standing in 1996. It was located on the north side of Charlton Street between the Avenue of the Americas and Varick Street. The house was the 15th house from the NW corner of Charlton Street and Avenue of the Americas. The house was once owned by Aaron Burr (ERA 45:500; PEM).

Joshua Parker (1809–80) was one of the first people converted by Elijah Fordham and Parley P. Pratt in 1837–38. He was baptized by Elijah Fordham on Jan. 9, 1838, when he was 28 and still single. Parker was a

Joshua Parker

cabinet maker and carpenter and had cabinet shops in the vicinity at 199 Varick Street (1830–31); 48 Vandam Street (1831–32), and 266 Hudson Street (1833–36) (NYD; PEM).

When David Rogers's home became too small to hold meetings, Joshua Parker joined with Rogers to acquire a larger meeting place. In 1844, at age 34, Joshua Parker married Drusilla Dixon Hartley in Nauvoo, and they eventually had 12 children. The family immigrated to Salt Lake City in 1852, where Joshua continued his cabinet making and carpentry work (PPM 1086).

Joshua Parker home site, 29 Charlton St.

■ **88. JOSHUA PARKER CABINET SHOP SITE.** Joshua Parker's first cabinet shop was at 199 Varick Street. Parker had his business here during 1830 and 1831. The shop was located in the fourth 25-foot-wide building from the SW corner of West Houston and Varick Streets (NYD; PEM; see also site no. 87).

■ **89. WANDLE MACE HOME SITE.** Wandle Mace (1809–90) resided at 13–15 Bedford Street when he was introduced to the restored gospel of Jesus Christ by Elijah Fordham and Elder Parley P. Pratt in 1837. At the time of this writing, both of these buildings were still extant (ERA 45:500, 522).

Parley P. Pratt indicated that Mace lived at 13 Bedford Street, and the New York City directory (1837–38) lists the Mace home site as 15 Bedford (JWMa 20). He probably owned both houses, which were side-by-side. These two houses are on the west side of Bedford Street between Downing and West Houston Streets. The houses are the fifth and sixth 25-foot-wide houses from the SW corner of Bedford and Downing Streets. No. 13 of 1837 was No. 19 in 1995 (NYD 1837–39, 413; PEM 1854; APPP 171).

During the time Wandle Mace was living at 13–15 Bedford

Street and was investigating the truthfulness of the gospel (ca. Nov. and Dec. 1837), his one-year-old son, Charles, became ill. The physician called the sickness "inflammation of the brain." Parley P. Pratt called it "the last stages of brain fever." The doctors had given up—the baby was having spasms and was near death—when the Maces decided to try "Mr. Pratt's religion." Wandle walked in the rain to Pratt's residence and asked him to bless his child. Perhaps he knew of Pratt's recent healing miracles (Pratt had healed a cripple who "arose and walked"). A woman who had been bedridden for four years with "dumb palsy" also "arose and walked" when blessed by God

Wandle Mace home site (1837–38), 13–15 Bedford Street, Greenwich Village. The building in the center was No. 13 (now 19) and the building on the right was No. 15 (21).

through Parley. Whatever else he knew, Wandle Mace had faith in God and His servant Parley P. Pratt.

When Pratt arrived at the Mace home, neighbors and relatives were already there to comfort the Maces, expecting the child to die. Parley first prayed, then he asked Wandle Mace to "lay on hands" with him, which he did. Parley rebuked the disease in the name of Jesus Christ, and the next day by 10:00 A.M., the child was well and playful. Written in the margin of Wandle Mace's journal are these interesting words: "Parley told me in Florence [NE] in 1856 that this was the only time he had asked a man not a member of the church to lay hands on the sick" (JWMa 17). A short time after the miracle, Mace and his family were baptized. Two years later in Quincy, IL, this child, named Charles, died at age three (JWMa 40).

A Mrs. Dexter, her daughter, and her daughter's baby were living upstairs in the Maces' home. Mrs. Dexter had come to NYC to escape her husband, and needed help as she cared for her daughter and grandchild who were seriously ill, with little hope of recovery. As Mrs. Dexter watched Parley administer to the Maces' baby, Charles, she said, "If this child can be healed, my daughter can" (JWMa 18). Two days after little Charles was healed, Wandle Mace wrote in his journal:

> Mrs. Dexter sent for Elder Pratt, who brought with him Elijah Fordham, also an elder. Together they sang a hymn to soft pleasant music. . . .
>
> After singing Elder Pratt offered up prayer, and he then explained the principles of the Gospel as he had done on the previous occasion. The sick woman listened attentively, and at her request, Elders Pratt and Fordham administered to her and also her babe. And they began to amend from that hour. . . . She was healed every whit [the baby was also healed]. Truly there was great rejoicing in my house, No 13 Bedford Street. (JWMa 18–20; APPP 171–72)

"In a short time after these miracles were performed [Dec. 1837], Elder Pratt appointed a day for baptizing in the East River, about two miles from my home," wrote Mace in his journal (JWMa 20–21). The party probably walked SE on Houston Street and were baptized approximately just north of where the Williamsburg Bridge now stands. (See site no. 60 for related information.)

In Apr. 1838 Elder Parley P. Pratt left the city with a small company of Saints for Missouri. His brother Orson Pratt having arrived from the West, took charge of the mission. Wandle Mace wrote concerning the arrival of Orson Pratt:

> And very soon after he arrived, he [Orson Pratt] ordained me an Elder and while his hands was upon my head, he broke out in tongues—I had never heard a manifestation of the gift of tongues before—after the tongues he said "You are of the seed of Joseph and the tribe of Ephraim" . . . He placed me to preside over the branch, while he traveled and preached and organized other branches of the church. While in the city himself and wife and little child, made their home at my house. This was the first branch of the Church of Jesus Christ of Latter-day Saints organized in New York City, and was composed of persons like myself, all young in the church, and they were very backward or diffident in speaking in public consequently most of the labor of preaching the gospel fell on me. We held

meetings three times on Sunday and one meeting during the week. (JWMa 21–22)

On Sept. 11, 1838, the Wandle Mace family and the David W. Rogers family with loaded horse-drawn wagons, went to Quincy, IL. Elder Orson Pratt, president of the mission, accompanied them across the river and traveled some distance with them before he bade them farewell (JWMa 26; BWM; EXWM; see site no. 26 for related information).

■ **90. WANDLE MACE COACH MAKER'S SHOP SITE.** Wandle Mace had a coach maker's shop at 161 West Broadway. This building is the third from the SW corner of Houston Street and West Broadway. (See site nos. 26 and 89 for related information.)

● **91. NEW YORK UNIVERSITY.** The principal campus of New York University is located immediately SW of Washington Square in the center of Greenwich Village. Most of the buildings of the main campus are in the vicinity of West 4th Street and Greene Street.

New York University is the largest private university in the world. It was founded in 1831 by Albert Gallatin, who was the Secretary of the Treasury under President Thomas Jefferson. NYU has 14 colleges and more than 45,000 students.

● **92. GREENWICH VILLAGE.** Greenwich Village is located in an area bounded approximately by Spring Street on the south and 14th Street on the north. On the east and west it is bounded approximately by Broadway and Greenwich Street, respectively. Its heart is Washington Square and the area just to the west of it.

The streets are not in a grid pattern like the rest of NYC because the village dates back to 1696 when British colonists settled here and named it after the English town of Greenwich.

In the 1830s, the area became fashionable as prominent families built town houses here. Eventually industry developed on the waterfront and Irish and Chinese immigrants settled here. Lower rents attracted artists and writers who followed the example of Edgar Allan Poe, who lived at 85 West 3rd Street in 1845.

The village still has its artists, intellectuals, students, theaters, movie houses, and rock and jazz musicians. It is especially interesting to visit Greenwich Village on Sundays or in the evening.

Other People, Events, and Places of Interest in the New York City Area

THE AMBITIOUS JAMES ARLINGTON BENNETT

James Arlington Bennett appeared suddenly in the history of the Church on Oct. 16, 1841, when he sent a letter from Arlington House, Long Island, NY, to James Gordon Bennett, the founder and editor of the *New York Herald*. James Arlington Bennett told James Gordon Bennett that he had received a letter from Joseph Smith before this time and that he, James Arlington Bennett, was "the friend of all good Mormons, as well as other good men" (HC 5:170–72). On Apr. 12, 1842, Joseph Smith appointed Willard Richards to write an "Epistle of the Twelve to the Saints in America." The epistle declared, among other things, that James Arlington Bennett, of Arlington House, Long Island, was appointed "Inspector-General of the Nauvoo-Legion, with the rank and title of Major-General" (HC 4:593). Shortly after that, on Apr. 22, 1842, the University of the City of Nauvoo conferred an honorary degree of LL.D. on General James Arlington Bennett (HC 4:600–601). Bennett wrote to **Joseph Smith** from Arlington House at Long Island on Aug. 16, 1842. He said: "Your polite and friendly note was handed to me a few days since by Dr. Willard Richards, who I must say, is a very fine specimen of the Mormon people, if they are all like him; and indeed I think him a very excellent representative of yourself, as I find he is your most devoted admirer and true disciple. He spent two days with me, and from his arguments, and from his mild and gentlemanly demeanor, almost made me a Mormon" (HC 5:112).

Bennett spoke of meeting a Brother Foster and Dr. Bernhisel. He said Foster was without guile. Of the two he said, "These are men with whom I could associate forever, even if I never joined their Church or acknowledged their faith." James Arlington Bennett continued his letter to Joseph Smith, saying:

> General John C. Bennett [the first mayor of Nauvoo] called on me last Friday and spent just two hours. . . . He, however, proposed to me to aid him, whether serious or not, in arranging materials for publishing "An Exposition of Mormon Secrets and Practices" which I promptly refused. . . . He [John C.

Bennett] gave Bennett of the *Herald* his commission, which I opposed from the very first; and you now see, by that paper, the sport which that man has made of it. I tell you there is no dependence on the friendship of that editor, when his interest is at issue. I am assured that James Gordon Bennett is going to publish, conjointly with John C. Bennett, on half profit, the exposition against you and your people, which is going to contain a great number of scandalous cuts and plates. But don't be concerned; you will receive no injury whatever from any thing any man or set of men may say against you. The whole of this muss is only extending your fame, and will increase your numbers ten-fold. . . .

My respects to your amiable lady and all friends; and believe me as ever, though not a Mormon, your sincere friend,

James Arlington Bennett. (HC 5:112–14)

A Boston firm, Leland and Whiting, published John C. Bennett's anti-Mormon book, *The History of the Saints, or an Exposure of Joseph Smith and Mormonism.* (See the entry on Leland and Whiting in the Massachusetts section of *Sacred Places,* vol. 1, for more information.)

James Arlington Bennett then wrote to the editor of the *Herald,* and contradicted false anti-Mormon reports. Joseph Smith answered James Arlington Bennett's letter and bore testimony that "'Mormonism' is the pure doctrine of Jesus Christ; of which I myself am not ashamed" (HC 5:152). It is a long and beautiful letter, and expresses the genuineness of Joseph Smith's character (HC 5:156–59). A letter of Sept. 1, 1842, from James Arlington Bennett shows in his own words that he had "been long a Mormon in sympathy alone, and probably can never be one in any other way" (HC 5:163).

On Aug. 29, 1843, **Brigham Young** visited James Arlington Bennett and family and stayed the night at their home. On the next day, Bennett was baptized in the Atlantic Ocean at Coney Island by Brigham Young (HC 5:556). Within two months of his baptismal date, it was found from a letter that Bennett considered his baptism a farce. He wrote to Joseph Smith on Oct. 24, 1843, and said: "You are no doubt already aware that I have had a most interesting visit from your most excellent and worthy friend, President B. Young, with whom I have had a glorious frolic in the clear blue ocean; for most assuredly a frolic it was, without a moment's reflection or consideration" (HC 6:71–72). He proceeded to tell Joseph Smith about his own mathematical mind, reassured his friendship, then suggested that he could become governor of the State of Illinois through the Prophet's influence. The Prophet Joseph wrote a scathing reply and indicated beautifully the integrity of himself, the gospel, and the Church (HC 6:73–78).

In a letter to James Arlington Bennett written on Mar. 4, 1844, Brother Willard Richards said, "General Smith says, if he must be President, Arlington Bennett must be Vice-President. . . . Consequently, your name will appear in our next paper as our candidate for Vice-President of the United States" (HC 6:231–33). It was later determined that Bennett was of foreign birth, and was not eligible. The position was then offered to Colonel Solomon Cope of Paris, TN, but for some reason he did not accept; so the next choice was Sidney Rigdon, who by that time had moved from Nauvoo to Pennsylvania and was not in harmony with the Church (CHC 2:207).

By June 1845, the true colors of James Arlington Bennett were showing more brightly when he sent a letter to Brigham Young and applied to be consecrated a general of the Nauvoo Legion, that he might "fight Napoleon's battles over again, either in Nauvoo or elsewhere." Of this request, Brigham Young said, "This wild spirit of ambition has repeatedly manifested itself to us by many communications received from various sources, suggesting schemes of blood and empire, as if the work of the Lord was intended for personal aggrandisement" (HC 7:429). However, in spite of Bennett's selfish ambitions, by Oct. 1845 he was in Nauvoo and held the title of general and met with the Twelve at Elder Taylor's house in a council meeting. They were involved in making decisions concerning the move west to find a new home for the Saints. Bennett "expressed himself opposed to our selling out to gratify the mob, and would rather see us fight and maintain our ground" (HC 7:483). Four days later he said "that he would cross the Rocky Mountains with us [the Saints] in the spring" (HC 7:488). But apparently his heart was not with the Saints. On Nov. 18, Brigham Young said: "I received a letter from James Arlington Bennett urging me to appoint him military commander-in-chief in the church, the spirit of the letter shows a thirst for personal aggrandizement unbecoming a servant of God" (HC 7:528). From the *History of the Church* it appears that this was the

end of the relationship between the leaders of the Church and James
Arlington Bennett.

WILLIAM S. GODBE AND THE CHURCH OF ZION (GODBEITES)

William S. Godbe, owner of the first drugstore in Salt Lake City, and
his friend E. L. T. Harrison, were both active in Church services in
the early 1860s. Godbe was the president of one of the quorums of
seventy, and Harrison was a member of a seventies quorum. But by
1868 these two men had feelings against the Church.

In the summer of 1868, Godbe went east to purchase merchandise for his business, and he took his friend Harrison with
him. By the time they reached NYC by train, they had concluded
that the Book of Mormon was not credulous, and that Brigham
Young was a "hopeless case." Mormonism, they concluded, was "a
crude jargon of sense and nonsense, honesty and fraud, . . . a
religion as unlike their conceptions of the teachings of Christ, as
darkness is to light" (CHC 5:260). When they arrived in New York
City, they decided to get answers from Deity while in their hotel
room. They formulated questions, and claimed that "a band of
spirits came to them, and held converse with them as friends would
speak with friends" (HC 5:261). With pencil in hand, they took
down the answers, and when they returned to Salt Lake City, they
established a rival church named "The Church of Zion." Amasa M.
Lyman became a member of their group, which lasted for a short
period of time and then faded away (CHC 5:258–71).

SEYMOUR B. YOUNG, RUDGER CLAWSON, AND WILLARD YOUNG

Seymour Bicknell Young enrolled in Oct. 1871 in the University
Medical College of New York, and in Mar. 1874 received his
diploma as a medical and surgical graduate from that famous institution (BE 1:200–202). He later became one of the First Seven
Presidents of Seventies (1882–1924).

Rudger Clawson, an Apostle from 1898–1943, spent the most
part of two years (1875 to 1877) in New York City as a private secretary to the Honorable John W. Young, then president of the Utah
Western Railway Company (BE 1:174–78).

Willard Young, born Apr. 30, 1852, to Brigham Young and
Clarissa Ross, was the first Mormon to graduate from the United

States Military Academy at West Point, located about 60 miles north of the center of Manhattan. Beginning in 1879 he was an instructor of civil engineering for four year at West Point. In 1891 he became the president of the Young University in Salt Lake City and from 1906 to 1915 was president of the LDS University. After serving as state engineer for Utah, he lived in NYC from 1889 to 1902 where he was general manager of the National Contracting Company. While he was general manager, the company constructed one of the great wheel pits for electric power development at Niagara Falls, built a tunnel under the bay between Boston and East Boston, and erected a dam near Glen Falls, NY, on the Hudson River. From 1902 to 1906 he was in private practice in Salt Lake City, then in 1919 became the superintendent of Church building activities (BE 3:575–76).

BROOKLYN, EASTERN STATES MISSION HEADQUARTERS, AND B. H. ROBERTS

On Nov. 22, 1839, Parley P. Pratt wrote to Joseph Smith and told him that there was a strong branch of the Church on Long Island (HC

Old LDS mission home in Brooklyn, NY, at 273 Gates Avenue. (1988)

4:22). A branch of the Church was organized in Brooklyn in the spring or summer of 1840, with George J. Adams as branch president.

In June 1842, branch meetings were held regularly in Brooklyn at **The Academy,** on the corner of Jay and Sands Streets, near the SE end of the Manhattan Bridge. Meetings were held at 10:30 A.M., 3:00 P.M., and 7:30 P.M. (ThP June 8, 1844, 2). Church services may also have been held at the offices of the *Log Cabin* on Fulton Street in Brooklyn. The *Log Cabin* was started in 1840 by Horace Greeley to further the political fortunes of William Henry Harrison and other Whig party candidates.

In 1854, when John Taylor went to NYC to preside over the Eastern States Mission, direct immigration, and publish *The Mormon*, he lived in Brooklyn. Because of the Utah War of 1857, missionaries were withdrawn for a time from New York. When a conference was held in Brooklyn on Apr. 9, 1865, there were 254 members in the New York Conference (JH Apr. 9, 1865).

Old LDS chapel (now used by the Evening Star Baptist Church) in Brooklyn, NY, next to the mission home on the corner of Gates and Franklin Avenues. (1988)

In Jan. 1893, Job Pingree of Ogden, UT, was set apart as a missionary to go to NYC to reopen missionary work in that area. He was joined by Elder Seymour B. Young Jr.

A two-story brick **mission home** was built in Brooklyn at 273 Gates Avenue, and an

Inside the old LDS chapel in Brooklyn. (1988)

LDS chapel was built on the corner of Gates and Franklin Avenues, next to the mission home. The chapel was decorated with a beautifully painted frieze of Mormon symbols, such as the beehive, the Book of Mormon, etc. Although the Evening Star Baptist Church occupied the chapel in 1996, the chapel is still decorated with the Mormon symbols. The former mission home serves as the pastor's rectory. The former LDS chapel is about ½ mile directly south of the Hasidic Jewish section of Brooklyn, which is just south of the east end of the Williamsburg Bridge. About 10,000 Jews live in this area.

Brigham H. Roberts (1857–1933) was the mission president of the Eastern States Mission from 1922 to 1927. The mission included New York, Pennsylvania, West Virginia, Maryland, Washington, D.C., and the New England states. Roberts's hope was to establish a branch of Jewish converts, but this did not happen. He wrote *Rasha the Jew* while he was mission president.

B. H. Roberts was an immigrant from Britain who crossed the plains at age 10. At age 31, he was a General Authority in the

Church as one of the seven Presidents of the Seventy. Three years before his death, his six-volume *A Comprehensive History of the Church,* a history of the Church during its first one hundred years, was published.

On one occasion in the hallway of the mission home, B. H. Roberts was surrounded by a group of missionaries who were asking him questions. One of the elders asked Roberts a question about the life and teachings of the Prophet Joseph Smith. John Emmet wrote of this occasion, "All of a sudden he [Roberts] looked up and raised his hands up and said, 'Brother Joseph, I have fought for you, I have defended you, I have loved you . . .' and made one of the most spiritual and emotional outbursts. It impressed me so. I have never heard a stronger testimony of the Prophet" (BHR 388).

After being released as mission president in Apr. 1927, Roberts returned to NYC and trained the new mission president, Henry H. Rolapp during the month of May. He then spent six months doing little else but working on his writings titled *The Truth, The Way, The Life.* This was a part of Roberts's major effort to systematize his doctrinal writings. During these six months, he lived alone at 380 Riverside Drive, in New York City, and followed a strenuous routine. He arose at 5:00 A.M., collected notes and wrote outlines for two hours as he worked on what he hoped would be the climax of his doctrinal writings, as he said, "crystallizing practically all my thought, research, and studies in the doctrinal line of the Church." After breakfast, he took a walk along the Hudson River. At 9:00 A.M. his typist came for dictation, which was given as he paced back and forth. Some days he dictated with hardly a pause for four consecutive hours. Roberts had worked intermittently on this project for 30 years, and at last he was pleased to be closer to finishing it. When he returned to Salt Lake City he still had more work to complete his writings, but he died July 27, 1933, and his doctrinal writings were not published until 1994, when *BYU Studies* published them as *The Truth, The Way, The Life* (BHR 434; IJWW).

THE MORMON PAVILION AT THE 1964 NEW YORK WORLD'S FAIR

President David O. McKay described the Mormon Pavilion at the New York World's Fair of 1964 in Flushing Meadows as "one of the most unique and effective missionary efforts in its [the Church's] history" (ERA 68:1170).

The Mormon Pavilion near the entrance of the fair was high-lighted with a triple-towered facade of the Salt Lake Temple complete with a gold-leafed statue of the angel Moroni. Inside the building was the *Christus*, a 12-foot-high statue by Danish artist Thorvaldsen. Murals, paintings, dioramas, and exhibits set the theme of the pavilion—"Man's search for happiness with the gospel as the way of life."

During the 12 months of the fair, approximately 6 million people visited the Mormon Pavilion, and nearly 100,000 copies of the Book of Mormon were sold. Many people were later converted as a result of their introduction to the Church at the Mormon Pavilion. **Florence Elliot Doyle,** the first woman stockbroker on Wall Street, visited the Mormon Pavilion and later joined the Church (see site no. 27).

In addition to the immediate and visible benefits, there were secondary benefits that are immeasurable. Dr. Richard O. Cowan, history professor at Brigham Young University, concluded that "experience gained at the New York fair enabled the Church to transform its bureaus of information, renamed 'visitors' centers,' into more effective tools for teaching the gospel" (TCTC 287; ERA 67:279–89; 68:1092–93, 1169–71).

NEW YORK METROPOLITAN MUSEUM AND THE PAPYRUS MANUSCRIPTS

Dr. Aziz S. Atiya, Egyptian scholar and faculty member at the University of Utah, was conducting research in May 1966 at the New York Metropolitan Museum of Art when he discovered 11 Egyptian papyri that for more than 100 years had generally been presumed lost. The papyri included Facsimile No. 1 of the Book of Abraham, as well as drawings and hieroglyphics that have likenesses to Facsimiles Nos. 2 and 3.

Dr. Atiya negotiated with the museum for the ownership of the papyri, and the papyri were a gift to the Church from the Metropolitan Museum of Art, but an anonymous donation by a friend of the museum covered the cost of the gift. **President N. Eldon Tanner,** counselor in the First Presidency, accepted the 11 papyri for the Church in Nov. 1967.

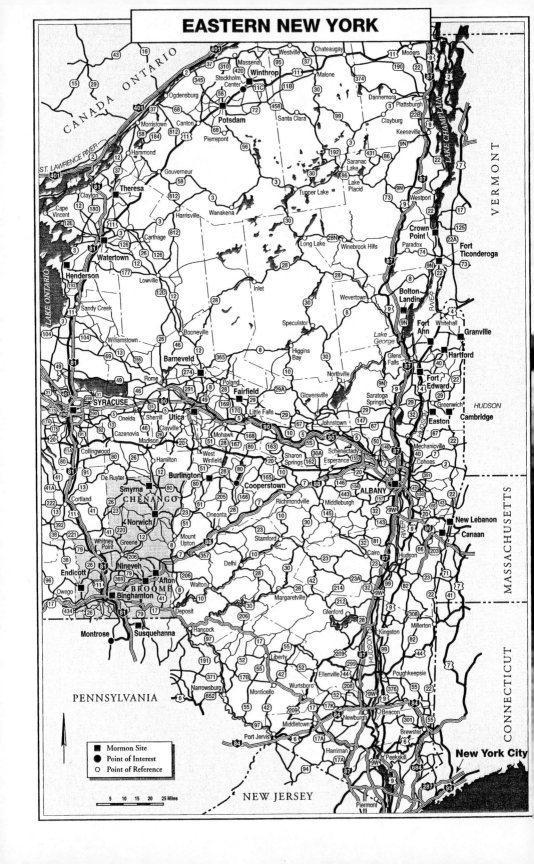

EASTERN NEW YORK

EASTERN NEW YORK

Larry C. Porter

Columbia County

■ CANAAN AND NEW LEBANON TOWNSHIPS, COLUMBIA COUNTY—**Home of the Parley P. and Orson Pratt Family**

Hudson, the county seat of Columbia County, is situated 27 miles south of Albany. Canaan and New Lebanon Townships are located in the NE corner of Columbia County. Canaan Township was first formed as "King's District" on Mar. 24, 1772, and changed to Canaan, Mar. 7, 1778. The township of New Lebanon was formed from Canaan Township on Apr. 21, 1818. New Lebanon Township is located 25 miles NE of the city of Hudson and 24 miles SE of Albany. The village of New Lebanon is situated at the junction of U.S. 20 and State 22. The area now within New Lebanon Township is where the Obediah and Jared Pratt families lived.

THE JARED PRATT FAMILY IN CANAAN/NEW LEBANON TOWNSHIPS. Jared Pratt was born to Obediah and Jemina Tolls Pratt in Canaan on Nov. 25, 1769. In the early 1790s, Jared married Polly Carpenter of the township of Canaan. Polly died giving birth to a daughter, Mary, born in Feb. 1793. On July 7, 1799, Jared again married and brought his bride, Charity Dickinson, back to Canaan, where their first son, Anson Pratt, was born on Jan. 9, 1801. The Jared Pratt family next moved to Otsego Co., NY, where two more sons were added to the family, William Dickinson at Worcester on Sept. 3, 1802, and **Parley Parker,** born Apr. 12, 1807, at Burlington. Jared then took his family to Hartford, Washington Co., where **Orson Pratt** was born on Sept. 19, 1811 (LOP 4–8).

The Jared Pratt family returned to Canaan from Hartford sometime in 1815–16 and located in the northern part of Canaan Township, which became New Lebanon after 1818. Orson and his older brother Parley were boarded out in 1822 to work for others and to make their own way. Orson did not return again to live at home (LOP 10–13).

In 1826 Parley traveled to Lorain Co., OH, where he took up a homestead in Amhurst Township near South River (now South Amherst). The following year, 1827, Parley returned to the Canaan/New Lebanon area and married his childhood sweetheart, **Thankful Halsey** of Canaan, on Sept. 9. When the couple returned to Ohio in October, Parley's brothers, Nelson and Orson, went with them. Orson labored independently and spent the winter of 1827 in South River (South Amherst) at the home of Eliphalet Redington. By 1829 he had returned to the state of New York and eventually hired out in the Canaan area, earning enough to board at a school where he learned geography, grammar, and surveying (LOP 14–16; APPP 27–30).

Orson frequently petitioned the Lord for direction. He said: "In the silent shades of night, while others were slumbering upon their pillows, I often retired to some secret place in the lonely fields or solitary wilderness, and bowed before the Lord, and prayed for hours with a broken heart and contrite spirit; this was my comfort and delight. The greatest desire of my heart was for the Lord to manifest His will concerning me" (ThC 12:42).

After selling their property on the Black River in Lorain Co., OH, Parley P. Pratt and his wife, Thankful, went to visit their family in the New Lebanon/Canaan area in Aug. 1830.[1] As they passed along the **Erie Canal,** Parley was impressed by the Spirit of the Lord to send Thankful on to their folks while he disembarked at Newark, Wayne Co., NY, near Palmyra. There he met with **Elijah Hamlin,** a Baptist deacon who had a copy of the newly published **Book of Mormon** (LOP 17). Parley said, "As I read, the spirit of the Lord was upon me, and I knew and comprehended that the book was true, as plainly and manifestly as a man comprehends and knows that he exists" (APPP 20). After having met Hyrum Smith in Palmyra, Parley was subsequently taken to the Peter Whitmer farm

---

[1] The acreage containing the old Pratt home in the northern part of Canaan Township was divided off and became New Lebanon Township in 1818 (see LOP 10).

in Fayette, Seneca Co., where Oliver Cowdery baptized him in Seneca Lake "about the 1st of September 1830" (APPP 27).

In answer to Orson Pratt's prayers for the Lord "to manifest His will concerning [him]," Parley P. Pratt returned to the Canaan/New Lebanon area preaching the Book of Mormon and the tenets of the Restoration in Sept. 1830 (ThC 12:42–43). Orson accepted the word gladly and was baptized on his nineteenth birthday, Sept. 19, 1830, by his brother. Although Parley attempted to teach the gospel to other family members and friends and even to a Quaker Community at New Lebanon, all remained aloof. Parley and Orson soon joined the body of the Church in western New York and met the prophet Joseph Smith at the Peter Whitmer farm in Fayette, NY, in Oct. 1830 (APPP 28–31; ThC 12:42–43).

Parley was later designated as one of the original members of the **Quorum of the Twelve Apostles** in this dispensation and served in that capacity from 1835 to 1857. He was certainly one of the most significant of the Mormon proselyters, writers, and thinkers to emerge during the early years of the Restoration. Parley P. Pratt published some 31 separate works during his lifetime. "Through the great and enduring legacy of his writings, hymns, songs, and poems, Parley Parker Pratt continues to inspire each new generation with the image of his indomitable spirit" (APPP Classics Edition [1985] xix–xxviii; see also EPPP).

Orson was also selected as one of the original members of the Quorum of the Twelve Apostles in 1835. When Orson's earthly ministry ended on Oct. 3, 1881, Wilford Woodruff offered this most appropriate eulogy:

> It would be impossible to give the history of that great man, or to depict the glory that awaits him. It would take the trump of the sixth angel to do that. . . . Brother Pratt had lived longer in this Church, traveled more miles and preached more sermons than any man in it. He had baptized thousands, and fulfilled the revelation given to him through the Prophet Joseph Smith, November 4th, 1830 [D&C 34]. His garments were clear from the blood of this generation. He had studied and written more upon the Gospel and upon science than any man in the Church. He had now gone home. It was all right. (ThC 12:460–61)

JOHN VAN COTT IN CANAAN/NEW LEBANON. John Van Cott, a cousin of Parley and Orson Pratt, was born in Canaan, Columbia Co., to

Losee and Lovinia Pratt Van Cott on Sept. 7, 1814. Parley P. Pratt was especially fond of his Aunt Lovinia, who lived close to his family's home in Canaan, and with whom Parley boarded during his 16th year (APPP 21–22, 43, 45). Parley preached the gospel to the Van Cott family in 1830, but with little apparent success. However, the seed sown by Elder Pratt eventually bore fruit. In Sept. 1845 Parley baptized John Van Cott at Nauvoo, IL. John was later ordained a seventy on Feb. 25, 1847, and on Oct. 8, 1862, was sustained as one of the **first seven Presidents of the Seventy** by John Taylor. He died in Salt Lake City on Feb. 18, 1883 (APPP 21–22, 43, 45; DNCA 1995–96:60; BE 1:198-99).

John Van Cott

Albany County

■ **ALBANY—A Crossroads for Many Activities Associated with the Restoration**

Albany, capital of the State of New York, is located in NE New York. The settlement was incorporated by patent on July 22, 1686. The Dutch styled it "New Orange." It became a village on Apr. 9, 1804. Albany lies on the west bank of the Hudson River, near the river's head of navigation, and at the eastern terminus of the Erie Canal.

In Feb. 1828, when **Martin Harris** took a copy of the transcript of characters from the gold plates to show to learned men (Drs. Samuel Latham Mitchill and Charles Anthon in New York City), he stopped in Albany and visited with **Luther Bradish.** Bradish was an assemblyman from Franklin Co., NY, and a brother to Chloe Bradish Robinson, wife of Dr. Gain Robinson who was a well-known physician in Palmyra. This was probably more than a social call, however, as Luther Bradish, a graduate of Williams College and a noted scholar and statesman, spoke several languages and had an interest in antiquities (ORPM 41–42; RFF; BYUS 10, no. 2 [spring]:328–30).

By revelation, **Newel K. Whitney** was sent to Albany to preach the gospel and to sound a warning note to the people should they reject the message (D&C 84:112–14). As directed, he performed this missionary service during the latter half of 1832 (EH 211).

Because of its strategic location at the eastern terminus of the Erie Canal and the waters of the upper Hudson River, many of the Saints trafficked through Albany as emigrants or while performing a wide variety of assignments and functions. Illustrative of the countless numbers is the mournful return of the Twelve Apostles in 1844 following their notification of the martyrdom of the Prophet and Hyrum Smith at Carthage, IL. On July 24, Elders Brigham Young, Heber C. Kimball, Orson Hyde, Orson Pratt, Wilford Woodruff, and Lyman Wight met at Albany and then continued their journey by railroad, canal, stage, and steamboat to reach Nauvoo on August 6, 1844. Orson Hyde stopped momentarily in Kirtland and came on later (MHBY 171).

Washington County

■ EASTON TOWNSHIP—**Birthplace of Martin Harris, One of the Three Witnesses to the Book of Mormon Plates**

Easton Township is located on the east bank of the Hudson River in Washington County. The small community of Easton is situated 29 miles north of Albany on State 40.

Technically, when Martin Harris was born on May 18, 1783, his birthplace was in Albany Co. and the Saratoga District, which district had been formed Mar. 24, 1772. Saratoga was later made a township on Mar. 7, 1788. Easton Township, embracing the birthplace of Martin, was formed from Saratoga and Stillwater Townships on Mar. 3, 1789. Easton Township was then annexed from Albany Co. to Washington Co. on Feb. 7, 1791 (GNYS 591, 680–81). Martin's parents were Nathan and Rhoda Lapham Harris (see Palmyra, NY, for additional information on Martin Harris and his family).

Martin Harris

■ HARTFORD, HARTFORD TOWNSHIP—**Birthplace of Orson Pratt, Apostle**

Hartford is located near the center of Washington Co., 56 miles NE of Albany on State 40.

Orson Pratt

Orson Pratt, son of Jared Pratt and Charity Dickinson, was born in Hartford on Sept. 19, 1811, where he lived until about his fourth year. His father then returned to the familiar environs of Canaan, Columbia Co. The family was situated in the northern part of Canaan Township, which became New Lebanon when that township was formed in 1818. Orson and his older brother Parley were "boarded out" in 1822 to work for others and to make their own way. Orson did not return again to live at home (LOP 8–13; for more information on Orson Pratt see also Canaan and New Lebanon Townships).

■ FORT EDWARD—**Solomon Mack and the French and Indian War**

Fort Edward is located on the east bank of the Hudson River 46 miles north of Albany and four miles south of the village of Hudson Falls on U.S. 4.

Solomon Mack (1732–1820), father of **Lucy Mack Smith,** enlisted at the age of 21 at Lyme, CT, to fight for the English Crown (King George II of Great Britain) in the **French and Indian War** (1756–63). Under the command of Colonel Whiting he marched with his regiment to Fort Edward. Solomon participated in a "severe battle, fought at Half-way Brook in 1755" (HJS 2). He became too ill to continue and was sent to Albany to recuperate.

In 1757 he had two teams of oxen "in the King's service." Going out from Fort Edward in search of three of his oxen, which were missing, Solomon encountered four Indians, "armed with scalping knives, tomahawks and guns." He was alone on the road save for a man named Webster, traveling some 20 rods behind him. Solomon described his dilemma: "I saw my danger, and that there was no way to escape, unless I could do it by stratagem; so I rushed upon them, calling in the mean time at the top of my voice, Rush on! rush on my boys! we'll have the devils. The only weapon I had was a walking staff, yet I ran toward them, and as the other man appeared just at that instant, it gave them a terrible fright, and I saw no more of them" (HJS 2). Joseph Smith Jr. later used this same tactic to disperse "a large company of men, well armed" who were about to rush the Smith's Manchester frame home in search of the golden plates in 1827 (HJS 112).

■ FORT ANN

Fort Ann is located 12 miles NE of Fort Edward at the junction of U.S. 4 and State 149.

Solomon Mack was at Fort Ann in July 1758 where he and his unit had retreated following a devastating defeat of the English at the hands of the French defenders of Fort Ticonderoga on July 8. The occupants of the fort were suddenly alerted by their sentry that "the enemy was all around us." Major Israel Putnam, with Major Robert Rogers bringing up the rear, led Solomon's unit against the enemy. A company of Indians ambushed Putnam's men about ¾ mile from the fort. Major Putnam was captured at the outset and would have been killed by the Indians if a French lieutenant had not rescued him. Solomon recalled, "The enemy rose like a cloud, and fired a whole volley upon us, and as I was in the foremost rank, the retreat of my company brought me in the rear, and the toma-hawks and bullets flew around me like hail stones." During the retreat Solomon saw a man who was badly wounded and paused to help. He stated, "The Indians were close upon him; nevertheless I turned aside for the purpose of assisting him, and succeeded in get-ting him into the midst of our army, in safety." Half of the company was killed, wounded, or captured at Fort Ann (HJS 3–4).

■ GRANVILLE TOWNSHIP

Granville Township is located on the NE border of Washington Co. The community of Granville is situated near the Vermont border at the junction of State 22 and State 149.

Solomon Mack said he used the money that he received for his services in the French and Indian War to purchase property. He stated, "I contracted for the whole town of Granville, in the state of New York," 1,600 acres of wilderness. The deed stipulated that he would build a number of log houses for homestead lots. Unfortunately, he cut his leg and had to hire a man to help him fulfill the contract. The man was paid for his work in advance and "ran away with the money, without performing the labor." As a result Solomon lost the land and his earnings. Following this disastrous season he and his bride, Lydia Gates, moved to Marlow, NH, in 1761 (HJS 5; JSN 9–10).

Warren County

■ BOLTON LANDING—**Home of John Tanner**

Bolton Landing is situated on Lake George, in north-central Warren Co. on State 9N. The John Tanner two-and-one-half story frame home still stands in the village of Bolton Landing. The home is on the west side of Lake Shore Drive (State 9N) at the south end of the village. It is now used as a bed and breakfast inn called Ronnegan's (PS; JTHF 15, 39).

John Tanner was born on Aug. 15, 1778, at Hopkinton, RI, the son of Joshua and Thankful Tefft Tanner. John Tanner first moved his family to North West Bay, six miles north of Bolton, in 1818. He

John Tanner home, Bolton Landing. The home dates from the early 1800s. (1960)

subsequently located in the village of Bolton Landing in 1823. Through industry he acquired substantial holdings in the area. A son, Nathan Tanner, said that his father had 2,200 acres, much of it in timber (DJT 12–13; JTHF 40).

During Aug. and Sept. 1832, **Elders Jared** and **Simeon Carter** were proselyting in the town of Bolton. John Tanner attended their meeting with an eye to discredit the Mormons. However, he was so impressed by their teachings that he invited them to his home. John told the elders that he was ready to be baptized but would have to forestall that ordinance because of a seriously diseased leg, which had left him crippled and unable to walk. At this point, "one of the Elders asked him if he did not think there was power enough in the gospel of Jesus Christ anciently to heal all manner of disease, to which he replied in the affirmative. He was then asked if he did not think that the same cause produced the same effect in all ages, and if there was not sufficient power in the gospel to heal him." John Tanner replied that "such a thought had not occurred to him, but he believed that the Lord could heal him." At this juncture Jared Carter "then arose and commanded him in the name of Jesus Christ to arise and walk." John stated, "'I arose and threw down my crutches, and walked the floor, back and forth—back and forth, praising God, and I felt light as a feather'" (JTHF 47).

Jared Carter journalized that this healing took place on Sept. 17, 1832. That very night John is reported to have walked ¾ mile to Lake George where Simeon Carter baptized him into the Church. Other accounts have specified that his baptism occurred the next day and yet another stated that John read the Book of Mormon first and then, after a two-week period, the elders returned and performed the baptism (JTHF 38–50, 53).

John Tanner and his family left Bolton Landing for Kirtland, OH, in Dec. 1834. There he "became the instrument in the hands of God to contribute means, by which the partially constructed Kirtland Temple and grounds were saved from passing out of the hands of the Saints by a foreclosure of the mortgage" (BE 2:800). John Tanner was a major contributor to the financial operations of the early Church at

Nathan Eldon Tanner (1898–1982), Counselor to four Church Presidents.

a very critical moment (JTHF 71–82). He died in Salt Lake City (Fort Union area) on Apr. 13, 1850.

President Nathan Eldon Tanner (1898–1982), an Apostle and a Counselor in the First Presidency of the Church to Presidents David O. McKay, Joseph Fielding Smith, Harold B. Lee, and Spencer W. Kimball, was a direct descendant of John Tanner (DJT 170).

Essex County

■ FORT TICONDEROGA

The site of Fort Ticonderoga is situated on a peninsula on the west bank of Lake Champlain 2.1 miles east of the village of Ticonderoga, which is at the junction of State 9N and State 22.

On July 5, 1758, **Solomon Mack** was a member of an English expeditionary force that embarked by water from the ruins of Fort William Henry at the south end of Lake George to capture the French-held Fort Ticonderoga on Lake Champlain. Commander of the 15,000-man force was Major General James Abercrombie, and second in command was Brigadier Lord Augustus Howe. The next day the army landed on the western shore with the intention of marching around the rapids of Lake George as they ran NE and then turn west to Ticonderoga. This would allow them to attack the French fort from the rear. Lord Howe and Major Israel Putnam were out with a reconnoitering party when they ran into a French unit also on reconnaissance. Solomon explained, "We had a bloody and hot engagement with the enemy, in which Lord Howe fell at the onset of the battle" (HJS 3; TWOA 57).

The 4,000 French defenders had constructed a huge breastwork on the ridge behind the fort standing eight to nine feet high. Firing platforms had been built behind it, and the line was zigzagged so that the front could be swept with a devastating flanking fire. General Abercrombie unwisely chose a direct assault on what proved to be an impregnable position. The English attempted to storm the French fortification on July 8. Solomon Mack described the action: "We marched to the breastworks, but were unsuccessful, being compelled to retreat with a loss of five hundred men killed and as many more wounded. In this contest I narrowly escaped—a musket ball passed under my chin, within half an inch of my neck. The army then returned to Lake George, and, on its way thither, a large scouting party of the enemy came round by Skeenesborough, and, at Half-way Brook, destroyed a large number of both men and teams" (HJS 3; TWOA 57–58). Solomon and his unit retreated to the comparative safety of Fort Ann.

- **CROWN POINT**

Crown Point State Historic Site is located on the NW side of the Crown Point peninsula on Lake Champlain, five miles directly north of the village of Crown Point. From the village, proceed north on State 9N and 22 to its juncture with County Road 903. County Road 903 will take you to the site of the Fort Crown Point ruins. .

At Crown Point was a stone fort built by the French to help control the waterway on Lake Champlain. In 1759 the French abandoned the fort in an effort to strengthen their defenses at Quebec. The English then occupied and expanded the fortification. **Solomon Mack** reported, "In the spring of 1759, the army marched to Crownpoint, where I received my discharge" (HJS 5).

CENTRAL NEW YORK

Larry C. Porter

Herkimer and Oneida Counties

■ **FAIRFIELD TOWNSHIP, HERKIMER COUNTY—Birthplace of Lyman Wight, Apostle**

Fairfield Township is located in north-central Herkimer Co. The village of Fairfield is situated at the junction of State 29 and State 170.

Lyman Wight, the son of Levi and Sarah Corbin (Cardin) Wight, was born in Fairfield Township on May 9, 1796. He married Harriet Benton in Henrietta, NY, on Jan. 5, 1823. About 1826, Lyman moved his family to Warrensville, OH. In 1829 he joined with **Sidney Rigdon,** a Campbellite, and in 1830 moved to Kirtland. There he became associated with

Lyman Wight

Isaac Morley of Kirtland Township, a fellow Campbellite, in a common stock covenant. Lyman was converted to Mormonism and baptized by Oliver Cowdery on Nov. 14, 1830, at the time the missionaries to the Lamanites came through Ohio on their way to Missouri and the Indian Territory.

Lyman helped in the recruitment of the members of **Zion's Camp** and marched with "Hyrum's Division" from Michigan to Missouri in 1834. He was later called to the Quorum of the Twelve Apostles and was ordained by Joseph Smith on Apr. 8, 1841, at Nauvoo. In Mar. 1845, Lyman took about 150 followers from the Black River area in Wisconsin and journeyed to Texas. Having broken his alignment with the Twelve under Brigham Young, he was excommunicated from the Church on Dec. 3, 1848. Lyman Wight died at Dexter, Medina Co., TX, on Mar. 31, 1858. He is buried at Zodiac, TX, four miles south of Fredericksburg, Gillespie Co., TX (RPJS 82–83; BE 1:93–96; BYUS 31, no. 1 [winter and spring]: 119–48).

■ UTICA, ONEIDA COUNTY

The city of Utica is located on I-90 at the eastern edge of Oneida County.

ATTEMPTED ROBBERY OF LUCY MACK SMITH. Joseph Smith Sr. left Norwich, VT, in 1816 and went to Palmyra, NY, where he found conditions favorable and sent a man by the name of Caleb Howard to bring **Lucy Mack Smith** and the children on to Palmyra. At or near Utica (Lucy says 20 miles west of Utica while Joseph Jr. recorded the event at Utica), Caleb Howard, who had spent all of Father Smith's money in drinking and gambling, attempted to run away with the wagon and team. When alerted to Howard's intentions, Lucy summoned Caleb before witnesses at the inn and declared to those present, "Gentlemen and ladies, please give your attention for a moment. Now, as sure as there is a God in heaven, that team, as well as the goods, belong to my husband, and this man intends to take them from me, or at least the team, leaving me with eight children, without the means of proceeding on my journey." Then, turning to Caleb, she said, "Sir, I now forbid you touching the team, or driving it one step further. You can go about your own business; I have no use for you. I shall take charge of the team myself, and hereafter attend to my own affairs." In a resolute frame of mind Lucy shepherded the family to Palmyra where they arrived with barely two cents in cash (HJS 62–63; see also BYUS 10, no. 3 [summer]:481–82).

BOOK OF MORMON COPYRIGHT. In accordance with the 1790 U.S. Copyright Act, **Joseph Smith Jr.** made application through the auspices of the government at Utica, i.e., **Richard Ray Lansing,** clerk of the United States District Court for the Northern District of New York, to secure the copyright of the Book of Mormon on June 11,

1829. The document preserves this important date and event in history as recorded:

> BE IT REMEMBERED, That on the eleventh day of June in the fifty third year of the Independence of the United States of America, A.D. 1829 Joseph Smith Junior of the said District, hath deposited in this Office the title of a book the right whereof he claims as author in the words following, to wit: The Book of Mormon. . . . [signed] R. R. Lansing. (COLC)

It is not certain whether the copyright application was sent through the mail or hand-carried by someone to Lansing's office in Utica. Richard R. Lansing was a long-term resident of Utica until 1829 or shortly thereafter. The New York census for 1830 places him in New York City where the partnership of Lansing, Munroe & King organized an importation business. Lansing, MI, is named for Richard Ray Lansing (POU 332–34; see also copyright page in front of GNY and p. 535, courtesy of Richard L. Anderson).

THE PROPHET JOSEPH SMITH IN UTICA. Taking a line boat on the Erie Canal from Buffalo, the Prophet Joseph Smith, Oliver Cowdery, Sidney Rigdon, and Hyrum Smith arrived in Utica on July 29, 1836. Here they boarded "the first passenger car on the new road," for Schenectady. It took the party six hours to go 80 miles on the Albany & Schenectady Railway, the first railroad in New York, having been in operation since Sept. 1831 (HC 2:463).

DISTRICT CONFERENCE HELD IN UTICA. On July 29, 1843, a conference of the various branches in the region of Utica was held at the city home of "Sister Monroe." **Elder John P. Greene** presided over the four branches representing seven elders, five priests, six teachers, two deacons, and 159 members. **Elder Jacob Boyce** represented the branch in the city of Utica which consisted of four elders, one priest, two teachers, one deacon, and forty-seven members (T&S 4:300–302).

■ **BARNEVELD, ONEIDA COUNTY—Birthplace of Apostles John E. Page and Daniel H. Wells**

The Village of Barneveld (formerly Trenton), Trenton Township,

John E. Page
(Courtesy of RLDSLA)

Oneida Co., is located 11.2 miles north of Utica on State 12 (immediately SW of the junction of State 12 and State 365).

John Edward Page, first child of Ebenezer and Rachel Page, was born Feb. 25, 1799, in Trenton Township. He later embraced the gospel and was baptized in Brownhelm, Lorain Co., OH, on Aug. 18, 1833, by Elder Emer Harris (brother of Martin Harris). John E. Page and Lorain Stevens were married on Dec. 26, 1833. They moved to Kirtland, OH, in the fall of 1835. In 1836–37 John labored as a missionary in Leeds Co., Upper Canada. It is estimated that he was instrumental in baptizing approximately 600 persons during this two-year mission (see SP 1:157–58).

John was ordained as one of the Quorum of the Twelve Apostles on Dec. 19, 1838, at Far West, MO, under the hands of Elders Brigham Young and Heber C. Kimball. Following the death of his first wife and two children in Missouri, he married Mary Judd about Jan. 1839. John later fell into disharmony with the Twelve and in 1846 chose to support the claims of James J. Strang. He was excommunicated from the Church on June 26, 1846. Page later affiliated with the Hedrickites in Nov. 1862. John E. Page died near Sycamore, De Kalb Co., IL, on Oct. 14, 1867 (MS 27:103–104; RPJS 232–33; DPOR 39–40).

Daniel Hanmer Wells was born in Trenton (now Barneveld) on Oct. 27, 1814, the only son of Daniel Wells and Catherine Chapin. He moved to Illinois in 1834. There he married Eliza Rebecca Robison on Mar. 12, 1837, at Commerce (later Nauvoo). Daniel first met the Prophet Joseph Smith in the spring of 1839, and a strong bond grew between the two men. He owned considerable land in the area of Commerce, including 80 acres on the bluff, which he sold to the Mormons.

It was not until Aug. 9, 1846, that Daniel was baptized into the LDS faith.

Daniel H. Wells
(Courtesy of USHS)

Elder Almon W. Babbitt performed the ordinance in the Mississippi River. Daniel participated as one of the principal defenders of the Saints in the Battle of Nauvoo, Sept. 10–17, 1846. "Squire" Wells accompanied Brigham Young to Utah in 1848. Following the death of Jedediah M. Grant, President Young selected Daniel as his Second Counselor in the First Presidency of the Church on Jan. 4, 1857. He was released at the death of Brigham Young on Aug. 29, 1877. Daniel H. Wells died on Mar. 24, 1891, in Salt Lake City, while serving as President of the Manti Temple (DHW 20–31, 39–51, 233–34, 409).

Onondaga County

■ **SYRACUSE—Burial Site of John F. Boynton, Apostle**

The city of Syracuse is located at the junction of I-90 and I-81. From I-90 go north on I-81 to I-690. From I-81 turn east on I-690 and take exit 14. Proceed north on Teall Avenue to Grant Boulevard. Woodlawn Cemetery is on the NW corner of Teall Avenue and Grant Boulevard. The main entrance to the cemetery is at 800 Grant Boulevard. **John Farnham Boynton** is buried in Lot 42, Section 34, and his headstone is on the SW corner of Section 34. The cemetery is of sufficient size that the visitor will want to get directions from the Woodlawn Cemetery office.

John Farnham Boynton was born Sept. 20, 1811, in Bradford, Essex Co., MA. The Prophet Joseph Smith baptized him in Sept. 1832, and Sidney Rigdon ordained him an elder. He was later ordained as one of the original members of the Quorum of the Twelve Apostles on Feb. 15, 1835, at Kirtland, OH. John became disaffected over financial conditions associated with the **Kirtland Safety Society Bank** and was subsequently excommunicated in 1837.

He visited Salt Lake City in 1872 and met with President Brigham Young and others. Visiting with Elder Erastus Snow, an Apostle, he was reminded that he had ordained Elder Snow a teacher at age 16, and that Elder Snow had been preaching the gospel ever since. John Boynton responded to Elder Snow in a congratulatory tone, "Stick to it, for it is good" (BE 1:91).

John died of "congesting of lungs with angina [pectoris]" at 315 Highland Place in Syracuse on Oct. 20, 1890, age 79, and was buried in the Woodlawn Cemetery (DFB; NYDH).

Jefferson County

■ HENDERSON TOWNSHIP—**Cyrus Bates Home**

The Cyrus Bates home still stands and is located two miles SW of the community of Henderson, Jefferson Co., at Alexander Corners, the intersection of State 3 and CR 152, in the township of Henderson. The home is approximately 250 yards north of the Alexander Corners intersection on the west side of the road on State 3. The colonial-style home was built by Cyrus Bates about 1826. It is constructed of cut bedrock limestone with walls two feet thick (GLR).

As the Twelve Apostles performed their extended mission in the summer of 1835, **Orson Pratt** and **John F. Boynton** reached Sackets Harbor on June 7, and preached a sermon at the home of William Bates in nearby Henderson Township. They then proselyted extensively in the area. **Sarah Marinda Bates,** the daughter of Cyrus Bates, also of Henderson Township, applied to Elder Pratt for baptism. Orson administered the ordinance to her on June 18, 1835. Elder Pratt then began a courtship of Sarah Marinda by letter. The following year he was again performing missionary labors in Henderson. Orson proposed matrimony to Sarah and the couple were married at the Cyrus Bates household on July 4, 1836. Elder Luke S. Johnson performed the wedding. The Bates home became a focal point for the Church in the area (LOP 42–43, 47–48; GLR).

■ WATERTOWN—**Birthplace of Zina Diantha Huntington Young, General President of the Relief Society**

The city of Watertown, Jefferson Co., is located on I-81 at exits 45 and 46.

William Huntington cleared 300 acres near Watertown for farming and also constructed a one-and-one-half-story stone house for the comfort of his family. William and his wife, Zina Baker

Huntington, had nine children. **Zina Diantha,** the seventh of the Huntington children, was born on Jan. 31, 1821, in Watertown. Of Huntington's other children, "the first two children, Chauncey and Nancy, were twins; Nancy died as an infant. Another daughter, Adaline, also died in childhood. The other children were Dimmock, William, Oliver, John, and Prescendia [Prescindia]" (EL 44).

A neighbor, Joseph H. Wakefield, with whom William often discussed religion, was excited enough about the accounts of the "golden bible" then circulating in their neighborhood that he went to see

Zina Diantha Huntington Young, third general president of the Relief Society (1888–1901).

the Prophet Joseph Smith. Wakefield returned with a copy of the Book of Mormon. Commenting on this situation, William's daughter Zina recalled, "One day on my return from school I saw the Book of Mormon, that strange, new book, lying on the window sill of our sitting-room. I went up to the window, picked it up, and the sweet influence of the Holy Spirit accompanied it to such an extent that I pressed it to my bosom in a rapture of delight, murmuring as I did so, 'This is the truth, truth, truth!'" (EL 45).

Zina's parents received baptism in Apr. 1835 at the hands of Elder Thomas Dutcher. Zina, however, waited until later in the year when Hyrum Smith and David Whitmer came to their home. Hyrum baptized her on Aug. 1, 1835. Dimmock, a brother, and his wife, Fanny, were also baptized at the same time. The family generally embraced the new faith, but Chauncey, the eldest son, was never converted and chose to remain in New York when the family gathered to Kirtland in 1836. Prescindia, a sister who had married Henry Bailey Jacobs (a Mormon convert of 1832) and lived 18 miles south of Watertown in Loraine, Jefferson Co., also went to Kirtland in May 1836 with the family. Prescindia was baptized in Kirtland on June 6, 1836, and confirmed by Oliver Cowdery (EL 46–47, 49; WM 206–7).

Zina D. Huntington later became a plural wife of Joseph Smith and then **Brigham Young.** Following the death of Eliza R. Snow Young in 1888, she was called to be the third general president of the Relief Society (Apr. 8, 1888–Aug. 28, 1901).

■   Theresa—**Birthplace of David W. Patten, Apostle**

The village of Theresa is located three miles east of I-81 at exit 49 on State 411 in north-central Jefferson County.

David Wyman Patten was born Nov. 14, 1799, to Benenio (Benoni) Patten and Abigale (Edith) Cole in Theresa. First hearing of the Book of Mormon in 1830, David was later baptized by his brother, John Patten, in Green Co., IN, on June 15, 1832. As a missionary in 1833, he raised up a branch of 18 members in Orleans Township, Jefferson Co., and baptized eight converts at Henderson, Jefferson Co.(EM 3:1068).

While en route to Canada in Apr. 1833, Brigham Young stated, "I went to Theresa, Indian River Falls, near Ogdensburgh, where I found brother David W. Patten preaching the Gospel to his friends in that neighborhood; tarried four or five days; preached five discourses and baptized seven persons, among whom were brother Patten's mother, brothers [Archibald and Ira] and sisters [Polly was one of them], Warren Parrish [a brother-in-law] and wife [Betsy]," and also another brother-in-law, (Mr. Cheeseman). David Patten had prepared them all to be baptized by Brigham Young (MHBY 1:6).

David W. Patten was ordained a member of the original Quorum of the Twelve Apostles at Kirtland, OH, on Feb. 15, 1835. While leading a company of Saints intent on rescuing three brethren who had been kidnapped by the Missouri mob-militia, David was mortally wounded at the Battle of Crooked River in Ray Co., MO, on Oct. 25, 1838. While his life still lingered, he was carried to the nearby home of Stephen Winchester in Caldwell County. The Prophet, other brethren, and David's wife, **Phoebe Ann Babcock,** were summoned. Heber C. Kimball recorded David's parting plea to his wife, "Whatever you do else, O, do not deny the faith!" And then he prayed, "Father I ask thee, in the name of Jesus Christ, that thou wouldst release my spirit and receive it unto thyself." Speaking to those around him, he made a final request, "Brethren, you have held me by your faith, but do give me up and let me go I beseech you." Brother Kimball said, "We then committed him to God, and he soon breathed his last, and slept in Jesus without a groan" (CTA 218–48).

St. Lawrence County

St. Lawrence Co. lies in northern New York and is the largest county in the state. On its northern and NW boundaries are the St. Lawrence River and Canada. St. Lawrence Co. was created from Oneida Co. on Mar. 3, 1802. **Asael (Asahel) and Mary Duty Smith,** with their sons, Jesse, Asael (Asahel) Jr., Samuel, Silas, John, and daughter Susan (Susanna) had moved here from the area of Tunbridge, VT, over a period of years ranging from 1806 to the 1820s. Jesse Smith reportedly didn't come to the Township of Stockholm until some 17 years after the removal of his parents from Tunbridge (JH Feb. 14, 1859). **Joseph Smith Sr.,** who came out of Vermont in 1816 and chose to locate in Palmyra, was not the first of his father's family to migrate to New York as is often supposed (RSNY 15).

In Aug. 1830, Joseph Smith Sr. took his 14-year-old son, Don Carlos, on a proselyting mission, to see his father's family in St. Lawrence Co. and to introduce them to the gospel through the pages of the Book of Mormon (HJS 172–76; JD 5:103–4).

■ THE VILLAGE OF POTSDAM AND POTSDAM TOWNSHIP—Home of Silas, Samuel, John, and Susan (Susanna) Smith

The village of Potsdam is located 10 miles NE of Canton, the county seat, and is situated at the junction of U.S. 11 and State 56. Potsdam is the focal point for the surrounding township of that name.

Silas Smith (1779–1839), son of Asael Smith Sr. and **Mary Duty,** purchased 73.27 acres of land in the Township of Potsdam on Oct. 24, 1806. He moved to Potsdam following his marriage to **Ruth Stevens** of Royalton, VT, in Jan. 1806. Silas served as commissioner of highways in 1808 and fence viewer in 1809. It appears that Silas's unmarried brothers, **Samuel** and **John,** and their unmarried sister, **Susan (Susanna),** were also living in his household at this time (RSNY 21–24).

In 1810 Silas moved his family to the Township of Stockholm, St. Lawrence Co. Silas and his brother Asael Jr. associated with the Presbyterian congregation in Stockholm. Silas's wife, Ruth, died in East Stockholm on Mar. 14, 1826. She is buried in the **Union Cemetery,** Buckton, NY (see Union Cemetery, p. 114). None of

Ruth's children ever became affiliated with the LDS Church. Silas then married Mary Aikens on Mar. 4, 1828. Due to the seed sown by his brother Joseph in Aug. 1830, Silas was baptized into the Mormon faith on June 19, 1835, and migrated to Kirtland, OH, in 1836. Silas and his family were driven from Missouri and crossed the Mississippi River into Illinois on Feb. 21, 1839. He died at the age of 58 on Sept. 13, 1839, in a temporary settlement of the Saints called Pike City (Mormon Town), located just 2½ miles east of Pittsfield, Pike Co., IL, on U.S. 106. Silas was the branch president at the time of his death (SSS 1–2; RSNY 21–24).

Susan (Susanna) Smith (1773–1849) was living in Potsdam in the fall of 1836, when her two missionary brothers, **Joseph Smith Sr.** and **John Smith,** visited her. Joseph attempted to proselyte her with the Book of Mormon. However, it was reported, "We . . . found our sister Susan full of popularity and pride" (GAS 21). Susan never embraced Mormonism. She was strongly influenced by Jesse Smith, the eldest brother, who was very antagonistic toward the Prophet Joseph and the Book of Mormon. Susan continued to live in Potsdam, dying there on Mar. 22, 1849 (RSNY 27–28; IWP v. N–Z).

In 1810 **John Smith** (1781–1854) resided in Potsdam, apparently with Silas. He was appointed an overseer of highways for the

"Uncle" John Smith (1781–1854)

township on Mar. 3, 1810. John purchased 100 acres of land on Nov. 13, 1810. He married **Clarissa Lyman** on Sept. 11, 1815. They were members of the First Congregational Church at Potsdam. While living on the family farm on the Raquette River their son, **George A. Smith** (1817–75), attended school in the village of Potsdam. George A. said that his mother and father "spared no pains to impress my mind from my infancy with the importance of living a life of obedience to the principles of the religion of heaven, which they taught to me as well as they understood it" (ThI 81:7; ThC 4:3). **Joseph Smith Sr.** and **Don Carlos Smith** stayed several nights with John and his family in Aug. 1830. Mormon missionaries later called on John's family in Sept. 1831 and baptized Clarissa. John was later baptized on Jan. 9, 1832, by Solomon Humphrey and was confirmed and ordained an elder by Joseph H. Wakefield.[1]

George A. Smith described the prevailing situation at the time of his father's baptism:

> His neighbors all believed that baptism would kill him [physicians had pronounced him in the last stages of consumption]. I cut the ice in the creek, and broke a road for forty rods through the crust on two feet of snow; the day was very cold; the neighbors looked on with astonishment, expecting to see him die in the water, but his health continued improving from that moment. During the evening he had a vision of the Savior. The next day he visited his barn. He soon commenced traveling and preaching. His former Christian friends denouncing him as crazy, saying that the improved condition of his health was the result of insanity; and were greatly surprised that a crazy man should know more about the Bible than they did. (JH Jan. 9, 1832)

On Mar. 29, 1833, John attempted to preach in the "**Yellow School-house**" in Potsdam but an unruly assembly forced him to desist (MS 27:438).

John Smith and his family started for Kirtland on May 1, 1833. They were accompanied by Brother Moses Bailey and family. Also joining the caravan were Brother Norman D. Brown, and his father and mother, who were members of the Church from Parishville. The small company arrived at their destination on May 25, 1833 (ThI 81:74–75). John and his brother Joseph Sr. returned to the Postsdam/East Stockholm area in 1836 as missionary companions. **Jesse Smith,** in a moment of spite, swore out an execution against Joseph Sr. and "levied upon his horse and wagon." However, Silas Smith, who was here on business, stepped forward and paid the required 50 dollars (JH May 10, 1836). John subsequently became the president of the Adam-ondi-Ahman Stake in Daviess Co., MO,

---

[1] Solomon Humphrey, originally a Baptist, was convinced of the truthfulness of the gospel by Don Carlos Smith during Don Carlos's Aug. 1830 visit to St. Lawrence Co. Solomon traveled from Stockholm to western New York, where he met the Prophet Joseph during the fall of 1830. He was baptized and ordained an elder. Solomon later accompanied Lucy Mack Smith as she led the Fayette Saints to Kirtland in May 1831. He marched with Zion's Camp and afterwards died in Clay Co., MO, in Sept. 1834 (HC 4:393; JD 5:104; HJS 195–96; M&A 1:176).

the Zarahemla Stake, Lee Co., IA, the Nauvoo Stake in Hancock Co., IL, and the Salt Lake City Stake of Zion in Utah. John also served as Patriarch to the Church (1847–54). He administered 5,560 patriarchal blessings (ERA 48:337). Interestingly, among those blessings was one given to a non-Mormon, Col. Thomas L. Kane, at Council Bluffs, IA. Kane had given the Church significant aid in the recruitment of the Mormon Battalion in 1846. When Kane became deathly ill, John Smith helped nurse him back to health during a two-week period in Aug. 1846. "Uncle" John Smith died in Salt Lake City on May 23, 1854. He was the only son of Asael Sr. to live to see the West, although the families of Asael Jr. and Silas did immigrate to Utah after the deaths of the fathers (RSNY 24–26; ERA 48:337; EM 2:779; BE 1:184).

John's son, **George A. Smith,** was baptized on Sept. 10, 1832, by Joseph H. Wakefield and confirmed by Solomon Humphrey and Elder Wakefield (HC 1:285; ThI 81:11, 14; see also JH Feb. 14, 1859). George later became an Apostle on Apr. 26, 1839, at age 21. He served in the First Presidency under Brigham Young (1868–75).

George A. Smith

Birthplace of George A. Smith, Potsdam, NY. (Courtesy of LDSCA)

George A. Smith's son, **John Henry Smith** (1848–1911), was ordained an Apostle on Oct. 27, 1880, and called as Second Counselor in the First Presidency on Apr. 7, 1910. John Henry's son, **George Albert Smith** (1870–1951), was ordained an Apostle on Oct. 8, 1903, and ordained and set apart as the eighth President of the Church on May 21, 1945. Exceptional results were set in motion by that early missionary journey of Joseph Sr. and Don Carlos Smith in Aug. 1830.

■ BAYSIDE CEMETERY—**Burial Site of Samuel Smith**

Potsdam's **Bayside Cemetery** is located on the east side of the road .7 mile south of the junction of U.S. 11 and County 59 (which is also Clarkson Avenue/West Hannawa Road). The entrance to the cemetery is set back in and could easily be missed because of the houses that front the road. Also the cemetery is of sufficient size and pattern that the visitor should obtain directions to **Samuel Smith's grave** from the Sexton's House at the entrance. Samuel is buried in Section I (alphabetical letter I), Lot 86. Samuel's headstone is on the east side of the cemetery on an "island" created by two roadways. The stone is lying flush with the ground and reads, "Samuel Smith died May 2, 1830 in his 53rd yr." He reportedly died of consumption (tuberculosis). Samuel's wife, Frances, who died of pneumonia at age 75, is buried beside him as are others of his family.

Samuel (1777–1830), son of Asael Sr. and Mary Duty Smith, purchased 44.87 acres of land in the Township of Potsdam on Aug. 31, 1810. He was appointed clerk of election on Mar. 27, 1815, and school inspector on Mar. 5, 1816. Samuel had married Frances Wilcox in Feb. 1816. Unfortunately, Samuel died on May 2, 1830, just a few months before his brother, Joseph Smith Sr., brought the Book of Mormon to the family in St. Lawrence Co. during Aug. 1830. We are left to wonder what his disposition might have been in regard to his brother's message of salvation (ORS).

● POTSDAM PUBLIC MUSEUM

The Potsdam Public Museum is part of the civic center complex and is located on the north side of Elm Street at the junction of Elm and Park Streets in the village of Potsdam. They have a collection of research materials including record books, diaries, newspapers, photographs, and manuscripts relating to the development of the village, town, and county.

■ UNION CEMETERY—Burial Site of Asael Smith Sr. and His Son Jesse Smith

To locate the **Union Cemetery** in Buckton, Stockholm Township, proceed nine miles NE of the village of Potsdam to the hamlet of Stockholm Center at the junction of U.S. 11 and U.S. 11C. From Stockholm Center go east on U.S. 11C for 1.1 miles to East Part Phelix Road and turn right (south) for 1.8 miles to the front entrance of the Union Cemetery. The cemetery is on the left (east) side of the road. Some members of the Smith family are in lot 28. From the front entrance walk east to the second row of headstones then go right (south) for 14 yards. There you will first find the headstone of **Jesse Smith** (1768–1853), older brother of Joseph Smith Sr., followed by that of **Asael Smith Sr.** (1743–1830), father of Joseph Smith Sr. and grandfather of the Prophet Joseph Smith. Asael Smith's headstone (which spells his name "Asahel") states that he died Nov. 1, 1830, at age 87 years, while Jesse's stone specifies that he died Mar. 16, 1853, at age 81 years, 10 months, and 20 days. **Mary Duty Smith's** gravesite is conspicuously absent, as she died in Kirtland, OH, on May 27, 1836. Mary Duty is buried in the cemetery immediately north of the Kirtland Temple. Among the others in lot 28 of the Union Cemetery are **Hannah Peabody,** wife of Jesse Smith, and **Ruth Stevens,** wife of Silas Smith (1781–1826), and Silas's two infant children. There are also other family members in the second and third rows from the road. Still others are buried in lots 44 and 45.

■ WINTHROP

Today the village of Winthrop in Stockholm Township houses the town hall and records for the area of East Stockholm where the Asael Smith Sr. family lived. Winthrop is located 12 miles NE of Potsdam at the junction of U.S. 11 and State 420.

Asael Smith Jr. and his wife, **Elizabeth Schellinger,** moved from Vermont to East Stockholm in 1809. They were baptized into the Mormon faith on June 29, 1835, by Lyman E. Johnson. The family moved to Kirtland, OH, in May 1836. After the exodus of the Saints from Missouri the family, relocated to Illinois. Asael Jr. was a member of the Zarahemla Stake high council in Lee Co., IA. He also was ordained as a stake patriarch in Nauvoo on Oct. 7, 1844. Andrew Jenson, assistant Church historian, informs us that in 1845 "the Patriarchal office, according to the hereditary order, belonged to Asahel Smith; but as his health was poor, he is not known to have taken any active part in the office of presiding Patriarch" to the Church (BE 1:182). While journeying to the Rocky Mountains, Elizabeth died on Oct. 12, 1846. She was followed by Asael Jr. who died at Iowaville, IA, on July 21, 1848 (RSNY 28–29).

It is not certain when Asael (Asahel) Sr. and Mary Duty Smith arrived in East Stockholm from Tunbridge, VT. Heber C. Kimball said that "Silas and John removed their parents to St. Lawrence Co. N.Y., and took care of them until the day of their death, in turns of five years each. . . . John took care of his parents the first five years, Silas the second, and John the third, and then Silas kept them until their death" (JH Feb. 14, 1859). Asael and Mary were both being cared for in the household of Silas Smith in East Stockholm in 1830 when Asael Sr. died.

In Aug. 1830, Joseph Smith Sr., accompanied by his son Don Carlos, traveled to St. Lawrence Co. to share the newly restored gospel with his parents and other members of the family. Joseph Smith Sr. had a very pleasant visit with his brothers John, Silas, and Asael Jr., but from the outset he had trouble with his elder brother, Jesse. When Joseph attempted to talk about the discovery and translation of the Book of Mormon, Jesse exclaimed, "If you say another word about that Book of Mormon, you shall not stay a minute longer in my house, and if I can't get you out any other way, I will hew you down with my broadaxe" (HJS 172–76; JD 5:103–4).

It is most interesting to note the eventual outcome of this visit. In May 1836, **Mary Duty Smith,** nearly 93 years old, was taken to Kirtland, OH, in a small company led by Asael Jr. and Silas Smith. Embarking by boat from Ogdensburg, St. Lawrence Co., they traveled SW along the St. Lawrence River into Lake Ontario, and on to Rochester. From there they took a barge on the Erie Canal to Buffalo. Asael Jr. and Silas continued overland, but Elias Smith, Asael's son, took Mary Duty and some others on the steamboat *Sandusky* across Lake Erie to Fairport Harbor, OH. The company was then transported to Kirtland (JSN 113). Mary Duty was there for a brief period with four of her sons, Joseph Sr., Asael Jr., Silas, and John. All of her sons save Jesse had joined the Church.

The Prophet wrote of the arrival of his grandmother:

> She had come five hundred miles to see her children, and . . . was much pleased at being introduced to her great grand-children. . . . My grandfather, Asael Smith, long ago predicted that there would be a prophet raised up in his family, and my grandmother was fully satisfied that it was fulfilled in me. My grandfather Asael died in East Stockholm, St. Lawrence county, New York, after having received the Book of Mormon, and read it nearly through; and he declared that I was the very prophet that he had long known would come in his family. (HC 2:442–43)

Having arrived on May 18, and greeting her family, Mary Duty Smith "fell asleep without sickness, pain or regret," on May 27, 1836 (HC 2:442–43). She was never baptized. There were some problems because of the strenuous objections from her son, Jesse Smith (HC 2:442). Mary Duty's grandson, Jesse Nathaniel Smith, son of Silas, said that "she had expressed a desire to be baptized, but being infirm it was not done. She was 93 years old" (JJNS 5).

Otsego, Chenango, and Broome Counties

■ **BURLINGTON, OTSEGO COUNTY—Birthplace of Parley P. Pratt**

Burlington, Otsego Co., is located 12 miles west of Cooperstown (home of the **National Baseball Hall of Fame**) on State 80.

Parley P. Pratt
(Courtesy of USHS)

Parley Parker Pratt, the third son of Jared and Charity Dickinson Pratt, was born in the town of Burlington on Apr. 12, 1807. Sometime between 1807 and 1810, Jared moved his family to the town of Hartford, Washington Co., NY, just 17 miles SE of Lake George (LOP 8–9; see also Canaan and New Lebanon Townships for more information on Parley P. Pratt).

■ SMYRNA TOWNSHIP/COLD BROOK AREA, CHENANGO COUNTY

The Township of Smyrna, formerly part of Sherburne Township, is located in north-central Chenango Co. The principal community is the village of Smyrna at the intersection of State 80 and CR 20.

John Young, father of Brigham Young, homesteaded in Smyrna. When John Young moved his family here from Whitingham, VT, in 1804, they located at what was then the township of Sherburne. However, when the township of Smyrna was formed from Sherburne on Mar. 25, 1808, the Youngs became part of the newly created town of Smyrna. We don't know precisely where they lived initially, but Joseph Young stated that in 1807 they moved to Cold Brook (LOL 14–15; BYNY 2).

The Young family located on Cold Brook in "Dark Hollow." The site of Cold Brook and Dark Hollow is located 3.5 miles SW of Smyrna on CR 20, 21, and 10. At the intersection of CR 21 and CR 10 is a metal historical marker on the south side of the road, placed in commemoration of Chenango County's Bicentennial in 1982. The marker reads, "BRIGHAM YOUNG. Site of boyhood home of Brigham Young, Mormon leader, is one-half mile no[rth] on Cole Rd. The family went on to western N.Y." Dark Hollow is ½ mile NW of the intersection of CR 21 and CR 10 on CR 10 (Cole Rd.), on the west side of the road. There is no marker or physical feature at Dark Hollow. The precise site of the Young Home is unknown.

Local historians Richard F. Palmer and Karl D. Butler affirmed, "Joseph Young's account concurs with the local tradition that the Youngs lived near Cold Brook in a rural neighborhood called 'Dark Hollow,' about three miles southwest of the village of Smyrna." Palmer and Butler also indicated that the family remained here until "the winter of 1813" (BYNY 2–3).

● NORWICH, CHENANGO COUNTY

Norwich, the county seat, is located at the intersection of State 12 and State 23.

Important regional research facilities are located at Norwich, including the **Guernsey Memorial Library** at 3 Court Street and the **Chenango County Historical Society,** at 45 Rexford Street.

■ AFTON (FORMERLY SOUTH BAINBRIDGE), CHENANGO COUNTY

The village of Afton is located 25 miles NE of Binghamton on I-88, at the exit to Afton on State 41. When the Prophet Joseph Smith was in this village, it was known as **South Bainbridge.**

JOSEPH SMITH AND EMMA HALE ELOPEMENT. Joseph Smith, at age 21, was married to Emma Hale, age 22, on Jan. 18, 1827, in South

Joseph Smith and Emma Hale. (Courtesy of RLDSLA)

Squire Tarble's house in Afton, NY, where Joseph Smith and Emma Hale were married.

Fairgrounds at Afton, NY, where Squire Tarble's house site is located. (1978)

Bainbridge at the home of Squire Zachariah Tarble. The couple eloped after Emma's father, Isaac Hale, had refused Joseph his daughter's hand on the basis that "he was a stranger, and followed a business that I could not approve." Joseph explained that "owing to my continuing to assert that I had seen a vision, persecution still followed me, and my wife's father's family were very much opposed to our being married." After the ceremony in South Bainbridge, the newlyweds were taken by Josiah Stowell to Joseph's parents' home in Manchester, NY, where they stayed from Jan. to Dec. 1827 (NEW 186–94).

The Tarble house once stood at what is now the entrance to the Afton Fairgrounds on the east side of the Susquehanna River. The entrance is at the intersection of East Main Street and Evelyn

Avenue. A New York State Education Department sign at the site reads: "Mormon House, Joseph Smith, founder of the Mormon Church, was married in this house Jan. 18, 1827 to [Emma] Hale." The house was eventually sold at auction and torn down in July 1948. Charles Decker purchased two of the mantel pieces from the Tarble home in 1948. One is now at his home in Afton, and the other was donated to the Afton Historical Society Museum (CD).

THE PROPHET ON TRIAL IN SOUTH BAINBRIDGE. The Mar. 20, 1826, court trial of Joseph Smith Jr. also took place here, though the exact location is unknown. While Joseph was employed by **Josiah Stowell,** who lived three miles SW of the village, a misdemeanor charge was filed against the Prophet by Peter Bridgeman for being "a disorderly person." Joseph was arrested by Constable Philip De Zeng and the complaint was heard before Justice of the Peace Albert Neely. The writ stemmed from Joseph's participation with Josiah Stowell in an attempt to find buried treasure. Joseph was acquitted of the charge by Justice Neely (BYUS, 30, no. 2 [spring]: 91–108).

Beginning on June 28, and extending into the forepart of July 1830, Joseph Smith was the subject of a second trial in South Bainbridge. The exact location of the trial is not known. Joseph merely stated, "He [Constable Ebenezer Hatch] drove on to the town of South Bainbridge, Chenango County, where he lodged me for the time being in an upper room of a tavern" (HC 1:89). Some have supposed this to be the site of the Afton Inn of today. An inn was originally built on the site in 1823 by Alpheus and Josiah Wright. This tavern burned down in 1877 but was rebuilt by the owner, Erastus Sullivan. Whether this was the site of the trial is uncertain.

After the baptism of a number of persons at the Joseph Knight Sr. farm in Colesville, Broome Co., on June 28, 1830, Joseph Smith was arrested by Constable Ebenezer Hatch and taken to South Bainbridge for trial on the charge of being "a disorderly person, of setting the country in an uproar by preaching the Book of Mormon" (HC 1:87–88). In addition to the excitement created by the Book of Mormon in the neighborhood, the Mormons had baptized Deacon Josiah Stowell and two choir members from the Presbyterian Church. This had aroused considerable local resentment against the Prophet. He was arraigned on the misdemeanor charge before Justice of the Peace Joseph Chamberlin on July 1, 1830. The Prophet recorded that "Joseph Knight, had repaired to two of his neighbors, viz., James Davidson and John S. Reid, Esqrs., respectable farmers, men renowned for their integrity, and well versed in the laws of their country; and retained them on my behalf during my trial" (HC 1:89). Despite the best efforts of the prosecution to convict Joseph, he was pronounced "not guilty" at about twelve o'clock midnight. However, just a half hour after his discharge in Chenango Co. he was again arrested on a similar warrant from Colesville, Broome Co. (HC 1:91; 6:394-95; NEW, 203–5; see also Colesville Township herein).

■ **AFTON TOWNSHIP, CHENANGO COUNTY**

Afton Township is located 20 miles NE of Binghamton. In the days of the Prophet Joseph Smith this was part of Bainbridge Township and did not become Afton until Nov. 18, 1857, when it was divided off. It was here that Joseph was employed by Josiah Stowell Sr.

● **GUY CEMETERY.** The Guy Cemetery is located on State 7 on the south side of the road, 2.1 miles south of the village of Afton, and just 200 yards south of the railroad overpass that crosses State 7.

In this small rural cemetery Arad Stowel (only one *l*), Thomas Stowell, Hannah Stowel, Reuben Bridgeman, Seneca Reed, and other contemporaries of Josiah Stowell are buried. Josiah and his wife, Miriam Bridgeman Stowell, are not among them. They are buried in the Smithboro Cemetery, Tioga County, NY (NEW 208–9).

■ **JOSIAH STOWELL HOME AND FARM SITE.** The Josiah Stowell home is located at 323 SR 7, 3.1 miles south of the south boundary of the village of Afton on the north side of State 7, or 1.5 miles north of Nineveh when coming from the south on State 7. According to Charles Decker, Afton town and village historian, the existing two-story frame home is the one which belonged to Josiah Stowell (CD). It is privately owned.

Josiah Stowell visited **Joseph Smith Jr.** at his home in Manchester, NY, during Oct. 1825. Commenting on Stowell's visit, Joseph stated, "I hired with an old gentleman by the name of Josiah [Stowell], who lived in Chenango County, state of New York. He had heard something of a silver mine having been opened by the Spaniards in Harmony, Susquehanna County, state of Pennsylvania; and had, previous to my hiring to him, been digging, in order, if possible, to discover the mine. After I went to live with him, he took me, with the rest of his hands, to dig for the silver mine" (HC 1:17).

Isaac Hale said that Josiah Stowell's crew boarded at his home from about Nov. 1, to Nov. 17, 1825. It was there that Joseph first saw his future wife **Emma,** the daughter of Isaac Hale. The Prophet said, "Finally I prevailed with the old gentleman to cease digging after it [Spanish treasure]" (HC 1:17). Josiah Stowell then took Joseph as one of his hired hands to his farm below the village of South Bainbridge where he was employed as "a wool carder, and a farmer." Joseph apparently worked in one of Stowell's mills once located on Reed Creek, just 0.2 mile east of the Josiah Stowell Sr. home on State 7 (NEW 180). Although he was also hired to work for Joseph Knight Sr. five miles south on the Susquehanna River, Joseph said that he was married to Emma Hale on Jan. 18, 1827, "while I was yet employed in the service of Mr. Stoal" (HC 1:17).

Josiah Stowell Sr. joined the Church following its organization. He did not gather to Kirtland. In 1833 he had purchased land in Tioga Co., NY, and is identified as being buried in Smithboro (NEW 207–210). His headstone in lot 26 of the Smithboro Cemetery, Tioga County, NY, identifies his **death date as May 12, 1844,** and notes that he died at the age of 76 years. In a letter of Josiah Stowell Jr. to John S. Fullmer dated Feb. 17, 1843, Josiah Jr. added a note dictated to him by his aged father in defense of Joseph Smith saying, "He has binn acquainted with him [Joseph] 6 years & he never knew any thing of him but what was right als[o] know him to be a Seer & a Phrophet & Believe the Book of Mormon to be true & all these stories is fals[e] & untrue that is told about Joseph Smith" (CN May 12, 1985, 10).

■ COLESVILLE TOWNSHIP, BROOME COUNTY

Colesville Township is located on I-88, seven miles east of Binghamton, the county seat of Broome County. It was created from Windsor Township on Apr. 2, 1821, and is named after Nathaniel Cole Sr. The township is centrally drained by the Susquehanna River. Joseph and Polly Peck Knight moved their family to Colesville Township from Bainbridge Township, Chenango Co., NY, in about 1810. The Colesville Branch of the LDS Church was organized in this town in 1830, and the members emigrated together from here to Ohio in 1831.

■ **THE JOSEPH KNIGHT SR. FARM.** The Joseph Knight Sr. farm is situated in Colesville Township 16.7 miles NE of Binghamton. Take I-88 east from Binghamton to exit 6 and its junction with State 7.

Nineveh Village, Colesville Township, looking NE up the Susquehanna River. (1978)

Proceed NE on State 7 to Nineveh. The Joseph Knight Sr. farm is on the east side of the Susquehanna River, opposite Nineveh via the bridge at the village of Nineveh, and south 0.4 mile on CR 29. The Joseph Knight Sr. home no longer stands. On the Knight farm and set back in the hills to the east from CR 29, is a privately owned modern house and an artist's studio.

A local reminiscence of the **Joseph Knight Sr.** family and their Colesville holdings stipulated:

Nineveh Village, Colesville Township, looking west, with Pickerel Pond and the Joseph Knight Sr. farm in the foreground. (1978)

Just opposite of N[i]neveh, on the east side of the river, on what is now known as the Scott, or Henry P. Bush farm, in a little old, gray, frame house lived a poor man named Knight who worked hard to sustain his little family. At the outlet of Pickerel Lake, on this farm, Knight had a carding mill, the dam tranches and raceways being still visible. In this mill Knight toiled from day to day to eke out the scanty supply for his little ones. Some distance west of the carding mill on a slight rise of ground, stands an old barn, in which

Pickerel Pond, on the Joseph and Polly Knight farm, Colesville Township. (Photo by George E. Anderson, 1907; courtesy of LDSCA)

[Joseph] Smith later preached to his disciples, giving forth his doctrines and revealing the new truth. (NEW 183)

Joseph Knight Jr. indicated that his father was somewhat better off than the above description suggests, as he had built a gristmill and two carding machines, and at one juncture owned "three other farms and hired many hands" (NEW 184). **Joseph Smith Jr.** was among those employed in 1826. Joseph Knight Jr. further related, "My father said Joseph was the best hand he ever hired, we found him a boy of truth, he was 21 years of age. I think it was in November [1826] he made known to my father and I, that he had seen a vision, that a personage had appeared to him and told him where there was a gold book of ancient date buried, and if he would follow the directions of the Angel he could get it. We were told it in secret" (NEW 184).

During the winter of 1826–27, Joseph Knight Sr. loaned Joseph Smith his horse and cutter (sleigh) so that he could go down the Susquehanna River some 28 miles to visit his girl, Miss **Emma Hale,** at Harmony, PA. After Joseph's marriage to Emma on Jan. 18, 1827, the Prophet obtained the golden plates in Sept. 1827, and the young couple later moved to Harmony in Dec. 1827. There Joseph Knight Sr. continued his friendship and assistance. During the translation of the plates he literally came to the rescue of the Prophet and Oliver Cowdery, who found themselves impoverished in the spring of 1829. Knight stated, "I Bought a Barral of Mackrel and some lined paper for writing. And when I Came home I

Bought some nine or ten Bushels of grain and five or six Bushels taters [potatoes] and a pound of tea, and I went Down to see him [Joseph] and they ware in want. Joseph and Oliver ware gone to see if they Could find a place to work for provisions, But found none. They returned home and found me there with provisions, and they ware glad for they ware out" (BYUS 16, no. 4 [autumn]: 36).

EARLY CONVERTS AND BAPTISMS AT THE KNIGHT FARM. Following the publication of the Book of Mormon and the organization of the Church at Fayette, NY, on Apr. 6, 1830, the Prophet visited the Joseph Knight Sr. family in Colesville Township during that same month. Joseph stated: "Mr. Knight and his family were Universalists, but were willing to reason with me upon my religious views, and were as usual friendly and hospitable" (HC 1:81). Among those attending the meetings was **Newel Knight,** the son of Joseph Sr. Newel had refused the opportunity to pray vocally with the group. While attempting to pray by himself in the woods, he was overcome by an evil spirit which distorted and twisted his limbs. The Prophet was summoned to Newel's home and reported, "I rebuked the devil, and commanded him in the name of Jesus Christ to depart from him; when immediately Newel spoke out and said that he saw the devil leave him and vanish from his sight. This was the **first miracle** which was done in the Church, or by any member of it. . . . It was done by God, and by the power of godliness" (HC 1:82).

Many early converts were baptized at the Knight farm. The Prophet and Oliver Cowdery successfully proselyted among the

Joseph Knight Jr. (Courtesy of LDSCA).

Knight family and others in Colesville, and many were ready for baptism on June 28, 1830. **Joseph Knight Jr.** said a mob broke down the dam the brethren had built on a little stream that flowed from Pickerel Pond down to the Susquehanna River. The brethren rebuilt the dam and went ahead with their baptisms. Among those baptized at the Knight farm on June 28, 1830, were Emma Hale Smith, wife of the Prophet; Joseph Knight Sr. and his wife, Polly Peck; Hezekiah Peck, and his wife, Martha Long; William Stringham and his wife, Esther Knight; Joseph Knight Jr., Aaron Culver and his wife, Esther Peck; Levi Hall, Polly Knight, and Julia Stringham. Listed as being baptized on June 29 [June 28] were Sally Coburn, wife of Newel Knight (who had already been baptized at Fayette in May 1830), and Anna Knight De Mill (also DeMille), wife of Freeborn DeMill (BYUS 10, no. 2 [spring]: 372–73).

Joseph Knight Jr. recorded the circumstances immediately following the baptisms:

> When we were going from the water, we were met by many of our neighbors, pointing at us and asking if we had been washing sheep; before Joseph could confirm us he was taken by the officers to Chenango Co. [South Bainbridge] for trial, for saying that the Book of Mormon was a revelation from God; my father employed two lawyers [James Davidson and John Reid] to plead for him and cleared him; that night our wagons were turned over and wood piled on them, and some sunk in the water, rails were piled against our doors, and chains sunk in the stream and a great deal of mischief done. Before Joseph got to my Father's house he was taken again to be tried in Broome Co., Father employed the same lawyers who cleared him there. (BYUS 10, no. 2 [spring]: 373–74)

TRIAL OF JOSEPH SMITH AT COLESVILLE. The Prophet was first taken from Colesville, Broome Co., to South Bainbridge, Chenango Co., for a trial, which occurred on July 1, 1830. Being exonerated of the charges there, Joseph was again seized by an officer from Colesville, Broome Co., on another charge of disorderly conduct. As indicated by Joseph Knight Jr., his father rehired James Davidson and John S. Reid, who again defended the Prophet. Reid later declared that when asked to defend Joseph a second time he tried every means to be excused as he was much fatigued, but then stated, "A peculiar impression or thought struck my mind that I must go and defend him, for he was the Lord's anointed" (HC 6:395).

The Prophet was taken to a tavern in Colesville Township by the arresting constable. There are those who feel that Cole's Tavern SW of Harpursville on the SW corner of what is now the Colesville Road (or Farm to Market Road) and Watrous Road was the site of the second trial. The small settlement at these crossroads was the original Colesville. Cole's tavern was torn down in 1925 by Aaron Olmstead (HCJ 21–26). Joseph was once more acquitted, though the prosecution "sent out runners and ransacked the hills and vales, grog-shops and ditches, gathered together a company that looked as if they had come from hell, and had been whipped by the soot-boy thereof, which they brought forward to testify one after another, but with no better success" (HC 1:91–96; HC 6:395).

THE COLESVILLE BRANCH. The Colesville Branch of the Church was formed by the individuals who were baptized on June 28, 1830. Some 68 members of the Colesville Branch eventually emigrated from New York to Kirtland, OH, in April and May 1831. Obedient to the Jan. 2, 1831, commandment of the Lord to gather in Ohio (D&C 38:31–32), the Colesville Saints commenced selling their lands in anticipation of an exodus in the spring. An advertisement posted in the *Broome Republican* on behalf of Joseph Knight Sr. reads: "FOR SALE, THE farm lately occupied by Joseph Knight, situate in the town of Colesville, near the Colesville Bridge—bounded on one side by the Susquehanna River, and containing about one hundred and forty two acres. On said Farm are two Dwelling Houses, a good Barn, and a fine Orchard. Terms of the sale will be liberal—Apply to Wm. M. Waterman" (BYUS 10, no. 2 [spring]: 380).

Most of the members of the Colesville Branch, under the leadership of **Newel Knight,** met at Ithaca, NY, so they could travel together by water to Kirtland, OH, as a single company They embarked by steamboat from the inlet to Cayuga Lake on Apr. 25, 1831. Their journey took them 38 miles north on Cayuga Lake, still farther north by the Cayuga and Seneca Canal, and west to Buffalo on the Erie Canal. From Buffalo Harbor they were eventually able to sail on Lake Erie to Fairport Harbor, OH. They then went overland to Kirtland, where the company arrived in mid-May 1831. There the Colesville Branch was directed to the farm of Lemon Copley in Thompson Township, Geauga Co., OH, where they took up residence and began to improve that property under the Law of Consecration (NEW 296–308; see also TAF 63–71).

■ BINGHAMTON (CHENANGO POINT), BROOME COUNTY

The city of Binghamton (Chenango Point) is the county seat of Broome Co. and is located at the junction of I-81 and State 17. It was the site of early baptisms and the creation of a branch.

William W. Phelps, editor of *The Evening and The Morning Star,* informed his readership, under an item dated Dec. 24, 1832, that through one of his contacts he had "just learned, that brothers **Martin and Emer Harris** have baptized one hundred persons at Chenango Point [Binghamton], New-York, within a few weeks" (EMS Feb. 1833, 6). On May 25, 1835, Elders John Murdock and Lloyd Lewis were assigned to visit the branch at Chenango Point and assist in putting some things in order there (HC 2:224).[2]

● RESEARCH FACILITIES IN BINGHAMTON. Significant resources for regional research are located at the **Broome County Historical Society,** a constituency of the **Roberson Museum and Science Center,** 30 Front Street, Binghamton, and at the **Binghamton/ Broome County Public Library,** 78 Exchange Street, Binghamton. The Broome County historian's office is located in the library.

NOTE TO READER: Directly south of Broome County, NY, are Susquehanna County, PA, and old Harmony Township (now Oakland), where Joseph and Emma Hale Smith resided and where important historical sites exist. See pp. 262–76.

■ UNION TOWNSHIP, BROOME COUNTY—Birthplace of Jedediah M. Grant, Apostle and Second Counselor in the First Presidency

Union Township adjoins Binghamton to the NW. The villages of Johnson City and Endicott are located within Union Township on State 17C.

Jedediah Morgan Grant was born in Union Township to Joshua and Athalia Howard Grant on Feb. 21, 1816.[3] That same year the

---

[2] For a more extensive history of the Church in Binghamton and vicinity, see H. H. Christensen, *History of The Church of Jesus Christ of Latter-day Saints in the Binghamton, New York Area, 1825 through 1979* (Endwell, New York: n.p., n.d.).

[3] There is some conjecture as to the birthplace of Jedediah M. Grant. Five of Jedediah's siblings had been born in Windsor Township, Broome Co., NY. However, the family appears to have been living in Union Township, Broome Co. when Jedediah was born. (BE 1:56 ; MT 4; JMG 1).

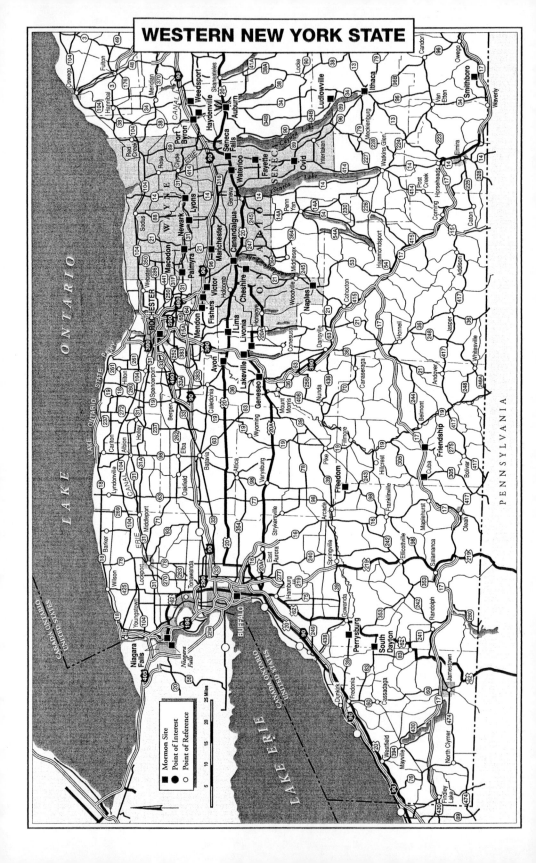

WESTERN NEW YORK STATE

family moved to a farm near Naples, Ontario Co., NY. By 1833 the family had relocated to Erie Co., PA. It was here that Mormon elders, first Amasa Lyman and Orson Hyde, and later John F. Boynton and Evan M. Greene, proselyted the family. Jedediah was baptized under the administration of Elders Boynton and Greene at Sherman's Corners, PA, on Mar. 2, 1833. The Grants immigrated to Chagrin, OH. Jedediah's sister, Caroline, married William Smith, brother of the Prophet

Jedediah Morgan Grant

Joseph, in Kirtland during the fall of 1833. Jedediah marched with Zion's Camp in 1834 (MT 4–9). Years later, he was ordained an Apostle and was sustained as Second Counselor in the First Presidency of the Church under the administration of President Brigham Young on Apr. 7, 1854. He died in Salt Lake City on Dec. 1, 1856.

Tompkins County

■ ITHACA

Ithaca is located at the junction of State Highways 96, 89, 79, and 366, at the south end of Cayuga Lake.

The members of the **Colesville Branch** were directed by the Lord to gather to Kirtland, OH, and vicinity at the Jan. 2, 1831, conference of the Church held at the Peter Whitmer Sr. farm in Fayette (D&C 38). Some 68 Saints responded to the call. Under the leadership of the branch president, Newel Knight, at least two groups of immigrants rendezvoused at Ithaca between Apr. 21 and 25, 1831. Jared Carter said that at Ithaca they "took water to go to the Ohio" (JCJ). The company could have arranged for steamboat passage on Cayuga Lake from the inlet at Ithaca to the northern end in the vicinity of Cayuga Bridge, some 40 miles distant, or contracted for a smaller through boat all the way to Buffalo. The Colesville Saints departed Ithaca on Apr. 25, 1831, and arrived at Cayuga Bridge (a mile-long wooden bridge which spanned from the village of Cayuga, Cayuga Co., to Bridgeport, Seneca Co., on the west side of the lake) on Apr. 26. The steamboats *Telemachus, De Witt Clinton,* and *Enterprise,* were involved in the lake traffic during this period. The *Telemachus* and *De Witt Clinton* were primarily used for passengers, while the *Enterprise* handled the towing of barges and canal boats. Given the financial situation of the company and the convenience of not having to unload and load their belongings at the north end of the lake, it is probable that they merely opted for a small through boat to Buffalo.

At the north end of Cayuga Lake the Colesville Saints then used the Cayuga and Seneca Canal to move through the Montezuma Marshes and on to the Erie Canal. They then traveled westward on the canal to Buffalo, where they secured ship's passage on Lake Erie for Ohio. Being delayed by ice freshets in Buffalo Harbor, Jared Carter led a small group of the Colesville Saints by land to Dunkirk, NY, where they took a steamboat to Ohio. The larger element of Colesville Saints finally reached Fairport Harbor, OH, on May 14, 1831, and then traveled 14 miles overland to Kirtland (NEW 296–308).

- **RESEARCH FACILITIES IN ITHACA. Cornell University** is located at Ithaca. The superb collections of the **John M. Olin and Carl A. Kroch Libraries** at that institution provide an invaluable resource to researchers and historians. Similarly, there are significant archival materials available at the **DeWitt Historical Society Tompkins County Museum** at 401 East State Street in Ithaca.

■ **WHITE SETTLEMENT CEMETERY—Reported Burial Site of Abigail Howe Young, Mother of Brigham Young**

The **White Settlement Cemetery** is located in Lansing Township, north of Ithaca and NW of Ludlowville. From the junction of State 34 and State 34B at the hamlet of South Lansing, continue NW on 34B 6.4 miles to the intersection of 34B and Jerry Smith Road. Go east on Jerry Smith Road .7 mile to Dates Road and then north on Dates Road ½ mile to the White Settlement Cemetery, which is on the right-hand (east) side of the road.

Joseph Young, brother of **Brigham Young,** stated that in 1813 his father, John Young, moved the family from the Township of Smyrna to the town of Genoa, Cayuga County. However, local historians Richard F. Palmer and Karl D. Butler suspect the Young family actually located some seven miles SW of Genoa, near Lansing or Lansingville. Brigham's mother, Abigail Howe Young, who had long suffered from consumption (tuberculosis), died on June 11, 1815. Palmer and Butler have uncovered "several historical accounts that indicate that she was buried near Lansingville, possibly in the old White Settlement Cemetery, a half mile west of that village" (BYNY 3–4, 89 note 16). Their research is ongoing.

Seneca County

■ OVID, OVID TOWNSHIP—**Birthplace of Zebedee Coltrin, One of the Seven Presidents of the Seventy**

Ovid, Seneca Co., is located 18 miles south of Waterloo at the intersection of State Highways 96, 414, and 96A.

Zebedee Coltrin was born in Ovid on Sept. 7, 1804, a son of John and Sarah Graham Coltrin. The Coltrins moved to Geauga Co., OH, in 1814, then to Strongsville, Cuyahoga Co., OH. In Jan. 1831 Elder Solomon Hancock came to the Coltrin home and preached. As Zebedee lay meditating on what he had heard that evening he said that, "the room became lighted up with a brilliant light and I saw a number of men dressed in white robes, like unto

Zebedee Coltrin

what we call temple clothes." The next morning he applied to Elder Hancock for baptism. Zebedee was baptized by Solomon Hancock in a pond near his father's farm on Jan. 9, 1831. They had to cut through ice one foot thick to make a hole. Zebedee Coltrin was among those who marched with Zion's Camp in 1834 and was later ordained in Kirtland as one of the **seven Presidents of the Seventy,** on Feb. 28, 1835. Zebedee was released from that presidency on Apr. 6, 1837, having previously been ordained a high priest. He died in Spanish Fork, UT, on July 21, 1887 (LZC 4–8, 28–32, 90).

Ovid is regionally famous for its "Three Bears." Seneca County actually has two shires, one at Waterloo and the other at Ovid. Waterloo has become predominant over the years, but Ovid still maintains "half-shire public buildings." They are situated on a knoll

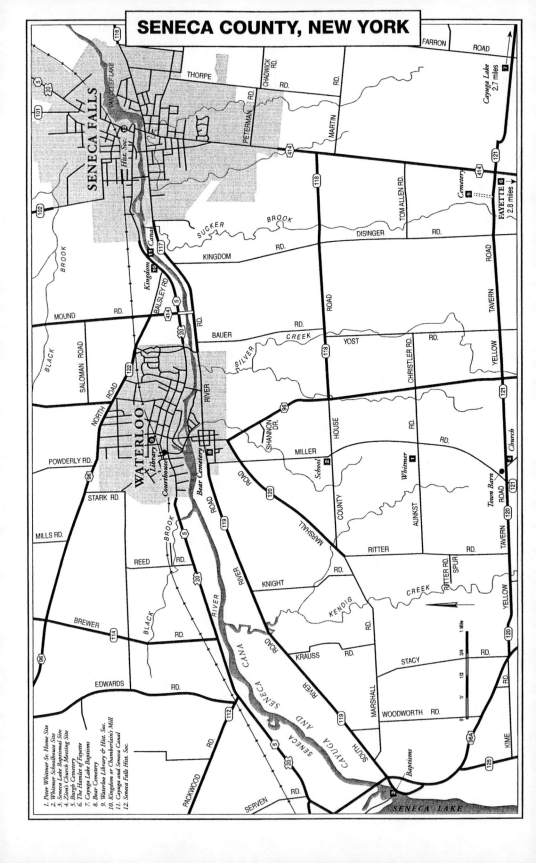

SENECA COUNTY, NEW YORK

SENECA FALLS

WATERLOO

SENECA LAKE

1. Peter Whitmer Sr. Home Site
2. Whitmer Schoolhouse Site
3. Seneca Lake Baptismal Site
4. Zion's Church Meeting Site
5. Burgh Cemetery
6. The Hamlet of Fayette
7. Cayuga Lake Baptisms
8. Bear Cemetery
9. Waterloo Library & Hist. Soc.
10. Kingdom or Chamberlain's Mill
11. Cayuga and Seneca Canal
12. Seneca Falls Hist. Soc.

Cayuga Lake
2.7 miles

FAYETTE 6
2.8 miles

fronting Courthouse Square in the village. Today the three buildings are commonly called "The Three Bears." The largest of the brick buildings, the courthouse, is called "Papa Bear." The next building to the south is the (new) county clerk's office, and is known as "Mama Bear." Next to this is the smallest of the three, the (old) county clerk's office, which is affectionately referred to as "Baby Bear." They were built in 1845, 1860, and 1845 respectively. The buildings are all built in the same architectural style and need to be seen to be fully appreciated.

■ FAYETTE TOWNSHIP

Fayette Township is located in Seneca Co., immediately south of the village of Waterloo on State 96. Fayette derives its name from the American Revolutionary War hero General Marquis de LaFayette. When first organized as a town on Mar. 14, 1800, it was known as Washington, Cayuga Co. On Feb. 12, 1803, the town of Junius was divided from Washington. Seneca Co. was created from Cayuga Co. in 1804, and Washington was within the confines of its borders. By an act of Apr. 6, 1808, the town name of Washington was changed to Fayette. Fayette Township is bounded on the north by the town of Junius, on the east by Cayuga Lake and Cayuga Co., on the south by the town of Romulus, and on the west by Seneca Lake and Ontario County. Local historian John S. Genung, vice president of the Waterloo Library and Historical Society, has given invaluable assistance through many years in identifying places and events.

■ 1. PETER WHITMER SR. HOME SITE, FARM, AND LDS VISITORS CENTER.

The Peter Whitmer Sr. farm is located in Seneca Co. three miles south of Waterloo on State 96 and .8 mile west on the north side of Aunkst Road. A colonial-style building housing a **visitors center** and **chapel** is on the site along with a **reconstructed log house** depicting the home of Peter Whitmer Sr. An

Peter Whitmer farm, aerial view looking NE. (Courtesy of LaMar C. Berrett, 1978)

original Greek Revival home, built in 1845–50 by John Deshler, a later owner of the property, is also at the site.

Many of the first settlers of what became known as Fayette were Pennsylvania Germans. Among the German immigrants making their residences in the township were members of the **Peter Whitmer Sr. family.** Peter Whitmer Sr. was born on Apr. 14, 1773, in

Harrisburg, PA. He moved his household to Fayette from Hamburg, PA, about 1809. How long they had been working the land where the present farm is now located is not known. A series of four warranty deeds dating from Apr. 14, 1819, to Mar. 7, 1827, however, conveys the 100 acres comprising the property to

Peter Whitmer Sr. farm, barn, and an 1845–50 Greek revival house. (1945)

the Whitmers. At the time of the restoration of the gospel, the Whitmer family consisted of Peter Sr., his wife, Mary Musselman Whitmer, and their children, Christian (married to Anna Schott, 1825), Jacob (married to Elizabeth Schott, 1825), John, David (married Julia Ann Jolly, 1831), Catherine (married Hiram Page, 1825), Peter Jr., and Elizabeth Ann (who would later marry Oliver Cowdery in Jackson Co., MO, 1832) (NEW 223–30; RSNY 149–50).

The reconstructed log house of Peter Whitmer Sr. has the unique distinction of being on the exact site where The Church of Jesus Christ of Latter-day Saints (then simply the "Church of Christ" or the "Church of Jesus Christ") was organized on Tuesday, Apr. 6,

1830. Six men were chosen to formally organize the Church "agreeable to the laws of our country, by the will and commandments of God." **Joseph Smith Jr., Oliver Cowdery, Hyrum Smith, Peter Whitmer Jr., Samuel H. Smith, and David Whitmer** were the six original members

Reconstructed log house of Peter Whitmer Sr. Fayette, Seneca Co., NY. (1980)

(D&C 20:1; HC 1:75–79; ENS 9 [Mar. 1979]: 42–45; ENS 19 [Feb. 1989]: 14–19).

David Whitmer indicated that on the day of organization his "father's 2 rooms were filled with members—about 20 from Colesville, 15 from Manchester Church and about 20 from round-about Father Whitmers. About 50 members & the 6 Elders were present" (JEdS Jan. 2, 1887). The Prophet Joseph Smith described the initial proceedings of that April day: "Having opened the meeting by solemn prayer to our Heavenly Father, we proceeded, according to previous commandment, to call on our brethren to know whether they accepted us as their teachers in the things of the Kingdom of God, and whether they were satisfied that we should proceed and be organized as a Church according to said commandment which we had received. To these several propositions they consented by a unanimous vote" (HC 1:77).

Joseph then ordained Oliver Cowdery an elder and Oliver in turn ordained Joseph to that same office. The two men administered the sacrament for the first time in this dispensation and followed that sacred ordinance by laying their hands on those who had been previously baptized "that they might receive the gift of the Holy Ghost, and be confirmed members of the Church of Christ" (HC 1:77–78). A number of ordinations to priesthood offices were then performed. The Prophet summated these events by saying:

Organization of The Church of Jesus Christ of Latter-day Saints, April 6, 1830, in the Peter Whitmer home at Fayette, Seneca Co. (Courtesy of Robert T. Barrett)

After a happy time spent in witnessing and feeling for ourselves the powers and blessings of the Holy Ghost, through the grace of God bestowed upon us, we dismissed with the pleasing knowledge that we were now individually members of, and acknowledged of God, "The Church of Jesus Christ," organized in accordance with commandments and revelations given by Him to ourselves in these last days, as well as according to the order of the Church as recorded in the New Testament. (HC 1:79)

Joseph Smith recalled with some emotion, "Several persons who had attended the above meeting, became convinced of the truth and came forward shortly after, and were received into the Church; among the rest, my own father and mother were baptized, to my great joy and consolation; and about the same time, Martin Harris and Orrin Porter Rockwell" (HC 1:79; see also BYUS 16, no. 4 [autumn]: 37).

Orson Pratt exhibited very strong foresight concerning the original log house and its significance to future generations. He declared, "That house will, no doubt, be celebrated for ages to come as the one chosen by the Lord in which to make known the first elements of the organization of His Kingdom in the latter days" (RSNY 150).

Although the procedures carried out on Apr. 6, 1830, were done in accordance with the laws of the state of New York relative to organizing a religious society, the incorporation record for the "Church of Christ" has never been found, either in Seneca Co. (where the record should be) or in Albany, NY (ENS 8 [Dec. 1978]: 26–27).

For the **sesquicentennial celebration of the organization of the Church** in 1980, Church leaders determined to replicate the old Whitmer log house. The original home had long since disappeared, probably before the turn of the 20th century. Historians and archaeologists working together had pinpointed the exact location of where the Whitmer dwelling had once stood (ERA 73:16–25). Preparation of the site began in Mar. 1979. Using as models two log houses in the area, both documented to be over 150 years old, historical restorationists meticulously pieced together a beautiful reconstruction of the structure.

President Spencer W. Kimball and Camilla Eyring Kimball in the reconstructed log house of Peter Whitmer Sr. at Fayette, Seneca Co., for the sesquicentennial celebration of the organization of the Church, April 6, 1980.

The old Tillinghast log cabin in Romulus Township, Seneca Co., was used as a model for the new cabin. The replica log house was constructed precisely on the site of the first home and used the same dimensions, 20' x 30'. The new cabin, the visitors center, chapel, and the Deshler home (converted to a residence for missionary couples) were all dedicated by **President Spencer W. Kimball** on Apr. 6, 1980. The dedication was part of a telecast originating from the Whitmer farm and was broadcast by satellite to general conference at the Tabernacle on Temple Square, thus marking the 150th anniversary of the organization of the Church (ERA 73:16–25; BYUS 13, no. 1 [winter]: 172–201; CN Apr. 12, 1980, 5–6).

In addition to the organization of the Church on the Peter Whitmer Sr. farm, many other significant events associated with the restored Church occurred at the Whitmer farm in this formative period.

(1) In the first part of Apr. 1829, Oliver Cowdery and Samuel H. Smith stayed with Oliver's friend, David Whitmer, on their way to Harmony, PA, to offer assistance to Joseph Smith Jr., who was translating the Book of Mormon. This visit and an exchange of letters awakened a deep interest in the Whitmer family concerning the Prophet and his work (HC 1:32n).

(2) In June 1829, Joseph Smith and Oliver Cowdery moved to the Whitmer home to complete the last portion of the translation of the Book of Mormon. Here, in June 1829, the **angel Moroni** delivered the gold plates to Joseph at the farm after having transported them from the Prophet's home in Harmony, PA, for purposes of safe keeping (HJS 149–50).

(3) David Whitmer maintained that his mother, **Mary Musselman Whitmer,** had said that she was shown the gold plates by a man, apparently Moroni. Mary was reportedly concerned about the increased toil to which she was subjected by the presence of so many "guests" (including Joseph Smith, Emma Smith, and Oliver Cowdery) during the translation process. The appearance of the angel with the plates was designed to quiet her apprehensions (DEN Nov. 16, 1878; CHC 1:127; MS 49:773; JSR 99–100; WBM 71).

(4) David Whitmer stated that the translation of the Book of Mormon was completed with the help of the Whitmers, Oliver Cowdery, and Joseph's wife, Emma, at the Whitmer home between June 1 and July 1, 1829 (KCDJ June 5, 1881).

(5) While Joseph Smith lived in the Whitmer home, he applied for the copyright for the Book of Mormon on June 11, 1829, through Richard R. Lansing, Clerk of the Northern District Court, whose office and residence in 1829 was at Utica (HC 1:58–59n; POU 332–34).

(6) As predicted by the ancient prophet Nephi, **three witnesses—Oliver Cowdery, David Whitmer, and Martin Harris**—saw and testified of the truthfulness of the gold plates, which the angel Moroni showed to them (see 2 Ne. 27:12; see also Ether 5:2–4).

The Three Witnesses

During this experience they also heard a voice from heaven as a divine witness and saw other plates, the breastplate, the sword of Laban, the Urim and Thummim, and the Liahona (see "The Testimony of Three Witnesses" at the front of the Book of Mormon).

David Whitmer gave considerable information regarding the approximate time and physical setting of their experience. He indicated that this miraculous event took place in the latter part of June 1829, "about noon" of that particular day. Joseph directed the witnesses to a "spot near by, previously designated to him by his angelic visitant." David specified that the witnesses "went about 40 rods from his Fathers house" and that

The Three Witnesses as portrayed on the Angel Moroni Monument, located on the Hill Cumorah. (Sculpture by Torlief S. Knaphus)

the chosen spot was a "pasture, cleared of underbrush, at a point equally distant between two public highways." David notes that they "were seated on a log waiting for the promised manifestation, having previously knelt in prayer." The mention of being "equally distant between two public highways" apparently has reference to the junction of what are today the Aunkst and Miller Roads, which intersect a few hundred yards SE of the Peter Whitmer Sr. home site. If this is a correct assessment it would mean that the witnesses went out approximately 40 rods (220 yards) in an easterly direction from the log house. The information provided by David, however, is sufficiently vague that the exact place remains uncertain. Martin Harris had withdrawn from the others just prior to the first visitation. He was later joined by Joseph Smith; to them the angel Moroni again appeared and displayed the plates and artifacts seen by the other witnesses. Here again the exact site is indistinct from the descriptives (CHC 1:142; HJS 151–55; HC 1:57–58; NEW 239–43; DWI 175–76, 250–51).

Very soon after the above event, Joseph Smith directed an additional **eight witnesses** to assemble at the Smith home near Palmyra, NY, where they were able to both see the ancient engravings and actually handle the gold plates. The angel Moroni was not visibly present, however (HJS 151–55; NEW 242–43).

(7) Twenty revelations found in the Doctrine and Covenants were received at the Peter Whitmer farm by the Prophet between June 1829 and Jan. 1831 (sections 14–18, 20–21, and 28–40).

(8) The voice of the Lord was heard by Joseph Smith, Oliver Cowdery, and David Whitmer in the chamber (bedroom) of the Whitmer home in June 1829, outlining in detail the procedures which should be followed in organizing the Church some 10 months later (HC 1:60–61).

(9) First under the authority of the Aaronic Priesthood and later employing the power of the Melchizedek Priesthood, baptisms were performed in the area of the Whitmer farm from June 1829 to the time of the Saints' leaving New York for Ohio in May 1831. Seneca Lake, the Seneca River, Cayuga Lake, Kendig Creek, Silver Creek, and Thomas Creek are all cited as locations where baptisms were performed during this general time period (for information about baptisms in Seneca County see NEW 253–68).

(10) Joseph and Emma Smith were living at the Whitmer farm

in June 1829, when application was first made to Egbert B. Grandin in Palmyra to publish the Book of Mormon.

(11) The first three conferences of the Church were held on the Whitmer farm on June 9, 1830, Sept. 26, 1830, and Jan. 2, 1831 (HC 1:84–86, 110, 140).

(12) Oliver Cowdery, Peter Whitmer Jr., Parley P. Pratt, and Ziba Peterson, as **missionaries to the Lamanites,** left from the Whitmer farm on their missionary journey via Kirtland, OH, to Independence, MO, and finally on to the borders of the Lamanites in the unorganized Indian Territory (HC 1:118–20).

(13) Here **Sidney Rigdon** was called to act as a scribe for Joseph on the inspired version, or Joseph Smith Translation, of the Bible (see D&C 35).

(14) From the Whitmer farm the Prophet and Sidney Rigdon were directed by the Lord to "[strengthen] up the church whithersoever it is found" (D&C 37:2). Under the Prophet's direction and in obedience to the Lord's revelation, **Sidney Rigdon** gave noteworthy sermons in Waterloo, Colesville, Canandaigua, and Palmyra (NEW 287–90).

(15) The Fayette home of the Whitmers served essentially as the headquarters of the Church from the organization on Apr. 6, 1830, to the latter part of Jan. 1831, when the Prophet left for Kirtland, OH (RSOH 2–5).

(16) The first call for the Church membership to gather as a collective body was received by the Prophet at the Whitmer farm— "go to the Ohio" (D&C 37; 38:32).

(17) The Peter Whitmer Sr. family left their Fayette farm and departed Seneca Co. in the forepart of May 1831, for Kirtland, OH (NEW 311–22).

(18) In the 20th century the Church purchased the 100-acre original Whitmer farm from Joseph H. and Valara F. Manges on Sept. 25, 1926 (NEW 370).

■ **2. SITE OF THE WHITMER SCHOOLHOUSE (RED SCHOOLHOUSE), DISTRICT NO. 17.** The site of the Whitmer Schoolhouse, District No. 17, is located at the NW corner of the junction of Miller Road and CR 118 (County House Road) in Fayette Township (JSGe). It is immediately north of the existing Waterloo Mennonite Church meetinghouse, which is situated on the SW corner of the same intersection.

During 1830 and 1831 preaching services were held at the Peter Whitmer home and were also reportedly held in the Whitmer Schoolhouse, near Martin Miller's house. Grattis C. Deyoe, a contemporary of the Whitmers, recalled, "I remember Jo[seph] Smith, the Mormon prophet, when he had only twelve followers and they met together for services in an old red house two miles south of the village." The old schoolhouse, sometimes called the **"Red Schoolhouse,"** has since been removed (CHST 48; GHSW 18, 20, 21).

■ **3. SENECA LAKE AND SENECA LAKE OUTLET.** Seneca Lake forms much of the western border of Seneca Co., extending 40 miles from north to south, and varying in width from two to four miles. It is one of the famous Finger Lakes of western New York. The modern-day outlet of Seneca Lake is located .3 mile west of the junction of State 96A and CR 119 (South River Road) on CR 119.

Historical accounts from the Prophet Joseph Smith indicate that Seneca Lake was the principal place of baptism in Seneca Co. during 1829–30. One account specifies that some baptisms were performed "in Seneca Lake near the Outlet" (NEW 256). Today, the existing outlet, where the Seneca River flows out of the lake, is not where it was in the 1830s, but it does give access to the lake in the same sector.

In June 1829, Joseph Smith baptized his brother Hyrum Smith and David Whitmer in Seneca Lake; at the same time, Oliver Cowdery baptized Peter Whitmer Jr. These particular baptisms were performed under the authority of the Aaronic Priesthood. The Prophet stated that "from this time forth many became believers, and some were baptized whilst we continued to instruct and persuade as many as applied for information" (HC 1:51). Others known to have been baptized in Seneca Lake following the organization of the Church were Hiram Page, Katharine (Catherine) Whitmer Page, Christian Whitmer, Anne (Anna) Schott Whitmer, Jacob Whitmer, and Elizabeth (Eliza Schott) Whitmer, who were baptized by Oliver Cowdery on Apr. 11, 1830. On Apr. 18, 1830, Oliver baptized Peter Whitmer Sr., Mary Musselman Whitmer, William Jolly, Elizabeth Jolly, Vincent Jolly, Richard B. Peterson (Richard Ziba Peterson), and Elizabeth Anne Whitmer in Seneca Lake (HC 1:81). Shortly after the first general conference of the Church held June 9, 1830, David Whitmer baptized John Poorman,

John Jolly, Julia Anne Jolly, Harriet Jolly, Jerusha Barden Smith, Katherine (Catherine) Smith, William Smith, Don C. Smith, Peter Rockwell, Caroline Rockwell, and Electa Rockwell here (HC 1:86). On about Sept. 1, 1830, Parley P. Pratt said that he was "baptized by the hand of an Apostle of the Church of Jesus Christ, by the name of Oliver Cowdery. This took place in Seneca Lake, a beautiful and transparent sheet of water in Western New York" (APPP 42). Seneca Lake is certainly noted for its clarity and great beauty.

■ **4. SITE OF THE ZION'S CHURCH MEETINGHOUSE OF THE GERMAN REFORMED CHURCH.** The Zion's Church Meetinghouse once stood on the SE corner of the intersection of CR 121 (Yellow Tavern Road) and Watts Road in Fayette Township. The site is immediately SE of the existing Fayette Town Office Building and the town barns.

The Peter Whitmer Sr. family were initially members of the German Reformed Church. On Aug. 3, 1811, the German inhabitants of the central and western parts of Fayette, of German Reformed and Lutheran denominations, organized a society under the title "Zion's Church." The first building was constructed of logs and was used until it was destroyed by fire on Feb. 7, 1835 (some four years after the Whitmers had gone with the Mormons to Kirtland, OH). A new house of worship, the "Jerusalem Church," was constructed and then dedicated on Nov. 13, 1836 (MCSC 101–2). The Jerusalem Church no longer exists today, but the old cemetery adjacent to the site of the former meetinghouses remains in a stand of trees. There are many interesting inscriptions on the headstones (MCSC 101–2).

Rev. Diedrich Willers ministered to the Whitmers commencing in 1821. When that family was later drawn to the Mormon persuasion he tried to intercede, but to no avail. In June 1829 Rev. Willers learned that Joseph Smith was at the Whitmer home and in the process of translating ancient plates by the use of "spectacles." He stated, "Upon receiving this report, I hurried immediately to Whitmer's house to see this man, in order to learn the actual source of his story and to find out how it might be possible to nip this work in the bud. However, I received the reply from Whitmer's father that Smith had already departed to take his translation to the press" (NYHi July 1973, 326–27).

- **5. BURGH CEMETERY**—The Burgh Cemetery is located in Fayette Township on the north side of CR 121 (Yellow Tavern Road), .3 mile west of its junction with State 414. There is a "Burgh Cemetery" sign at the entrance and the cemetery itself is set back from CR 121 about .3 mile to the north via a dirt road.

   Rev. Diedrich Willers is buried in the SW corner of the Burgh Cemetery; his grave is identified by a tall granite obelisk. Rev. Willers was born in Bremen, Germany, Feb. 6, 1798. He died May 13, 1883, having been a pastor of the Reformed German congregations of Seneca County for 60 years. At the behest of his congregations, Rev. Willers read the Book of Mormon and reported his findings in 1829. He also philosophically mused on the rise of Mormonism, "Past centuries have also had their religious monstrosities, but where are they now? . . . They have dissolved into the ocean of the past and have been given the stamp of oblivion. The Mormonites, and hopefully soon, will also share that fate." Rev. Willers labored most conscientiously for some 40 years to protect his flock, and his name is yet highly revered locally for his steadfastness and exceptional service to mankind (NYHi July 1973, 327–33; RSNY 161).

- **6. CHRIST CHURCH.** The hamlet of Fayette is located at the junction of State 414 and CR 124. Within the community the original structure of Christ Church still stands with some additions. The meetinghouse is situated on the NE corner of the junction of State 414 and CR 124. It currently houses the United Church of Fayette. The community was once called Bearytown for Henry Beary, one of the first settlers.

   Rev. Diedrich Willers entered on his pastorate in Apr. 1821. The stone structure of Christ Church was erected in 1823 and dedicated on June 6, 1824. The tower and belfry were added in 1882. Rev. Willers presided here until his resignation on Jan. 1, 1882. During this time he also served some five additional congregations in a variety of locations in Fayette Township. When confronted with the menace of Mormonism among members of his congregation, particularly the **Peter Whitmer Sr. family**, he wrote a letter to two professors in the Theological Seminary of the Reformed Church at York, PA, "This upstart sect calls itself The True Followers of Christ; however, because they believe in the Book of Mormon, they bear the name Mormonites. For the past several Sundays many people of both sexes have been immersed by them, and so many during the week that their numbers in the region hereabouts may amount to at least 100 persons. They have their own preachers whom I know; Oliver Cowdery by description and David Whitmer (the so-called Angel-viewer) personally" (NYHi July 1973, 331).

■ **7. CAYUGA LAKE.** Cayuga Lake is 40 miles long and varies from one to 3½ miles in width. It lies between Seneca and Cayuga Counties and extends some 10 miles into Tompkins Co. to the south. Some baptisms of early Saints occurred in this body of water, but the exact sites are unknown.

Thomas B. Marsh, later the senior member of the original Quorum of the Twelve Apostles in this dispensation, moved from Charleston, MA, near Boston, to Palmyra, NY, in Sept. 1830. He had first been introduced to Mormonism by Martin Harris, who gave him 16 pages of the Book of Mormon in the fall of 1829 at the Grandin Printing Shop in Palmyra. During Sept. 1830, he was baptized in Cayuga Lake by David Whitmer and ordained an elder by Oliver Cowdery a few days later at the home of Peter Whitmer Sr., in Fayette (DN Mar. 24, 1858, 18). The precise site of Marsh's baptism is not known.

■ **VILLAGE OF WATERLOO**

The village of Waterloo is situated at the junction of State Highways 96 and 5 and U.S. 20 and State 5 in Seneca County. It is just three miles north of the Peter Whitmer Sr. farm in Fayette Township, and is the seat of Seneca County.

Waterloo was where the Whitmers did a majority of their trading. Of general interest is the fact that Waterloo is the home of **Memorial Day.** The custom of observing Memorial Day by a floral demonstration and the delivery of orations and recitations of poems in words of tribute to our war dead originated here. On May 5, 1866, in Waterloo, the first Decoration Day observance was held. The graves of every soldier, sailor, and marine had flowers placed upon them. On May 5, 1868, General John A. Logan, Commander in Chief of the Grand Army of the Republic, expanded the commemoration by issuing his famous General Order No. 11, which officially set aside May 30 as Decoration Day (HVW 184–85).

■ **8. BEAR CEMETERY.** The Bear Cemetery (named after Samuel Bear) is located on the south side of Waterloo, just west of the intersection of West River Street (CR 117), and Market Street. The headstone of **Anna Schott Whitmer Hulett** is in the fourth row from the west edge of the cemetery and the seventh stone north from the south edge. The stone reads, "Anna Schott, Wife of Sylvester Hulett, Died Nov. 19, 1866, Ae. 65 Yrs., 7 Mo., 21 Ds."

Anna Schott married Christian Whitmer on Feb. 22, 1825, at Fayette. She and Christian Whitmer were both baptized by Oliver Cowdery in Seneca Lake on Apr. 11, 1830. Christian Whitmer died on Nov. 27, 1835, at age 38 in Clay County, MO, of a "severe affliction upon one of his legs." Anna then married another Mormon elder, Sylvester Hulett. She later returned to Fayette and died at age 65 in the home of her brother, Vincent Schott (HC 1:81; M&A 2:240; FWR 269; SFR Nov. 24, 1866).

● **9. WATERLOO LIBRARY AND HISTORICAL SOCIETY.** The Waterloo Library and Historical Society is located in Waterloo at 31 East Williams Street. The **Terwilliger Museum** is associated with that facility. The Historical Society has an important collection of documents, books, and newspapers relating to the area.

■ **SENECA FALLS TOWNSHIP**

Seneca Falls Township was formed from the town of Junius on Mar. 26, 1829. It lies four miles east of Waterloo, and is bounded in part on the east by Cayuga Lake. The Seneca River flows east and north through the center of the town, its valley dividing the town into two distinct parts.

■ **10. THE KINGDOM, OR CHAMBERLAIN'S MILLS.** The Kingdom, or Chamberlain's Mills, is located in Seneca Falls on U.S. 20 and State 5 (the old Turnpike Road), just east of the junction of that roadway and CR 122 (Balsley Road) which comes in from the NW between Waterloo and Seneca Falls. Although once a budding hamlet, the Kingdom no longer exists as a community. Its identity has been virtually swallowed up by a modern-day business district, and only a vestige of the name can still be traced. The former Kingdom primarily embraced the area to the east of Balsley Road, beginning with the existing Liberty Plaza, and to the south on both sides of the Seneca River. A New York State Education Department historical marker identifies the site of the "Kingdom Cemetery" on the north side of U.S. 20 and State 5, which was once the old Turnpike Road. The marker reads, "Kingdom Cemetery reserved in deed to Thomas Lawrence. Here until 1856 were mills, distilleries, taverns, school, justice ct., Masonic Lodge, race track." No evidence of the cemetery can be found today. The few remaining headstones, once visible in 1946–47, were gathered up and removed during the interim (JSGe). "Here Lewis Birdsall erected the first brick house in Seneca County about 1808" (AHB). It stood into the 1970s when it was torn down. On the south side of the Seneca River at the SW corner of the intersection of Kingdom Road and CR 117 is the "Kingdom Tavern." The existing structure is thought to be period, not as a tavern, but as a private dwelling in the 1820–1830s (JSGe). There was a dwelling on this site in the days of the Kingdom (AHB).

When **Joseph Smith Sr.** and his wife, **Lucy,** were forced to leave their Manchester farm in 1829, they lived for several months in their former log house in Palmyra Township, which was then occupied by **Hyrum Smith.** In Oct. and Nov. 1830 they moved to what Lucy Mack Smith described as "Waterloo," in Seneca County. However, local historians have placed them in a small settlement that was located between the villages of Waterloo and Seneca Falls called the Kingdom, or Chamberlain's Mills. Initially in the town of Junius, by 1830 the Kingdom was within the boundaries of the town of Seneca Falls. Over the years it has been known as Little Skoi-Yase, Chamberlain's Mills or Dam, and the Kingdom. After the 1850s the once bustling mill community gradually declined until the Kingdom became only the name of a bridge crossing the Seneca River at this point (AHB). Now even the bridge has been torn down.

Lucy Mack Smith said that they were well received in their new home:

> We moved into a house belonging to an individual by the name of Kellog. Shortly after arriving there, we were made to realize that the hearts of the people were in the hands of the Lord; for we had scarcely unpacked our goods, when one of our new neighbors, a Mr. Osgood, came in and invited us to drive our stock and teams to his barn-yard, and feed them from his barn, free of cost, until we could make further arrangements.

Many of our neighbors came in, and welcomed us to Waterloo. Among whom was Mr. Hooper, a tavern-keeper, whose wife came with him, and brought us a present of some delicate eatables. Such manifestations of kindness as these were shown us from day to day, during our continuance in the place. And they were duly appreciated, for we had experienced the opposite so severely, that the least show of good feeling gave rise to the liveliest sensations of gratitude. (HJS 189)

The 1830 Census for the town of Seneca Falls lists Pontius Hooper, Fuller Kellog, and Leonard W. Osgood. These men appear to have been the persons named by Lucy. Pontius Hooper was a tavern keeper in the Kingdom for many years. One of the earliest town meetings for the town of Junius was held in his house at the Kingdom (HVW 78).

In the evenings the Smith home became host to a devotional service for "some dozen or twenty persons." The service consisted of singing, praying, and some preaching. Joseph Smith Jr. attended periodically and was speaking to the gathering on Dec. 10, 1830, when **Sidney Rigdon** and **Edward Partridge** first arrived from Kirtland, OH, to meet the Prophet. Joseph baptized Edward Partridge the next day in the Seneca River, which ran just across the road to the south of the Smith home. The Fayette Branch gathered at the Smith home in early May 1831 for their departure to Kirtland, OH. Lucy Mack Smith was appointed to lead the Ohio-bound company of Saints (HJS 195–208; NEW 268–73, 311–22).

■ **11. CAYUGA AND SENECA CANAL.** The Cayuga and Seneca Canal can be observed on the south side of U.S. 20 and State 5 as it parallels that roadway between the villages of Waterloo and Seneca Falls.

It was from the Joseph Smith Sr. home on the Cayuga and Seneca Canal (Seneca River) at the Kingdom that **Lucy Mack Smith** directed the loading and exodus of the Fayette Branch from Seneca Co. to Kirtland, OH, about May 3–4, 1831, in response to the Lord's direction to his Saints (D&C 37:1–4 and 38:31–32, 42). Lucy described the situation: "When the brethren considered the spring sufficiently open for traveling on the water, we all began to prepare for our removal to Kirtland. We hired a boat of a certain Methodist preacher, and appointed a time to meet at our house, for the purpose of setting off together; and when we were thus collected, we numbered eighty souls. The people of the surrounding country came and bade us farewell, invoking the blessing of heaven upon our heads" (HJS 195).

On their canal boat the Fayette Saints proceeded east along the Cayuga and Seneca Canal, through the village of Seneca Falls, and then NE to the north end of Cayuga Lake. From that point they traveled generally north through the Montezuma Swamps and into the Erie Canal. The Saints could then go west on the Erie Canal to Buffalo and take passage by steam or sailboat on Lake Erie to Fairport Harbor, OH, from where they traveled 12 miles overland to Kirtland (NEW 314–16).

■ **VILLAGE OF SENECA FALLS**

The village of Seneca Falls lies immediately east of Waterloo on U.S. 20 and State 5. The Fayette Branch passed through Seneca Falls on a canal barge in May 1831 on the Cayuga and Seneca Canal, where there is a 40-foot descent within a distance of one mile. Five locks made their passage possible.

● **12. SENECA FALLS HISTORICAL SOCIETY.** The Seneca Falls Historical Society is situated in a Queen Anne style mansion at 55 Cayuga Street/U.S. 20 and State 5 in the village of Seneca Falls. The society houses an important collection of area historical books and documents. The mansion also features 23 elaborately furnished rooms, which reflect Victorian appreciation of exquisite workmanship. Their period clothing collection is exceptional.

Cayuga County

■ **AUBURN**

Auburn is located at the junction of U.S. 20 and State 38.[4]

■ **BRIGHAM YOUNG AND THE HISTORIC SEWARD HOUSE.** The home of **William Henry Seward** is located in Auburn at 33 South Street.

---

[4] The author is highly indebted to Richard F. Palmer of Tully, NY, and Karl D. Butler of Ithaca, NY, for introducing them to various dwelling places of Brigham Young. Their authorship of *Brigham Young, The New York Years,* 1982, has opened the entire spectrum of the Young family in New York to all of us.

Following the death of Brigham Young's mother, Abigail Young, in the Genoa/Lansingville area on June 11, 1815, Brigham's father, John Young, moved his remaining children to the "Sugar Hill" district in Steuben County (presently Schuyler Co.), near the settlement of Tyrone. There John married Hannah Dennis Brown sometime between 1815 and 1817. Brigham left home in 1817 for the Auburn area and began to work on his own (BYNY 4–6, 11).

In Auburn, Brigham apparently apprenticed himself to John C. Jeffries, a carpenter, painter, and glazier. In that capacity Brigham worked on numerous construction projects in the vicinity of Auburn, the most noted of which was the house of Judge Elijah Miller, father-in-law of William Henry Seward. The home was built in 1816–17. Brigham Young is reported to have constructed the ornate mantel for the fireplace in the parlor and to have assisted in painting the house (BYNY 12–13).

The William H. Seward mansion, which Brigham Young helped build in 1817, in Auburn. (1993)

William H. Seward moved into the house in 1824 and lived here with his wife, Frances Miller, for nearly half a century. He became governor of New York, U.S. Senator, secretary of state in the cabinets of Presidents Lincoln and Johnson, and the key figure in the negotiations for the purchase of Alaska. He was also a principal figure in the founding of the Republican Party. The Seward House is now a very interesting museum with original furnishings and has exceptional guide service. There is a fee. The museum is not open on Sundays or major holidays.

■ HAYDENVILLE, MENTZ TOWNSHIP

The Haydenville home of **Brigham Young** still stands at a point six miles north of Auburn on State 38 where it intersects with Hayden Road or 1.3 miles south of Port Byron on State 38 at the intersection of State 38 and Hayden Road. The house, with a mailing address of 8182 State St., Port Byron, NY, is a 1½-story frame home

Brigham Young home in Haydenville,
Mentz Township, Cayuga County. (1993)

on the hillside directly east of the intersection. The home is privately owned.

Brigham Young worked in the pail factory that once stood immediately across the road from his home to the west. He was reportedly working in that factory when first introduced to **Miriam Works.** William Hayden said that Brigham "was first employed at painting pails, the work being done in a manner so satisfactory as to call forth many compliments from the proprietor, Mr. Parks" (BYNY 18).

■ PORT BYRON

The home of **Brigham and Miriam Works Young** in Port Byron is seven miles north of Auburn and near the three-way intersection of State 31, State 38, and CR 56 (Rochester, Main, and Utica Streets). On the NE corner of that intersection is a small, triangular-shaped cement island with benches and memorial plaques, one of which reads, "BRIGHAM YOUNG THE MORMON PROPHET lived in this house 100 yds East of here in 1831 [Brigham Young was living in the township of Mendon, Monroe Co., in 1831]. He was baptized a Mormon In 1832 at Mendon, N.Y. State Education Department, 1932." The house referred to is actually 125 yards SE, where the north and west

Brigham and Miriam Works Young's rented
home, at Port Byron, Mentz Township. (1999)

sides of the home can be seen across the parking lot opposite the triangular monument. The front of the house faces south and is situated 100 yards north of the intersection of Pine and Seneca Streets on the east side of Seneca Street, which dead ends at the home. The home is privately owned.

Unable to find sufficient work in Auburn, Brigham Young moved to Port Byron on the Erie Canal in about 1824. (He had purchased a one-acre lot in Port Byron in 1823, but apparently never made use of it.) He worked at a variety of jobs including painting and building boats and worked in a pail factory at Haydenville, Mentz Township, immediately south of Port Byron. On Oct. 5, 1824, Brigham married Miss Miriam Angeline Works from the Township of Aurelius, which is five miles west of Auburn. Brigham and Miriam apparently spent the first months of their marriage living in Haydenville. They then moved to Port Byron. During the five years that the Young family remained in the Port Byron/Aurelius/Haydenville area they are reported to have lived in a number of dwellings among which is the home identified above. Their first daughter, Elizabeth, born on Sept. 26, 1825, was said to have been born in Port Byron (BYNY 17–21). The Youngs left Port Byron for Oswego, NY, in 1828, and from there went to Mendon, NY, in 1829 (BYNY 23).

BRUTUS TOWNSHIP—Birthplace of Horace S. Eldredge, One of the Seven Presidents of the Seventy

Brutus Township is located seven miles north of Auburn. The principal community within the township is the village of Weedsport, which is situated on State 31.

Horace S. Eldredge, the son of Alanson Eldredge and Esther Sunderlin, was born in the township of Brutus on Feb. 6, 1816. He first heard the gospel in 1836 and was baptized soon afterwards. He married and settled near Indianapolis, IN, in 1836, but in the fall of 1838 he joined the Saints at Far West, MO. At the time of the forced exodus of

Horace S. Eldridge

the Mormons, he returned to Indiana in Dec. 1838. Horace then gathered with the Church in Nauvoo during 1840. He was ordained a seventy in Nauvoo on Oct. 13, 1844, and was sustained as one of the **first seven Presidents of the Seventy** on Oct. 7, 1854, in Salt

Lake City. Horace became one of the foremost businessmen in Utah Territory. He died in Salt Lake City on Sept. 6, 1888 (BE 1:196–97; DNCA 1995–96:60).

WESTERN NEW YORK

Larry C. Porter

Ontario and Wayne Counties, Including Manchester and Palmyra Townships

South of Palmyra along Canandaigua Road (State 21)

■ THE VILLAGE OF MANCHESTER, ONTARIO COUNTY

Manchester is located 25 miles SE of Rochester and immediately south of I-90, at exit 43, on State 21.

The village of Manchester was certainly familiar to the Joseph Smith Sr. family; however, that portion of Manchester Township north of the village became an area especially significant to the Smiths and to the rise of the Restoration.

■ MANCHESTER TOWNSHIP, ONTARIO COUNTY

Manchester Township was originally part of Farmington Township. In 1820, the year of the **First Vision** and at the time the Joseph Smith Sr. family was making final arrangements to article for or purchase their 100-acre farm in Lot 1, the acreage was still in Farmington Township. However, in 1822 the township name was changed to Manchester (GNY 302; HOC 180). The Joseph Smith Sr. farm and the existing **frame home, the Sacred Grove,** and **the Hill Cumorah** are all located in Manchester Township. The nearby village of Palmyra in Palmyra Township was about two miles north of the Smith farm and became the primary community for the Smiths rather than the village of Manchester six miles to the south.

The following historical sites are located between the villages of Manchester and Palmyra on State 21 North.

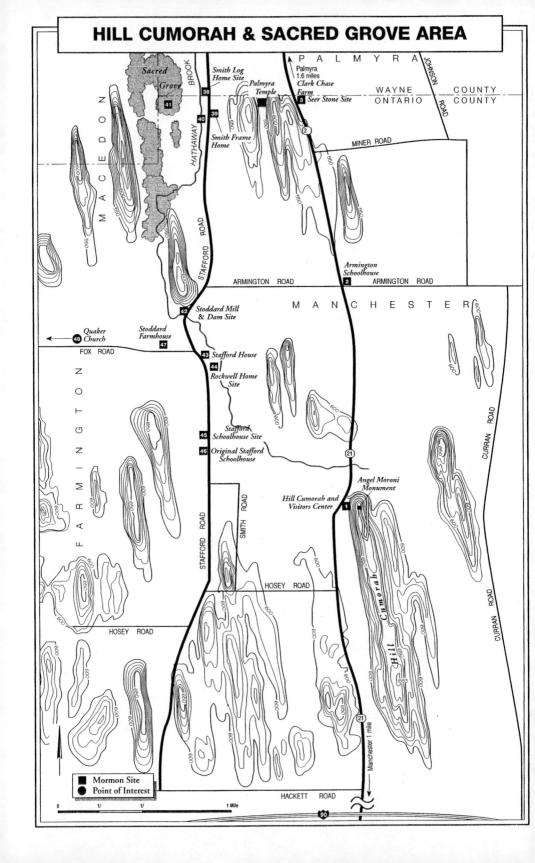

HILL CUMORAH & SACRED GROVE AREA

Sacred Grove
41

MACEDON

Smith Log Home Site
38
Palmyra Temple
Smith Frame Home
40 **39**

BROOK

HATHAWAY

STAFFORD ROAD

P A L M Y R A

Palmyra 1.6 miles
Clark Chase Farm
3 Seer Stone Site

JOHNSON ROAD

WAYNE COUNTY
ONTARIO COUNTY

2

MINER ROAD

Armington Schoolhouse
2
ARMINGTON ROAD
ARMINGTON ROAD

M A N C H E S T E R

42 Stoddard Mill & Dam Site

Quaker Church
48
FOX ROAD

Stoddard Farmhouse
47

43 Stafford House

44 Rockwell Home Site

F A R M I N G T O N

CURRAN ROAD

45 Stafford Schoolhouse Site

46 Original Stafford Schoolhouse

21

Angel Moroni Monument

Hill Cumorah and Visitors Center
1

STAFFORD ROAD

SMITH ROAD

HOSEY ROAD

Hill Cumorah

CURRAN ROAD

HOSEY ROAD

■ **Mormon Site**
● **Point of Interest**

0   1/   1/   1 Mile

21 Manchester 1 mile

HACKETT ROAD

90

The Hill Cumorah, Manchester Township. From this hill, Joseph Smith received the golden plates of the Book of Mormon, Sept. 22, 1827. Aerial view looking east. (Photo by LaMar C. Berrett, 1978)

■ **1. Hill Cumorah.** The Hill Cumorah and its visitors center are located on State 21, just 2.3 miles north of I-90 at exit 43, on the east side of the road. It is four miles south of Palmyra's Main Street on State 21.

The Hill Cumorah is referred to as a glacial "drumlin." There are literally hundreds of drumlins in upstate New York that "were created during the ice age when sand, gravel, clay, boulders, etc., were dragged along under the moving glacier and, at some friction point, deposited on top of the existing terrain" (RSNY 71–72). The Hill Cumorah has a peak about 117 feet GPS (Global Positioning System) above ground level and is one of the highest drumlins in the area.

The Hill Cumorah and visitors center, Manchester Township, looking east. (1930s)

In preparation for the final battle of the Nephites and Lamanites, Mormon and his soldiers marched "to the land of Cumorah" and pitched their tents "round about the hill Cumorah" (Morm. 6:4). Mormon stated that he hid the records of the Nephites "in

An engraving of the Hill Cumorah, looking south. (1841)

the hill Cumorah" except for a few plates which he gave to his son Moroni (Morm. 6:6). According to Parley P. Pratt, Oliver Cowdery declared that the Book of Mormon record "was hid in the earth by Moroni, in a hill called by him, Cumorah, which hill is now in the State of New York, near the village of Palmyra" (APPP 55–56; RSNY 73–74).

The **angel Moroni** visited **Joseph Smith** three times in the family's log house on the night of Sept. 21, 1823. During these appearances Moroni showed Joseph in vision the exact place to go on the Hill Cumorah to find certain **gold plates** containing a record of the ancient inhabitants of the American continent and a fulness of the gospel as delivered to them by Jesus Christ. The next day Moroni again appeared to Joseph as he was going to the house from the field where he had been working. Joseph said that Moroni "again related unto me all that he had related to me the previous night" (JS—H 1:49). He also instructed Joseph to tell his father of the heavenly visits, which Joseph did. Joseph Sr. told his son "that it was of God, . . . and [to] do as commanded" (HC 1:14–15).

On that same day, Sept. 22, 1823, Joseph walked three miles to the Hill Cumorah. He described to Oliver Cowdery the place where the plates were buried as being slightly south of the north end of the hill, on the west side, not far from the top (M&A 2:195–96). There he removed the lid from a stone box and found within it the gold plates and the Urim and Thummim, which were attached to a breastplate. There the angel Moroni gave Joseph instructions. He was shown an

Sculpture of Joseph Smith receiving the plates of the Book of Mormon from Moroni on the Hill Cumorah, Sept. 22, 1827. It was sculptured about 1950 by Torlief S. Knaphus, a convert from Norway, and is preserved by the Wilford C. Wood Foundation. (1967)

open vision of Satan and his host so that he would know the reality of that unseen world of evil. Moroni told Joseph he could not take the plates at that time, but that he should make a series of annual visits to the hill each successive Sept. 22 to receive additional directions (JS—H 1:50–53; M&A 2:195–96).

The Hill Cumorah, looking south. (Photo by George E. Anderson, 1907; courtesy of LDSCA)

Joseph was again at Cumorah for appointed meetings with Moroni in the years 1824–26. Then on Sept. 22, 1827, the fourth year, Joseph obtained the gold plates, the Urim and Thummim, and breastplate from Moroni. Joseph said that the angel instructed him "that I should be responsible for them; that if I should let them go carelessly, or through any neglect of mine, I should be cut off; but that if I would use all

The Hill Cumorah, looking south. (Photo by George E. Anderson, 1907; courtesy of LDSCA)

my endeavors to preserve them, until he, the messenger, should call for them, they should be protected" (HC 1:18).

After the golden plates were translated, Joseph Smith and Oliver Cowdery delivered the plates back to the angel Moroni (JS—H 1:60). Brigham Young and others indicated that this exchange with Moroni took place at the Hill Cumorah. The hill apparently opened up and Joseph and Oliver walked into a large and spacious room. Many wagon loads of plates were in the room, and the unsheathed sword of Laban lay across gold plates on a table. The "Messenger" was there to receive the plates (JD 19:38; 4:105; JWW 6:508–9; JJNS Feb. 1874:217). The Prophet Joseph did not detail the circumstances of the return other than to simply say, "When, according to arrangements, the messenger called for them, I delivered them up to him; and he has them in his charge until this day" (JS—H 1:60).

In a series of land purchases from 1923 to 1928, the LDS Church acquired the principal portion of the Hill Cumorah and surrounding farmland. The purchases, which totaled 487 acres,

The Hill Cumorah and billboard.

included the 97-acre Inglis, or "Cumorah," farm, acquired on Oct. 16, 1923, and the 220-acre Bennett farm and the 170-acre Samson, or "Mormon Hill," farm, both acquired on Feb. 17, 1928 (ERA 31:682–87; NEW 70).

During the 20th century many visitors, programs, and pageants have memorialized the significant historical events of the past that transpired at the Hill Cumorah. Some of these commemorative occasions are highlighted herein:

Dec. 26, 1905. **President Joseph F. Smith** and party, while returning from the dedication of the Joseph Smith Monument at Sharon, VT, stopped at Palmyra and drove to Cumorah. They climbed to the top of the hill and there sang a heartfelt rendition of "An Angel from on High." Junius F. Wells informs us that President Smith then prayed "that every one present might feel the solemnity and sacredness of the place, and of the occasion . . . that each one present might feel a deep sense of the responsibility in spreading that message of truth which had lain so long concealed in this hill" (PAD 66–67).

Oct. 31, 1911. Two hundred members of the **Tabernacle Choir** plus fifty others sang "An Angel from on High" while on the crest of Cumorah (ERA 15:237).

1922. **President B. H. Roberts** of the First Council of Seventy and president of the Eastern States Mission had his missionaries walk the three miles from the Joseph Smith Sr. farm to the Hill Cumorah for a program of "well-written slogans" (ERA 71:25).

Sept. 17, 1923. **Willard W. Bean** purchased 97½ acres from James H. Inglis, which included land going halfway up the west side of the Hill Cumorah and "the entire apron or flat between the hill and the highway" on the west side. Willard Bean transferred this property to the LDS Church on Oct. 16, 1923 (AWB pt. 2, 31–32; WCLD 327:470–471).

Sept. 21–22, 1923. **President B. H. Roberts** and 200 missionaries were part of an aggregate of 2,000–3,000 persons who gathered at the Hill Cumorah for the centennial anniversary of the revealed existence of the Book of Mormon plates in Sept. 1923. **President Heber J. Grant** was the principal speaker. Elder James E. Talmage recorded that on Sun., the 23rd, over 1,250 individuals took part in "the sacred Hosanna shout" from Cumorah's height (CHC 6:522–26; ERA 71:25–26; JJET Sept. 23, 1923).

Sept. 1927. The Eastern States Mission under **President Henry H. Rolapp** celebrated the 100th anniversary of the delivery of the plates to Joseph Smith by Moroni. President Heber J. Grant and other General Authorities were present (CHC 6:525; PBC 14).

1928. The principal portion of the Hill Cumorah and three surrounding farms were acquired by the Church in 1928. The first **Book of Mormon Pageant** in the area was staged, but it was held at the Joseph Smith Sr. farm and not the Hill Cumorah (ERA 31:687; 71:24–27; PBC 14).

1928–29. Because the Hill Cumorah had been stripped bare of trees, it was reforested with 31,000 evergreen and hardwood seedlings in 1928–29 under **Willard W. Bean's** direction. Other plantings followed (ERA 32:468; PBC 14; ENS 15 [June 1985]: 29).

Jul. 21, 1935. On Sunday morning a dedicatory program marked the unveiling of the **Angel Moroni Monument** on the highest point of the Hill Cumorah. The bronze statue, gilded with gold leaf, commemorated the coming forth of the Book of Mormon through the instrumentality of a heavenly being. It was sculptured by Torlief S. Knaphus. **President Heber J. Grant** dedicated the 10' 4" statue of Moroni atop its granite shaft. The overall height of the memorial is 39' 3". Four bronze plaques depicting key events associated with the advent of the Book of Mormon surround the base of the monument (ERA 38:542–45; CN June 29, 1974, 2; NEW 71).

Erection of the Angel Moroni Monument on the Hill Cumorah, 1935. (Courtesy of LDSCA)

The Angel Moroni Monument on the Hill Cumorah.

General Authorities at the dedication of the Angel Moroni Monument on the Hill Cumorah, July 21, 1935. In addition to Church President Heber J. Grant, who dedicated the monument, future Presidents George Albert Smith and David O. McKay were present. (Courtesy of LDSCA)

President Heber J. Grant and Elder David O. McKay at the dedication of the Angel Moroni Monument, July 21, 1935. (Courtesy of LDSCA

Jul. 25, 1936. Although Book of Mormon pageants had been performed by Eastern States missionaries at the Joseph Smith Sr. farm as early as July 1928, it was not until July 25, 1936, that the first Book of Mormon Pageant was presented at the base of the west slope of the Hill Cumorah. The audience sat on the hillside and the stage was behind the bureau of information. However, beginning in 1937 the audience sat at the base of the hill while the performers were on the side of the hill. Harold I. Hansen was the pageant's director, a position he would hold for the next 40 years.

Many drama directors, missionaries, actors, musicians, sound and lighting technicians, and volunteer laborers have worked hard through the years to make the Book of Mormon Pageant an exceptional production. The *Buffalo News* has referred to the pageant as a "Living Monument to Religious Volunteerism." It is currently titled the **"Historic Hill Cumorah Pageant"** and is truly

"America's Witness for Christ." A series of approximately seven performances are scheduled annually over a two-week period in July, playing to tens of thousands of spectators (ERA 71:27; PBC 14–15; CN Jul. 27, 1986, 6, June 25, 1977, 6, Jul. 16, 1977, 4, 14, Jul. 30, 1988, 6, 10, Jul. 17, 1993, 11, 14).

Harold I. Hansen, Book of Mormon Pageant director for many years, and members of the cast at the Hill Cumorah.

Aug. 29, 1937. The beautiful **bureau of information** (visitors center) was designed to resemble the architecture of ancient America. It was dedicated by **Elder John A. Widtsoe** of the Twelve on Aug. 29, 1937 (RSNY 80–81). New construction on the site was completed in 2000.

Crowds attending the Book of Mormon Pageant, at the Hill Cumorah. (1975)

Apr. 8–12, 1976. The statue of the angel Moroni on the crest of the Hill Cumorah was taken down, its gold leafing was refurbished, it was replaced on its pedestal, and it was rotated 90 degrees from its north-facing position (since 1935) to the west, where it now overlooks the pageant seating area (CN Apr. 17, 1976, 3).

■ **2. ARMINGTON SCHOOLHOUSE.** The Armington Schoolhouse, Manchester Union School District No. 10, stands on the NE corner of the junction of State 21 (Canandaigua Road) and the Armington School Road 1.1 miles north of the Hill Cumorah, and 2.9 miles south of Main Street in Palmyra on State 21 (Canandaigua Road). It is privately owned.

This cobblestone school, constructed of field cobbles, was built in 1846 as indicated by the date-stone on the south end at the point of the gable. It was named after Benjamin Armington (HOC 179). Some have believed that this was the site of an earlier schoolhouse where Oliver Cowdery taught the Smith and other neighborhood children during the 1828–29 school year. However, conclusive evidence to the contrary can be documented showing that Oliver Cowdery was at the schoolhouse located on the Stafford Road in Dist. No. 11 (see Stafford Schoolhouse site).

■ **3. CLARK CHASE FARM.** A **seer stone** used by **Joseph Smith Jr.** was said to have been discovered on the Clark Chase farm 1.2 miles north of the Armington Schoolhouse or 1.5 miles south of the

The Clark Chase farm, Manchester Township, looking SE from the point where the Ontario-Wayne County line crosses State 21. The original Chase farmhouse and well were on the left side of this photo, in the immediate foreground and near the road. (1966)

Four Corners intersection in the village of Palmyra on State 21 (Canandaigua Road).

Martin Harris stated that "the Prophet possessed a Seer Stone, by which he was enabled to translate [the Book of Mormon] as well as with the Urim and Thummim" (CHC 1:128–29; ORPM 19; MUV 240; PV 238; MS Feb. 6, 1882, 86).

Joseph was digging a well on the Chase farm with his older brothers, Alvin and Hyrum, in Sept. 1819 (Willard Chase said 1822) when the seer stone was uncovered. The well was reportedly in the NW corner of the field next to the road on the east side of State 21, and immediately south of the Ontario-Wayne County line. That line is also the Manchester-Palmyra township line. The Clark Chase home stood near the road on the east side and the well was in the proximity of the house (WCJ Dec. 20, 1917, 3).

Palmyra Village

■ **PALMYRA TOWNSHIP, WAYNE COUNTY**

Palmyra Township is considered one of the oldest towns in western New York. In the winter of 1789 Captain John Swift and John Jenkins negotiated with the Phelps and Gorham Purchase Company headquartered at Canandaigua, NY, and procured a tract of land embracing the present-day townships of Palmyra and Macedon.

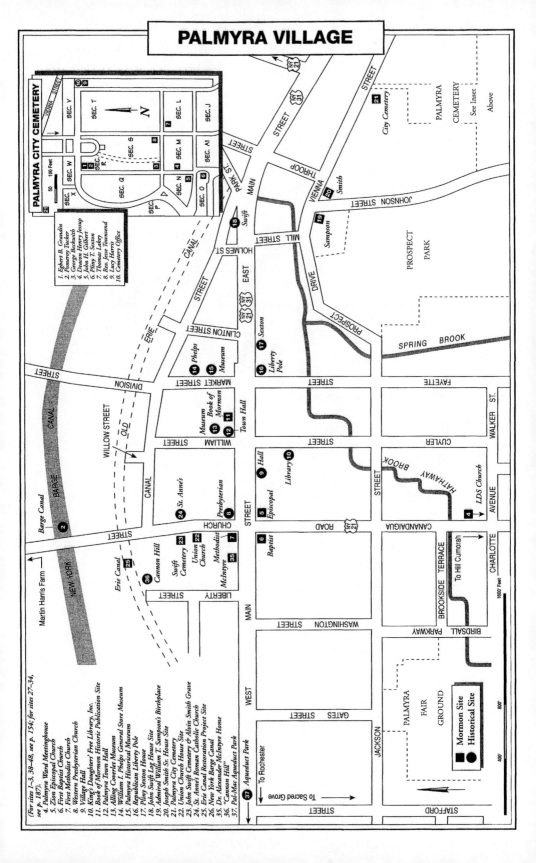

PALMYRA VILLAGE

PALMYRA CITY CEMETERY

1. Egbert B. Grandin
2. Pomeroy Tucker
3. George Beckwith
4. Deacon Henry Jessup
5. John H. Gilbert
6. Pliny T. Sexton
7. Thomas Lakey
8. Rev. Jesse Townsend
9. Lucy Harris
10. Cemetery Office

(For sites 1–3, 38–48, see p. 154; for sites 27–34, see p. 187.)

4. Palmyra Ward Meetinghouse
5. Zion Episcopal Church
6. First Baptist Church
7. First Methodist Church
8. Western Presbyterian Church
9. Village Hall
10. King's Daughters' Free Library, Inc.
11. Book of Mormon Historic Publication Site
12. Palmyra Town Hall
13. Alling Coverlet Museum
14. William I. Phelps General Store Museum
15. Palmyra Historical Museum
16. Republican Liberty Pole
17. Pliny Sexton House
18. John Swift Log House Site
19. Admiral William T. Sampson's Birthplace
20. Joseph Smith Sr. House Site
21. Palmyra City Cemetery
22. Union Church House Site
23. St. Anne's Roman Catholic Church
24. John Swift Cemetery & Alvin Smith Grave
25. Erie Canal Restoration Project Site
26. New York Barge Canal
35. Dr. Alexander McIntyre Home
36. "Cannon Hill"
37. Pal-Mac Aqueduct Park

■ Mormon Site
● Historical Site

■ **VILLAGE OF PALMYRA, WAYNE COUNTY**

The village of Palmyra is located 6.3 miles north of I-90, exit 43, on State 21. From the Hill Cumorah it is four miles north on State 21.

The village of Palmyra was first called Swift's Landing (also Swift-town) after John Swift, and still later was named Tolland. However, at a meeting on Jan. 1, 1796, the name of Palmyra (after the ancient Syrian city) was selected for both the township and the primary village. At the time of its formation, Palmyra Township was part of Ontario County. However, Palmyra

Aerial view of Palmyra Village with the steeples of four churches at one intersection.

became a part of Wayne County when that unit was formed from Ontario and Seneca Counties, Apr. 11, 1823. The Joseph Smith Sr. family located in the village of Palmyra in 1816, and the Book of Mormon was later published here on Mar. 26, 1830 (PV 11–15, 219; PBC 3; RSNY 1–13; NEW 36–37, 92).[1]

■ **4. PALMYRA WARD HOUSE.** The Palmyra Ward house is located on the east side of the street at 1150 Canandaigua Road (State 21), near the south edge of the village of Palmyra. It is just .8 mile south of Main Street from the Four Corners Churches in the village of Palmyra.

The establishment of what is now the Palmyra Ward is a fascinating study of perseverance and sacrifice on the part of numerous Saints. In Feb. 1915 Elder Willard Washington Bean and his wife, Rebecca Peterson, were called on a special mission by the First Presidency to act as caretakers of the Joseph Smith Sr. farm in Manchester, NY. The call was for "five years or longer" and initiated a new Mormon presence in the Manchester-Palmyra community. Their mission lasted twenty-five years (WBFP 87–89; WBFR).

---

[1] The author is indebted to Donald L. Enders, senior curator of the Museum of Church History and Art in Salt Lake City, and Robert O. Lowe, Palmyra village and town historian, for insights willingly shared.

Main Street of Palmyra, Wayne County. The letters BM *are on the third-floor window of the E. B. Grandin Building, where the Book of Mormon was first published. (Photo by George E. Anderson, 1907; courtesy of LDSCA)*

The first converts to Mormonism in the community were Mr. and Mrs. Charles Collins, in 1921. A Sunday School class was formed at the Joseph Smith Sr. home on Stafford Road in 1922, and the Palmyra Branch of the Church was organized in 1925. On Jan. 15, 1961, President David O. McKay dedicated the existing meetinghouse. Samuel J. Ferguson served as branch president in the Cumorah District. The following year, on Jan. 14, 1962, Palmyra was organized as a ward in the newly formed Cumorah Stake (PBC 107–12, 172; CN Jan. 21, 1961, 3; CN Jan. 27, 1962, 6; ENS 15 [June 1985]: 26–29).

● **THE FOUR CORNERS CHURCHES**

The Four Corners Churches in Palmyra at the intersection of Main St. and State 21.

The Four Corners Churches are located in the village of Palmyra at the junction of State 21 and Main Street, with Church Street going north from the corner. The Episcopalian Church occupies the SE corner, the Baptist Church the

SW corner, the Methodist Church the NW corner, and the Presbyterian Church the NE corner.

Although it is often supposed that these church houses (one or more) were extant when the Prophet and his family were interacting with the village of Palmyra, this is not the case. Although the denominations themselves existed within the community, none of these four houses of worship had been completed during the time the Joseph Smith Sr. family was here. The Prophet and Emma left New York for Kirtland, OH in the latter part of Jan. 1831, and other Smith family members were all in Kirtland by May 15, 1831. The earliest of the Four Corners Churches was not completed until 1832, so none of them would have been a familiar landmark to the Smith family.

■ **5. ZION EPISCOPAL CHURCH, 1873 MEETINGHOUSE ON THE SE CORNER.** Early services were undoubtedly conducted by missionary Davenport Phelps. The parish was first organized on June 23, 1823. Initial meetings were held at the old brick Academy building on Church Street on the same lot where St. Anne's Roman Catholic Church stands. The church on the SE corner of Main Street and Canandaigua Road was finished and consecrated in 1873. It was built in the English Gothic style using red stone from Medina, NY (LWCNY 194–95; PV 253–54).

Rev. John A. Clark, rector of Zion Episcopal Church and contemporary of the Prophet Joseph Smith, said that in the autumn of 1827 **Martin Harris** visited him in his Palmyra home and stated that Joseph Smith had recently taken from the earth a golden bible, "and two transparent stones, through which, as a sort of spectacles, he could read the Bible" (GBTW 222–24).

■ **6. THE FIRST BAPTIST CHURCH OF PALMYRA, 1871 MEETINGHOUSE ON THE SW CORNER.** The First Baptist Church of Palmyra was organized May 29, 1800, at the home of Lemuel Spear. In subsequent years a number of meeting places were used by that society, including the old Union Church house, which they occupied from 1834 until it burned on Nov. 14, 1838 (WSP Nov. 17, 1838). On Feb. 24, 1839, a committee voted to secure a site for the location of a new building at the SW corner of Main and Canandaigua Streets. The meetinghouse was built of stone and was dedicated on Jan. 28, 1841. However, in 1870 the old stone church was torn down and the present structure was erected. The current church house was dedicated on Mar. 29, 1871 (LWCNY 192–93; PV 250–51).

Joseph Smith specified that among those initiating the revivals in the early 1820s were the Baptist Society, the Methodists, and the Presbyterians. Joseph stated that he "attended their several meetings as often as occasion would permit" (JS—H 1:8). It seems very probable that he would have listened to the Baptist revivalists from both the Palmyra and Manchester congregations.

■ **7. FIRST METHODIST CHURCH, 1867 MEETINGHOUSE ON THE NW CORNER.** It is not known exactly when Methodism was first preached in Palmyra. However, it was apparently about 1808 or 1809 when the initial congregation was formed. For a period of years they met for worship in homes, schoolhouses, barns, tents, and groves and then in a succession of meetinghouses. On July 23, 1866, ground was broken for a new meetinghouse on the site of the former Ainsworth Tavern, at the NW corner of Main and Church Streets. The completed building was dedicated on Oct. 31, 1867 (PV 251–53; LWCNY 194–95).

Joseph Smith said that a religious revival occurred in the Palmyra-Manchester area in the period of 1820. It began with the Methodists but also involved the Presbyterians and Baptists. The Prophet attended their several meetings; however, he said, "In process of time my mind became somewhat partial to the Methodist sect, and I felt some desire to be united with them" (JS—H 1:8). Orsamus Turner stated that Joseph caught "a spark of Methodism in the camp meeting, away down in the woods, on the Vienna road" (HPGP 214). Although Joseph did not join the Methodist faith, both Oliver Cowdery and William Smith affirmed that it was a Methodist preacher and visiting revivalist from the Susquehanna District, Rev. George Lane, who caused Joseph's mind to become awakened. Rev. Lane was apparently one of the catalysts which moved the Prophet to pray in the Sacred Grove. Joseph Smith would have had contact with members of Methodist congregations in both Palmyra and Manchester Townships during this period (BYUS 9, no. 2 [spring]: 321–40; M&A Dec. 1834, 42; DN Jan. 20, 1894, 11).

● **8. WESTERN PRESBYTERIAN CHURCH, 1832 MEETINGHOUSE ON THE NE CORNER.** The first religious services held by the Presbyterian

Church in the township of Palmyra were conducted in private homes during 1792 and then in the local schoolhouse by the fall of 1793. In 1807 worship was enjoyed in a newly erected meetinghouse in East Palmyra. On Feb. 26, 1817, two churches were formed, the Presbyterian Church of East Palmyra, which remained in the old building, and the Western Presbyterian Church of Palmyra, which occupied the Union Church on Church Street (see site no. 15 for the Smith family involvement with this denomination). In 1831 a lot on the NE corner of Main and Church Streets was purchased from George Beckwith, and construction of a new meetinghouse commenced. Rev. Samuel W. Whepley had charge of the pastorate during the building phase. The congregation continued to occupy the old Union Church House until 1832 when their present brick meetinghouse was completed at the Four Corners. This place of worship, still in use today, is the oldest standing structure in the village (PV 249–50; LWCNY 191–92; PBC 95).

- **9. PALMYRA VILLAGE HALL.** The Palmyra village hall is located on the south side of East Main Street at 144. The structure was completed in early Jan. 1868 (PV 282). The upper floor was at one time used as an opera house.

- **10. KING'S DAUGHTERS' FREE LIBRARY, INC.** The King's Daughters' Free Library, Inc., is located at 127 Cuyler Street, on the west side of the street near Main. Cuyler Street is one block east of the intersection of Canandaigua and Main Streets and the Four Corners Churches. It was built in 1850 by Carlton Rogers. Pliny T. Sexton later acquired the home, and when he died in 1924 he left the property to the King's Daughters' Society. It houses a wonderful circulating library for the community and an excellent collection of newspapers and historical and genealogical materials related to Palmyra and the vicinity (PBC 46–47, 56, 172).

- **11. BOOK OF MORMON HISTORIC PUBLICATION SITE.** The Book of Mormon Historic Publication Site is located on the north side of the street at 219 East Main, between William and Market Streets. It serves as the **LDS visitors center** in Palmyra.

  In 1828 **Grandin's publishing business and bookstore** were housed in the west end of a newly built, three-story, 85-foot-long structure called Thayer and Grandin's Brick Row, later named

Egbert B. Grandin Bookstore and Printing Office, Palmyra, 1907. The letters BM
*on the third-story window identify the room where the 1830 edition of the Book of
Mormon was published. (Photo by George E. Anderson, 1907; courtesy of LDSCA)*

Exchange Row in 1831. The four-bay building was constructed by
Grandin's brother, Philip Grandin, and the Thayer brothers, Joel
and Levi (DLE; ENS 28 [Sept. 1998]: 34). A description of the exterior features of this "business mall" of the day specifies that "its
federal-style brick facade with arched doorways and fan windows

was painted with a nearly
translucent Venetian red glaze
and striped with a white lead
paint to simulate brick laid in a
Flemish bond pattern. Capped
with a white balustrade across
its full length, the crisp red
structure exhibited a rather
grand appearance" (ENS 28
[Sept. 1998]: 34).

Beginning in the fall of
1828, E. B. Grandin rented the
three-level space from his
brother. This included the first
three-story bay on the west side
(DLE). The printing press was

*Site of Egbert B. Grandin Bookstore
and Printing Office, Palmyra. (1998)*

Egbert B. Grandin, publisher of the original 1830 edition of the Book of Mormon.

located on the third floor of the building. A book bindery was situated at the rear of the bay on the second floor; it was under the foremanship of Luther Howard. Here the printed sheets of books were folded into book-size pages, sewed, cut, and then bound. The front portion of the second story was occupied by a lawyer named Thomas P. Baldwin. On the first floor was the Palmyra Bookstore, where copies of the Book of Mormon were to be sold to the public. It was in this building that the Book of Mormon was first printed between mid-Aug. 1829 and Mar. 26, 1830 (JSPM 53; ENS 10 [July 1980]: 48–50; CN Oct. 30, 1982, 3; ENS 19 [Feb. 1989]: 43–47; DLE).

In June 1829 Joseph Smith and others first made application to **Egbert Bratt Grandin** for the printing of the Book of Mormon manuscript. Grandin was a Palmyra publisher of the local newspaper, the *Wayne Sentinel,* and a book printer. He initially refused Joseph's request on moral and religious grounds but was eventually persuaded to undertake the project of printing 5,000 copies of the book for $3,000. Martin Harris offered the necessary security through a mortgage agreement with Grandin dated Aug. 25, 1829 (JSPM 51–52).

Typesetter's footprints in the Grandin printing office. (1988)

Many others helped in the printing process. John H. Gilbert acted as chief compositor (typesetter) for the Book of Mormon. He and J. H. Bortles did the presswork until Dec. 1829, when a journeyman pressman, Thomas McAuley (or "Whistling Tom" as he was known) was employed to work with Bortles in finishing the presswork. Pomeroy Tucker acted as office foreman and read proof on many pages of the work. Daniel Hendrix also read proof and periodically set some type, and William Van Camp reportedly served as one of the compositors. J. N. T. Tucker claimed he was a practical printer on the project; however, John Gilbert thought Tucker was not part of the crew that printed the Book of Mormon. A young boy, Franklin P. Rogers, assisted; Lucy Smith mentioned that a son of Dr. Gain C. Robinson was also employed. Albert Chandler assisted Luther Howard in binding the books (JSPM 53–54; LS 112; DLE).

John H. Gilbert, chief compositor (typesetter) of the 1830 edition of the Book of Mormon.

After Joseph Smith and Oliver Cowdery had completed the original translation of the Book of Mormon, Oliver made a second copy, or printer's manuscript, as a protection against loss. The printer's manuscript was primarily used at the press from which to set type. The original manuscript, however, was also employed for 72 pages (Helaman 13 through Mormon). This was apparently done during a time when Oliver was copying from the original manuscript to the printer's copy but lagged behind the demands of the printer for copy (JSPM 71–75).

On Oct. 2, 1841, the Prophet placed the original manuscript in the SE cornerstone of the Nauvoo House, in Nauvoo, IL. Unfortunately, the stone receptacle leaked and the document was badly water damaged by the time Lewis C. Bidamon, the second husband of Emma Hale Smith, found it in 1882. Bidamon began giving some of the better-preserved portions of the manuscript away. The LDS Church in Salt Lake City, UT, has acquired approximately 25 percent of the original manuscript. The Wilford Wood heirs have 2–3 percent in a fragmented condition. The

Printer's manuscript of the Book of Mormon. This copy of the original (1 Nephi 7:12–16), was written in longhand by Oliver Cowdery in order to avoid using the original manuscript during printing. (Courtesy of RLDSLA)

University of Utah Archives also has a small segment (half a leaf). The bulk of the manuscript was destroyed by moisture. Fortunately, the printer's manuscript is intact and in good condition at the RLDS Library-Archives in Independence, MO. Joseph Smith III obtained the document from George W. Schweich, grandson of David Whitmer, on Apr. 18, 1903 (DN Sept. 27, 1882, 3; JSPM 65–75; SH June 1, 1881, 354).

After Joseph Smith initiated the printing contract with Grandin and got the project underway, he spent the majority of the publication period at his homestead in Harmony, PA, with Emma. Local supervision of the printing was carried out primarily by Oliver Cowdery and Hyrum Smith, with the regular assistance of Martin Harris.

It is interesting that on Oct. 8, 1829, a copy of the King James Version of the Bible printed by the H. and E. Phinney Company at Cooperstown, NY, was purchased from Grandin. The flyleaf bears the handwritten inscription, "The Book of the Jews And the Property of Joseph Smith Junior and Oliver Cowdery Bought October the 8th 1829, at Egbert B Grandins Book Store Palmyra Wayne County New York. Price $3.75 Holiness to the Lord." Joseph Smith used this copy in what would later be called the Joseph Smith Translation of the Bible (APT 26, 56).

While the Book of Mormon was being printed, a man by the name of **Abner Cole** was using the press on evenings and Sundays to publish a newspaper entitled the *Reflector.* Cole violated the copyright covering the Book of Mormon by printing some extracts from the work. Warned by Joseph Smith of impending legal action against him, Cole desisted. However, he continued a critical commentary on the book and the progress of Mormonism in the community (BYUS 10, no. 2 [spring]: 315–20; JSPM 57–58).

During the printing operation, unbound pages from the Book of Mormon were often used by Joseph Smith and his followers as part of their proselyting endeavors. Martin Harris and Oliver Cowdery gave Stephen S. Harding "the first and second chapters of the *Book of Mormon.*" The Prophet Joseph reportedly took some copy to show to his in-laws in Harmony. Oliver Cowdery gave several sheets to his brother Warren Cowdery. Thomas B. Marsh received 16 pages from Martin Harris, and Solomon Chamberlain later received 64 pages during a visit to the Grandin Print Shop in the fall of 1829 (PP 49; PJE 73–89).

On Mar. 26, 1830, the first copies of the Book of Mormon were made available for public sale in the Grandin's Palmyra Bookstore. Five thousand copies of the Book of Mormon were printed for $3,000. The book initially sold for $1.75 per copy (later reduced to $1.25) but a

Uncut sheets of the 1830 edition of the Book of Mormon. (Photo courtesy of Wilford C. Wood)

local boycott of the book curtailed sales and forced Martin on Apr. 7, 1831, to sell 151 acres of his farm in Palmyra Township to liquidate the mortgage (JSPM 59–60; MH 38–39, 99).

The original single-pull Smith patented improved press used in the printing process was acquired by the Church in 1906 (ENS 13 [Dec. 1983]: 42) and is currently on display in the Museum of Church History and Art in Salt Lake City.

On Dec. 15, 1978, following negotiations by President Milton A. Barlow with Mr. and Mrs. Paul I. Cherry, the Church purchased the three-story building space once occupied by Grandin's Bookstore and Printing Office, along with what had been the adjoining bay to the east. By agreement the Church

The single-pull Smith patented improved press used in the printing of the 1830 edition of the Book of Mormon at the E. B. Grandin Printing Shop (Courtesy of LDSCA)

was to take possession on Mar. 1, 1979. The building opened as a visitors center in 1982 (CN Nov. 18, 1978, 7; Oct. 30, 1982, 3; WCLD 725:387). Two beautiful portraits of Egbert B. Grandin and his wife, Harriet Rogers, painted in 1843 by Alonzo Parks, were donated to the Church in 1980 by Grandin's descendants and are now on display in the center (ENS 10 [July 1980]: 49). Following

2½ years of extensive renovation, the Grandin Press Building has been restored to appear as it did at the time of the 1829–30 printing of the Book of Mormon. President Gordon B. Hinckley dedicated the **Book of Mormon Historic Publication Site** during commemorative services held at the Palmyra Ward meetinghouse March 26, 1998, the 168th anniversary of the Book of Mormon's release (CN Mar. 28, 1998, 3, 11; Apr. 4, 1998, 3, 12).

■ **THAYER AND GRANDIN'S BRICK ROW.** The three-story building known as Thayer and Grandin's Brick Row (in 1831 renamed Exchange Row) on the north side of Main Street between William and Market Streets not only housed the E. B. Grandin Bookstore and Press in the west bay of the structure, but also contained other commercial and business outlets in adjoining bays to the east. **Sidney Rigdon** preached in one of the third-story units in the building. Pomeroy Tucker said Sidney Rigdon was allowed to preach in "the hall of the Palmyra Young Men's Association, in the third story of Exchange Row, . . . upon the earnest entreaty of [Martin] Harris." Sidney's discourse was based on verses from Chapter III of the 1830 edition of the Book of Mormon (or 1 Nephi 13:40 in the present edition) (ORPM 76–77; NEW 289).

● **12. PALMYRA TOWN HALL.** The Palmyra town hall is situated on the NE corner of Main and William Streets at 201 East Main.

● **HISTORIC PALMYRA, INC.** Historic Palmyra, Inc., was established in 1967 as a nonprofit organization dedicated to community service and historic preservation. They administer the Alling Coverlet Museum, William Phelps General Store Museum, and Palmyra Historical Museum.

● **13. THE ALLING COVERLET MUSEUM.** The Alling Coverlet Museum at 122 William Street houses the largest collection of hand-woven bed coverlets (bedspreads) in the United States. They are approximately 80 x 90 inches in size and are often referred to as the "American Tapestry." They are woven from homespun wool along with cotton or linen. The flax and wool were raised by the early settlers and were cleaned, sorted, and spun prior to weaving. Colors for the dyes were brewed from local weeds, roots, and flowers.

Several types of weaves were used to make the coverlets, which were woven on large looms.

Martin Harris was a prize-winning weaver of fine coverlets. In the *Ontario Repository* for Oct. 29, 1822, and Nov. 11, 1823, the annual Ontario Agricultural Society Premiums list "Domestic Manufactures—to Martin Harris, Palmyra, for the best cotton and woollen coverlet, $5.00." The museum houses no weavings of Martin Harris.

Mrs. Harold Alling of Rochester, NY, collected coverlets over a 35-year period, and 230 of her pieces are on display in the museum. Mrs. Henry W. Griffith of Palmyra donated the two-story brick building which once housed the *Palmyra Courier-Journal.* The museum opened on July 4, 1976. It is open daily from 1:00 to 4:00 P.M., June 1 through Sept. 16. There is no admission fee (PBC 131–33).

● **14. WILLIAM I. PHELPS GENERAL STORE MUSEUM.** The William Phelps General Store Museum at 140 Market Street is housed in a three-story brick building constructed about 1845 by Isaac Gardner in a decorative Anglo-Italian style with a balcony of cast iron and iron front pillars. William I. Phelps (no known relation to William W. Phelps of the early Church) purchased the building in 1866, and it was owned by the Phelps family until 1975. The Phelps family operated a grocery business on the main floor of the building from the late 1860s until the 1940s. The upper stories were living quarters. The current restoration takes the visitors back to the 1890s and introduces them to the merchandise of a turn-of-the-century mercantile store. On weekends from June through Sept., visitors may see the store on the main floor and the Phelps's home on the upper floors (CN Nov. 30, 1986, 5; PBC 130–31, 133–35; ROL).

● **15. PALMYRA HISTORICAL MUSEUM.** The Palmyra Historical Museum at 132 Market Street is housed in the two-story **St. James Hotel,** which was always known as "Rifenberg's" and was built by John Rifenberg about 1898 (PBC 138–40). The museum, which opened in 1978, features a display of elegant furniture, children's toys, dolls, household furnishings, and other articles from Palmyra's past. Of significance to researchers are the historical sources housed here. The museum's archives hold certain Palmyra town and village records, day books, ledgers, other miscellaneous documents, and the Sanford D. Van Alstine collection. It is open weekends from 1:00 to 4:00 P.M., June through Sept.

● **16. REPUBLICAN LIBERTY POLE.** The Republican Liberty Pole (Palmyra Village flagpole) is located at the SE corner of East Main and Fayette Streets.

A liberty pole had been standing on this block for many years when, in 1892, the Republican Party erected a new one measuring 150' (some say 170') high to fly the party banner. There was a steel latticework work of 100', which was topped by an extended pole of 50'. The Republicans gave it to the village. The pole was "found to be too high for the wind" and so was shortened to 135' (PV 65; PNY 34; ROL).

● **17. PLINY SEXTON HOUSE.** The Pliny Sexton House is located at 322 East Main Street. A New York State Education Department historic marker has been placed on the curb in front of the structure.

Pliny Sexton (1796–1881) built this Italian-villa-style house in 1827. He and his wife, Hannah Van Alstine, were members of the Society of Friends (Quakers). He was primarily engaged in the hardware and banking businesses (LWCNY, 18–20). His son, Pliny T. Sexton (1840–1924), was born in this home.

Pliny Sexton's daughter married David S. Aldrich. David, as a young clerk in a dry goods store in Palmyra, is reported to have sold Joseph Smith Jr. "his first decent suit of clothes" (PV 125). Apparently Martin Harris procured a "new black suit" from Aldrich for Joseph at the time the Prophet was returning to Harmony in 1829 after making the contractual arrangements with E. B. Grandin to print the Book of Mormon (ORPM 56).

During the Civil War, Pliny Sexton's brick home became a station on the Underground Railroad from the southern states to Canada. It is said that as many as 40 slaves were known to have taken refuge here at one time (WCJ Nov. 10, 1921).

The Pliny Sexton home is one of a limited number of residences on Main Street still standing from the Joseph Smith period. It is not open to the public.

● **18. JOHN SWIFT LOG HOUSE SITE.** John and Rhoda Swift's 1789 log home site is at the junction of Main and Canal Streets. Lodge No. 248 F&A Masons has placed a historic marker on Main Street to designate the site. John Swift and John Jenkins bought tract 12, range 2, now Palmyra Township, in the winter of 1789 from agents of the Phelps and Gorham Purchase Company. Swift was the first pioneer in Palmyra. He built a log house and a storehouse at this location in the summer of 1789 (PBC 3). He was the first moderator of the initial town meeting, the first supervisor, the first pound master, and the first captain of the local militia company.

■ **19. REAR ADMIRAL WILLIAM T. SAMPSON'S BIRTHPLACE.** The birthplace of Rear Admiral William T. Sampson is on the SW corner of Vienna and Johnson Streets at 112 Vienna Street. A New York State Education Department historical site marker is in front of the house.

William T. Sampson was the son of James Sampson and Hannah Walker. He was born in Palmyra on Feb. 9, 1840. After graduating from the Naval Academy at Annapolis, MD, he saw action in the Civil War and the Spanish American War, rising to the rank of rear admiral during the latter conflict, in which he commanded the North Atlantic Squadron. William T. Sampson purchased the "Mormon Hill Farm" in 1879. It encompassed the north end and east side of the Hill Cumorah and consisted of 170 acres. His brother, George Sampson, operated the farm. After the admiral's death the property was acquired by Pliny T. Sexton, a Palmyra banker (PV 246, 276–79).

Admiral Sampson passed away on May 6, 1902. His funeral services were conducted in Washington, D.C., with President Theodore Roosevelt in attendance. He is buried in Arlington National Cemetery.

■ **20. TRADITIONAL HOMESITE OF THE JOSEPH SMITH SR. FAMILY.** Local tradition identifies the SE corner of the intersection of Johnson and Vienna Streets at 202 Vienna Street as the approximate site of the Smith home following the 1816 arrival of the Joseph Smith Sr. family in Palmyra from Norwich, VT (ABCHP 18–19; HSP 14; NEW 38). However, the authors cannot find any "hard facts" to substantiate this location. But we do find the Smiths very early on West Main Street in the village of Palmyra.

The Palmyra road tax list, beginning with Apr. 1817 (nothing listed for 1816, the year of their arrival), places Joseph Smith Sr. in Road District 26, in the vicinity of William Jackways and Gain Robinson, who lived on West Main Street. The exact site of the home is not presently known. The road tax list for District 26 shows Joseph Sr. at the same location in 1818 and 1819. But in 1820 his name appears at the end of District 26 on Stafford Road, placing the family in Palmyra Township, near the Palmyra-Farmington (later Manchester) township line (OCAR). This indicates that the move to the site of their log house on Stafford Road may have occurred sometime in either 1819 or 1820.

Joseph Smith Sr. and the older sons hired themselves out in the village and farming area on day-labor jobs such as gardening, harvesting, and well digging to earn some substance with an eye to procuring a piece of land. Father Smith also opened a small foods shop, his merchandise "consisting of gingerbread, pies, boiled eggs, root-beer, and other like notions of traffic." Lucy augmented the family's income by painting oil-cloth coverings for tables and stands (ORPM 12; HJS 63–64).

■ **21. PALMYRA CITY CEMETERY.** The Palmyra City Cemetery is located on Vienna Street. The main entrance has an archway gate on the south side of the road, opposite 273 East Vienna Street. There is also a Johnson Street entrance on the west side of the cemetery. The Palmyra City Cemetery ("New Cemetery") was established in 1844 (PV 264).[2]

Tombstone of Egbert B. Grandin in the Palmyra City Cemetery.

Burial sites of particular interest to Latter-day Saint visitors are noted as follows (see the Palmyra City Cemetery insert on p. 163):

(1) **Egbert Bratt Grandin,** publisher of the Book of Mormon, his wife, **Harriet Rogers,** and two sons are buried in the northern end of Sec. R, in a small fenced enclosure with cement posts, connecting iron bars, and suspended metal chains. The lot borders on the road running along the north side of Sec. R, Lot 111. Egbert B. Grandin died of pneumonia on Apr. 16, 1845, at age 39 (WSP Apr. 23, 1845).

---

[2] The author is indebted to Roger Weaver, Palmyra City Cemetery superintendent, and Robert O. Lowe, Palmyra village and town historian, for introducing him to the cemetery plots of a number of notable figures of Palmyra's past.

(2) The gravestone of **Pomeroy Tucker,** the shop foreman for the publication of the Book of Mormon, is located in Sec. R, Lot 113, immediately south of the tombstone of his brother-in-law, Egbert B. Grandin. A polished stone with an open book and Masonic symbols on top mark the Tucker family plot. Tucker's personal tombstone is just 3 yards SW of the polished marker. He died June 30, 1870.

(3) **George Beckwith's** headstone is located in the SW corner of Sec. R, Lot 126. He died on Dec. 20, 1867, at age 78. Beckwith was one of three men delegated by the Presbyterian Church to call on **Lucy Smith, Hyrum Smith,** and **Samuel Harrison Smith,** who had joined that denomination, and direct them to be silent on the subject of the Book of Mormon. Lucy replied, "Deacon Beckwith, if you should stick my flesh full of faggots, and even burn me at the stake, I would declare, as long as God should give me breath, that Joseph has got that Record, and that I know it to be true." These Smith family members had not been active in that denomination for the previous eighteen months because of important developments in the rise of Mormonism. They were subsequently excommunicated from that congregation on March 29, 1830 (HJS 160–61; JSFV 182–83).

(4) **Deacon Henry Jessup** is buried in Sec. M, Lot 178. His headstone is on the first row of headstones facing the road on the west side of that section and is the thirteenth from the north line of the section. He died on Jan. 4, 1854, at age 77. Deacon Jessup was an original trustee of the Western Presbyterian Church of Palmyra at its incorporation on Mar. 18, 1817 (PWC 41). He, along with George Beckwith (see above), was one of the elders of that church who tried, unsuccessfully, to convince Lucy Smith, Hyrum Smith, and Samuel Harrison Smith to renounce their belief in the Book of Mormon and return to activity in the Presbyterian congregation (JSFV 182–83; HJS 158–63).

(5) The grave of **John Hulburd Gilbert,** the compositor (typesetter) of the first edition of the Book of Mormon, is located in the SE corner of Sec. N, Lot 319, 17 yards west of the east line of that section. John was born on Apr. 13, 1802, and died Jan. 26, 1895, at age 92. His wife, Chloe P., and nine of their children and grandchildren are also buried there. The headstone was donated by BYU's Religious Education Faculty and staff and by friends of the university, and dedicatory services were held at the gravesite on

Jul. 22, 1990. Prior to this time no existing headstone marked his resting place.

(6) **Pliny Titus Sexton's** grave can be found in Sec. O, Lot 320, just 5 yards north of the cemetery flagpole. Pliny T. Sexton was born on June 12, 1840, the son of Pliny Sexton (1796–1881), who is buried immediately east of his son's gravesite. Pliny T. died on Sept. 5, 1924.

Pliny T. was a lawyer and president of the First National Bank of Palmyra. He procured from John H. Gilbert, compositor of the Book of Mormon, a full set of printer's form proof sheets from the original edition of the Book of Mormon, unbound and uncut. These sheets were later purchased by Wilford C. Wood of Bountiful, UT, from Mrs. Clara Giese. They are currently located in the LDS Church Museum of History and Art in Salt Lake City. (ERA 45:638). The Smith press on which the Book of Mormon was printed was at one time acquired by Pliny T. Sexton. It was later purchased by the LDS Church (ENS 13 [Dec. 1983]: 42).

Pliny T. Sexton owned the northern end of the **Hill Cumorah** and the next adjoining farm along the east side of the hill, which were later secured by the LDS Church from his heirs. The Church also purchased from his estate the Grange Hall on Cuyler Street in the village of Palmyra where the Mormons once held their services (AWB, Pt. 2, 43–45). Until his death, Pliny T. Sexton owned the entire Exchange Row, part of which was the old Egbert B. Grandin Bookstore and Printing Shop, where the Book of Mormon was printed (PV 80).

(7) **Thomas Lakey** (1793–1864) is buried in the NW corner of Sec. L, Lot 427. Thomas purchased the 151 acres of the Martin Harris farm which was used to finance the printing of the Book of Mormon (see site no. 29 below).

(8) **Jesse Townsend's** grave is located in the SE corner of Sec. S, Lot 22. There is an 8-inch-high cement retainer around his gravesite. Reverend Townsend died in Palmyra on Jul. 14, 1838, at age 73 (WSP July 18, 1838). He became the pastor of the Western Presbyterian Church of Palmyra on Aug. 29, 1817 (LWCNY 192). In Apr. 1820, he moved his family to Illinois where he gave missionary service for a season. Reverend Townsend may have participated in the revivalistic activity involving the Joseph Smith family in the early spring of 1820, but this is not a certainty because of his early

departure that year. He did profess to know the Smith family and of the activities of Joseph Smith (LJTC Aug. 16, 1834; MUV 261–62).

(9) **Lucy Harris's** grave is in the John Strong/Rufus Harris family burial plot. It is the first lot south of and is adjacent to the Palmyra Cemetery Office in Sec. U, Lot 564. Those known to be buried in that plot are (1) Lucy Harris, who was born May 1, 1792, and died in the summer of 1836, at age 44. She was the wife of **Martin Harris** and was personally involved in the loss of the 116-page manuscript of the Book of Mormon (PCIR; HJS 131; HC 1:21; CHC 1:109–14). (2) Lucy Harris, the mother of Lucy Harris above, who died in 1824 at the age of 72 years. (3) There are eleven other Harris family members also buried in the plot (PCIR; MHS 176-77).

The **Cemetery Office** has information on a walking tour of the cemetery featuring the gravesites of some 17 significant Palmyrans (generally individuals other than those named above). Foremost of these are the gravesites of **Ambrose and Clarissa Wilcox Hall,** great-grandparents of Sir Winston Leonard Spencer Churchill, are buried in the SW corner of Sec. S. They were the parents of a daughter, Clarissa, who married Leonard Jerome. The Jeromes had a daughter, Jennie, who married Lord Randolph Churchill. Jennie was the mother of **Sir Winston Churchill, Prime Minister of Great Britain** (1940–45; 1951–55).

■ **22. Site of the Union Church House and the Western Presbyterian Church of Palmyra.** Members of the Western Presbyterian Church of Palmyra first met in 1817 at the Union Church, which was once located on the west side of Church Street, .1 mile north of the Four Corners junction of State 21 and 31. It stood immediately south of the General John Swift Memorial Cemetery at what is today approximately 127 Church Street (PV 262).

The Western Presbyterian Church of Palmyra was "set off" from its parent society at East Palmyra on Feb. 26, 1817, with 56 members. Rev. Jesse Townsend was installed as the first pastor on Aug. 29, 1817. The congregation met for worship services in the Union Church, which had been built as a nondenominational meetinghouse in 1811 on land donated by John Swift. It served the community not only as a meetinghouse but also as the town hall. The church house measured 40' x 50' and was surmounted by a steeple. It was constructed of wood and painted white with green shutters (LWCNY 192; PV 247).

Lucy Mack Smith, and her children **Hyrum, Sophronia,** and **Samuel Harrison** were all converted to Presbyterianism during the Palmyra-Manchester revivals of 1820 and worshiped in that building. It is very probable that in his quest for truth Joseph Smith Jr. also attended meetings here with his family, especially because of the "importunities and exertions" of his mother mentioned by William Smith (WSM 6–7; JS—H 1:7).

When **Alvin Smith** died on Nov. 19, 1823, arrangements were made by his family for his services to be held in this building, and a "vast concourse of people" attended (HJS 89). Reverend Benjamin Stockton of the Presbyterian Church preached the funeral sermon (ENS 17 [Aug. 1987]: 70). Alvin was buried in the adjoining General John Swift Memorial Cemetery, or "Swift Burying Ground," to the north.

With the exception of Sophronia, who had married Calvin W. Stoddard and moved to Macedon Township, the Smiths' names were on the rolls of this Presbyterian congregation until Mar. 29, 1830, when they were excommunicated. Their removal occurred just three days after the Mar. 26 publication of the Book of Mormon. They had, however, discontinued their activity some 18 months earlier in anticipation of the marvelous events then unfolding in relationship to the restoration of the church of Jesus Christ on the earth (JSFV 66–70, 182–83).

The Presbyterians continued to occupy the Union Church house until 1832 when their present brick meetinghouse was constructed on the NE corner of Main and Church Streets at the Four Corners.

Members of the Baptist Church next occupied the Old Union Church, or Presbyterian meetinghouse, from 1834 until it burned to the ground in a spectacular blaze on the morning of Nov. 14, 1838. The fire was apparently caused by "the deposite of ashes in a wooden vessel" (WSP Nov. 17, 1838).

■   **23. GENERAL JOHN SWIFT MEMORIAL CEMETERY.** The General John Swift Memorial Cemetery is on the west side of Church Street, opposite St. Anne's Roman Catholic Church. The small cemetery is situated on a rise 20 feet above the level of the street. It has a retaining wall with steps leading to the top at the SE corner of the cemetery.

In 1793 a log schoolhouse was built at the site on land donated by John Swift. This was followed in 1811 by the erection of a non-denominational church, Union Church, at that location (see site no. 23). At that same time, the log schoolhouse was removed, and the ground was used for a village cemetery (General John Swift Memorial Cemetery), which was situated directly north of the Union Church (PWC 31; PV 247, 265).

During the War of 1812, John Swift was commissioned as a brigadier general of the New York Volunteers. In the campaign of 1814 at Queenston Heights, Upper Canada (later Ontario Province), he led a force against Fort George. While reconnoitering the enemy's position he captured a British picket-post of about 60 men. One of the prisoners produced a pistol and fatally wounded General Swift. His tombstone states that he was "killed by the Enemy of his Country July 12, 1814 near Newark in U[pper] C[anada]." At first, he was buried in the region of conflict. Several years afterward, the citizens of Palmyra exhumed his body and returned his remains to this burial plot (LWCNY 169). His resting place is marked by a headstone and bronze plaque (PV 262).

The headstone of Alvin Smith, a brother of the Prophet Joseph, can be found on the southern edge of the Swift Cemetery just 106 feet in from the entry stairway. The thin stone has been adhered to a strong granite backing to preserve it. The epitaph reads, "In memory of Alvin, son of Joseph and Lucy Smith, who died Nov. 19, 1823, in the 25 year of his age." Lucy Mack Smith said that "a vast concourse of people" attended his funeral (HJS 89). Although Alvin was not a member of any church, his funeral was held in the Union Church House, then occupied by the Western Presbyterian Church of Palmyra. Lucy Mack Smith, two sons, and a daughter were

Headstone of Alvin Smith, brother of the Prophet Joseph Smith, located in the Swift Cemetery in Palmyra. (1965)

To the Public.

WHEREAS reports have been industriously put in circulation, that my son *Alvin* had been removed from the place of his interment and dissected, which reports, every person possessed of human sensibility must know, are peculiarly calculated to harrow up the mind of a parent and deeply wound the feelings of relations—therefore, for the purpose of ascertaining the truth of such reports, I, with some of my neighbors, this morning repaired to the grave, and removing the earth, found the body which had not been disturbed.

This method is taken for the purpose of satisfying the minds of those who may have heard the report, and of informing those who have put it in circulation, that it is earnestly requested they would desist therefrom; and that it is believed by some, that they have been stimulated more by a desire to injure thh reputation of certain persons than a philanthropy for the peace and welfare of myself and friends.   JOSEPH SMITH.

Palmyra, Sept. 25th, 1824.   57

Announcement concerning Alvin Smith in the Wayne Sentinel, *Sept. 30, 1824.*

members of that congregation. Reverend Benjamin Stockton preached the funeral sermon (ENS [Aug. 1987]: 70). Lucy recalled the great feeling of remorse that gripped the entire family: "We all with one accord wept over our irretrievable loss, and we could 'not be comforted, because he was not'" (HJS 89).

Alvin was a believer in the gold plates and the importance of that sacred record. On Jan. 21, 1836, while in the Kirtland Temple, the Prophet saw Alvin in vision and learned from the Lord that his brother would eventually receive the celestial degree of glory (ENS 17 [Aug. 1987]: 70; HJS 87; HC 2:380–81; D&C 137).

The remains of Alvin were not allowed to rest in peace. As early as Sept. 1824, about one year after his death, a vicious rumor began to spread that the Smith family had allowed the removal and dissection of Alvin's body for medical research. In order to "ascertain the truth" Joseph Smith Sr. and some of his neighbors "repaired to the grave, and removing the earth, found the body which had not been disturbed." With both hurt and irritation Father Smith reported the circumstances in the *Wayne Sentinel,* Sept. 30, 1824, and severely chastised those who would "deeply wound the feelings of relations."

● **24. ST. ANNE'S ROMAN CATHOLIC CHURCH.** St. Anne's Roman Catholic Church is located on the east side of Church Street, .1 mile north of the Four Corners junction between State 21 and 31 in the village of Palmyra.

Father O'Riley of Rochester said the first mass in Palmyra. Reverend Edward O'Conner of Canandaigua established St. Anne's Catholic Church in 1849. Reverend O'Conner purchased the old brick academy on Church Street from William Aldrich in 1848 or 1849. This building was used until 1860, at which time the present brick church, measuring 60' x 40' feet, was constructed on the same lot. The house was blessed by Bishop Timon in Feb. 1861. On St. Anne's Day, July 26, 1864, the cornerstone was consecrated and laid by the Very Reverend Michael O'Brien, vicar general of the diocese of Buffalo. The various construction phases were finally completed in 1870, and the house was dedicated by the Right Rev. Bernard J. McQuaid on Oct. 23 of that year. The congregation later added a belfry, bell, and vestibule in 1903 (PV 254–55).

■ **25. ERIE CANAL RESTORATION PROJECT.** An Erie Canal restoration project site is located on the west side of Church Street, .2 mile north of Main Street and the Four Corners churches. Here one can get a feel for the general measurements of the canal, which was 4' deep, 28' wide at the bottom, and 40' wide at the surface. This restored segment no longer functions as a canal but is an excellent preservation of the bed of the old Erie, which ran just north of Canal Street. Note the towpath running along the north side of the canal where horses or mules pulled the freight boats and packets. Today joggers can run all the way to Macedon along the path.

The route of the Erie Canal, or "Clinton's Big Ditch," named after Governor **De Witt Clinton,** ran from Albany, NY, on the Hudson River to Buffalo, NY, on Lake Erie—a distance of 363 miles. The rise in elevation from the level of the Hudson River to Lake Erie at Buffalo was 565 feet. This necessitated the construction of 83 locks to move the boats up or down the canal. Surveys were completed in 1816, and work began at Rome, NY, on July 4, 1817. The gates at Lockport, NY, were opened on Oct. 24, 1825, and transportation became possible over the entire length.

On Oct. 26, 1825, the *Seneca Chief,* the first boat to navigate the entire canal, left Buffalo with Governor Clinton and a group of dignitaries on board. Cannons were fired in each community along the route to New York City to announce the opening of the canal (see "Cannon Hill"). The Erie Canal, with its packets, line boats, and freighters, changed the pattern of transportation in America. Instead of costing $100 to ship a ton of freight from Albany to Buffalo, on the canal it cost only $10, and the price soon dropped to $7. Packet boat passage in the 1820s cost four cents a mile including meals, or three cents without (EC 5, 8–14; EWW 87, 214; SA July 1976, 118–22).

The Saints utilized the Erie Canal extensively to facilitate their missionary labors, emigration, and private endeavors. In the spring of 1830, Oliver Cowdery journeyed east along the Erie Canal with copies of the Book of Mormon on a proselyting mission. Abner Cole stated, "The apostle to the Nephites (Cowdery) has started for the east, on board a boat, with a load of 'gold bibles,' under a command . . . to declare the truth (according to Jo[seph] Smith,) 'in all the principal cities in the Union'" (REF June 1, 1830:28).

When the call to gather to Ohio came to the New York Saints (D&C 37 and 38), the Colesville, Fayette, and Manchester Branches of the Church all used the Erie Canal as a primary avenue during their April-May 1831 movement to Kirtland, OH and vicinity (NEW 296–322).

Joseph Smith, Oliver Cowdery, Sidney Rigdon, and Hyrum Smith traveled on the Erie Canal in the latter part of July 1836, when the Prophet and his party were en route from Kirtland to Salem, MA (HC 2:463).

● **26. NEW YORK BARGE CANAL.** The 348-mile New York Barge Canal runs on the north side of the village of Palmyra today. It can be seen from the bridge on Church Street, just .3 mile north from Main Street Palmyra and the Four Corners Churches, or at the Pal-Mac Aqueduct Park, located at 555 West Main Street in Palmyra (see site no. 37 below).

Work began on the Barge Canal in 1905 and was completed in 1918. Sometimes the bed of the Old Erie Canal was used by the new and enlarged waterway and sometimes not. The Barge Canal is now 125' wide and 12' deep. When motorized barges were introduced early in the 20th century, sections of the route were shifted to rivers. From Waterford, NY, to its new terminus at North Tonawanda, NY, the canal extends 348 miles and rises through 34 state locks and two federally operated locks, one at Troy and the other at Buffalo, NY (PV 297; PBC 5–8).

North of Palmyra

■ **27. CARPENTER CEMETERY (LANGDON CEMETERY).** The "Carpenter Burying Ground" is located on private property 1 mile north of the intersection of Main and Church Streets. North of the village, Church Street becomes Maple Avenue. At 1944 Maple Avenue, on the east side of the road, between two houses, is the small burying ground. **Calvin Stoddard,** the husband of **Sophronia Smith,** a sister

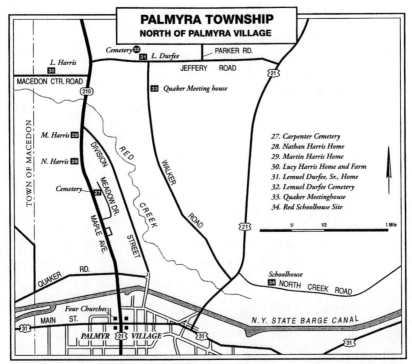

PALMYRA TOWNSHIP
NORTH OF PALMYRA VILLAGE

27. Carpenter Cemetery
28. Nathan Harris Home
29. Martin Harris Home
30. Lucy Harris Home and Farm
31. Lemuel Durfee, Sr., Home
32. Lemuel Durfee Cemetery
33. Quaker Meetinghouse
34. Red Schoolhouse Site

of the Prophet Joseph Smith, is buried here. Calvin preached Mormonism in Palmyra and vicinity. His tombstone is in the second row of markers from Maple Avenue and is the fourth stone from the north. He died Nov. 19, 1836. Sophronia next married William McCleary in Ohio on Feb. 11, 1838 (ENS 9 [Mar. 1979]: 42).

■ **28. NATHAN HARRIS HOME SITE.** The home site of Nathan Harris, father of Martin Harris, is 1.1 miles north of the Four Corners in Palmyra on the west side of the road at 1971 Maple Ave. The home is privately owned. Both Don Enders and Bob Lowe are of the opinion that this is the site where the Nathan Harris farm home stood, but they are reluctant to specify that the existing frame home is the original dwelling house without further research and proper verification (DLE; ROL).

Nathan Harris purchased 600 acres from John Swift just north of Swift's Landing (later Palmyra) on Feb. 3, 1794. Nathan and Rhoda Lapham Harris with their children, then numbering seven, moved first into a log house which they built at the north end of Wintergreen Hill (Walton Hill). Nathan later built a frame house at the site identified above. Nathan and Rhoda and their son Preserved are specifically named as being among those to whom Martin Harris was allowed to show the 116 pages of Book of Mormon manuscript, which were subsequently lost in June–July 1828. Nathan and Rhoda Harris went to Ohio where they joined with their children who had espoused the Mormon faith, i.e., Martin, Emer, Preserved, and Naomi (whether Nathan and Rhoda themselves were baptized is a point in question). Nathan died in Mentor, OH, just above Kirtland, on Nov. 17, 1835. His funeral was in the home of Preserved Harris in Mentor on Nov. 18. The Prophet Joseph Smith is reported to have preached the funeral sermon. Rhoda Harris died at Mentor on Oct. 11, 1849 (MH 12–13; MHS 5, 9; HC 1:20–22; MHT Sept. 4, 1998).

■ **29. MARTIN HARRIS HOME SITE AND FARM.** The Martin Harris farm is located 1.4 miles north of Palmyra and the famous Four Corners

Martin Harris farm and home site near the village of Palmyra, NY. This farm was mortgaged to secure payment of the publication of the Book of Mormon.

intersection of Main and Church Streets. Church Street becomes Maple Avenue on the north side of the village limits. The site of the Martin Harris farm home is on the west side of the road at 1962 Maple Avenue. A New York Education Department marker identifies the location. Martin's original home, a 1½-story white frame house, in which he lived until 1831, burned down in 1849. The present cobblestone house, built by William Chapman, replaced Martin's old frame house in 1849–50 (MHS 50–51). The existing house and property are now owned by the Church. This beautiful structure is currently being used to house missionary couples and is not open to the public.

The Martin Harris farm initially consisted of 320 acres, a portion of which had originally been the north part of his father, Nathan's, 600-acre tract. Martin obtained 150 acres of this large tract from his father and brother Emer Harris during 1813–14. He also acquired additional acres totaling the 320 acres (MHS 10).

Martin married his first cousin, **Lucy Harris,** on Mar. 27, 1808, in Palmyra. At least four children were born to this marriage—Lucy, Duty, George B., and Elizabeth. Martin served briefly in the War of 1812 in Pardon Durfee's company of the New York Militia. By 1824, Martin and Lucy had built a 1½-story frame home, containing seven to eight rooms on the west side of the road. There were farm buildings directly east of the home (on the east side of Maple Avenue) (MHS 10, 179; MHPF).

Martin Harris, friend of the Prophet Joseph Smith

Martin hired Joseph Smith Sr. and his son Hyrum to dig and curb a well and cistern at the Harris home in 1824. It was at this time that Martin became aware of the activities of Joseph Smith Jr. (MH 16–17n). One of four known wells on the farm is immediately in front of and to the east of the kitchen of the cobblestone house. According to local tradition this is the well and cistern dug by the Smiths.

In Nov. 1825, Martin deeded 80 acres and another farmhouse from his holdings to his wife, Lucy Harris, through her brother, Peter Harris, leaving 240 acres. Lucy continued to live with Martin until early in 1831, in spite of their domestic difficulties (see site no. 30 below).

The 116 pages of manuscript from the translation of the Book of Mormon were brought to Martin's home site soon after Martin left Harmony, PA, on June 14, 1828. The manuscript was shown to Martin's immediate family and then, without approval, to other individuals. It was subsequently stolen from him sometime in June or July 1828. The theft was apparently carried out by Martin's own wife, Lucy, and Flanders Dyke. Dyke had just married Martin's daughter Lucy on May 8, 1828. The manuscript has never been found. Because of these circumstances Martin was no longer allowed to assist the Prophet as scribe (HC 1:20–29; D&C 3, 10; MHS 27–35, 179).

Martin took out an 18-month mortgage on his farm on Aug. 20, 1829, as security for the payment of $3,000 to Egbert B.

Grandin for the publication of 5,000 copies of the Book of Mormon. On Apr. 7, 1831, Martin sold 150¼ acres to Thomas Lakey to obtain the needed $3,000 to pay off the mortgage. Lakey was to pay Martin in a series of installments extending to October 1832. However, a third party sped up the payment process for all parties. In 1831 John Graves, accompanied by his wife, Jane, and widowed daughter, Mrs. Christina Graves Grainger, had come to the Palmyra area from England. Mrs. Grainger brought with her $3,000 in gold coins, wrapped in a money belt around her waist. On Jan. 28, 1832, John Graves purchased the Harris farm from Thomas Lakey, paying $3,300. Thomas Lakey pocketed the additional $300 sales price and paid Martin Harris the requisite $3,000 in gold. This amount was passed on to E. B. Grandin to retire the debt owed for the printing of the Book of Mormon (MH 37–39, 97–100; MHS 49–50; MTPa; WCLD 11:128–29).

After the deaths of John Graves in 1841 and his wife, Jane, in 1849, the farm rightfully passed to his daughter, Christina Graves Grainger, who had married William Chapman in 1835. It was just as the couple was about to take possession of the farm in 1849 that the old frame home of Martin Harris burned down. The Chapmans immediately contracted to build the existing 2½-story cobblestone house. Robert Johnson was the mason. The water-rounded, variously colored cobbles were hauled from the shore of Lake Ontario, 20 miles to the north. Some fieldstones were used in the rear wall of the house. Over 700 cobblestone structures were built in the counties south of Lake Ontario. Wayne County had the highest number, more than 150. The William Chapman home is on the registry of the Cobblestone Society, Childs, NY (MHS 49–51; MH 37–39, 97–100; CLNY 4–5, 39; CM 175–76).

Martin Harris left Palmyra with some 50 Saints from the Manchester Branch who traveled to Kirtland, OH, in May 1831 via the Erie Canal and Lake Erie (WSP May 27, 1831; NEW 321). He experienced extended difficulties with his Church membership but eventually went to Utah in 1870 and was rebaptized at Salt Lake City on Sept. 17, 1870. Martin died at Clarkston, UT, on July 10, 1875. Martin Harris Jr. reported to the First Presidency of the Church that his father was buried with "his Book of Mormon in his right hand and the Doctrine and Covenants in his left" (MH 50–75; MHS 77–80, 90).

On May 13, 1937, Willard W. Bean, residing in the Joseph

Smith Sr. frame home in Manchester, made arrangements on behalf of the Church for the purchase of 88.06 acres of the original Martin Harris farm, including the Chapman cobblestone home on the site where the Harris frame home once stood (DN May 18, 1937, 16; WCLD 319:122).

■ **30. Lucy Harris Home and Farm.** The Lucy Harris home and farm are on private property. From the Martin Harris farm and home site go north on Maple Avenue ½ mile, across the railroad tracks, to Macedon Center Road (County 209). Turn west and travel .3 mile to the two-story frame home on the north side of the road at 2827 Macedon Center Road (a Macedon Township line sign is on the west border of the property). It is believed that the west side of the existing home is the original house, which was deeded in 1825 to Lucy Harris by her husband, Martin Harris (through Lucy's brother, Peter Harris), along with 80 acres lying on the north side of the road, as a security measure for Lucy. There was an old Dominion law which prohibited a direct transfer of property by a husband to his wife (see also PV 195; MH 19 n. 2, and 95–96; MHS 17).

Sometime previous to May 1831, Martin and Lucy separated over a series of issues which reached their culmination when Martin sold a large portion of the farm to pay the mortgage he owed E. B. Grandin for the publication of the Book of Mormon. Lucy took the children and moved to this farm (MH 43; MHS 51).

Lucy Harris was born May 1, 1792, the daughter of Rufus and Lucy Harris. Rufus was a brother of Martin's father, Nathan, making Martin and Lucy first cousins. She belonged to the Society of Friends (Quakers) as did her brother Peter, who was said to be a minister in that faith. Early services were held in his home (JSFV 64). Lucy died in the summer of 1836. Martin married Caroline Young on Nov. 1, 1836, in Kirtland, OH. Caroline was a daughter of John Young Jr., brother of Brigham Young. Martin and Caroline had seven children. In 1856 Caroline and the children moved to Utah, while Martin, refusing to go, remained behind. In the West, Caroline married John Catley Davis on Jan. 16, 1860 (MHT).

Martin lived primarily in the Kirtland area until 1870, then he, too, moved to Utah. He was rebaptized and continued to bear strong testimony of the Book of Mormon. Martin died in the home of Martin Harris Jr., his namesake by Caroline, in Clarkston, UT, July 10, 1875 (MHS 10, 17, 62, 176–77; MH 13, 58–59, 74–75).

■ **31. LEMUEL DURFEE SR. HOME.** The Lemuel Durfee Sr. home is located on private property. From the intersection of Maple Avenue and Jeffrey Road, the Durfee home is .4 mile to the east at 3105 Jeffrey Road on the north side at the top of the hill. Lemuel Durfee Sr. and his son (whom Lucy Mack Smith refers to as the "high sheriff"), interacted in the affairs of the Joseph Smith Sr. family in 1825. The Smiths had made every exertion to make the annual mortgage payment on their one-hundred-acre farm in Manchester Township by the due date that year. An understanding which they had with Zachariah Seymour, the land agent for the Nicholas Evertson estate, to meet their annual obligation was nullified when Seymour died and a new agent was appointed. The new agent was convinced by a neighbor, Russell Stoddard, and others to sell the property to them. However, appeals by the Smiths to the new land agent and the involvement of the "high sheriff" resulted in a separate arrangement which was more advantageous to the Smiths in terms of their continued residence on the farm. Though they ultimately lost the farm (Dec. 20, 1825), which was sold to the "high sheriff's" father, Lemuel Durfee Sr., the Smiths were allowed by that old gentlemen to remain on the property under a long-term rental agreement in return for the performance of specified tasks and making improvements on the property. Joseph Smith Sr. and his family finally left the farm in the spring of 1829, moving in temporarily with their son Hyrum, who occupied the old Joseph Smith Sr. log house just over the line in Palmyra Township (LS 59–64; HJS 92–99; WSM 12–14; NEW 104).

● **32. LEMUEL DURFEE CEMETERY.** The Lemuel Durfee family burying ground is situated 120 yards west of the Durfee home and 110 yards straight north of the Jeffrey Road on the rise, surrounded by an iron picket fence. Lemuel Durfee Sr. is buried here, having died on Aug. 8, 1829, at age 71 (WCJ July 25, 1918, 3; PV 189). It is on private property.

● **33. PALMYRA SOCIETY OF FRIENDS (QUAKER) MEETINGHOUSE SITE.** The Orthodox Quaker Meetinghouse was located .1 mile east of the Lemuel Durfee home on Jeffrey Road and .2 mile south on the east side of Walker Road. A five-foot steel post is all that remains of a New York State Education Department historical marker that marked the site. The 24' x 40' structure is gone. However, a rectangular stone foundation plainly marks the meetinghouse's location just above the fence line on the rise a few yards from the road (JSFV 64; PV 191, 256–58).

The Palmyra Society of Friends (Quaker) meetinghouse originally stood on the Durfee farm. The Durfees were Quakers, as was Martin Harris's wife Lucy. Martin himself was reported to have been an Orthodox Quaker at one juncture. Peter Harris, Lucy's brother, was a Quaker preacher. In 1828 Elias Hicks, a noted Quaker from Long Island, came through this part of the country and preached new doctrine, causing a split among the congregations of the Friends. Lemuel Durfee followed the Hicksite Faction rather than continuing as an Orthodox Quaker (JSFV 64; PV 191, 256–59; ROL). At the time of the separation between the Orthodox Quakers and the Hicksites, a second Quaker meetinghouse was constructed in the field across the road from the first, again on Durfee property. The exact location is unknown (ROL).

■ **34. RED SCHOOLHOUSE SITE.** From the junction of State 21 and North Creek Road in the NE sector of the village of Palmyra, the red schoolhouse once stood .3 mile east on North Creek Road on the north side of the highway. The laid-rock foundation of the old school is still very visible. The home immediately east of the school's foundation is number 3539 North Creek Road. The old foundation is located on private property (ROL).

Orsamus Turner, a contemporary of Joseph Smith Jr., stated that the red schoolhouse on Durfee Street (North Creek Road) was the scene of some lively discussions during their boyhood days. Orsamus affirmed, "He [Joseph Smith] used to help us solve some portentous questions of moral or political ethics, in our juvenile debating club, which we moved down to the old red schoolhouse on Durfee street [North Creek Road], to get rid of the annoyance of critics that used to drop in upon us in the village" (HPGP 214).

■ **35. DR. ALEXANDER MCINTYRE HOME.** The home of Dr. Alexander McIntyre is on the north side of the street at 109 West Main Street. This house is the first structure west of the First United Methodist Church at the Four Corners. It is a private home.

The house was built by Dr. McIntyre probably in the early 1820s and is one of the oldest homes in Palmyra. The early origin of the home is reflected in that it has nearly no setback from the sidewalk on Main Street (PBC 79).

Dr. McIntyre served as an assistant surgeon in the War of 1812, and was on duty at Niagara. He attended General John Swift when the General was shot and mortally wounded by a British prisoner at Queenston Heights, Upper Canada. "McIntyre was standing by his side and he fell into his arms" (PV 16; MHWC 279).

Dr. McIntyre was the Joseph Smith Sr. family physician. Unfortunately, he was away at the time Alvin Smith contracted bilious colic on Nov. 15, 1823. He was one of five eminent physicians who assembled at the Smiths' on Nov. 17, in an effort to relieve the obstruction created by an overdose of calomel that had been administered by a Dr. Greenwood. Dr. McIntyre and his uncle, Dr. Gain C. Robinson, performed an autopsy on Alvin's body following his death on Nov. 19, 1823, which revealed the cause of death (HJS 86–89).

In 1827, Dr. McIntyre refused to take command of a mob of some 50 men who requested that he lead them on an attack designed to seize the "Gold Bible" from Joseph Smith. Similarly, he warned the Prophet of 40 men who had collected as a mob to ambush him while on his way to Palmyra to "draw writings" with E. B. Grandin for the publication of the Book of Mormon in 1829 (HJS 118–19, 155–56).

● **36. CANNON HILL.** Cannon Hill is at the north end of Liberty Street, which leads north off of West Main Street just one block west of the Four Corners Churches in Palmyra. Cannon Hill lies between the north end of Liberty Street and Church Street. It is on private property and is not readily accessible.

For the celebration of the grand opening of the **Erie Canal,** cannons were placed along its banks from Buffalo to Albany and along the Hudson River to New York City. As Governor De Witt Clinton started from Buffalo on the *Seneca Chief,* Oct. 26, 1825, the first gun was fired, and then the next, all the way to New York City. Palmyra's cannon was fired from Cannon Hill (PV 294–95; PBC 5).

● **37. PAL-MAC AQUEDUCT PARK.** The Pal-Mac Aqueduct Park at 555

West Main Street, .7 mile west of the Four Corners Churches, is partly in Palmyra and partly in Macedon townships, thus the name Pal-Mac. Originally a wooden aqueduct spanned Ganargua Creek at this point, but in 1856 a 90-foot stone aqueduct built by Thomas Richmond took its place. It is one of the best preserved of the 19 aqueducts along the length of the canal (PBC 6; PV 295). Existing Locks 29 (Palmyra) and 30 (Macedon) can be seen here as part of the present-day Barge Canal. Complete with picnic tables, the park is a pleasant place to eat.

South of Palmyra along Stafford Road

Stafford Road goes south from West Main Street in Palmyra at a point .4 mile, or 3 blocks west, of the Four Corners Churches.

■ **38. SITE OF JOSEPH SMITH SR. LOG HOUSE.** The site of the Smith log home and Welcome Center at 843 Stafford Rd. is 1.6 miles south of West Main Street in Palmyra on the Stafford Road. The home stood 25 feet west of Stafford Road and 30 feet north of the Palmyra-Manchester Township line, which is the north fence line of the Joseph Smith Sr. Manchester farm. It is about 230 yards north of the existing Joseph Smith Sr. frame home. There is a reconstructed log house at the site with visitor parking in a lot immediately to the NW. On Mar. 27, 1998, President Gordon B.

Reconstructed log house of Joseph Smith Sr., Palmyra Township. (1998)

Hinckley dedicated the newly rebuilt Smith log house during morning services at the site. In the course of his remarks President Hinckley stated, "This will do away with the legend that has somewhat grown up among us that the other house [the Joseph Smith Sr. frame house] was the place where Moroni visited the Prophet. It was in this place and in the upstairs room that that event occurred" (CN Apr. 4, 1998, 3, 6).

In 1969 the author found a recording of the "Minutes of the survey of a public Highway beginning on the south line of Township No. 12, 2d range of townships in the town of Palmyra, three rods fourteen links southeast of Joseph Smith's dwelling house." The surveyors, Isaac Durfee and Lumon Harrison, Commissioners of Highways, shot their azimuth and made initial calculations while standing in the middle of Stafford Road on what was then the Palmyra-Farmington (later Manchester) town lines on the "13th day of June 1820," the very year of the First Vision (NEW 42–43). The author mentioned these "minutes" to Dr. Dale L. Berge of the BYU Anthropology Department, who was conducting a dig of the site of the Peter Whitmer Sr. log house site in Fayette, Seneca Co., NY, in the summer of 1969. He was very interested in the prospect of identifying the exact site of the Smith home. In 1982 Dr. Berge joined forces with Dr. LaMar C. Berrett, who was then serving as director of the Church history area of the BYU Religious Studies Center and who had independently been gathering data on the site and making aerial photographs of the area. Dr. Berrett

Archaeological dig at the site of the Joseph Smith Sr. log cabin in Palmyra Township, Wayne County, July 1982. Persons left to right in the background are Dale L. Berge, archaeologist and director of the dig, T. Michael Smith, and Don L. Enders. In the foreground (left to right) are Larry C. Porter and LaMar C. Berrett.

arranged funding for Dr. Berge and his crew, and an excavation of the site was carried out that same year. The location of the log house was verified. It confirmed the fact that the Smiths' 1½-story log house was indeed in Palmyra Township, immediately north of the 100-acre farm they contracted, or articled for, probably in the summer of 1820 (ENS 15 [Aug. 1985]: 24–26). Interestingly, the 1820 census lists the Smiths in

Farmington Township rather than Palmyra. Both towns were in Ontario County at that time and the Farmington census taker was apparently unable to make a distinction as he crossed the line into Palmyra.

From Aug. 8 to 23, 1997, a highly important follow-up field excavation was carried out by the LDS Church Historical Department under the direction of T. Michael Smith, assisted by Donald L. Enders. Both of these trained archaeologists were members of the original crew in 1982. Invaluable additional data and artifacts were retrieved. Some of the best evidences of the foundational walls were discovered in the previously unexcavated bulkheads. Enders has reported that the 1½-story home was 28' long and 18½' wide (DLE Nov. 25, 1999). The bedroom addition constructed off the NW corner of the house was 10 x 6 square feet (TMS).

The Smiths may have begun erecting the log house as early as the winter of 1817–18. Sources place the Smith home on that site by 1818 or 1819 (ENS 15 [Aug. 1985]: 16; JSPM 214–16). The log house was a 1½-story structure. At first there were two rooms on the ground level, a kitchen, or "keeping room," on the south, and a parlor, or "best room," which doubled as a bedroom, on the north. A little later the Smiths added a bedroom wing, built of sawed slabs, off the NW corner. A steep, narrow stairway led to an overhead garret that had been divided into two apartments (ENS 29 [Sept. 1998]: 30–32; ENS 15 [Aug. 1985]: 16, 26; ORPM 15; PV 219; NEW 40–42). This was home to Joseph and Lucy Smith and their nine children: Alvin, Hyrum, Sophronia, Joseph Jr., Samuel Harrison, William, Catherine, Don Carlos, and Lucy (HJS 336–46).

It was from this home that Joseph Smith Jr. went into the woods and received the First Vision of the Father and the Son in the early spring of 1820 (JS—H 1:5–20).

In this log house Joseph's sister, Lucy, was born July 18, 1821. She was the last child of Joseph Sr. and Lucy Mack Smith (HJS 345–46).

On the night of Sept. 21–22, 1823, the angel Moroni appeared to

The angel Moroni appeared to the seventeen-year-old Joseph Smith in the Joseph Smith Sr. log home in Palmyra Township, Sept. 21–22, 1823.

Joseph Smith Jr. three different times in this house and instructed him concerning the gold plates and the future work that God had for him to do. A revelation, Doctrine and Covenants 2, was written as a result of this visit. The next day Moroni appeared to Joseph a fourth time near the home and a fifth time at the Hill Cumorah (JS—H 1:29–53; ENS 15 [Aug. 1985]: 18; D&C 2).

Alvin Smith, Joseph's older brother, died here on Nov. 19, 1823, after a Dr. Greenwood administered a heavy dose of calomel which lodged in his upper bowels and created a blockage that culminated in death. As he lay dying, Alvin admonished young Joseph, "I want you to be a good boy, and do everything that lies in your power to obtain the Record. Be faithful in receiving instruction, and in keeping every commandment that is given you." Alvin is buried in the General John Swift Memorial Cemetery in Palmyra (HJS 86–89; ENS 17 [Aug. 1987]: 58–72; see also D&C 137:5–9).

Hyrum Smith and his wife, Jerusha Barden, occupied this log house after their marriage on Nov. 2, 1826, until the fall of 1830. Two daughters were born to them during this time Lovina, on Sept. 16, 1827, and Mary, on June 29, 1829 (ENS 15 [Aug. 1985]: 20; HSP 39–40, 57, 102–3).

When Joseph Smith Sr. and Lucy were required by the new owners to leave the Manchester farm in the spring of 1829, Lucy said, "We now began to make preparations to remove our family and effects back to the log house which was now occupied by Hyrum" (LS 99; ENS 15 [Aug. 1985]: 20–22).

The Smiths were again living in this log house when their son Joseph and members from the Whitmer and Page families, as Lucy

The Eight Witnesses were shown the Book of Mormon plates in June 1829 while Joseph Smith was living in the log home. This depiction of the event is found on the Angel Moroni Monument on the Hill Cumorah.

Mack said, "came [from Fayette] to make [them] a visit." Male members of the company then "repaired to a little grove where it was customary for the family to offer up their secret prayers." It was in that "little grove" that Joseph Smith showed the **eight witnesses**— Christian Whitmer, Jacob Whitmer, Peter Whitmer Jr., John Whitmer, Hiram Page,

Joseph Smith Sr., Hyrum Smith, and Samuel H. Smith—the ancient record. The eight men "looked upon the plates and handled them" (LS 110; HC 1:52–59).

In this house **Oliver Cowdery** completed copying in longhand the **printer's copy of the Book of Mormon** from the original manuscript. From this site Oliver Cowdery and Hyrum Smith supervised the first publication of the Book of Mormon, at the E. B. Grandin Printing Shop in Palmyra from Aug. 1829 to Mar. 1830 (ENS 15 [Aug. 1985]: 20–21).

This house became the focal point for the branch of the Church formed in the Manchester-Palmyra area during 1830. The Prophet was visiting here from his Harmony home when sections 19, 22, and 23 were given in March-April 1830.

Hyrum Smith left the log house to preside over the Colesville Branch in Broome Co., NY, in Sept.-Oct. 1830. Mother and Father Smith also left at this same time and moved to the Waterloo (Kingdom) area in Seneca Co. (NEW 109–10). The log house had completely disappeared before the turn of the 20th century.

On June 18, 1930, the LDS Church purchased from the Federal Land Bank, in Springfield, MA, 16.2 acres on which this log house had been situated in Palmyra Township. By that time it had been generally forgotten that the Joseph Smith Sr. log house had once stood on this very piece of land.

■ **39. JOSEPH SMITH SR. FRAME HOME.** The existing Smith frame home is located 1.7 miles south of Palmyra's West Main Street on what was then the east side of the original Stafford Road in Manchester Township. Today the road has been curved around the home to the east as a safety factor to protect those visitors who formerly had to cross a dangerous public road in order to get to the Sacred Grove. In 2000 the house was restored to its condition at the time of the Smith occupancy, 1825–29. Missionaries serve as guides at the home.

Under the management of Alvin

Joseph Smith Sr. frame home in Manchester Township, Ontario County. (1992)

Smith, the framework of the two-story dwelling had been raised by
Nov. 1822 (HJS 85). After the death of Alvin on Nov. 19, 1823,
Russell Stoddard, a neighbor, supervised the construction (ENS 15
[Aug. 1985]: 19). The house was still not completed in Oct. 1825,
when Josiah Stowell came to visit Joseph Jr. (HJS 91). However, it
was undoubtedly finished to a degree that was compatible with the
Smiths' means by the latter part of 1825 or early 1826. The Smiths
apparently occupied the home from 1825 to the spring of 1829.

Joseph Smith Jr. went from this frame home to the Hill
Cumorah for his annual visits with Moroni in 1825, 1826, and 1827.

In Oct. 1825 Josiah Stowell of Chenango Co., NY, probably
came to this home and employed Joseph to dig for him in an
attempt to find purported Spanish silver in Harmony Township,
Susquehanna Co., PA (HC 1:17; NEW 121–28).

The Smiths lost their ownership of this Manchester home and
farm in 1825 when they were unable to make the mortgage payment. Lemuel Durfee Sr. purchased the farm on Dec. 20, 1825.
The Smiths then became tenants on what had been their own farm
until they left in the spring of 1829 (NEW 104–10; ENS 15 [Aug.
1985]: 19–22).

Joseph brought his bride, **Emma Hale,** to this frame home following their marriage on Jan. 18, 1827, in South Bainbridge,
Chenango Co., NY. Joseph farmed with his father that season (HC
1:17).

The Prophet and Emma went from here to the Hill Cumorah
during the early morning of Sept. 22, 1827, when Joseph received
the gold plates from Moroni. Joseph initially hid the plates in the
woods, but later placed them in a chest belonging to Hyrum, then
under a hearthstone in this home. When a mob attacked the home
to get the plates the Smith family staged a counterattack and scared
them away (HJS 102–12). The plates were then hidden in the flax
(also flags) in the loft of the cooper's shop across the road to the
west of the frame home. Josiah Stowell and Joseph Knight Sr. were
house guests during some of these proceedings (HJS 102–3,
112–13). Here, in this home, Joseph's mother, Lucy, handled the
breastplate with the permission of her son (HJS 111).

Sophronia, Joseph's sister, married Calvin Stoddard Dec. 2,
1827, while residing here (HJS 336).

Because of persecution, and to ensure the safety of the gold plates, Joseph and Emma moved from here to the home of Isaac Hale in Harmony, PA, during Dec. 1827 (HC 1:19).

As a teacher in the Manchester Union School District No. 11, which encompassed the Smith home, Oliver Cowdery boarded here with the family during the winter of 1828–29 (see site no. 45).

Oliver and Samuel H. Smith left from this house for Harmony, PA, in the first part of April 1829. Oliver started working as Joseph's scribe on the Book of Mormon manuscript on Apr. 7, 1829 (IBMW 51–52; HC 1:32–33).

In early April 1829, Joseph Sr. and Lucy began to make preparations to move their family back to the log house some 230 yards north of their new house and on the west side of the Stafford Road in Palmyra Township. This was the home in which they had formerly lived and which was now occupied by Hyrum. The precise date of this removal is unknown, but it was apparently not long after Oliver and Samuel left for Harmony to join the Prophet (LS 110; ENS 15 [Aug. 1985]: 20).

Elder George Albert Smith purchased the 100-acre Manchester farm and frame home on June 10, 1907. An additional 39 acres were also purchased on the west in Macedon Township in 1907. Title for both acquisitions was conveyed to the Presiding Bishop on Dec. 7, 1916. On a lease agreement the former owner, William A. Chapman, worked the farm for several years. At the call of the First Presidency, Willard W. Bean, a boxer nicknamed the "Fighting Parson," his wife, Rebecca, and their two children occupied the old Smith farm in 1915 and remained until 1939. During their tenure another 16 acres were added on the north in 1930 (LNY 7–15, 50–51; CHC 6:427; ENS 15 [June 1985]: 26–29).

■ **THE 100-ACRE MANCHESTER FARM.** The Smiths did not actually contract, or article, for their 100-acre farm in Lot 1 of Farmington Township (later Manchester) until 1820, probably in the summer of that year. Zachariah Seymour acted as land agent for the heirs of Nicholas Evertson in the transaction from his office in Canandaigua. Pomeroy Tucker and Orsamus Turner remembered the Smiths occupying their log house adjoining the farm (in Palmyra Township) as early as 1818 and 1819–20, respectively (JSPM 215). It is possible that they were allowed by the agent for the Evertson estate to do some preliminary work on the farm acreage even before the 1820 contract became a binding agreement (DLE).

Joseph Smith Sr. Manchester farm, looking NE. The Sacred Grove is the 10-acre square of trees in the left center of the photo. The Joseph Smith Sr. frame house is at the end of the pathway leading east from the Sacred Grove. (Photo by LaMar C. Berrett, 1978)

Structures on the farm once included a frame house, a barn, and a cooper's shop (for barrel-making). It also probably had a granary, a smokehouse, and other outbuildings (ENS 15 [Aug. 1985]: 17; JSPM 213). The restored frame home and newly reconstructed barn and cooper's shop occupy the site. The framework for the 1820s barn comes from the original barn on the John Young (father of Brigham Young) farm in Mendon, NY.

William Smith said that during the time they were there, the family cleared some 60 acres of "the heaviest timber" (DN Jan. 20, 1894, 11). As they cleared the land they built stone fences by piling the larger stones on the boundaries of the fields and along property lines. The perimeter of the farm is 1⅜ miles (JSPM 219). Most of these stone fences have disappeared but remnants can still be seen at various locations about the farm, including walls east and NE of the frame home. At least four wells have been found on the farm; they were probably dug by the Smiths.

The primary crops grown on the land were wheat, corn, beans, and flax. An apple orchard of 200 trees was also laid out, and a large garden plot was maintained. From 1,200 to 1,500 sugar maple trees were tapped, producing about 1,000 pounds of sugar annually

(ENS 15 [Aug. 1985]: 17; JSPM 213, 223).

The first Book of Mormon pageant in the area was produced by John W. Stonely and Florence Bushman (Zobell) in 1928. The presentation was staged at the Sacred Grove on the Joseph Smith Sr. farm and not at the Hill Cumorah (ERA 71:24–27; PBC 14).

The Willard Bean family at a rock fence behind the Joseph Smith Sr. frame home in the 1920s or 30s. (Courtesy of Wilford C. Wood)

■ **PALMYRA NEW YORK TEMPLE.** The 100th announced temple and the 77th dedicated House of the Lord was constructed at 2720 Temple Road, Palmyra, NY. Temple Road, a new east-west road, connects State 21 and Stafford Road. The structure is situated on the NE corner of the original 100 acres which were once part of the farm belonging to Joseph Smith Sr. in Manchester, Ontario Co. The temple

The Palmyra New York Temple, Apr. 6, 2000.

grounds also extend to the north into Palmyra Township, Wayne Co. Immediately to the west of the temple are the sites of the reconstructed log house of Joseph Smith Sr., the Smith's white frame home, and the Sacred Grove beyond.

President Gordon B. Hinckley and others visited the prospective location on Jan. 22, 1999, with President David L. Cook of the Rochester New York Palmyra Stake. Wearing boots and using a four-wheel-drive vehicle they reached the proposed point. President Cook said that after President Hinckley had surveyed the area and been involved in "personally walking the ground," he announced to those with him, "This is a good site." The First Presidency informed local priesthood leaders of the decision by letter on Feb. 9, 1999. And at a special adult fireside held on Sunday, Feb. 14, 1999, President Cook told his stake membership the marvelous news. Accompanied by President Thomas S.

Monson, President Hinckley conducted groundbreaking exercises for the New York Palmyra Temple on May 25, 1999. President Hinckley observed on that occasion, "This is where the First Vision occurred and I think it appropriate that we build a House of the Lord on this ground. . . . I regard this temple as perhaps the most significant, in one respect, in the entire Church. It was right there in the Sacred Grove where it all began." Following his remarks, President Hinckley dedicated the site. He then invited the ecclesiastical leaders from the area, seven stake presidents and two mission presidents, to join him and President Monson in the ceremonial groundbreaking. The 10,900-square-foot temple, serves some 18,000 members (DLC; CN Feb. 20, 1999, 3, 6, 10; May 20, 1999:3).

The dedication of the temple took place on the 170th anniversary of the organization of the Church, Apr. 6, 2000. Proceedings were broadcast via satellite to approximately 1,300 stake centers and other facilities in the United States and Canada. An estimated 1.3 million members participated in the respective broadcasts during the day. This constituted the largest viewing audience of such an event in the history of the Church. President Hinckley was accompanied by his wife, Sister Marjorie P. Hinckley, and President Boyd K. Packer and Elder W. Craig Zwick. (CN Apr. 15, 2000, 1, 3, 6–9). In his dedicatory prayer President Hinckley affirmed:

> It was here, on this land which the Smiths once farmed, it was here in the Grove below and to the west that Thou, the Almighty God of the universe, and Thy Beloved Son, the resurrected Lord, appeared to the boy Joseph Smith. This wondrous event parted the curtain that had been closed for centuries. This marvelous appearance, which is the foundation of Thy work in this dispensation, brought back to earth a knowledge of the one true God and the resurrected Lord. (CN Apr. 15, 2000, 7)

■ **40. HATHAWAY BROOK.** Hathaway Brook (also known as Crooked Creek or Crooked Brook) runs through the Joseph Smith Sr. farm, immediately west of the existing frame home. The path to the Sacred Grove passes over the brook by bridge.

Early baptisms reportedly occurred in the brook. Parley P. Pratt mentions attending a meeting in Joseph Smith Sr.'s home in Manchester and states that after the Sunday services "we repaired from the meeting to the water's edge, and, at [Joseph's] request, I baptized several persons" (APPP 31). This appears to have taken place somewhere along Hathaway Brook, presumably in the proximity of the Smith home. However, the baptisms could have taken place farther south at the Russell Stoddard sawmill and dam site on Hathaway Brook (see

Hathaway Brook, west of the Joseph Smith Sr. frame house in Manchester Township. Baptisms were performed within the area of this photo after a dam was built to deepen the water. The barns on the right were located SW across the road from the Joseph Smith Sr. frame home. The older barn is in the right foreground.

site no. 42). While going out to the Sacred Grove on Dec. 26, 1905, William A. Chapman pointed out to President Joseph F. Smith's party a place on Hathaway Brook where he said a dam had once been constructed for the performance of baptisms in an early day (PAD 66–67; ERA 9:380).

More recently, other baptisms have taken place on the farm. For instance, on Sept. 23, 1923, Willard W. Bean dammed up Hathaway Brook just west of where the old barns stood, flooded an area, and baptized his little daughter Palmyra Bean (Packer). Palmyra was born at the farm in 1915. He also baptized two children from the Palmyra Branch of the Church, William Wilson Morgan and his sister Hazel Maud Morgan. Elder James E. Talmage, here for the 100th anniversary of Moroni's first appearances to Joseph Smith, confirmed Palmyra Bean a member of the Church during services held that same evening in a "great tent." President Heber J. Grant, who presided at the meeting, confirmed William Wilson Morgan a member. Elder Rudger Clawson was also present and confirmed Hazel Maud Morgan (PBP; WBFR; JJET Sept. 23, 1923, 53; TCR 767, 770–71).

■ **41. THE SACRED GROVE, SITE OF JOSEPH'S FIRST VISION.** The Sacred Grove is situated ¼ mile west of both the Joseph Smith Sr. Palmyra log home and the frame home on the Manchester farm. A merging pathway from the Welcome Center and the log house will take

The Sacred Grove, aerial view, looking east.
The Sacred Grove is in the lower part of the
photo. (Photo by LaMar C. Berrett, 1978)

A country lane to the Sacred Grove, with boys
fishing in Hathaway Brook. (Photo by George
E. Anderson, 1907; courtesy of LDSCA)

The Sacred Grove. (Photo by
George E. Anderson, 1907;
courtesy of LDSCA)

you directly west to the grove. Another path connects the grove and the frame home.

The Sacred Grove is called "one of the last surviving tracts of primeval forest in western New York state." It is a 10-acre grove today and its trees include maples, beech, hophornbeam, wild cherry, ash, oak, hickory, and elm. In the grove there are still trees that were fully grown in Joseph's day. Many are more than 200 years old. Some of these trees are 90 to 100 feet in height (ENS 20 [Apr. 1990]: 14–17).

When the party of Joseph F. Smith visited the Smith farm and Sacred Grove on Dec. 26, 1905, they met William A. Chapman, whose father, Seth T. Chapman, had purchased the farm on Apr. 2, 1860. They learned that this wood lot had been kept in its native state for more than 70 years and that "no ax [had] been laid at the roots of [the] trees" save to remove the dead and decaying timber. Mr. Chapman explained that his father was told "that this was the particular piece of wood in which Joseph Smith claimed to see a vision; and his father had never felt disposed to mar its sacred silence or beauty" (ERA 9:380–81; PaD 66; ENS 20 [Apr. 1990]: 16).

In the 1820s the Palmyra-Manchester area was embroiled in revivalism. Joseph Smith said that it primarily involved the Methodists, Presbyterians, and Baptists. Lucy Mack Smith and her children, Hyrum, Sophronia, and Samuel Harrison,

Camp Meeting in the West, *1830, by A. Rider. (Courtesy of Library of Congress)*

were proselyted to the Presbyterian faith (JS—H 1:5–7).

Not knowing which church to join, Joseph read James 1:5: "If any of you lack wisdom, let him ask of God, that giveth to all men liberally, and upbraideth not; and it shall be given him." Inspired, Joseph sought the Lord in humble prayer. Going out into the privacy of the woods, he knelt down and prayed.[3] His petition was answered by the appearance of God the Father and His Son, Jesus Christ. Joseph was instructed to join none of the existing sects and was told

The First Vision in the Sacred Grove. (Courtesy of LDSCA)

that in due time the fulness of the gospel should be made known to him (JS—H 1:8–20; JSFV 172; NEW 45–64).

Joseph declared the truths of the First Vision throughout his life. On June 16, 1844, just 11 days before his martyrdom at

---

[3] Various accounts record Joseph's going into the "wilderness," to the "silent grove," or to "a secret place in a grove, but a short distance from his father's house." He described going into "the woods where my father had a clearing, and went to the stump where I had stuck my axe when I had quit work, and I kneeled down, and prayed" (JSFV 155–76). The term "Sacred Grove" was apparently not used by the Prophet but applied to the site at a later time. When Richard W. Young visited the Joseph Smith frame home (ca. June 1882), he commented that "In the vicinity were several extensive patches of woods, one of which was doubtless the scene of the supplications of the boy Joseph" (ThC 4:20). The precise spot where the Father and the Son appeared to the young Joseph is unknown. (For significant recitals of Joseph Smith's First Vision see *BYUS* 9, no. 2 (spring):275–96; JSFV 155–79.)

Carthage, IL, he sermonized to the Saints in Nauvoo, "I have always declared God to be a distinct personage, Jesus Christ a separate and distinct personage from God the Father, and that the Holy Ghost was a distinct personage and a Spirit: and these three constitute three distinct personages and three Gods" (HC 6:474).

March to the Sacred Grove, Sept. 23, 1923, led by flag bearer and followed by (left to right) Andrew Jenson, President Heber J. Grant, and Joseph Fielding Smith. The celebration was for the 100th anniversary of Moroni's first visit to Joseph Smith.

■ **42. RUSSELL STODDARD SAWMILL AND DAM SITE.** The Russell Stoddard sawmill and dam site is 2.9 miles south of West Main Street, Palmyra, on Stafford Road, or 1.2 miles south of the Joseph Smith Sr. frame home. The sawmill was situated near the west side of Stafford Road, where a branch of Hathaway Brook (Crooked Creek) flows under the road. The site is on private property, gained by a small access road leading off of Stafford Road on the west side.

After Russell Stoddard had built the mill a neighbor informed him "that there would not be power enough to run the mill, and he would furnish the first log and give him the lumber if he would saw it." Because of insufficient power, the mill was never used. However, the dam proved to be a boon to the Mormons, who, according to Thomas L. Cook, used it as an early baptismal site (PV 220). Both Parley P. Pratt and Ezra Thayer spoke of baptisms being performed in that general area but they didn't specify Stoddard's mill pond as the site of the baptisms in which they were involved (APPP 45; SH Oct. 1862 3:79–80). Neither the mill or the dam exist today.

■ **43. WILLIAM STAFFORD HOME.** The William Stafford home is reportedly the one on the east side of Stafford Road, about 1.4 miles south of the Joseph Smith Sr. frame home, or 50 yards south of the junction of Fox and Stafford Roads at 405 Stafford Road. It has every appearance of being a home that was contemporary with the time period of the Smith family (DLE). Thomas Cook wrote that the old William Stafford home had burned down (PV 221). However, Don Enders of the Church Historical Department is of the opinion that the home still stands at the above address and that Cook has mistakenly identified the burning of another home in the vicinity as being that of William Stafford (DLE). It is on private property.

William Stafford stated that in 1820 the Joseph Smith Sr. family lived in Palmyra Township "about one mile and a half from my residence" (MUV 237). C. M. Stafford said that the Joseph Smith Sr. family "settled on one hundred acres one mile north of our house" (NTAM Apr. 1888, 1). The Stafford children attended school with the Joseph Smith Sr. children. Both the Stafford School and the Stafford Road derive their names from William Stafford.

■ **44. PROBABLE ORIN AND SARAH WITT ROCKWELL FAMILY HOME SITE.** The probable site of the Orin Rockwell family home is 1.5 miles south of the Joseph Smith Sr. frame home on Stafford Road. The home was reportedly on the east side of the road on the William Stafford property and may have been at the site of a house which once stood about 120 yards SE of the existing home of William Stafford (see site no. 43). According to the 1820 census, the Rockwell family lived next to William Stafford on Lot No. 5, and may have been renting from him (DLE). Today, the purported Rockwell home is just a mound of stone, earth, and ashes. The Shortsville and Manchester Fire Departments exercised a "controlled burn" of the dilapidated structure in 1991 or 1992 (EBB).

Orrin Porter Rockwell, the son of Orin (the father spelled his name with one *r*) and Sarah Witt Rockwell, was born on June 28, 1813, in Belcher, Hampshire Co., MA. The Rockwells came out of Belcher in 1817, and settled in Manchester, NY. Caroline Rockwell (Mrs. M. C. R. Smith), Porter's sister, stated that the family lived "one mile [south on Stafford Road] from the Mormon Smith family, and I attended school with their children" (NTAM Apr. 1888, 1).

The Smith and Rockwell families befriended one another, and the Prophet Joseph and his mother and father were often in the Rockwell home for visits. On such occasions young Orrin reportedly "listened with delight to all that was said. He even begged his mother to allow him to sit up and keep the pine torch burning," so that he wouldn't miss the interesting conversation (CS Aug. 31, 1935, 7). Orrin, it was said, picked berries and gathered and sold wood in order to raise money for the printing of the Book of Mormon. Porter and his mother, Sarah Witt, were among the first to be baptized into the Restored Church (CS Aug. 31, 1935, 7; NEW 259).

Although Porter Rockwell was 7½ years younger than the Prophet Joseph, the two became close companions and remained so to the time of the Prophet's martyrdom in 1844. Porter has become a legendary figure in LDS Church history (PR).

■ **45. SITE OF THE STAFFORD SCHOOLHOUSE.** The site of the schoolhouse where **Oliver Cowdery** taught the children of the Smith family and other neighborhood children is located 3.7 miles south of Main Street, on the west side, at 498 Stafford Road, or 1.9 miles south of the Joseph Smith Sr. frame home. A later cobblestone schoolhouse now occupies the same location. At the top of the gable on the east side above the front entrance is a date-stone bearing the inscription "DIST. NO. 11, 1848." The 1848 cobblestone schoolhouse was in continuous use for classroom instruction until July 25, 1949, when it was discontinued (EEL). Edward B. Beavers, a Latter-day Saint, now owns the cobblestone schoolhouse and has made it into his private home.

The 1848 cobblestone school on the site of the Stafford Road Schoolhouse, where the children of Joseph Smith Sr., including Joseph Smith Jr., went to school, and where Oliver Cowdery taught, Manchester Township. (1993)

School books used by Joseph Smith Jr. and his brothers and sisters. From left to right, the books are an English reader, an arithmetic book, and a book of gospel songs. (Photo courtesy of Wilford C. Wood Foundation)

Some have supposed that Oliver Cowdery taught in a schoolhouse once located at the site of the existing 1846 Armington Schoolhouse (see site no. 2). However, historians have distinctly identified the Stafford Schoolhouse on Stafford Road as the site where Oliver was the schoolmaster (HONY 415; MED No. XXXIII). BYU religion professor Richard L. Anderson shared with the author conclusive statements by contemporaries of the Smith family tying them to the Stafford School. C. R. Stafford asserted, "Our

Inscription on arithmetic book: "Joseph Smith's Book January 31st, 1818" and signature "Catherine." (Courtesy of Wilford C. Wood Foundation)

school district was called the Stafford District because of sixty scholars enrolled, forty were Staffords. The road on which they lived is now called Stafford street. The Mormon Smith family lived near our house. I was well acquainted with them, and attended school with the younger children." C. M. Stafford affirmed that he had attended school with "Harrison" (Samuel Harrison Smith), Catherine, "Bill" (William Smith), and "Carlos" (Don Carlos Smith). Mrs. Sylvia Walker stated that "I attended school to Oliver Cowdery with Carlos, Sam, Bill, Catherine, and Lucy Smith. . . . Jo[seph], Hyrum and Sophronia, the other children, were older" (NTAM Jan. 1888, 3; and Apr. 1888, 1).

Lyman Cowdery, a brother of Oliver Cowdery, came into the Manchester area in 1828 and made a teaching application to Hyrum Smith, a trustee of the district school. Lyman's application was approved for the coming school season of 1828–29. However, it became necessary for him to withdraw, and he suggested Oliver as his replacement. This was acceptable to the trustees, and upon examination they hired Oliver. During his teaching appointment (approximately from Oct. 1828 to Mar. 1829) Oliver boarded at the Smiths' Manchester frame home. There he learned from Joseph Smith Sr. the facts concerning the gold plates (HJS 138–42; HC 1:32).

In this same time period, the Prophet stated that he had been praying for a scribe to aid him in the translation of the plates and that the "Lord appeared unto a young man by the name of

Oliver Cowd[e]ry and shewed unto him the plates in a vision and also the truth of the work . . . therefore he was desirous to come and write for me" (PJS 1:10). Oliver acknowledged the circumstances under which he received the manifestation (HC 1:35; see also D&C 6:15–16, 22–24). After receiving his salary for teaching, Oliver left the school district in the first part of April and in company with Samuel H. Smith walked 125 miles to Harmony, PA, where he met the Prophet Joseph Smith for the first time on Apr. 5, 1829. Two days later he was acting as scribe for Joseph (LS 98–100; HC 1:32–33).

Locally it is believed that when the new cobblestone schoolhouse was constructed in 1848, the original schoolhouse in which Oliver had taught was moved .1 mile to the south where it now forms the SE corner of the existing frame home on the west side of the road at 520 Stafford Road (see site no. 46).

46. ORIGINAL STAFFORD SCHOOLHOUSE. The original frame schoolhouse in which Oliver taught was apparently moved .1 mile south

and is now attached to the SE corner of the existing frame home immediately south of the 1848 cobblestone school on the west side of the road at 520 Stafford Road. The home is privately owned.

Edward B. Beavers, a local Church member, has inspected the frame home and is of the opinion that the SE section of that four-part house may well be the portion that once constituted the old frame school-house. Edward stated that

The original Stafford schoolhouse, Manchester Township, where Oliver Cowdery taught some of the children of Joseph Smith Sr. The SE portion of the existing structure is the old schoolhouse. It was moved here from the site where the 1848 cobblestone school is now located. (1993)

"it is of post and beam construction, wooden pegs etc., and could have been easily moved (EBB). Mr. Earl E. Lupold, at 551 Stafford Road, Manchester, lived in the frame home at 520 Stafford Road from 1944 to 1992 and also owned the cobblestone school for many years. He likewise believes that the frame home is in all probability the old frame schoolhouse. His deed shows that the District No. 11 schoolhouse on the original site was constructed of wood. He stated that the foundations of both the cobblestone school and the frame home are constructed of cobblestones and were probably laid about the same time, facilitating the move of the wooden schoolhouse onto the cobblestone foundation to the south—if such were the case. The frame home has rounded ceilings characteristic of a schoolroom while most homes in the area have square ceilings (EEL).

■ **47. RUSSELL STODDARD FARMHOUSE.** The Russell Stoddard farmhouse is located on Fox Road in Manchester Township. It is 1.3 miles south of the Joseph Smith Sr. frame home on Stafford Road and .1 mile west on the north side of Fox Road. The rear wing of the two-story Russell Stoddard farmhouse is the oldest portion, having been built in the early 1820s. The Stoddard farm at one time totaled 250 acres (PV 220–21).

When Alvin Smith died on Nov. 19, 1823, the Joseph Smith Sr. frame home, which Alvin had commenced for his parents in 1822, was not yet finished. Russell Stoddard, a neighbor living at this farm, was employed as the principal carpenter. He assisted the Smiths in their home's completion, which probably occurred in the latter part of 1825. Russell F., the son of Russell Stoddard, later reported that his father was the man, helped by others, who had built the home (DLE; JSPM 221). Russell Stoddard wanted to purchase the Smiths' home and farm, offering $1,500 for it. The offer was refused by the Smiths. Russell Stoddard and some associates next tried to wrest the property away from the Smiths by misrepresenting certain facts to the land agent at Canandaigua (HJS 94–99). Not having the necessary money to meet the immediate mortgage demand and not wishing to see the farm lost to Mr. Stoddard, Joseph Smith Sr. recommended another course. At Joseph's request, "Lemuel Durfee [Sr.] paid for the property and the Smiths continued to occupy it, paying rent considerably in labor" (NEW 104–10; HJS 94–99).

● **48. 1816 FARMINGTON SOCIETY OF FRIENDS (QUAKER) MEETINGHOUSE.** To see the 1816 Quaker Church, travel 1.3 miles south from the Joseph Smith Sr. frame house on Stafford Road to the junction of Stafford and Fox Roads. Turn west on Fox Road (crossing into

1816 Farmington Society of Friends (Quaker)
Meetinghouse in Farmington Township. (1993)

Farmington Township) and drive for 3.4 miles to Sheldon Road. Turn right (north) and follow the long, westerly curve of Sheldon Road to its junction with County Road 8 and the Allen-Podgham Road. An existing 1876 Quaker meetinghouse and cemetery are on the NE corner of that junction. The building is occupied by an active Society of Friends today. From that point the 1816 Quaker meetinghouse is .1 mile north of the junction on County Road 8, on the west side of the road. The building originally stood near the NW corner of the intersection, but in 1926 it was moved 165 yards north and down the hill to its present location. It is privately owned and is currently being used as a storage shed for potatoes (JSFV 61–64; HONY 1:322–23; CRB).

This 1816 Farmington Society of Friends meetinghouse of hand-hewn cedar is the only structure still standing in the proximity of the Joseph Smith Sr. farm (the Smith farm is about five miles east) which was used as a house of worship at the time of the First Vision in 1820 (JSFV 63).

Lucy Mack Smith referenced the family's interaction with certain Quakers who were in the general area (HJS 97–99, 179–81).

■ VILLAGE OF NEWARK

Newark is located nine miles east of Palmyra on State 31. **Parley P. Pratt** and his wife, Thankful Halsey, were passing through Newark on the Erie Canal in Aug. 1830 on their way to the Canaan/New Lebanon area of eastern New York. At Newark, Parley was impressed by the Spirit to get off the packet boat and send Thankful ahead to their destination. He called on an old Baptist deacon named Elijah Hamlin, who introduced him to a "very strange book" that had just been published—the **Book of Mormon.** Parley said, "I read all day; eating was a burden, I had no desire for food; sleep was a burden when the night came, for I preferred reading to sleep." Journeying to the old log house of the Smiths in Palmyra Township (they had lost the Manchester frame home), Parley was entertained by Hyrum Smith who presented him with a copy of the Book of Mormon. He said of his reading experience, "I esteemed the Book, or the information contained in it, more than all the riches of the world." Convinced of its truthfulness, Parley soon returned and "demanded baptism." Hyrum and Parley then walked the 25 miles to the Peter Whitmer farm in Fayette. Here Parley recounted, "About the 1st of September, 1830, I was baptized by the hand of an Apostle of the Church of Jesus Christ, by the name of Oliver Cowdery. This took place in Seneca Lake, a beautiful and transparent sheet of water in Western New York" (APPP 36–42).

■ LYONS AND LYONS TOWNSHIP

The village of Lyons, the Wayne County seat, is located 15 miles east of Palmyra at the junction of State 14 and State 31.

William W. Phelps was imprisoned in Lyons on Apr. 30, 1830. Some evidence suggests that this incident occurred in Apr. 1831 (see RSNY 211). William W. Phelps wrote, "I was thrown into prison at Lyons, N.Y., by a couple of Presbyterian traders, for a small debt, for the purpose, as I was informed, of keeping me from joining the Mormons'" (M&A 1:97).

A branch of the Church was organized by Brigham Young in Lyons. On Apr. 1, 1833, while making his way to Canada on a proselyting mission, Brigham Young passed through "Lyons-town," where he and his brother Joseph Young had taught the gospel at an earlier time. He affirmed, "I remained preaching, and baptized thirteen and organized a Branch of the Church, among whom was a young man, Jonathan Hampton, whom I ordained a Priest and took with me" (MHBY 6 [1801–44]).

Members of the Quorum of the Twelve Apostles passed through the Lyons area in June of 1835 and met in council in the neighboring township of Rose. They had come with the original intent of forming a conference. However, they concluded, "There being so few of the brethren in that region, it was resolved that it was not necessary to establish a conference" at that time (HC 2:225).

A branch was again organized at Lyons consisting of "two elders, 1 priest, 1 teacher, and 22 members," in early May 1843 (HC 5:384).

- **KEY RESEARCH FACILITIES LOCATED AT LYONS.** An important resource facility for regional research is located at the **Wayne County, New York Office of Tourism and History,** 9 Pearl Street (Wayne County Offices), Lyons. Deborah J. Ferrell, County Historian, has been especially helpful on this project.

    The **Wayne County Historical Society Museum** at 21 Butternut St., Lyons, has valuable records and exhibits.

◼ PILGRIMPORT—HOME OF SOLOMON CHAMBERLIN

In the village of Lyons, at the intersection of State 14 and Canal Street, follow Canal Street through the village to the NE. This road will take you to the small settlement of Pilgrimport, Lyons Township, the home of Solomon Chamberlin (sometimes spelled Chamberlain). The home is located one mile NE of the village of Lyons at the three-way junction of CR 244 (Pilgrimport Road), CR 245 (Lock Berlin Road), and Bishop Road. Chamberlin's home is a 1½-story

Solomon Chamberlin home in Pilgrimport, Lyons Township. (1992)

frame home (once a period tavern) and still stands on the NE corner of that intersection. It is privately owned. The dry bed of the original Erie Canal can be seen directly across the street to the south, running parallel to the road. While traveling along the Erie Canal from the township of Lyons en route to Upper Canada (Ontario Province) in the fall of 1829, Solomon took lodging for the night at a farmhouse south of the village of Palmyra. The householders told him of a "gold bible" which had been found by Joseph Smith who lived just ½ mile away. Solomon called on the Smith home and there met members of the Smith and Whitmer families. For two days they instructed him "in the manuscripts of the Book of Mormon." He went with them to the Grandin Press, where they gave him 64 pages of the Book of Mormon. These he carried with him into Canada and he stated, "I preached all that I knew concerning Mormonism, to all both high and low, rich and poor." Speaking of the time of organization of the Church on Apr. 6,

1830, Solomon declared, "A few days after [the organization] I was baptized in the waters of Seneca Lake by Joseph Smith" (BYUS 12, no. 2 [spring]: 314–17).

Phinehas and Joseph Young, brothers of Brigham and preachers for the Reformed Methodist Church, were pursuing their journey to Kingston, Canada, and stopped at the Lyons home of their old acquaintance Solomon Chamberlin. Phinehas stated:

> We had no sooner got seated than he [Solomon] began to preach Mormonism to us. He told us there was a Church organized, and ten or more were baptized, and every body must believe the Book of Mormon or be lost. I told him to hold on, when he had talked about two hours setting forth the wonders of Mormonism—that it was not good to give a colt a bushel of oats at a time, . . . but it made little difference to him, he still talked of Mormonism. (MHBY xix–xx [1801–44])

Solomon, himself once an exhorter for the Reformed Methodists, also went to a conference of that denomination at Manlius, Onondaga Co., where about 40 of their preachers were present. When he attempted to convince them of the truth of the Book of Mormon, they utterly rejected him and ordered him off the premises. However, he said that there were two of their number, "Brigham and his brother Phinehas Young," who "did not oppose me but used me well" (BYUS Spring 1972, 317). Solomon Chamberlin (Chamberlain) remained true to the Church throughout his life. He died at New Harmony, Washington, Co., UT, on Mar. 26, 1862.

Ontario and Monroe Counties

● **1. VALENTOWN MUSEUM AND COUNTRY STORE.** A focal point for information on historical locations in this vicinity can be found at the Valentown Museum and Country Store in Victor Township. The museum and country store are located on the NE corner of the junction of High Street and Valentown Road which is ¼ mile north of I-90 exit 45, just east off of State 96, and immediately east of the East View Mall on what is called Valentown Square.

For many decades the owner and proprietor of the Valentown Museum and Country Store has been J. Sheldon Fisher, the former

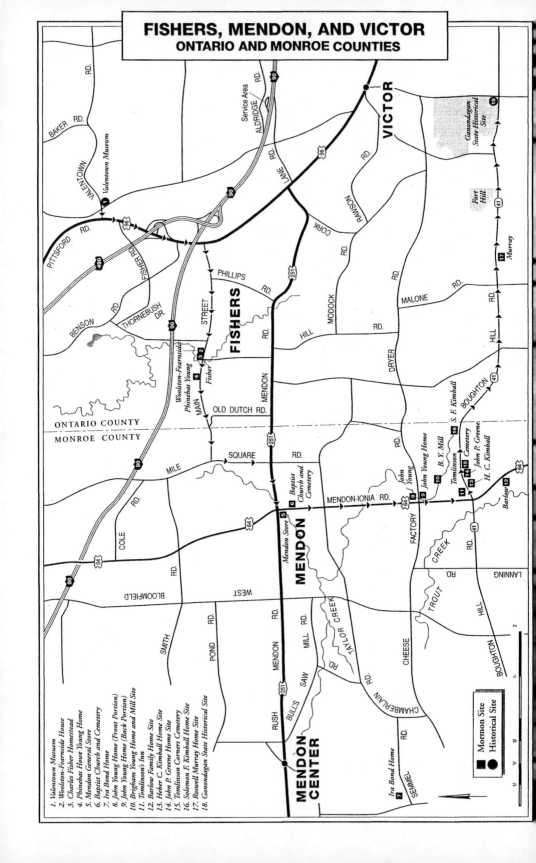

FISHERS, MENDON, AND VICTOR
ONTARIO AND MONROE COUNTIES

1. Valentown Museum
2. Woolston-Fearnside House
3. Charles Fisher Homestead
4. Phinehas Howe Young Home
5. Mendon General Store
6. Baptist Church and Cemetery
7. Ira Bond Home
8. John Young Home (Front Portion)
9. John Young Home (Back Portion)
10. Brigham Young Home and Mill Site
11. Tomlinson's Inn
12. Barlow Family Home Site
13. Heber C. Kimball Home Site
14. John P. Greene Home Site
15. Tomlinson Corners Cemetery
16. Solomon F. Kimball Home Site
17. Roswell Murray Home Site
18. Ganondagan State Historical Site

Mormon Site ■
Historical Site ●

Ontario County historian and an archaeologist. Mr. Fisher is exceptionally well versed in the local history and well acquainted with the Mormon habitation in the area.[4] However, the museum and store, along with historical documents and papers, have now been placed under the direction of the Victor Historical

Valentown Museum and Country Store, Victor Township (1966)

Society. These holdings are an invaluable index to an era and are well worth seeing.

■ **VILLAGE OF FISHERS, VICTOR TOWNSHIP, ONTARIO COUNTY**

The village of Fishers is located one mile west of the intersection of State 96 and County Road 42. It derived its early name, "Fisher's Station," from Charles Fisher, who moved here in 1817. Brigham Young was employed in the community as a carpenter, painter, and glazier. Phinehas Howe Young rented a home in Fishers for a brief period.

■ **2. WOOLSTON-FEARNSIDE HOUSE.** This home is located on the north side of the street at 7864 Main in Fishers. Brigham Young is reported to have built this house in 1829 (JSF).

■ **3. CHARLES FISHER HOMESTEAD.** Local historian Sheldon Fisher stated that this home, on the north side of the street and set back from the road at 7868 Main, had its windows glazed by Brigham Young. He also said that his progenitor, Charles Fisher, bought craft work from Brigham (JSF).

■ **4. PHINEHAS HOWE YOUNG HOME.** At one juncture, Phinehas Howe Young is said to have rented this home on the north side of the street at 8026 Main in Fishers (JSF).

---

[4] The author is indebted to Sheldon Fisher for his past friendship and invaluable assistance over a succession of years in identifying certain key Mormon sites.

■ **VILLAGE OF MENDON, MONROE COUNTY**

The village of Mendon is located at the intersection of State 64 and State 251 in Monroe County. Mendon was not incorporated until Apr. 12, 1833, the year that the widower Brigham Young moved with his two daughters, Elizabeth and Vilate, to Kirtland, OH.

■ **5. MENDON GENERAL STORE.** Brigham Young traded services in the Mendon General Store, which still stands in the village of Mendon

on the SW corner at the intersection of State 64 and State 251 (JSF). An $18.50 promissory note signed by Brigham Young on Mar. 16, 1830, to Milton E. Sheldon, owner of a general store in Mendon, reads: "In good Kitchen Chairs at Fifty Cents apiece, well done off painted and Bottomed according to the usual mode of doing off such chairs." The reverse side of the note is endorsed to show that "Brigham, on

Mendon General Store on the SW corner of the intersection of State 64 and State 251, in Mendon, where Brigham Young, Heber C. Kimball, and other members of the Church purchased goods. The store is in the top left corner of this photo. (1966)

the request of the owner of the note, had made a picket fence and worked 'on A. Parks Barn.'" The Sheldon General Store account book also shows that Brigham took $4.36 of merchandise in June 1829 and $2.34 in Aug. 1829 (BYAM 17–18).

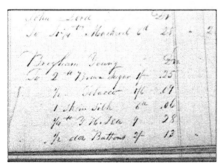

Brigham Young purchases, recorded in the day book of the Mendon General Store. (Courtesy of Wilford C. Wood)

The day book of the Mendon General Store records the purchase and charging habits of many Saints in the area. **Heber C. Kimball** was one of the customers. Drawing on the day book of M. E. Sheldon for 1831 (now in the Wilford C. Wood Museum, Bountiful, UT), biographer Stanley B. Kimball commented on the commodities available to **Vilate Kimball,** wife of Heber C. Kimball:

Vilate did a lot of sewing and made many of the clothes for the family. From a local merchant she purchased for herself and her two children basics like calico, gingham, buttons, thread, indigo, and cloak clasps; for Heber plain shirting, green flannel, cambric, and mull. But once in a while she would

Heber C. Kimball purchases, recorded in the day book of the Mendon General Store. (Courtesy of Wilford C. Wood)

splurge on pretty things, like blue satinette for William, and velvet, lace, and some silk twist for herself and Helen. Heber bought staples like iron, logwood, a scythe, as well as rifle powder, tobacco, and whiskey. The family also used nuts, pepper, tankey tea, and raisins and tried to ward off illness with the panacea of the day—sulphur and molasses. (HCKM 12, 22 n. 7)

Some dishes from the Milton Sheldon store are in the LDS Church Museum of Church History and Art in Salt Lake City (JSF).

■ **6. Baptist Church and Cemetery.** The Baptist meetinghouse and adjoining cemetery were located .2 mile south of the intersection of State 64 and State 251 on the east side of State 64. The meetinghouse has long since disappeared, but the Mendon Cemetery is still used today as a burial ground. Numbers of early Mormon converts, including Heber C. and Vilate Kimball, had been members of the Baptist congregation. As indicated in the "Historical Sketch of the Baptist Church in Mendon," the denomination suffered some severe trials during the period 1833–35, and "they were under the painful necessity of excluding several of the members for imbibing the heresy Mormonism" (HCKM 14, 24 n. 33).

■ **Mendon Township, Monroe County**

Mendon Township, Monroe Co. (originally in Ontario County), was created from Bloomfield, Ontario Co., on May 26, 1812. It is situated 12 miles south of Rochester.

Brigham and Miriam Angeline Works Young brought their daughter Elizabeth (born Sept. 26, 1825, at Port Byron, NY) to Mendon Township from Oswego, NY, in the spring of 1829. According to Brigham Young biographers Richard F. Palmer and Karl D. Butler, Brigham and Miriam had been preceded into the Mendon area by other members of the Young family. Susannah Young Little, a widow (later Mrs. William B. Stilson), relocated in nearby Canandaigua about 1825. By 1826, Rhoda Young and her husband, John Pourtenous Greene, were in Bloomfield, Ontario Co., seven or eight miles south of Mendon. In Sept. 1827 the Greenes were living in Mendon and then apparently moved back to Bloomfield where Samuel H. Smith called on them and left a copy of the Book of Mormon in June 1830. However, they were again living in Mendon Township when the 1830 census was taken. Father John Young and his second wife, Hannah Brown, had moved from Tyrone, NY, to Mendon in 1827. Louisa Young and her husband, Joel H. Sanford, came about this same time. Phinehas Howe Young, who had been living in Cheshire, Ontario Co., just south of Canandaigua, for some three years, came to Mendon in 1829 but is listed as being in Victor in 1830. Lorenzo Dow Young apparently had lived briefly in Mendon but returned to his former home in Hector during the latter part of 1829. Still others of the family, including John Young Jr. and Joseph Young were in Mendon in 1831. Fanny Young and her husband Roswell Murray, were living in the vicinity of Mendon (just over the line in Victor Township) in 1832, the year of their marriage (BYNY 23–24; MHBY viii; DN Mar. 31, 1858).

■ **7. IRA BOND HOME.** The home of Ira Bond still stands on the north side of Semmel Road just .1 mile east of the junction of Semmel Road and Quaker Meetinghouse Road in Mendon (JSF).

Ira Bond and his wife, Charlotte Wilcox, were members of the Mendon Branch. After their immigration to Kirtland, OH, Ira presided over the deacons in that community. He was among those who labored diligently in the construction of the Kirtland Temple. Ira died in 1887 and is buried with his wife, Charlotte, and daughter, Mary E., in the SE corner of the Kirtland Temple Cemetery (HC 2:206, 371; WTSL 17–18).

■ **8. JOHN YOUNG HOME (FRONT PORTION).** The farm and home of John Young, father of Brigham Young, are located 1.6 miles south of the village of Mendon on State 64 (Mendon-Ionia Road) at its junction with Cheese Factory Road. The **front portion** of the house on the NE corner of the intersection of State 64

Home of John and Hannah Brown Young, in Mendon. This is the original front portion of the home. (1998)

and 981 Cheese Factory Road is the front part of John Young's original home. At some juncture it was separated from the back portion of the house at 984 and moved across the street to its present location. A lean-to was built on the east side of the structure in later years. An 1820s barn, apparently the original John Young barn, was built just east of this house. The LDS Church recently disassembled the barn and moved it to the Joseph Smith Sr. farm at Manchester, NY. There, portions of its superstructure have been utilized in the careful reconstruction of a handcrafted 19th century barn by Randy Nash, a historical restoration expert (JSF; DLE).

■ **9. JOHN YOUNG HOME (BACK PORTION).** The **back portion** of the original John Young home at 984 Cheese Factory Road is where the complete house once stood on the SE side of the junction of State 64 and Cheese Factory Road. A new front, empire style in design, was later added to the original back section. The two homes are owned by The Church of

Home of John and Hannah Brown Young, in Mendon. The part of the house on the left was the original back portion of John's home. (1992)

Jesus Christ of Latter-day Saints, but are occupied by private parties.[5]

John Young moved to Mendon from Tyrone, NY, in 1827. He initially purchased eight acres in the SE corner of the township; in 1830 he acquired an additional 45 acres. Historian Anah B. Yates said that Brigham Young built the home that still exists on the site for his father. Joseph Young and Lorenzo Dow Young lived here with their father part of the time. On Apr. 5, 1832, John Young Sr. was baptized into the Latter-day Saint faith in Columbia, Bradford Co., PA, by Daniel Bowen. (Brigham stated that it was Ezra Landon [MHBY vi]. However, Phinehas, who was there, said that it was Daniel Bowen [MHBY xxiv; PEN 82 n. 49].) Phinehas was baptized that same day by Elder Ezra Landon. The next day, Joseph Young was also baptized by Daniel Bowen (MHBY xxiv; BYNY 24, 25, 95n; BYAM 16; HIB 60). John moved to Kirtland, OH, in June 1833. His wife, Hannah, refused to accompany him at the time, staying with family in Tyrone, NY. However, after nearly two years apart she relented and joined him in Kirtland. When the Youngs left Kirtland to follow the Church to Missouri, she apparently again returned to her family in New York and remained with them (BYNY 76–77).

■ **10. BRIGHAM YOUNG HOME AND MILL SITE.** The site of what was a combination home and mill, or woodworking shop, of Brigham and Miriam Works Young is located .2 mile east of the John Young home on Cheese Factory Road and about 450 yards south of the road on a small stream. There is virtually nothing left of what was a two-story structure (a mill on the bottom and dwelling on top) save some submerged wooden pilings or footings in the stream where Brigham had built a sizable undershot waterwheel to power his mill machinery. Some evidence also remains of an archaeological dig conducted by J. Sheldon Fisher (NYHi Oct. 1980, 431–46). The site is owned by the LDS Church.

---

[5] Lynn A. Skabelund, a building contractor and developer from Logan, UT, visited the old John Young farm and the Brigham Young mill site with friends while touring LDS Church history sites. Finding that the farm was up for sale, he made arrangements to purchase the property. The transaction was completed on Jan. 31, 1979, with the purchase of 73 acres from Robert H. and Marian J. Hutchinson of Mendon Township. Lynn was later joined by his brother, Dr. Robert E. Skabelund, in procuring the land, the two homes, and the barn. They subsequently turned these holdings over to the LDS Church for the amount of their original purchase on Dec. 28, 1983 (LAS Jan. 23, 1996).

The Brigham Young home and mill were situated on the property belonging to Brigham's father, John Young Sr. A contemporary, George Allen, described a visit to the log structure:

> His house and shop stood some 80 rods from the highway, nothing but a footpath led to it. . . . I followed this path which lay along the side of a beautiful little stream of clear water noted for the speckled trout it contained. A dam had been thrown across this stream and a sufficient

Brigham Young home and mill site on the creek running through the John Young farm, Mendon. Wood, brick, pottery, and miscellaneous debris mark the site. (1966)

> water power obtained to run a turning lathe in his shop.
>
> On arriving at the house and shop I ascended a rickety outside stair case and was bidden to come in. Pulling a leather string and lifting a wooden latch, enabled me to open the door and I entered.
>
> There was only one room in the house, which served for a bedroom-kitchen-sitting room and parlor. . . . There was a bed in one corner, a cupboard for dishes in another, a table and a few splint bottom chairs. (BYNY 26)

Brigham Young stated that he moved to Mendon with his wife, Miriam, and little daughter, Elizabeth, in the spring of 1829. Miriam gave birth to a second daughter, Vilate, on June 1, 1830. It was during the spring of 1830 that Brigham first saw a copy of the Book of Mormon—a copy Samuel H. Smith placed with Brigham's brother Phinehas in Apr. 1830. Brigham also mentioned reading from a second copy of the Book of Mormon which Samuel

Timbers and other debris of Brigham Young's home and mill. (1977)

Chair and brick made by Brigham Young in Mendon.

Brick made by Brigham Young with his initials in it. (1966)

placed on loan in the home of Brigham's sister Rhoda Young Greene during June 1830. He was likewise proselyted at a very early juncture by an old friend from the Methodist Reformed Church, Solomon Chamberlin (Chamberlain), who preached to both Brigham and Phinehas from the Book of Mormon (BYUS 12, no. 2 [spring]: 317).

It remained, however, for Elder Eleazer Miller and other elders from Columbia, Bradford Co., PA, to complete the conversion of Brigham Young. These elders had first proselyted among the Young family in 1831, and Elders Eleazer Miller and Alpheus Gifford returned again in Apr. 1832. During the intervening time, there had been an exchange of visits when members of the Young family journeyed to Columbia and met with the branch of the Church there on two different occasions.

By Apr. 1832 Brigham Young was prepared for baptism at the hands of Elder Miller. He said of Eleazer's great humility:

> If all the talent, tact, wisdom, and refinement of the world had been sent to me with the Book of Mormon, and had declared, in the most exalted of earthly eloquence, the truth of it, undertaking to prove it by learning and worldly wisdom, they would have been to me like the smoke which arises only to vanish away. But when I saw a man without eloquence, or talents for public speaking, who could only say, "I know, by the power of the Holy Ghost, that the Book of Mormon is true, that Joseph Smith is a Prophet of the Lord," the Holy Ghost proceeding from that individual illuminated my understanding, and light, glory, and immortality were before me. I was encircled by them, filled with them, and I knew for myself that the testimony of the man was true. (JD 1:90)

On Sunday, Apr. 15, 1832, Brigham Young was baptized in Mendon Township by Eleazer Miller. (Numbers of histories have recorded his baptism as being on Apr. 14, 1832, but Brigham Young specifically corrected this to be Apr. 15 [see JD 9:219].) Remembering that meaningful event, he said, "I recollect the Sunday morning on which I was baptized, in my own little mill stream." Brigham also recalled that Elder Miller confirmed him at the water's edge, after which, he said, "We returned home, about two miles, the weather being cold and snowy; and before my clothes were dry on my back he laid his hands on me and ordained me an Elder, at which I marvelled. According to the words of the Savior, I felt a humble, child-like spirit, witnessing unto me that my sins were forgiven." Miriam was baptized "about three weeks afterwards" (MHBY 2–3; RSNY 184–85).

Brigham Young and Heber C. Kimball spent the summer of 1832 preaching Mormonism in the surrounding townships of Hector, Henrietta, Reading, Hornby, Patten, Avon, and Warsaw (BYAM 33). Before Brigham left, he placed Miriam, sick with consumption (tuberculosis), in the Heber C. Kimball home under the watchful care of Heber's wife, Vilate, a niece of Brigham. Miriam, age 27, died at the Kimball home on Sept. 8, 1832, leaving Brigham with the two little girls, Elizabeth and Vilate. Brigham said of Miriam, "In her expiring moments she clapped her hands and praised the Lord, and called upon brother Kimball and all around to praise the Lord. After my wife's death I made my home at bro. Kimball's" (MHBY 3).

Brigham, his brother, Joseph, and Heber C. Kimball went to visit the Prophet Joseph Smith in Kirtland in Sept. 1832. After his return he made two missionary journeys into Canada and on the latter occasion formed a Canadian company of converts, which he led to Kirtland in July 1833. Returning to Mendon he settled his business and in Sept. 1833 moved his family from western New York to Kirtland, OH (MHBY 3–7).

■ **11. TOMLINSON'S INN.** Tomlinson's Inn is located on the NE corner of Tomlinson Corners, at the junction of State 64 and Boughton Hill Road (CR 41). The Victorian front portion of the existing home was added in later years, while the elongated structure extending towards the east on the back end of the house is the old Tomlinson Inn. In an attempt to preserve the Mormon legacy

Tomlinson's Inn, Mendon. The extension on the east side of this home, as shown in the right side of this 1993 photo, is the original inn.

associated with the old inn, David L. Cook, president of the Rochester New York Palmyra Stake, purchased the inn and converted it into a bed-and-breakfast. Visitors are welcome to tour the historic structure.

It was here that **Samuel H. Smith** sold a copy of the **Book of Mormon** to **Phinehas H. Young** in Apr. 1830, saying, "There is a book, sir, I wish you to read." Samuel then said, "If you will read this book with a prayerful heart, and ask God to give you a witness, you will know of the truth of this work." Supposing that he would expose the erroneous nature of the work Phinehas stated, "I commenced and read every word in the book the same week. The week following I did the same, but to my surprise I could not find the errors I anticipated, but felt a conviction that the book was true." This copy then began to circulate through the family, going initially to his father, John Young Sr., and then to his sister, Fanny Murray, (MHBY xvii–xix). Nathan Tomlinson, a convert to Mormonism, was the owner of the inn.

Many of the meetings connected with the Mendon Branch were conducted in this structure after the branch was organized in the spring of 1832. The members of the Mendon Branch have been identified as follows: John Young Sr. and his wife, Hannah; Edward Young; Brigham Young, his wife, Miriam, and their two daughters; Phinehas H. Young, his wife, Clarissa Hamilton, and their five children; Louisa Young, her husband, Joel H. Sanford, and their five children; Rhoda Young, her husband, John P. Greene, and their seven children; Susannah Young, her husband, William B. Stilson, and their four children; Fanny Young, and her husband, Roswell Murray; Joseph Young; Heber C. Kimball, his wife, Vilate (daughter of Roswell Murray and his deceased wife, Susannah), and their two children; Ira Bond and his wife, Charlotte; Rufus Parks; John Morton and his wife, Betsey; Nathan Tomlinson and wife; Israel Barlow; Annis Barlow; Jonathan Watson Barlow; Truman Barlow; George Lockwood; Anis Lockwood; Rhoda Lockwood; Julia A. Lockwood; Ezra Thayer and Hiram Page (perhaps missionaries in the area); and Isaac Flummerfelt, his wife, and their family (BYNY 68–69; IBS 102–3; HFT May 18, 1922).

Heber C. Kimball lived near the Tomlinson Inn, and in all probability the inn was the meeting place referred to by Heber when he described the sister Saints coming from nearby Victor Township to worship on the Sabbath Day:

> Women would come from Victor, a distance of three miles, to the town of Mendon, New York, where I lived; and I have seen them walk barefooted until they came near where I lived, and then they would put on their white stockings and shoes to go into meeting; and when they came out of meeting and had passed off a little out of sight, they would pull off their shoes and stockings and go home barefooted, for the purpose of saving their fine shoes and stockings which they had spun and knit out of flax. (BYNY 69)

■ **12. HOME SITE OF ANNIS GILLETT BARLOW AND HER SON ISRAEL BARLOW.** The home site of Annis Gillett Barlow and her son Israel Barlow is located on State 64 (the Mendon-Ionia Road), on the west side of the road about ½ mile south of the intersection of the Boughton Hill Road and State 64. Local historian J. Sheldon Fisher stated that what he believed to be the original Barlow house "stood vacant and neglected for many years and the exact location has now been obliterated by new housing" (JSF). There is apparently no land deed.

Annis Gillett Barlow's family consisted of both Barlows and Lockwoods as a result of two marriages. Each of these families were represented among the early membership of the Mendon Branch. A son, **Israel Barlow,** was a licensed exhorter for the Methodist Reformed Church at the time of his baptism by Brigham Young on May 16, 1832. The family moved to Ohio in about 1831 or 1832. Israel was recruited as a member of Zion's Camp in 1834, and in Feb. 1835 he was named as one of the seventy men comprising the First Quorum of Seventy in Kirtland. He died as a patriarch in West Bountiful, UT, on Nov. 1, 1883 (IBS 76, 84, 99, 102–3; HC 2:63, 183, 203–4; BE 4:687).

■ **13. HEBER C. KIMBALL HOME SITE.** The precise location of the Heber C. Kimball home site is in the process of being determined.

After an exhaustive examination of land deeds in the area, local historian J. Sheldon Fisher believes that what some have identified as the home of Heber and Vilate on the NE corner of the junction of State 64 and Boughton Hill Road (directly west of the Tomlinson's Inn) is *not* the right home for the Kimballs. Rather, he is of the opinion that the Heber C. Kimball home is at 806 Boughton Hill Road, on the south side, just .2 mile east of Tomlinson Corners (the intersection of State 64 and the Boughton Hill Road). He stated that "the framework is still there although the exterior is greatly altered" (JSF). Offering yet another location, Stanley B. Kimball observed: "Land records suggest this first home was located about a quarter-mile east of 'Tomlinson's Corners' on the north side of Boughton Hill Road, where Heber eventually owned property on both sides of the road" (HCKM 11). Additional research of the site is ongoing.

Not long after his marriage to Vilate in 1822, Heber bought out the pottery business of his brother Charles S. Kimball and also occupied himself at the blacksmith's trade. Late in the fall of 1831 Heber and Vilate decided to unite with the Baptist Church and were baptized by Elder Elijah Weaver. However, their first sacrament with that denomination would be their last. In Nov. 1831 Alpheus Gifford, his brother, and four other friends who were investigating the gospel from Rutland, Tioga Co., PA, and Columbia, Bradford Co., PA, passed through the area on a visit to see the Prophet in Kirtland, OH. Heber C. Kimball and Brigham Young traveled together to the home of Phinehas Young in Victor Township to listen to the missionaries preach. Heber said, "I was convinced that they taught the truth, and I was constrained to believe their testimony. I saw that I had only received a part of the ordinances under the Baptist Church" (HCKM 14–17). However, his baptism into Mormonism did not occur until Apr. 16, 1832, when Alpheus Gifford again came through on yet another visit to Mendon from Pennsylvania. Alpheus broached the subject of his being baptized. Heber affirmed, "I jumped up, pulled off my apron, washed my hands and started with him with my sleeves rolled up to my shoulders, and went the distance of one mile where he baptized me in a small stream in the woods" (HCKM 19). Vilate was baptized two weeks later.

Brigham Young was blessed to enjoy one of the gifts of the Spirit while at Heber C. Kimball's home. It occurred just a few weeks after Brigham's baptism. While family prayer was being offered Elder Alpheus Gifford began speaking in tongues. Brigham affirmed, "Soon the Spirit came on me, and I spoke in tongues, and we thought only of the day of Pentecost, when the Apostles were clothed upon with cloven tongues of fire" (MHBY 3).

■ **14. JOHN P. AND RHODA YOUNG GREENE'S HOME SITE.** In 1827 John P. and Rhoda Young Greene were living very close to the Heber C. Kimball home, which was located on Boughton Hill Road. Although we do not know the exact site of the home, we know it was within 100 yards of the Kimball home.

Heber C. Kimball tells of a unique experience had by him and the Greenes next door on the night of Sept. 22, 1827:

> I had retired to bed, when John P. Greene, who was living within a hundred steps of my house, came and waked me up, calling upon me to come out and behold the scenery in the heavens. I woke up and called my wife and Sister Fanny Young (sister to Brigham Young), who was living with us, and we went out-of-doors. . . . We looked to the eastern horizon, and beheld a white smoke arise toward the heavens. . . . In this bow an army moved, commencing from the east and marching to the west. . . . After I became acquainted with Mormonism, I learned that this took place the same evening that Joseph Smith received the records of the Book of Mormon. . . . My wife, being frightened at what she saw, said, "Father Young [John Young Sr.], what does all this mean?" "Why, it's one of the signs of the coming of the Son of Man," he replied, in a lively, pleased manner. (LHCK 31–33)

Lucy Mack Smith stated that Samuel H. Smith called on the John P. Greene family in Bloomfield and left a copy of the Book of Mormon in their home during June 1830 (HJS 170). However, when the 1830 census was taken the Greenes were again living in Mendon Township. By 1832 the Greenes were residing in Warsaw, Wyoming Co., NY, and were proselyting in that area (MHBY xxxi).

■ **15. THE TOMLINSON CORNERS CEMETERY (SANDY HILL CEMETERY).** The Tomlinson Corners Cemetery is located on the south side of

The tombstone of Miriam Angeline Works Young, the first wife of Brigham Young, located in the Tomlinson Corners Cemetery, Mendon. (1966)

Boughton Hill Road .3 mile east of the junction of State 64 and the Boughton Hill Road (CR 41).

Miriam Angeline Works Young is buried right in the SW corner of the cemetery. Initially her marker was just a fieldstone with the "rudely cut letters M.Y." (HFT Feb. 2, 1922). However, the inscription on her modern granite tombstone reads, "Miriam Works Young, wife of Brigham Young, Born June 7, 1806 at Aurelius, New York. Died Sep. 8, 1832 at Mendon, New York." On the next row east from Miriam's grave is the burial site of Heber C. Kimball's parents, Solomon F. Kimball and Anna Spaulding. Solomon's original headstone has been preserved by adhering it to a modern-day granite marker. The modern inscription on the opposite side reads, "Solomon F. Kimball died July 9, 1825 age 50. Father of Heber C. Kimball and great grandfather of Spencer W. Kimball the 12th President of The Church of Jesus Christ of Latter-day Saints." Two of Heber and Vilate's children, Judith Marvin and Roswell Heber, are likewise interred in the cemetery. Also Heber's older brother, Charles S., and Charles's wife, Judith Marvin, are buried beside Solomon Kimball (HCKM 12, 22 n. 11).

■ **16. SOLOMON F. KIMBALL HOME.** The frame home of Solomon F. Kimball is located on the north side of the road at 933 Boughton Hill Road, and is .7 mile east from the junction of State 64 and the Boughton Hill Road (Tomlinson Corners), or just .4 mile east of the Tomlinson Corners Cemetery. The house is privately owned.

Solomon F. Kimball, the father of Heber C. Kimball and great-grandfather of President Spencer W. Kimball, died of consumption (tuberculosis) on July 8, 1825, at Heber's home. He had been preceded in death by his wife, Anna Spaulding, who also died of consumption that same year in West Bloomfield, NY, Feb. 25, 1825 (DN Mar. 31, 1858; HCKM 22, n. 11).

■ **VILLAGE OF VICTOR, ONTARIO COUNTY**

The village of Victor is located nine miles NW of Canandaigua on State 96. The township of Victor was taken from Bloomfield on May 26, 1812.

■ **17. ROSWELL MURRAY HOME SITE.** The Roswell Murray home site is located in Victor Township, 2.9 miles east of Tomlinson Corners at 7525 Boughton Hill Road (CR 41) on the south side of the road. This site is between the intersections of Strong and Malone Roads with Boughton Hill Road. The original Roswell Murray home burned, and the old camp schoolhouse was moved onto the site just 30 feet south of where the Roswell Murray home had stood. The camp schoolhouse is the existing home, and is privately owned (IAD).

Roswell and Susannah Fitch Murray brought their family from Florida, Montgomery Co., NY, to Ontario Co. about 1810, and subsequently bought the farm in what became Victor Township (HOC 201). In the summer of 1822 Heber C. Kimball was traveling Boughton Hill Road between the towns of Mendon and Victor. He stopped at the Murray household and requested a drink of water from Roswell, who was in the yard. Roswell drew the water from the well and requested his daughter Vilate to bring a glass from the house to serve the stranger. Impressed by the young lady, Heber soon found an excuse to return to the Murray home for yet another drink from "Milatie" or "My-Laty" as he called her (she was known to her family as "Laty"). More visits followed, and the couple was married on Nov. 7, 1822 (HCKM 10–11; LHCK 24–25).

Following the death of his first wife, Susannah Fitch, Roswell married Fanny Young, Brigham Young's sister, in Feb. 1832. The couple affiliated with the Mendon Branch of the Church when it was formed. Fanny was baptized by Elder Alpheus Gifford in Apr. 1832 (BYNY 69; MHBY viii). A local account indicates that "the Mormons held meetings in this neighborhood [Victor Township], using a barn for the purpose, and on one occasion the indignation of the people was shown by an attack with stones, and the assembly dispersed" (HOC 201–2).

After moving to Illinois, Roswell Murray returned to Victor for an extended visit with his family during the latter part of 1839. He had traveled part of the way with Brigham Young and Heber C.

Kimball, who were en route to missions in Great Britain. Roswell stayed in the home of his daughter, Lucretia, wife of Nathaniel Campbell, and died there in 1840. He was interred beside his wife in the cemetery on the Ellis farm (which Roswell had sold to the Ellis family) beside his first wife, Susannah, and other relatives (HCKM 67, 75; HVNY 16–17). The small family cemetery is located on a grassy knoll about 70 yards immediately SW of the existing home site. Its few headstones are now down and in disarray. Some of the remains of individuals have been removed and reburied in the Tomlinson Corners Cemetery in Mendon Township (IAD).

PHINEHAS HOWE AND CLARISSA YOUNG HOME. We do not know the exact location of the Phinehas H. Young family home site in Victor Township.

Phinehas Howe Young was living in Victor when Mormon missionaries came from Bradford, Columbia Co., PA, and proselyted in that region in 1831. Heber C. Kimball remembered, "About three weeks after I joined the Baptist church (Fall 1831), five Elders of the Church of Jesus Christ came from Pennsylvania to the house of Phinehas H. Young, in Victor. Their names were Eleazer Miller, Elial Strong, Alpheus Gifford, Enos Curtis and Daniel Bowen," (BYNY 66). As indicated earlier, these missionaries were among those instrumental in converting the Young family and numbers of their friends.

Phinehas Howe Young was baptized by Ezra Landon on Apr. 5, 1832, in Columbia, Bradford Co., PA, during a visit with the Saints in that area. Phinehas, his wife, Clarissa, and their five children were members of the Mendon Branch of the Church. The Phinehas Young family began their journey west to join the body of the Saints in Sept. 1832 (MHBY xxiv–xxv; BYNY 67–69; HIB 60–61).

●   **18. GANONDAGAN STATE HISTORIC SITE/FORT HILL.** The Ganondagan State Historic Site Visitors Center is located on the NW corner of the intersection of Boughton Hill Road (County Road 41) and the Victor-Holcomb Road (County Road 3), Victor Township.

Here is an opportunity to visit the site of an Iroquois community where thousands of Seneca lived 300 years ago. A video program surveys the history of Ganondagan, and illustrated signs mark the trails at significant locations.

■ **VILLAGE OF CANANDAIGUA, ONTARIO COUNTY**

Canandaigua is located seven miles SW of I-90, exit 43, on State 21 in Ontario County. The site was acquired by Phelps and Gorham as part of a 1788 purchase from Massachusetts, with the first settlers arriving in 1789. Ontario County was divided off from Montgomery County in 1789, with Canandaigua as the county seat. The village is beautifully situated at the outlet of Canandaigua Lake. Canandaigua is the site of many historical events of interest to Latter-day Saints.

JOSEPH SMITH SR. ARTICLED FOR LAND IN FARMINGTON TOWNSHIP THROUGH AN AGENT AT CANANDAIGUA. When the Smith family arrived in Palmyra from Norwich, VT, in 1816, Palmyra was part of Ontario County. In 1820, when Joseph Sr. articled for 100 acres in Lot 1 of Farmington Township (changed to Manchester Township in 1822), he went to Canandaigua to enter into an agreement with Zachariah Seymour, who had the power of attorney for the Nicholas Evertson estate, which owned the land. During the financially difficult year of 1825, the Smiths worked through John Greenwood, a lawyer who had replaced Seymour as agent, in an attempt to save their Manchester property. In spite of an intensive effort, they were unable to pay the mortgage and lost the farm that same year. They remained as renters on their former farm until the spring of 1829, when they were obliged to leave.

FATHER SMITH WAS IMPRISONED UNDER AN OLD NEW YORK DEBTOR'S LAW AT CANANDAIGUA. In Oct. and Nov. 1830, **Joseph Smith Sr.** was imprisoned in Canandaigua for 30 days because he could not pay a $14.00 debt owed to a Quaker who had purchased the note. The Quaker said that if Father Smith would agree to burn the copies of the Book of Mormon in his possession, the note would be voided immediately; but Joseph Sr. would not do this. Samuel H. Smith spent a night in jail with his father, trying to see to his needs. Lucy Mack Smith reported a redeeming element in all of her husband's difficulties: "He preached during his confinement there every Sunday, and when he was released he baptized two persons whom he had thus converted" (HJS 179–86; NEW 109–10).

WILLIAM W. PHELPS WAS CONVERTED BY THE BOOK OF MORMON WHILE LIVING IN CANANDAIGUA. William W. Phelps moved from Trumansburgh, NY, to Canandaigua in Apr. 1828 to edit a local community newspaper, the *Ontario Phoenix.* On Apr. 3, 1830, just

three days before the organization of the Church, William purchased a copy of the Book of Mormon. He sat up that first night comparing its contents with that of the Bible and had soon read the whole volume. He later declared:

William W. Phelps
(Courtesy of RLDSLA)

> By that book I learned the right way to God; by that book I received the fulness of the everlasting gospel; by that book I found the new covenant; by that book I learned when the Lord would gather scattered Israel; by that book I saw that the Lord had set his hand the second time to gather his people, and place them in their own land; by that book I learned that the poor Indians of America were some of the remnants of Israel; by that book I learned that the New Jerusalem, even Zion was to be built up on this continent; by that book I found a key to the holy prophets; and by that book began to unfold the mysteries of God, and I was made glad. (M&A Sept. 1835, 177–78)

Phelps paid a visit to the Prophet Joseph Smith at the Peter Whitmer Sr. farm in Fayette, NY, on Christmas Eve 1830, conversing at length with Joseph and a visitor from Ohio, Sidney Rigdon. Learning of the intention of the Saints to go to Kirtland, OH, William began to contemplate his personal commitment and obligations to the Restoration. In the summer of 1831 he resigned his editorship in Canandaigua. He then took his family to Kirtland, where he was baptized on June 10, 1831.

W. W. Phelps became the editor of *The Evening and the Morning Star* in Jackson Co., MO, and publisher of the Book of Commandments, which contained 65 revelations given through the Prophet Joseph Smith. During July 1834 he was called as a counselor to President David Whitmer in Clay Co., Missouri. Over 30 of his hymns were included in the 1835 hymnal (selected by Emma Smith) and 15 are yet retained in the 1985 hymnal. The reader will recognize such favorites as "The Spirit of God," "Praise to the Man," and "Now Let Us Rejoice" (RSNY 202–13; NEW 101–3).

SUSANNAH YOUNG LITTLE. Susannah Young Little, Brigham Young's sister, lived in Canandaigua. Susannah was widowed by the death of her husband, James Little, in 1822. She moved to Canandaigua from Aurelius, NY, in 1825. Susannah was subsequently married to William B. Stilson. She was baptized in June 1832. The Stilsons and their four children were members of the Mendon Branch and remained in the Canandaigua/Mendon area until their emigration west in 1832 (BYNY 23, 69).

● **THE ONTARIO COUNTY HISTORICAL SOCIETY.** The Ontario County Historical Society is located at 55 North Main Street in Canandaigua. The Society has an excellent manuscript collection in addition to its extensive library and museum.

■ **BRIGHAM YOUNG LIVED IN "NUMBER NINE."** "Number Nine" refers to School District No. 9 in the township of Canandaigua. The district embraced a small rural farming community located about three miles SW of the village of Canandaigua at the junction of County Road 32 and Wool House Road. Brigham Young lived in a house which was located on the west side of Wool House Road, about .3 mile south of the junction of Nott Road and Wool House Road. His employer, Mr. Jonathan Mack, lived on the opposite side. Brigham stated, "I helped to finish his new house, so that he moved into it before I left the place." The home built for Jonathan Mack by Brigham Young no longer stands, but the original Mack home still stands on the west side. Interestingly, in the census of 1830 the Brigham Young family is listed as living in both Canandaigua and Mendon townships (BYNY 26, 96 n. 44; JSF).

■ **VILLAGE OF CHESHIRE—Home of Phinehas Howe Young**

Cheshire is located 4.3 miles SW of the village of Canandaigua on State 21. **Phinehas H. Young** joined the Methodist Reformed Church in Apr. 1824 and subsequently visited the small settlement of Cheshire on a preaching assignment, having received a license to speak in public. A Methodist congregation of 45 members was soon raised up, and Phinehas moved his family to the community. Here he sustained himself by his own labors. After visiting his brother-in-law John P. Greene in Mendon and learning that numbers of his father's family were locating in that area, he established his home in Mendon during the spring of 1828 (MHBY xiv–xvii).

■ **ROCHESTER, MONROE COUNTY**

The city of Rochester is located seven miles north of I-90 at exit 46. It is the county seat of Monroe County. Rochester was incorporated as the village of "Rochesterville" on Mar. 21, 1817, and its name was changed to "Rochester" on Apr. 12, 1822. Rochester was enlarged and incorporated as a city on Apr. 28, 1834.

JOSEPH SMITH SOUGHT A PUBLISHER FOR THE BOOK OF MORMON. When Egbert B. Grandin of Palmyra initially refused to publish the Book of Mormon, Joseph Smith had to look elsewhere to print the work. The Prophet applied to Thurlow Weed, of Rochester, the former editor and publisher of the *Rochester Telegraph* and then the publisher of the *Anti-Masonic Enquirer.* Weed also refused to print the book. Joseph was persistent and on the following day, Thurlow said, "He came again, accompanied by Martin Harris, a substantial farmer residing near Palmyra, who adopted the Mormon faith, and who offered to become security for the expense of printing. But I again declined" (JSPM 51–52).

The Prophet then went to the Rochester office of Elihu F. Marshall, a book publisher who "gave his terms for the printing and binding of the book, with his acceptance of the proffered mode of security for payment." However, Joseph made a last attempt to secure the services of Egbert B. Grandin, who having reconsidered the proposition agreed to publish the Book of Mormon. Thus, the Rochester printing establishment of Marshall was bypassed (JSPM 52).

ORSON HYDE IN ROCHESTER. In the spring of 1836 several of the Apostles went into the state of New York to perform missions. Orson Hyde "labored in the vicinity of Rochester" before going into Canada to join Parley P. Pratt in the Toronto area (MS 26:790–91).

Livingston County

■ **LIMA—Birthplace of Mary Elizabeth and Caroline Amelia Rollins**

Lima is located at the junction of U.S. 20, State 5, and State 15A in Lima Township.

Mary Elizabeth Rollins was born in Lima to John P. Rollins and Keziah Keturah Van Benthuysen on Apr. 9, 1818. She was followed by her sister, Caroline Amelia Rollins, born May 1, 1820. When Caroline was six months old, her father died in a tragic shipwreck on Lake Ontario in Nov. 1821. Keziah's sister, Elizabeth, who had gone to Chagrin, OH, married Algernon Sidney Gilbert, an Ohio businessman, on Sept. 29, 1823. The couple established themselves in Mentor, OH, where Sidney set up a mercantile trade with Newel K. Whitney at Kirtland. To aid the widowed Keziah, Elizabeth and Sidney invited Keziah's son, John Henry Rollins, and her daughter, Mary Elizabeth Rollins, to live with them at an early juncture. By 1829 the Gilberts were also joined by Keziah and daughter Caroline.

In Kirtland the Gilbert and Rollins families embraced the gospel taught to them by Oliver Cowdery and other missionaries who visited with them during Oct. and Nov. 1830. In Oct. 1832, the combined household immigrated to Zion, Jackson Co., MO. It was Mary Elizabeth and her sister, Caroline Amelia, who courageously saved some of the loose, unbound sheets of the Book of Commandments from a mob as it pillaged the Saints' printing establishment in the Independence, MO, home of William W. Phelps on July 20, 1833. The sheets were later bound into books, and Sister Sally Phelps gave one to Mary Elizabeth, which she prized very highly (ASG 7–12; UGHM 17:196).

■ **VILLAGE OF LIVONIA—Home of the Alva and Sarah Burtts Beman Family**

Livonia is located at the junction of U.S. 20A and State 15, Livonia Township.

In Livonia, Alva (Alvah) and Sarah (Sally) Burtts Beman (Beaman) lived with their family. The Bemans were considered well-to-do. The Beman home was one of refinement and culture. The daughters received a good education and were gifted singers—

as was Alva. Three of the daughters married influential Church members: Artimesia married Erastus Snow, Mary Adeline married Joseph Bates Noble, and Louisa became a plural wife of the Prophet Joseph Smith. In the fall of 1846, after the martyrdom of the Prophet, Louisa married Brigham Young at Winter Quarters (ES 43, 736–37, 745; OPH 19:202–5).

Alva and his family became early converts to Mormonism. Alva was acquainted with the Prophet Joseph and his family at the time the plates of the Book of Mormon were being kept in the Smiths' Manchester home in Sept. 1827. Lucy Mack Smith said that Alva Beman (she called him Braman) came from the village of Livonia and assisted the Prophet in taking up a portion of the hearth and burying the "Record and breast-plate" underneath it for fear that the mob would come to the home that night in search of them (HJS 112). Martin Harris remembered the plates being put into "an old Ontario glass-box" when they were later taken from another hiding place in the Smiths' cooper shop. "Old Mr. Beman sawed off the ends, making the box the right length to put them in, and when they went in he said he heard them jink, but he was not permitted to see them," Harris recalled. "He told me so" (SH June 1, 1881, 167). The Bemans lived in both Livonia and Avon, Livingston Co.[6] (See Avon, for additional insights on the Beman family.)

During the spring and summer of 1830, Samuel Smith performed missionary labors in Ontario, Monroe, and Livingston Counties. On one of his returns to the area, he took his father and mother, Joseph Sr. and Lucy Mack Smith, with him. Their route took them as far as Livonia, where they stayed the night with the Alva Beman family and then returned home the next day (HJS 169–71).

■ THE "MORMON BARN," GENESEO TOWNSHIP

From the Livingston Co. junction of I-390 and U.S. 20A the **"Mormon Barn"** is 1 mile east on U.S. 20A at the junction of 20A and CR 28, north side of road. Or the barn is .4 mile west of Lakeville, Lavonia Township, on U.S. 20A. The "Mormon Barn"

---

[6] In the 1830 U.S. Census the Bemans are listed in Livonia. However, on Jan. 20, 1831, Alvah and Sally Beman sold their land in Livonia (see Deeds 10:30). They then purchased new acreage in the town of Avon that same year (Deeds 8:593).

stands just behind the McPhail House Bed and Breakfast at 5477 Lakeville Rd., Geneseo, NY. The barn and home are private property.

Roger Whittles (also Wattles), his wife, Sarah Mason, and their son David moved to the Lakeville area in 1797. They located at what developed as the intersection of the Canandaigua-to-Geneseo stagecoach route (east–west) and the Dansville-to-Rochester route (north–south). David, who married Sarah Smith in 1827, built a larger English barn that same year and attached it to the smaller barn. Soon after the organization of the Church, the Whittles received requests for the use of the barn, first as a shelter and then as a place of meeting. Reportedly, Joseph Smith and his brother Samuel "slept in the barn loft and held religious services on the barn floor." Sarah recalled the names of "Mr. Pratt, Beaman, Boynton, Risden [Rigdon?], [and] Bosley" as being associated with the meetings conducted in the barn. The names of Joseph Smith's parents, and later that of Freeman Nickerson, have also been linked to gatherings in the "Mormon Barn"[7](TMB 2, 4–5, 8–9, 16–27; BGC 131–33).

■ GENESEO, GENESEO TOWNSHIP

Geneseo, the county seat of Livingston Co., is located at the junction of U.S. 20A and State 39.

During a period from the summer of 1832 through July 1833, a succession of elders including Ezra Landon, Brigham Young, Lorenzo D. Young, and Heber C. Kimball, labored in the area (PEN 87, 89). In Jan. 1835 the branch of the Church in Geneseo was reported to have "24 members in good standing" (M&A 1:75).

■ AVON, AVON TOWNSHIP

Avon is located at the junction of U.S. 20 and State 39.

David W. Patten preached at the home of a Father Bosley in Avon during 1833. There was a man present who would neither be civil nor keep quiet. Elder Patten told the man to either be quiet or he would put him out. To that, the fellow replied, "You can't do

---

[7] Dr. Russell A. Judkins of State University of New York at Geneseo has been of tremendous assistance in opening up available research materials and resource facilities relative to this and other area sites.

it." Elder Patten then declared: "In the name of the Lord I will do it." At the same time, he walked up to the man, seized him with both hands, carried him to the door, and threw him out about 10 feet onto a pile of wood—which quieted him for the moment. From this circumstance went forth the saying: "David Patten had cast out one devil, soul and body" (BE 1:76–77).

On Mar. 17, 1834, a conference was held in the Beman home in Avon (the Bemans had lived in Livonia but now resided in Avon). Among those present were the Prophet Joseph Smith, Sidney Rigdon, Parley P. Pratt, Lyman Wight, John Murdock, Orson Pratt, and Orson Hyde. These brethren had come to "obtain young and middle-aged men to go and assist in the redemption of Zion, according to the commandment [recruitment of Zion's Camp]; and for the Church to gather up their riches, and send them to purchase lands according to the commandment of the Lord" (HC 2:44; D&C 103). Joseph Bates Noble of Avon was one of those recruited to march (BE 4:691).

The Bemans gathered with the Saints in Kirtland, OH, where Alva was chosen to preside over the elders quorum in Jan. 1836 (HC 2:370). Alva died in Kirtland on Nov. 15, 1837, and his companion, Sarah, died in Nauvoo on Sept. 29, 1840.

Allegany County

■ FRIENDSHIP—Residence of the Sidney Rigdon Family

The village of Friendship is located in west central Allegany Co. on State 17. It was here that Sidney Rigdon made his home following his 1844–47 difficulties with the Church of Christ in Pennsylvania.[8]

Sidney Rigdon, who had done much for Mormonism in the formative years of the Restoration as First Counselor in the First Presidency to the Prophet Joseph Smith, turned against the Twelve Apostles in Nauvoo, IL, following the June 27, 1844, martyrdom of Joseph Smith. His actions warranted his excommunication on Sept. 8, 1844 (T&S 5:647–55, 660–67; SR 355–58). Sidney then took his family to Pittsburgh, PA, where he initially organized his followers under the name of The Church of Jesus Christ of Latter Day Saints. However, in

---

[8] The author is indebted to Peggy Brown, Friendship town historian, for supplying key information on the Rigdons and locations of related sites.

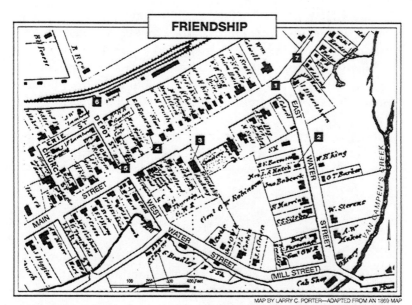

FRIENDSHIP

MAP BY LARRY C. PORTER—ADAPTED FROM AN 1869 MAP

their April conference of 1845, they adopted the name the Church of Christ (SR 367–77).

Beginning in Apr. 1845 an attempt was made to gather his people to the Cumberland Valley in south-central Pennsylvania, 1.5 miles west of Greencastle, Franklin Co. The 390-acre property had belonged to Andrew G. McLanahan and had been named by Andrew "Adventure Farm." Unable to obtain the monies required to maintain their payments, the farm was foreclosed in Aug. 1847 and sold

Sidney Rigdon
(Courtesy of RLDSLA)

at a sheriff's sale to the highest bidder, who turned out to be the previous owner, Andrew G. McLanahan. Rigdon had departed the community prior to the sale. With the Church of Christ in considerable disarray, Rigdon took his wife, Phebe, and family to a place near Cuba, NY, known as the Jackson Hill Farm. Since 1844 the farm had belonged to George W. Robinson, who had married Sidney Rigdon's daughter Athalia. In 1844 George had traded a farm in Nauvoo for the Jackson Hill Farm in New York. George and Athalia left the Rigdons to run the Jackson Hill Farm in 1847 while they moved into nearby Friendship. Unfortunately for the Rigdons, George decided to sell the farm in the hamlet of Cuba during the latter part of 1850. Sidney and Phebe had grown to feel a personal proprietorship over the farm and its loss was a blow to them. The Rigdons were then obliged to leave Cuba and make their home in Friendship with the Robinsons (SR 388–400; SRM 142–43).

■ **1. HOME OF GEORGE W. ROBINSON.** The spacious two-story frame home of George W. and Athalia Rigdon Robinson still stands on

the SE corner of East Main and East Water Streets at 51 East Main Street. Today it has been made into an apartment complex. The old porch has been taken off and the bars that once covered the windows of Robinson's private bank are now gone.

George W. Robinson home, Friendship.
(1992)

It was in this home that Sidney Rigdon and his wife, Phebe, initially resided with the Robinsons in Friendship. The Rigdons resided with George and Athalia in this home during the early 1850s and then moved to the home of their son-in-law, Edward B. Wingate. From 1837–40 George W. Robinson had served as a general recorder for the First Presidency under the Prophet Joseph Smith. However, he later turned against Joseph and the Brethren and chose to leave Mormonism. Robinson was very prosperous in his mercantile business. In partnership with Ira Hartshorn, George founded a private bank in the basement of his home in 1852. In 1864, George was instrumental in establishing the First National Bank of Friendship. He then moved out of the old Colwell store to a new home and banking institution. At this time Robinson gave this former home to his sister-in-law Lucy Ann Rigdon Hatch, the widow of Jeremiah Hatch. Since then it has been known as "the Hatch House" (HAC 715; SR 409 n. 9).

■ **2. HOME OF LUCY ANN RIGDON HATCH.** The 1865 home of Lucy Ann Rigdon Hatch, daughter of Sidney and Phebe Rigdon, still stands on the west side of the road at 15 East Water Street in Friendship, directly south on East Water Street from the George W. Robinson home. Lucy and her husband, Jeremiah Hatch, are buried near the Rigdons in the Maple Grove Cemetery (see site no. 7).

■ **3. THE FRIENDSHIP ACADEMY, SITE OF RIGDON LECTURES.** The Friendship Academy no longer stands. It was once located near where a home now stands at 21 East Main Street (PB). The Academy stood in the middle of the block on the south side of East Main Street, between West Water (formerly Mill Street) and East Water Streets, on the west side of the United Church of Friendship (formerly the old Baptist meetinghouse and cemetery).

The Friendship Academy burned down in 1893. It was a large three-story building with five recitation rooms, a library and spacious auditorium that seated a thousand persons, and a chapel. Jeremiah Hatch Jr., who married Sidney's daughter Lucy Ann Rigdon, was principal of the Academy from 1849 to 1854. Hatch arranged for Sidney Rigdon to deliver a series of lectures in the chapel on the subjects of history and geology (SR 401, 410 n. 15).

■ **4. SAMUEL AND PHEBE SPEARS HOME.** The Samuel Spears home still stands at 18 East Main Street on the north side. It is just east of the NE corner of the intersection of Main, Depot, and West Water (formerly Mill Street) Streets. The home is locally known as the Harry Buzzard House for the Buzzard family, who lived here for a good many years (MW).

Sometime following the 1880 census, the widow Phebe Rigdon moved into the home of her daughter Phebe and son-in-law Samuel Spears on Main Street. She was living here when she passed away at age 86 on Feb. 27, 1886 (SR 455–56). Sidney Rigdon was seemingly never a regular occupant of this home as some have supposed.

■ **5. FIRST NATIONAL BANK OF FRIENDSHIP.** The First National Bank of Friendship was located at 1 West Main Street on the NW corner of the intersection of Main, Depot, and West Water Streets (West Water St. was formerly Mill St.). Although remodeled several times the building is still standing, and is still a bank building—the Fleet Bank today (PB).

At the organizational meeting of Feb. 1, 1864, George W. Robinson was elected president of the First National Bank of Friendship. It was the first bank organized in Allegany County under the National Banking Act. Robinson continued as president until Feb. 14, 1870. He died on Oct. 2, 1878, and is buried in the Maple Grove Cemetery in Friendship (HAC 715; see site no. 7).

■ **6. EDWARD B. WINGATE HOME SITE.** The site of the home of Sidney's son-in-law Edward B. Wingate and daughter Sarah Rigdon Wingate is located just south of the railroad tracks on the east side of Depot Street at what was once 13 Depot Street. The location today is a part of the parking lot for the Friendship Fire Department building (PB). The original home of the Wingates burned to the ground on Monday, Mar. 21, 1881, during a fire that destroyed a substantial portion of the town. "Ned Wingate's residence and property" are specified among the losses (FNYWR Mar. 24, 1881).

In what appears to have been an ongoing dispute with George Robinson over the sale of the Jackson Hill Farm near Cuba, Sidney moved his family from the Robinson home to live with the Wingates on Depot Street. The move took place in the early 1850s. Sidney Rigdon never owned land in Friendship except for his simple plot in the Maple Grove Cemetery (SR 400).

Still filled with a desire to redeem Zion, Sidney Rigdon and Stephen Post, another former Latter-day Saint, combined their efforts to establish a new place of gathering. In a prophetic role, Sidney identified Attica, Marion Co., IA, as Zion, where Stephen Post and some others had taken up land. Rigdon, however, later designated the town of Emerson in the Red River Valley of southern Manitoba, Canada, as Zion, and a reduced number of his faithful followers, Stephen Post among them, again located there. Sidney and Phebe chose not to gather to either place but remained in Friendship throughout the remainder of their lives.

The intrepid Sidney Rigdon died at the Wingates' Depot Street home July 14, 1876, at age 82. In tribute to his father, John Wickliffe Rigdon later spoke of Sidney as "a man who had his fa[u]lts[,] he was subject to like passions as other men[,] yet he was a man who I believe always intended to do right even if he did sometimes miss his way" (SR 448–50). During Sidney's last illness, John asked his father if he were in any way connected with the Prophet Joseph Smith at the time of the translation of the Book of Mormon. Sidney replied, "I never knew anything about the *Book of Mormon,* nor of its translation until I received a bound volume of the book from the hands of Parley P. Pratt. Up to this time I had never before heard of the Book of Mormon, nor had I ever seen the Prophet Joseph Smith" (DN Apr. 6, 1912, 2).

The Rigdons' daughter, Sarah Rigdon Wingate, soon followed her father, dying in 1877. For a season Phebe continued to live with her son-in-law, Edward B. Wingate, who cared for her. However, in the 1880 census of Friendship, Phebe, age 80, is listed as being a "Mother in law" in the household of S. S. Hamilton and his wife, Sophiann, on Main Street. In that same census, Edward Wingate is listed as a "Father in law" in the household of Fred Oliver and family and apparently not in his home on Depot Street at that time. Whatever the circumstances of occupation were, the Edward B. Wingate family home on Depot Street was consumed by fire on Mar. 21, 1881 (FNYWR Mar. 24, 1881).

■ **7. MAPLE GROVE CEMETERY.** The Maple Grove Cemetery is located in the NE sector of the village of Friendship. From the junction of East Main and East Water Streets (where the first George W. Robinson home was on the SE corner) go east on Main .6 mile to Maple Grove Road, then north on Maple Grove Road .2 mile to the cemetery, which is on the right (east) side of the road. From the entrance proceed east to the first intersection and go north for 46 yards. Look 20 yards to the right (east) of the road for a tall obelisk that says "Hatch." Sidney and Phebe Rigdon are buried five yards east of that large monument. The inscription on their granite tombstone reads, "SIDNEY RIGDON, Born Feb. 19, 1793, Died July 14, 1876; PHEBE BROOKS, his wife, Born May 3, 1800, Died Feb. 27, 1886." Buried by the Rigdons are their daughter Hortense Antoinette (Nettie) Rigdon (on the south) and Edward B. Wingate (1820–87) and his wife, Sarah Rigdon (1824–77) to the immediate north. The Rigdons were related to the Hatches buried by the obelisk. Their daughter Lucy Ann Rigdon Hatch, 1833–77, and her husband, Jeremiah Hatch Jr., 1819–62, are interred immediately west of the Hatch monument. Just 65 yards farther north, and on the west side of the road, George W. Robinson (1814–78) and Athalia Rigdon (1821–1906) are buried.

It may be of some interest to readers to note that **John Wickliffe Rigdon,** Sidney's second son, rejoined the LDS Church in 1904. He was originally baptized at the age of nine by Hyrum Smith in Kirtland, OH, but for some reason was never confirmed. Decades later John, who had been living in New York City, was rebaptized into the Church on Sept. 8, 1904, at age 74. Elder John M. McFarlane baptized him in the Hudson River. John then came to Utah where he died on Apr. 5, 1912, in the W. H. Groves LDS Hospital at age 82. He is buried in the Salt Lake City Cemetery, Plat S, Block 36, Lot 4, Tier W, Grave 5. John's burial place was provided by the LDS Church (ERA 8:465–67; DN Apr. 6, 1912, 2; SLCI Bk. Q-RN; SLIR 32423).

Cattaraugus County

■ FREEDOM TOWNSHIP—**Home of the Warren A. Cowdery and Heman Hyde Families**

Freedom Township is the corner township in NE Cattaraugus County. It derives its name from the small village of Freedom, which had its origins in 1811.

The farms of **Warren A. Cowdery** and **Heman Hyde** adjoined one another in the township of Freedom. In 1830–31, Warren Cowdery received some proof sheets of the Book of Mormon from his brother, Oliver Cowdery, who was then supervising the printing of that scripture at the E. B. Grandin Bookstore in Palmyra, NY. Warren in turn shared those sheets with his neighbor, Heman Hyde, and family. Both families subsequently embraced the gospel (JWHy 6).

William Hyde stated that the Prophet visited Freedom while on a recruiting mission for Zion's Camp. "Early in the year 1834 Joseph Smith and Parley P. Pratt came to my father's house," he said. "They preached two or three times in the neighborhood, and conversed much in private. Before they left[,] my oldest brother [Heman T. Hyde] was baptized [Mar. 11, 1834] and went the same year to Missouri with Joseph Smith and many others in what was called the Zion's Camp" (JWHy 6; HC 2:42–43).

Of the above incident Parley P. Pratt explained: "We baptized a young man named Heman Hyde; his parents were Presbyterians, and his mother, on account of the strength of her traditions, thought that we were wrong, and told me afterwards that she would much rather have followed him to an earthly grave than to have seen him baptized. Soon afterwards, however, herself, her husband, and the rest of the family, with some thirty or forty others, were all baptized and organized into a branch of the Church—called the Freedom branch—from which nucleus the light spread and souls were gathered into the fold in all the regions round" (APPP 109–10).

Warren A. Cowdery was called to preside in Freedom and vicinity by the voice of the Lord through the Prophet Joseph Smith: "It is my will that my servant Warren A. Cowdery should be appointed and ordained a presiding high priest over my church, in the land of Freedom and the regions round about" (D&C 106:1).

On Apr. 3–4, 1835, a conference was held at Freedom with Sidney Rigdon of the First Presidency of the Church presiding and Warren A. Cowdery performing secretarial duties. There were 15 branches of the Church represented at the conference. As the respective branches reported their numbers, Heman Hyde responded with a count of 70 persons in the Freedom Branch (M&A 1:101–2).

The Quorum of the Twelve Apostles assembled in Freedom on May 22–25, 1835, and held a conference for that district with Elder David W. Patten presiding. The Apostles were on what has been termed the "first mission of the Twelve" in this dispensation, holding conferences in predesignated localities in New York, Canada, and New England, from May to Oct. 1835. The Freedom Conference was the second on their itinerary (HC 2:222–25, ChCh 11).

■ THE VILLAGE OF SOUTH DAYTON AND PERRYSBURG TOWNSHIP/DAYTON TOWNSHIP

The village of South Dayton is located on State 322 just 10 miles SW of the village of Perrysburg near the Cattaraugus/Chautauqua County line.

When a branch of the Church was first formed in the area (1833), it was part of Perrysburg Township; however, Dayton Township was taken off on Feb. 7, 1835, and the new township contained the old nucleus of the Perrysburg Branch, centered in the farming community of South Dayton.

■ FREEMAN NICKERSON HOME SITE. Between 1829 and 1831, Freeman Nickerson and other family members including Moses Nickerson and Eleazer Freeman Nickerson, owned some 573 acres in Lot 58 of the township of Perrysburg. Freeman Nickerson and his wife, Huldah Chapman, lived on their 228-acre farm, where the small community of South Dayton is now situated. The Nickerson home is described as being "a large house which stood on the site where Mrs. Hampton Phillp's House now stands [1906]. This house was

30 x 50 and three stories high. . . . [The Nickersons] owned the great house and all the land on which the village of South Dayton now stands." When the Nickersons moved they sold their property to the Smith brothers of Hanover, who then sold it to Homer Wheelock (SDN Aug 16, 1906).

Freeman Nickerson was converted to Mormonism in what was then Perrysburg Township by Zerubbabel Snow; he was baptized by the same in Apr. 1833. He went on an early mission to Kirtland, OH and vicinity. His sons, Eleazer Freeman and Moses Chapman Nickerson, had moved into the Mount Pleasant area of Upper Canada (now Ontario), and Freeman indicated to the Prophet Joseph Smith that he felt that a mission to these family members would be fruitful. With Freeman leading the way, Joseph Smith and Sidney Rigdon journeyed from Kirtland to Mount Pleasant during the fall of 1833. They went by way of Freeman's home in the township of Perrysburg, NY, arriving here on Oct. 12, 1833. That same day, the Prophet received the revelation that is now identified as D&C 100. It is listed in Church history as having been given in Perrysburg and as a result many visit the village of Perrysburg, supposing it to be the site of the revelation. D&C 100, however, was actually received in Freeman's home in the Township of Perrysburg at the geographical location that later became the village of South Dayton, Dayton Township. The next day the Prophet and Sidney Rigdon spoke to a large congregation here (HC 1:416–21).

RECRUITMENT OF ZION'S CAMP VOLUNTEERS. In response to the revelation recorded in D&C 103, calling for the recruitment of men to march with Zion's Camp to relieve the beleaguered Saints who had been expelled from Jackson County, MO, the Prophet and Parley P. Pratt arrived at the Freeman Nickerson home on Mar. 5, 1834. Joseph Smith related: "We called the church together, and related unto them what had happened to our brethren in Zion, and opened to them the prophecies and revelations concerning the order of the gathering to Zion, and the means of her redemption; and I prophesied to them, and the Spirit of the Lord came mightily upon me, and with all readiness the young and middle-aged volunteered for Zion" (HC 2:41–42).

Among the volunteers were Freeman Nickerson, Levi Stillman Nickerson, and Uriah (Uriel) Nickerson (ZCB 273).

THE BRANCH OF THE CHURCH IN PERRYSBURG TOWNSHIP. At a district conference of Church members held at Freedom, NY, on Apr. 3, 1835, Elder Freeman Nickerson of the Perrysburg Branch reported that there were "forty members in good standing" (M&A 1:101).

Freeman stayed true to the Church and was eventually a resident of Nauvoo. After the expulsion from Illinois, he died near the pioneer crossing at the Chariton River, Iowa Territory, on Jan. 22, 1847.

Erie County

■ **BUFFALO**

The city of Buffalo is situated in Erie Co., at the head of the Niagara River, the outlet of Lake Erie, and at "the foot" of the Great Lakes chain. It is readily accessible on I-90 in western New York. Buffalo was first settled in 1801. In 1814 it was burned by the British during the War of 1812. Buffalo is noted for its "secure harbor." The **Erie Canal** was opened from Buffalo to Albany in 1825. By reason of its strategic location, Buffalo became the crossroads of the Church.

MISSIONARIES TO THE LAMANITES. The Lord informed the Prophet Joseph Smith that one of the primary reasons that the plates of the Book of Mormon had been preserved for his generation was so "the Lamanites might come to the knowledge of their fathers, and that they might know the promises of the Lord" (D&C 3:18–20). In Sept.–Oct. 1830, four men were called to participate in a mission to the Lamanites: **Oliver Cowdery, Peter Whitmer Jr., Parley P. Pratt,** and **Richard Ziba Peterson** (D&C 28, 30, 32). They arrived in the Buffalo area in the latter part of Oct. 1830 (NEW 280). Here the missionaries visited among some members of the Seneca Nation who were located on the Buffalo Creek Reservation. This reservation was "situated east, and adjoining the city of Buffalo" (GSNY 371). Parley P. Pratt described their brief experience:

> After travelling for some days we called on an Indian nation at or near Buffalo; and spent part of a day with them, instructing them in the knowledge of the record of their forefathers. We were kindly received, and much interest was

manifested by them on hearing this news. We made a present of two copies of the Book of Mormon to certain of them who could read, and repaired to Buffalo. Thence we continued our journey, for about two hundred miles, and at length called on Mr. [Sidney] Rigdon. (APPP 47)

GATHERING PLACE OF NEW YORK SAINTS EN ROUTE TO KIRTLAND. Members of the Colesville, Fayette, and Manchester Branches of the Church in New York came to Buffalo on the Erie Canal and then embarked by boat out of Buffalo Harbor in May 1831, as the Saints emigrated to Kirtland, OH (NEW 296–322; see also OMP 101–4). Lucy Mack Smith arranged for passage for the Fayette Branch on a steamboat, but they were unable to proceed because of a mountain of ice that had piled up to the height of 20 feet in the harbor due to the prevailing winds. Undaunted, Lucy Mack Smith said to her fellow Saints:

> "Now, brethren and sisters, if you will all of you raise your desires to heaven, that the ice may be broken up, and we be set at liberty, as sure as the Lord lives, it will be done." At that instant a noise was heard, like bursting thunder. The captain cried, "Every man to his post." The ice parted, leaving barely a passage for the boat, and so narrow that as the boat passed through the buckets of the waterwheel were torn off with a crash, which, joined to the word of command from the captain, the hoarse answering of the sailors, the noise of the ice, and the cries and confusion of the spectators, presented a scene truly terrible. We had barely passed through the avenue when the ice closed together again. (HJS 204–5)

THE PROPHET JOSEPH SMITH AND COMPANY IN BUFFALO. The night of July 26–27, 1836, Joseph Smith, Sidney Rigdon, Hyrum Smith, and Oliver Cowdery lodged at the "Farmer's Hotel" in Buffalo before taking a line boat on the Erie Canal to Utica, NY, en route to Salem, MA (JH July 26, 1836; see also D&C 111).

1843 CONFERENCE. With Elder John P. Greene as chairman of a conference, representatives from 13 branches and some scattered members of the Church gathered at Buffalo on Sept. 1, 1843. It is difficult to determine how many persons were physically present, but a total of 257 members were reported as being in the respective branches including 58 elders, two teachers, and one deacon. **William H. Folsom** represented the Buffalo Branch with its five members, four elders, and one teacher (TS Sept. 15, 1843, 4:334–35). Brother Folsom, an 1842 New York convert, later became architect for the exterior of the Salt Lake Theatre, Salt Lake City Hall, and, along with Truman O. Angell, for the Salt Lake Tabernacle and the Salt Lake Temple. He likewise was architect for the Manti Temple and the Assembly Hall on Temple Square (CHFT 400; UTRP 149, 215).

Niagara County

■ NIAGARA FALLS, NEW YORK/NIAGARA FALLS, ONTARIO, CANADA

The city of Niagara Falls, NY, is located 20 miles NW of Buffalo. Its Canadian sister city, Niagara Falls, is directly across the border, separated by the Niagara River. Water from Lake Erie flows along the Niagara River for 34 miles into Lake Ontario. More than 12 million people visit Niagara Falls every year to view the tremendous natural spectacle. The falls are divided into two parts, the American Falls, which are 184 feet high and 1,064 feet wide, and the Canadian Horseshoe Falls, measured at 177 feet high, and 2,200 feet wide. The two sets of falls are divided by tiny Goat Island. Some 45 million gallons of water pour over the falls every minute. The Indians named the river and the falls "Niagara," or "thundering water."

The Niagara Falls area became an important route of passage for a succession of Mormon missionaries working in the western portion of Upper Canada. In mid-Oct. 1833, the Prophet Joseph Smith, Sidney Rigdon, and Freeman Nickerson passed through the Niagara Falls area on their way to proselyte among members of Elder Nickerson's family who had located at Mt. Pleasant, Upper Canada (now Ontario) (HC 1:416–21). On a later return to Canada the Prophet, Sidney Rigdon, and Thomas B. Marsh journeyed to Buffalo and on to Toronto during a short-term mission in the latter part of July 1837. (HC 2:502–3).

While on a mission to Canada in Apr. 1836, Parley P. Pratt,

Orson Pratt, and Freeman Nickerson arrived at Niagara Falls by
public coach. It was Parley's first visit and the falls "made a deep
and awful impression" on his mind. Commenting on the scene
before him, he asserted:

> We halted a short time to view this wonder of nature, and
> to adore that God who had formed a world so sublimely grand.
> The leaping of a mighty river of waters over a perpendicular
> fall of one hundred and sixty feet, the foaming and dashing of
> its white spray upon the rocks beneath; the rising cloud of mist
> with its glittering rainbow, the yawning gulf with its thousand
> whirlpools; all conspired to fill the contemplative mind with
> wonder and admiration, and with reverence to the Great
> Author of all the wonders of creation; while its everlasting roar
> which may be heard for many miles distant, seemed a lively
> emblem of eternity. (APPP 131)

Parley was so inspired by this stirring experience that he wrote
a lengthy poem with stanzas reflective of his mood. The poem
opens: "O, Niagara! Generations may pass in long succession; ages
may roll away and others still succeed; empires may rise and flour-
ish, and pass away and be forgotten; but still thy deafening, thy
solemn and awful voice is heard in one eternal roar" (APPP
131–32).

John Taylor, Isaac Russell, and other Toronto brethren visited
the Prophet Joseph Smith in Kirtland in Mar. 1837. After spending
some time with Joseph they returned by way of Queenston, Canada,
on the Niagara River, to the east of Niagara Falls. Desiring to
preach in Queenston, the elders retired to "a secluded spot under
a high cliff, just below Niagara Falls" and asked the Lord to help
them find a place. "While engaged in prayer, there, within hearing
of the mighty cataract, Elder Taylor spoke in tongues for the first
time." The full implication of the special knowledge he received
during that spiritual experience was kept secret by Elder Taylor.
Later that fall he was notified by the Prophet that he would be
called to fill a vacancy in the Quorum of the Twelve. "He had previously received a manifestation that he would be called to that
high office in the Church [while near Queenston below Niagara
Falls], but fearing that it might be from the devil he wisely kept it
hidden in his own breast" (LJT 41, 47–48).

Elders Oliver B. Huntington and Henry B. Jacobs were proselyting in the Buffalo/Tonawanda area in July 1843. While there
they traveled to Lewiston on the Niagara River and crossed over to
the Canadian side to see the site of Brock's Monument (Sir Isaac
Brock, a hero of Britain's war with the U.S. in 1812), "which had
been blown nearly down with powder, by a villain who was then in
Prison for attempting to blow up a steamboat." They then proceeded up the Niagara River toward the falls, visiting the "Devils
Hole, so called, where a British army overpowered an army of
French and Indians, and with the point of the bayonet forced them
off a precipice of 120 feet, where they were dashed to pieces, or
torn asunder in the tops of trees." Moving farther upstream they
witnessed a "great whirlpool, which is formed by nearly the whole
river, striking against a square bank." Oliver and his companion
proceeded to the falls and "spent the day in searching every crook
and corner about [them]." Overpowered by the grandeur of the
falls, Elder Oliver Huntington, recorded: "It surely is one of the
seven wonders of the world. A man may view them from morn until
eve and his mind is not satisfied. It is a scene; one which the narrow mind of man cannot comprehend" (JOBH pt. 1, p. 10).

Isaac C. Haight was at Niagara Falls on Nov. 1, 1845. He had
come from Nauvoo, IL, to New York to conduct some business for
the Brethren and for himself. Isaac related: "For the first time [I]
gazed on that great wonder of nature. My mind was filled with the
sublimity of the scene. The Great Niagara rolling, tumbling, foam-
ing, from its dizzy height into the abyss below, being beat into spray
on the rocks by the fall, displaying the rainbow in all its beauty and
grandeur. The scene is grand and imposing" (DIH Nov. 1, 1845,
24–25).

NOTE TO READER: Erie County, PA, which divides the extreme
western border of New York and the northeastern border of Ohio
on Lake Erie, is rich in LDS Church history. For information on
Erie County, PA, see pages 313–14 herein.

PENNSYLVANIA

Larry C. Porter

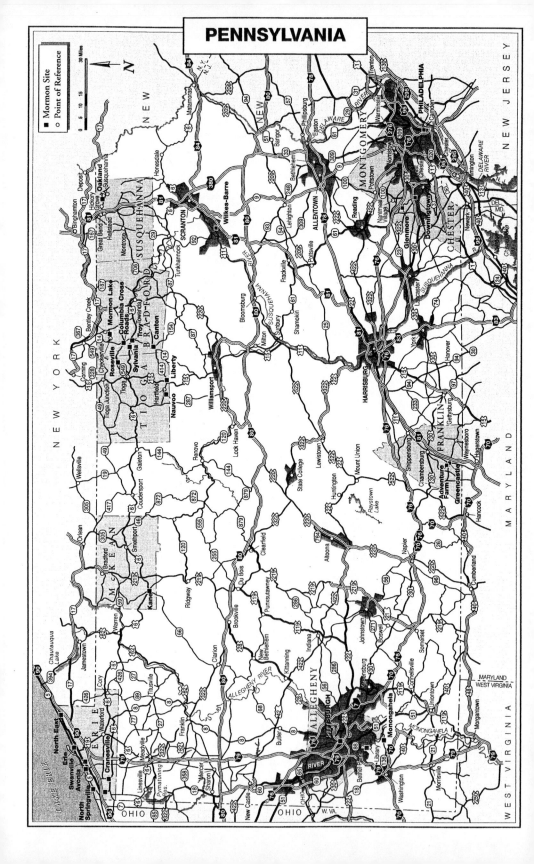

INTRODUCTION TO PENNSYLVANIA

William Penn, an English proprietor and devout Quaker, was granted the Province of Pennsylvania in 1681 by King Charles II of England in repayment of a debt owed Penn's father, Sir William Penn. It was to be a location where his fellow Quakers could enjoy freedom of worship and have a chance to govern themselves and develop their own way of life. Penn opened his colony to members of all religious faiths. French Huguenots, Germans, and Scotch-Irish were among those nationalities settling in the province. Pennsylvania was named by King Charles II for Sir William Penn; *sylvania* is the Latin word for "woods," thus "Penn's woods." Pennsylvania is known as the Keystone State because of its central geographical position among the thirteen colonies. It is likewise called the Quaker State, and is known as a refuge against religious discrimination.

The province's interior included lands claimed by the French. The Indians, who at one time had been generally peaceful with the colonists, became more hostile with the encroachment of western settlement. Much of the fighting of the **French and Indian War** (1754–63) took place in Pennsylvania. George Washington built Fort Necessity near Uniontown. An English general, Edward Braddock, suffered defeat and was killed by the French and their Indian allies on the Monongahela River in 1755. On Nov. 25, 1758, British General John Forbes captured Fort Duquesne from the French and renamed it Fort Pitt. In 1763 the war ended with a British victory, and the entire region of Pennsylvania was placed under the rule of Great Britain.

In the **Revolutionary War,** America's contest of will against the British Crown, Philadelphia became the meeting place for the **First Continental Congress** in 1774. On July 4, 1776, the **Declaration of Independence** was signed at Philadelphia by the Second

Continental Congress, and a provisional government prepared a
new **Constitution.** General George Washington's Continental Army
camped at Valley Forge from Dec. 19, 1777, to June 19, 1778.
Despite setbacks and defeats the American army eventually
prevailed. The Treaty of Paris ended the Revolutionary War on
Sept. 3, 1783.

The Constitutional Convention met in Philadelphia on
Dec. 12, 1787. Pennsylvania was the second state to ratify the
Constitution. The nation's capital was moved from Philadelphia to
Washington, D.C., in 1800. Likewise the capital of the state
of Pennsylvania was shifted from Philadelphia to Harrisburg on
June 18, 1812.

Latter-day Saints in Pennsylvania

Connecticut-born **Isaac Hale** came out of Vermont in about
1787. Journeying through the state of New York, he descended the
Susquehanna River as far as the Great Bend in what was then
Luzerne County, Pennsylvania. Finding the country much to his lik-
ing, he returned to Vermont, married Elizabeth Lewis, and with his
new bride came to the sparsely settled community of Willing-
borough, Luzerne County, Pennsylvania, about 1790. This area
eventually became Harmony, Susquehanna County, Pennsylvania.
It was here that **Joseph Smith Jr.** of Palmyra/Manchester, New York,
first visited the home of Isaac Hale in November 1825 while
employed by Josiah Stowell. Boarding in the Isaac Hale home, he
became acquainted with the comely daughter of Isaac, **Emma Hale.**
Joseph continued to court Emma from the state of New York, and
the couple was eventually married in January 1827. An important
link was thus formed with the state of Pennsylvania in the development of Mormonism. Commencing in December 1827, the Smiths
made their home in Harmony Township. Here the majority of the
translation of the Book of Mormon took place. Fifteen revelations
now recorded in the Doctrine and Covenants were received during
their tenure in that location (1827–30). The appearance of John
the Baptist on the banks of the Susquehanna resulted in the
restoration of the Aaronic Priesthood; a subsequent visit by the
ancient Apostles Peter, James, and John was marked by the con-
ferral of Melchizedek Priesthood keys on the heads of the Prophet

Joseph Smith and Oliver Cowdery. These events became the main-spring for the spread of Mormonism throughout the marvelous ethnic mix and diversified folk cultures represented among the populace of the Keystone State.

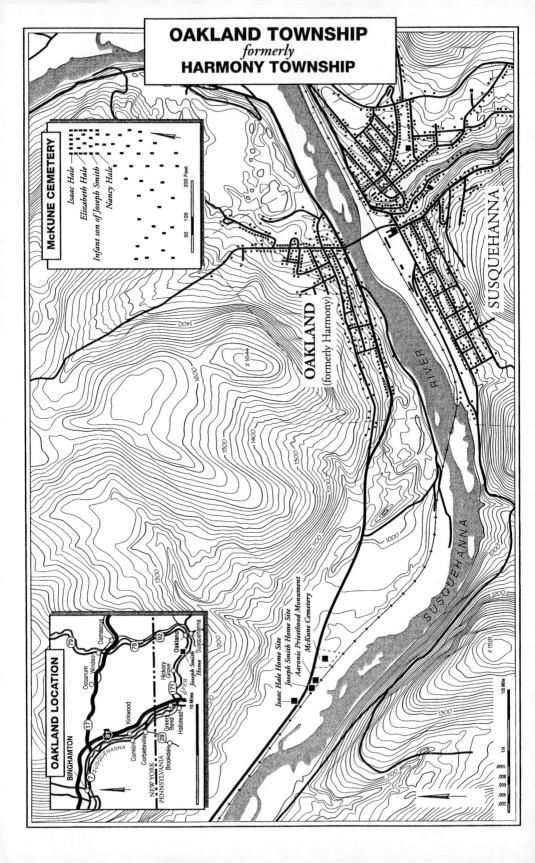

OAKLAND TOWNSHIP
formerly
HARMONY TOWNSHIP

McKUNE CEMETERY

Isaac Hale
Elizabeth Hale
Infant son of Joseph Smith
Nancy Hale

50 100 200 Feet

OAKLAND
(formerly Harmony)

SUSQUEHANNA

RIVER

SUSQUEHANNA

Isaac Hale Home Site
Joseph Smith Home Site
Aaronic Priesthood Monument
McKune Cemetery

OAKLAND LOCATION

BINGHAMTON

Oceanum
Windsor
Damascus

Occanum

Kirkwood

Conklin
Corbettsville
Brookdale

Hickory Grove

Green Bend
Hallstead

Joseph Smith Home

Oakland
Susquehanna

NEW YORK
PENNSYLVANIA

10 Miles

SUSQUEHANNA COUNTY

Larry C. Porter

■ HARMONY TOWNSHIP (NOW OAKLAND TOWNSHIP)

That portion of Harmony Township (now Oakland Township) of Mormon interest is located in the "Great Bend" of the Susquehanna River, Susquehanna Co. in NE Pennsylvania. The sites of the Isaac Hale and Joseph Smith Jr. homes, the Aaronic Priesthood Restoration Monument, and McKune Cemetery are clustered together just 6½ miles east of the Hallstead/Great Bend exit from I-81 on State 171 or just 1.8 miles west of the hamlet of Oakland on State 171. The homes of both Isaac Hale and Joseph Smith Jr. were in the rural area of the township of Harmony and never in the village of Harmony. The village of Harmony consisted

Looking NE, an aerial view of the area where the Book of Mormon was translated and the Aaronic Priesthood was restored. (Photo by LaMar C. Berrett, 1978)

The Susquehanna River in Oakland (formerly Harmony) Township.

of a few scattered houses on the opposite or east side of the Susquehanna River, just south of where Cascade Creek empties into the Susquehanna, and 3.2 miles to the NE of the Hale/Smith properties. The village no longer exists as an entity today.[1]

■ **AARONIC PRIESTHOOD RESTORATION MONUMENT.** The central feature from which directions can be given to the various historic sites in this immediate vicinity is the Aaronic Priesthood Restoration

The Aaronic Priesthood Restoration Monument in Oakland (formerly Harmony) Township.

Monument, located 40 yards south of State 171. The 23½-ton monument has an 8' x 6' x 1' polished base with a 12' monolithic shaft, up to four feet thick. Superimposed upon the shaft are three bronze figures in high relief depicting **John the Baptist** bestowing the Aaronic Priesthood on the heads of **Joseph Smith** and **Oliver Cowdery.** Dr. Avard Fairbanks sculptured the beautiful work. The stone is carnelian granite from Cold Springs, MN (CN May 14, 1960, 13).

The dedication of the monument took place on June 18, 1960. (Services were originally set for May 14, but circumstances beyond the control of those in charge of arrangements made the later date necessary.) More than 1,200 members and friends of the Church gathered for the occasion. Presiding Bishop Joseph L. Wirthlin

[1] The author is highly indebted to local historian Horace H. (Chris) Christensen of Endwell, NY, for his kind introduction of the writer to the respective sites in this locality over a succession of many years. Appreciation is also expressed to the Susquehanna County Historical Society and Free Library Association, Montrose, PA, for their invaluable assistance.

offered the dedicatory prayer. A chorus of 250 Aaronic Priesthood young men from the Eastern States Mission and stakes of the East participated in the memorial services. For historical purposes a box containing pertinent documents was sealed in the monument. The memorial was paid for by contributions from more than 60,000 members of the Aaronic Priesthood and their Church leaders (CN May 14, 1960, 13; June 18, 1960, 13; June 25, 1960, 10–11).

■ **ISAAC AND ELIZABETH HALE HOME SITE.** The site of the Isaac Hale homestead is 230 yards NW of the Aaronic Priesthood Restoration Monument on the north side of State 171 and about 20 feet into the undergrowth from the north edge of the paved road. There is a dirt road that goes north off of State 171 at that point and provides ease of access to the east side of the Hale home site. The original home was destroyed by fire sometime between 1873 and 1875. A replacement home built on the same site was torn down dur-

ing 1951–52 (NEW 130–31; see also OMP 156–57). What are believed to be the original rock foundation and cellar of the Hale home have been preserved by filling them in with layers of dirt to protect them from further deterioration and loss. All that is visible today is a grassy plain surrounded by a split rail fence and a marker identifying the site.

Home built about 1875 over the foundation of the Isaac and Elizabeth Hale home, in Harmony Township.

Isaac Hale visited what later became the township of Harmony as early as the fall of 1787. And by 1791 he and his brother-in-law, Nathaniel Lewis, brought their families and established themselves on the land. Isaac and his wife, Elizabeth, were the parents of nine children, the seventh of which was Emma. She was born July 10, 1804, and later became the wife of Joseph Smith.

Reverend George Peck, an elder in the Methodist Church, said of his old friend Isaac: "Hale was a mighty hunter. In fact, he came from Vermont, and fixed his home in this new region for the purpose of pursuing game in the Harmony Woods—the great forest which then stretched from the Susquehanna to the Delaware. He slaughtered about a hundred deer annually, most of which he sent to the Philadelphia market. He often killed bears and elks, as well as a great variety of smaller game, of the flesh of which I often partook at his table" (LTGP 67–68).

In the forepart of Nov. 1825, Joseph Smith Jr., his father, and others came to Harmony in the employment of Josiah Stowell of Chenango Co., NY. They were hired to dig for lost treasure in the earth. The crew boarded at the Isaac Hale home while in that vicinity. Stowell was convinced that a company of Spaniards had once "excavated from the bowels of the earth ore" in the hills near the home of Isaac Hale "and coined a large quantity of money," part of which they had left behind when they evacuated the locality (NEW 122–28).

Joseph Smith said that after a time he finally "prevailed with the old gentleman to cease digging after it [the Spanish silver mine]" (HC 1:17). Isaac Hale stated that Josiah and his hands left his place about Nov. 17, 1825. Joseph Smith was then hired by Mr. Stowell to work on his farm 3.1 miles south of the village of South Bainbridge, NY (NEW 128).

During the time he boarded in the Hale home, Joseph found himself attracted to Emma Hale, the "comely" daughter of Isaac. After leaving for Stowell's place and also during his later employment with Joseph Knight Sr. of Colesville, NY, Joseph Smith continued to go down the Susquehanna River some 28 miles to Harmony to court his girl. Joseph Knight Sr. said that he loaned Joseph a horse and cutter (sleigh) for that purpose (BYUS 16, no. 4 [autumn]: 32). His attentions to Emma led to matrimony on Jan. 18, 1827, at the home of Zachariah Tarble, Esq., in South Bainbridge, NY. Joseph's visits and eventual elopement with Emma had been strenuously objected to by Isaac Hale. (See the village of Afton [formerly South Bainbridge], Chenango County, NY, for the circumstances of their marriage.)

During an Aug. 1827 visit of Joseph and Emma to the Hales from the Smith family home in Manchester, NY, Isaac extended an invitation for the couple to come down and live with them on the Susquehanna. Because of mobocracy in the Manchester/Palmyra area and a desire to pursue the translation of the Book of Mormon, Joseph eventually accepted the hospitality of the Hales, arriving in Harmony in Dec. 1827.

Referring to the golden plates of the Book of Mormon, which Joseph kept concealed in a box, Isaac Hale declared: "If there was anything in my house of that description, which I could not be allowed to see, he must take it away" (SPR May 1, 1834). Unable to show the plates to anyone at that time, Joseph and Emma were obliged to establish their own homestead.

■ **JOSEPH AND EMMA SMITH HOMESTEAD.** The site of Joseph and Emma's homestead is situated 130 feet NW of the Aaronic Priesthood Restoration Monument. Much of the laid-rock foundation was still visible, two to three feet high, in 1960. "At that time the site was graded to put in the Aaronic Priesthood monument and they used the bulldozer to mound over the laid-rock foundation. The foundation was on top of the ground. There was no basement" (HHC). The rectangular shape of the homestead is still marked by a series of stones showing through the top of the mound.

The left portion of this building was the Prophet's home.

The center portion of this building was the Prophet's home.

The small two-story frame house that once stood here burned down in 1919. It is believed that a spark from a locomotive passing on the track south of the house may have been the cause of the fire. The original home was procured by Joseph and Emma from Jesse Hale, Emma's brother, and was moved onto the 13-acre parcel of land that Joseph purchased from Issac Hale. Among the notable events that took place in this home were the following:

Hand-carved model of Joseph and Emma Smith's home. (By Ralph B. Norton; courtesy Wilford C. Wood)

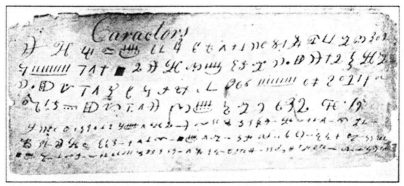

A transcript of Book of Mormon characters once belonging to the Whitmer family, now in the RLDS Archives.

(1) Joseph prepared a transcript of characters from the golden plates, which in Feb. 1828 Martin Harris took to **Dr. Charles Anthon** at Columbia College (now University) in New York City, and Dr. Samuel Latham Mitchill at Rutgers Medical College in New York City (which college was under the auspices of Rutgers College of New Jersey). This was in fulfillment of the prophecy of Isaiah 29 (BYUS 10, no. 2 [spring]: 325–52; PJS 1:9; see also Albany, NY, herein).

(2) Here the Prophet, with Martin Harris as scribe, translated **116 pages of manuscript** between Apr. 12 and June 14, 1828. Unfortunately, despite a sacred covenant, Martin lost the entire manuscript while on a visit to his home in the township of Palmyra, NY, in June–July 1828 (HC 1:20–28).

The Prophet Joseph Smith and scribe, Martin Harris. (Courtesy of Vernon Murdock)

(3) **Moroni** interacted with Joseph relative to the loss of the 116 pages. He initially took from Joseph the plates and the Urim and Thummim, and then returned them to the Prophet at the appropriate time, Sept. 22, 1828. Moroni later delivered the golden plates safely to Fayette, NY, during May–June 1829, when there were serious problems with a mob in Harmony (HC 1:21–23; HJS 135, 149–50).

(4) The first child of Joseph and Emma, a son, was born June

15, 1828. The child, however, died shortly after his birth and is buried in the nearby McKune Cemetery (see site no. 4).

(5) Fifteen revelations in the Doctrine and Covenants (sections 3–13, 24–27) were received here between July 1828 and Aug. 1830.

(6) Emma, her brother Reuben Hale, and Samuel Smith all gave brief assistance to Joseph as scribes (SH Oct. 1, 1879, 110; PJS 1:10).

(7) **Oliver Cowdery** arrived at Joseph's home on Apr. 5, 1829, and acted as scribe as Joseph translated the Book of Mormon, commencing Apr. 7, 1829. By about May 28, 1829, a majority of the Book of Mormon had been translated when, because

Emma Hale Smith, a scribe to Joseph Smith as he translated. (Courtesy of Vernon Murdock)

of mob activity, David Whitmer came down from Fayette and transported the two men to his father's home in Seneca Co., NY, where

Oliver Cowdery

they arrived on June 1, 1829. The translation was completed at the Whitmers' during the month of June (HC 1:48–49; KCJ June 5, 1881).

(8) Joseph Knight Sr. visited the home, bringing with him paper for the translation and badly needed food stores for the occupants (HC 1:47-48).

(9) The restoration of the Aaronic Priesthood by John the Baptist and the Melchizedek Priesthood by Peter, James, and John occurred while the Prophet was living in this home, although the actual events took place along the banks of the Susquehanna River during May 1829 (JS—H 1:68–74; D&C 128:20; ENS 25 [Dec. 1995]: 30–47).

(10) Chapter 1 of the Book of Moses in the Pearl of Great Price was received during June 1830.

(11) Joseph and Emma finally left their Harmony home during the last week of Aug. 1830. They were moved to the Peter

Detail from Translating the Golden Plates of the Book of Mormon, *by Dale Kilbourn. (Courtesy of LDSCA)*

Whitmer Sr. log house in Fayette, NY, by Joseph Knight Sr. in his wagon. The 13-acre farm and home were later sold by Joseph Smith to Joseph McKune Jr. on June 8, 1833, while the Prophet was living in Kirtland, OH (Deed Book 9:290, Susquehanna County Courthouse, Montrose, PA).

■ **McKune Cemetery.** The western edge of the McKune Cemetery is 80 yards east of the Aaronic Priesthood Restoration Monument. The graves of members of the Joseph Smith and Isaac Hale families are located 207 yards NE of the monument in the NE corner of the cemetery, and just 20 feet south of State 171. From the east edge of the cemetery Isaac Hale's headstone is the first on the sixth row going west.

Isaac Hale's inscription, which is becoming difficult to read, states, "Isaac Hale died Jan. 11, 1839, AE. 75 y's 10 mo. & 10 d's. The body of Isaac Hale, the Hunter, like the cover of an old book, its contents torn out, and stript of its lettering and gilding, lies here food for worms, yet the work itself shall not be lost for it will as he believed,

Tombstone of Alvin, infant son of Joseph and Emma Smith. (Photo by George Edward Anderson, 1907; courtesy of LDSCA)

appear once more in a new and more beautiful edition, corrected and amended." The lines of the epitaph were originally those of Benjamin Franklin (OMP 161–62; see also LBF 238). Isaac was buried on his own land at the time. Only later did it become the McKune Cemetery. Isaac's last will and testament stipulated, "I further desire my body buried on my own land back of the garden near the line betwixt me and Joseph

McKune Jr." (Will Book 1:178, Susquehanna County Courthouse, Montrose, PA).

The inscription on the next headstone to the south of Isaac's reads, "Elizabeth wife of Isaac Hale, Died Feb. 16, 1842, Aged 75 Years 2 mo. & 28 d's." Continuing to the south are two intervening headstones, those of Phoebe and Stephen Root, and then the slate headstone of Joseph and Emma's first child. The simple inscription reads, "In Memory of An Infant Son of Joseph and Emma Smith June 15th 1828." Little Alvin, as he was named, did not survive his birth. The Joseph and Emma Smith family Bible confirms his name as "Alvin" rather than Alva (or Alvah), as some have thought (BY).

Too often forgotten is the next headstone to the south of that of the "Infant Son," which reads, "In memory of Nancy Hale daughter of Jesse and Mary Hale who Died Jan. the 29th AD 1828 Aged two years and six months thirteen Days." The two little cousins both died that difficult year of 1828 and are buried side by side.

■ **THE RESTORATION OF THE AARONIC PRIESTHOOD ON THE BANKS OF THE SUSQUEHANNA RIVER.** Because of the position of the Isaac Hale and Joseph Smith properties in the "Great Bend" of the Susquehanna, they are said to be situated on the north side of that river. The Susquehanna runs through the valley 175 yards directly to the south of the site of the Joseph Smith homestead. It is probable that Joseph Smith and Oliver Cowdery went into the woods directly south of the Smith homestead, toward the river, and that both the appearance of John the Baptist and the subsequent baptisms of Joseph and Oliver occurred near Joseph's home. A path leading to the Susquehanna River on the south has been cleared through the trees and undergrowth commencing on line with the backside of the Aaronic Priesthood Restoration Monument. However, a

John the Baptist confers the Aaronic Priesthood on Joseph Smith and Oliver Cowdery near the Susquehanna River, Harmony Township, May 15, 1829 (D&C 13). (Painting by Dale Kilbourn; courtesy of LDSCA)

chain-link fence and "No Trespassing" signs have been placed between the monument and the river because visitors must cross a dangerous set of railroad tracks. Please observe the signs for your personal safety. Negotiations are now in process to provide a safe avenue for the visitor.

Regarding the important work of translation in which Joseph Smith and he were involved, Oliver Cowdery recorded, "These were days never to be forgotten—to sit under the sound of a voice dictated by the inspiration of heaven, awakened the utmost gratitude of this bosom! Day after day I continued, uninterrupted, to write from his mouth, as he translated with the Urim and Thummim, or, as the Nephites would have said, 'Interpreters,' the history or record called 'The Book of Mormon'" (JS—H 1: endnote, p. 58).

While translating 3 Nephi from the golden plates, the Prophet Joseph and Oliver became concerned over baptism and the authority to perform that ordinance. On May 15, 1829, as the two men prayed near the banks of the Susquehanna River, **John the Baptist,** an angelic personage, appeared to them. John the Baptist, a direct descendant of Aaron, the brother of Moses, had baptized the Savior in the meridian of time as an example to all mankind and "to fulfil all righteousness" (Matt. 3:13–17). The Prophet Joseph described the bestowal of the Aaronic Priesthood by John the Baptist:

> We still continued the work of translation, when, in the ensuing month (May, 1829), we on a certain day went into the woods to pray and inquire of the Lord respecting baptism for the remission of sins, that we found mentioned in the translation of the plates. While we were thus employed, praying and calling upon the Lord, a messenger from heaven descended in a cloud of light, and having laid his hands upon us, he ordained us, saying:
>
> *Upon you my fellow servants, in the name of Messiah, I confer the Priesthood of Aaron, which holds the keys of the ministering of angels, and of the gospel of repentance, and of baptism by immersion for the remission of sins; . . .*
>
> He said this Aaronic Priesthood had not the power of laying on hands for the gift of the Holy Ghost, but that this should be conferred on us hereafter; and he commanded us to go and be baptized, and gave us directions that I should baptize Oliver Cowdery, and that afterwards he should baptize me.

Accordingly we went and were baptized. I baptized him first, and afterwards he baptized me—after which I laid my hands upon his head and ordained him to the Aaronic Priesthood, and afterwards he laid his hands on me and ordained me to the same Priesthood—for so we were commanded.

The messenger who visited us on this occasion and conferred this Priesthood upon us, said that his name was John, the same that is called John the Baptist in the New Testament, and that he acted under the direction of Peter, James and John, who held the keys of the Priesthood of Melchizedek, which Priesthood, he said, would in due time be conferred on us, and that I should be called the first Elder of the Church, and he (Oliver Cowdery) the second. . . .

Immediately on our coming up out of the water after we had been baptized, we experienced great and glorious blessings from our Heavenly Father. No sooner had I baptized Oliver Cowdery, than the Holy Ghost fell upon him, and he stood up and prophesied many things which should shortly come to pass. And again, so soon as I had been baptized by him, I also had the spirit of prophecy, when, standing up, I prophesied concerning the rise of this Church, and many other things connected with the Church, and this generation of the children of men. We were filled with the Holy Ghost, and rejoiced in the God of our salvation. (JS—H 1:68–73; see also D&C 13)

Having been invested with the authority of the Aaronic Priesthood, they soon began to "reason out of the Scriptures" with family members and other acquaintances. Among the first to receive their ministrations was Samuel H. Smith, a brother of the Prophet, whom they baptized for the remission of his sins on May 25, 1829 (HC 1:44).

THE RESTORATION OF THE MELCHIZEDEK PRIESTHOOD. From available sources it is very difficult to determine the exact location of the site where the Melchizedek Priesthood was restored to Joseph Smith and Oliver Cowdery by the ancient Apostles **Peter, James,** and **John.** In an epistle to the Saints, the Prophet spoke of the significant events associated with the rise of Mormonism and declared, "The voice of Peter,

James, and John in the wilderness between Harmony, Susquehanna county, and Colesville, Broome county, on the Susquehanna river, declaring themselves as possessing the keys of the kingdom, and of the dispensation of the fulness of times!" (D&C 128:20). This means the restoration occurred some-where along an approximately 28-mile stretch between the Smith/ Hale properties in Harmony, PA, and that of Joseph Knight Sr. in Colesville, NY. If a statement of Addison Everett, an early member, is accurate, Joseph Smith told Bro. Everett and others that the restoration took place when he and Oliver were returning from Colesville. Joseph reportedly said: "We had some 16 or 17 miles to goe to reach our place

Joseph Smith and Oliver Cowdery receive the Melchizedek Priesthood from Peter, James, and John, 1829. (Painting by Kenneth Riley; courtesy of LDSCA)

of residence. . . . I heard the Name of the Banks of the Susquehanah river spoken, of. But where it was pla[c]ed I cannot t[e]ll" (LAE). Should Addison's account be correct, the 16–17 mile distance from Harmony would place the restoration site near the Susquehanna River in the township of Windsor, Broome Co., NY. The actual location of that event remains very obscure (ENS 26 [Dec. 1996]: 42–44). Of this same event Addison Everett further stipulated, "As the Mob spirit had not abated when they returned they had to remove to Father Whitmores at fayet[t]e Sen[e]ca Co to finish the Translation" (LAE; ENS 26 [Dec. 1996]: 43).

"The day, month, and year designation that so precisely identifies the restoration of the Aaronic Priesthood (15 May 1829) is absent in the case of the Melchizedek Priesthood. Evidence suggests a date within the 13-day period from 16 May to 28 May 1829," just before the removal of Joseph Smith and Oliver Cowdery to the Peter Whitmer Sr. farm, where they were situated by June 1, 1829 (ENS 26 [Dec. 1996]: 33).

Oliver Cowdery gave fervent testimony of his experiences with John the Baptist and Peter, James, and John to many. To Samuel W. Richards he stated:

While darkness covered the earth and gross darkness the people; long after the authority to administer in holy things had been taken away; the Lord opened the heavens and sent forth his word for the salvation of Israel. . . .

John the Baptist, holding the keys of the Aaronic Priesthood; Peter, James and John, holding the keys of the Melchisedek Priesthood, have also ministered for those who shall be heirs of salvation, and with these ministrations ordained men to the same Priesthoods. . . . Accept assurances, dear Brother, of the unfeigned prayer of him, who, in connection with Joseph the Seer, was blessed with the above ministrations, and who earnestly and devoutly hopes to meet you in the celestial glory. (DN Mar. 22, 1884)

MODERN-DAY ACQUISITION OF SOME KEY PROPERTIES IN HARMONY. A genuine service to the Church was performed by the late Wilford C. Wood of Woods Cross, UT, in the acquisition of valuable historical sites on the Susquehanna River in the 1940s. Brother Wood purchased about 100 acres of land known as the McKune Farm from Jessie M. Colwell on Oct. 17, 1946. This parcel of land contained the 13 acres which had originally belonged to Joseph and Emma Smith and on which the couple owned their first home. Brother Wood then conveyed his approximately 100-acre purchase to the Church on Feb. 7, 1947 (Deed Book 203:586; Deed Book 206:305, Susquehanna County Court-

President George Albert Smith and Wilford C. Wood, south of the Joseph Smith home, near the Susquehanna River, Harmony (now Oakland) Township, in 1948. (Courtesy of Wilford C. Wood Foundation)

house, Montrose, PA). Similarly, on June 4, 1948 Wilford C. Wood procured an additional 115 acres that included the land on which the Isaac Hale home had been situated. He in turn sold that parcel to the Church on July 16, 1948 (Deed Book 213:173; Deed Book 213:175, Susquehanna County Courthouse, Montrose, PA). And in preparation for the dedication of the Susquehanna Aaronic Priesthood

Restoration Monument in 1960, the Church acquired an additional
6.16 acres of riverfront property on May 15, 1959, from the Erie
Railroad Company covering the area where the Aaronic Priesthood
is presumed to have been conferred by John the Baptist on May 15,
1829 (ERA 63:339).

● SUSQUEHANNA COUNTY HISTORICAL SOCIETY AND FREE LIBRARY
ASSOCIATION. The Susquehanna County Historical Society and Free
Library Association has important regional historical and genealogi-
cal information. Their facilities are located at Monument Square,
Montrose, PA.

OTHER PENNSYLVANIA SITES

Larry C. Porter

Bradford and Tioga Counties

Bradford and Tioga Counties are located on the northern line of the state in NE and north-central Pennsylvania, and are immediately west of Susquehanna County.

■ **TROY, COLUMBIA, AND RUTLAND TOWNSHIPS**

Troy Township is located in west-central Bradford Co. with the borough of Troy as the principal community. Columbia Township is situated in NW Bradford Co. with the boroughs of Sylvania and Columbia Cross Roads as key communities. Rutland Township is located in NE Tioga Co. with the borough of Roseville as the primary community.

It was in the spring of 1831 that Alpheus Gifford of Rutland Township heard of the doctrines of the gospel as taught by the Prophet Joseph Smith. He was baptized and ordained a priest. He brought home five copies of the Book of Mormon and placed them with friends and family members. Soon after Alpheus went to see the Prophet in Kirtland and took with him friends from Tioga and Bradford Counties. These included his brother Levi Gifford, Elial Strong, Eleazer Miller, Enos Curtis, and Abraham Brown. Alpheus was ordained an elder while there. We also know that Enos Curtis and Elial Strong were baptized in Kirtland. Lyman Wight performed the ordinance for Enos Curtis. Eleazer Miller wasn't baptized until Dec. 1831 in Pennsylvania. On their return to Pennsylvania these brethren conducted extensive missionary work in Tioga and Bradford Counties. Among those baptized under their ministrations were Daniel Bowen in Columbia Township and Ezra Landon in Troy Township (PEN 67–73; PENR 32–34).

During the fall of 1831, Elial Strong, Brother Potter (possibly Robhard Potter of Columbia Township; see 1830 U.S. Census) and Brother Bowen (presumably Daniel Bowen), undertook a short-term mission to Shaftsbury, VT, where "a few received the work" (PEN 73; PENR 37).

In the winter of 1831 Alpheus Gifford, Enos Curtis, and Elial Strong from Rutland Township, and Eleazer Miller and Daniel Bowen from Columbia Township undertook a mission to Mendon, NY. Samuel H. Smith, brother of the Prophet Joseph, had previously paved the way for their labors by placing at least two copies of the Book of Mormon with the Phinehas H. Young and John P. Greene families in that area. These copies were circulated widely among other family members. The elders first visited Phinehas in the town of Victor and then spread to the larger Young and Kimball families in the area before going on to Warsaw, NY, and other locations (PEN 74–78).

Prompted by a desire to learn more of Mormonism, **Brigham and Miriam Young, Phinehas and Clarissa Young,** and **Heber C. Kimball** made an exchange visit with the Pennsylvania elders. They left Mendon about the Jan. 20, 1832, and traveled by horse and sleigh to Bradford County where they met with the people of the Columbia Branch. Brigham Young reported:

> We travelled through snow and ice, crossing rivers until we were almost discouraged; still our faith was to learn more of the principles of Mormonism.
>
> We arrived at the place where there was a small Branch of the Church; we conversed with them, attended their meetings and heard them preach, and after staying about one week we returned home, being still more convinced of the truth of the work, and anxious to learn its principles and to learn more of Joseph Smith's mission. The members of the Branch in Pennsylvania were the first in the Church who received the gift of tongues. (MHBY 2; PEN 79; PENR 38–39)

In the spring of 1832, Phinehas H. Young, Joseph Young, and

their father, John Young, again journeyed to the Columbia Branch. On Apr. 5 Phinehas and John were baptized by Ezra Landon and Daniel Bowen, respectively. And on the following day, Apr. 6, Joseph Young was baptized by Daniel Bowen. Returning to Mendon with the visitors or shortly thereafter, Alpheus Gifford and Eleazer Miller again began to proselyte. Brigham Young was baptized by Eleazer Miller on Apr. 15, 1832 (JD 9:219, LHCK 38). Heber C. Kimball was baptized by Alpheus Gifford on either Apr. 15 or 16, 1832. More than thirty persons were baptized in the Mendon/Victor area in the next few weeks (LHCK 37–38; PEN 83–84; see also Mendon, NY).

The intensity of missionary work from such small branches of the Church as those in Bradford and Tioga Counties is hard to imagine. During the summer of 1832, Eleazer Miller, Enos Curtis, Elial Strong, and an unnamed missionary from Rutland joined with Elders Phinehas and Joseph Young from Mendon and journeyed to Ernestown, Midland District, Upper Canada (now Ontario Province). They labored for about six weeks and were successful in baptizing many and raising up a branch of the Church (PEN 86; EMS May 1833).

In summating his and his friend Eleazer Miller's missionary successes during this period, Elial Strong recorded, "Brother Miller, an elder that has traveled with me in the two last routes, has baptized about twenty. I have baptized, in all thirty-five; nine in Rutland and Sullivan [Sullivan Township, east-central Tioga Co.]; four in Columbia; seven in Troy and three in Canton [Canton Township, SW Bradford Co.], Pennsylvania; five in Shaftsbury, Vermont; one in Chenango [Chenango Township, western Broome Co., NY], and one in Mendon, NY, and five in Ernest Town, Upper Canada" (EMS May 1833; PENR 40).

Concerning his early missionary labors, Elial Strong specified: "We have labored under some disadvantage, not having instructions till within a few months past, respecting this great work, other than the Articles [D&C 20 and 22], Book of Mormon, and the Comforter" (PENR 40–43).

Among those recruited for Zion's Camp in 1834 were Elial Strong and Levi Gifford from Tioga County and Eleazer Miller from Bradford County. Unfortunately, Elial Strong was one of the members of Zion's Camp who died of cholera in Clay County, MO, at the conclusion of the march (PEN 90–92).

■ **RIDGEBURY TOWNSHIP, BRADFORD COUNTY—Site of Mormon Lake and Mormon Hill**

Ridgebury Township is located in NW Bradford County. The northern border of the township is also the PA/NY state line. **Mormon Lake** and **Mormon Hill** are located in the SW corner of Ridgebury Township. Mormon Lake is 3.5 miles SW of the small community of Bentley Creek. Today Mormon Lake is a privately owned hunting, fishing, and recreation resort and is surrounded by numerous cabins and summer homes. Mormon Hill is the extended elevation running from west of Mormon Lake to the NE. From State 4013 (Burwick Turnpike) at Bentley Creek go west on Pennsylvania Rural Route System 4027 (Bucks Creek Road) to its intersection with Ridgebury Township Road 692 (Mormon Lake Road). Turn south and travel .9 mile to Mormon Lake on the west side of the road.

One of the converts to Mormonism in Ridgebury Township was Joel Campbell. Many of the Campbell family joined the Mormon faith. Mormon Lake was reportedly used for baptisms in the area (PEN 94–96).

■ **LIBERTY TOWNSHIP—Settlement of Nauvoo, Pennsylvania**

Liberty Township is in SE Tioga Co., and the small community of Nauvoo lies in the SW corner of that township. From the borough of Liberty go west four miles on State 414 to its intersection with Pennsylvania Rural Route System 58034 at Hartfield. Turn left or SW on 58034 (Nauvoo Road) for two miles to Nauvoo.

Daniel W. Canfield was proselyted to Mormonism and ordained an elder. His settlement was subsequently named Nauvoo about 1844 after the famed Nauvoo, IL. Some maintain that the name "Nauvoo" was applied by a prominent poet of Liberty Township, Lydia Jane Pierson, who chose the name "Because during the Mormon excitement a few persons living in the neighborhood became adherents of that faith, and went with the Mormons to Nauvoo, Illinois" (PEN 99–102; CEZ).

Luzerne County

■ **WILKES-BARRE—Home of Reverend George Lane**

Wilkes-Barre is located in NE Pennsylvania on I-81.

Reverend George Lane of the Methodist Episcopal Church was said to have had a direct role in the Palmyra/Manchester Revival

Reverend George Lane

of 1820. In 1819 he had been appointed Presiding Elder of the Susquehanna District of the Genesee Conference. In regard to Reverend Lane, Oliver Cowdery stated, "Much good instruction was always drawn from his discourses on the scriptures, and in common with others, our brother's [Joseph Smith Jr.'s] mind became awakened" (M&A 1:42; see also BYUS 9, no. 2 [spring]: 321–40).

William Smith, brother of the Prophet Joseph, confirmed Lane's influence:

> Rev. Mr. Lane of the Methodists preached a sermon on "what church shall I join?" And the burden of his discourse was to ask God, using as a text, "If any man lack wisdom let him ask of God who giveth to all men liberally." And of course when Joseph went home and was looking over the text he was impressed to do just what the preacher had said, and going out in the woods with child like, simple trusting faith believing that God meant just what He said, he kneeled down and prayed. (DEN Jan. 20, 1894:11)

Reverend Lane's older sister, Irene Lane, the wife of David Foote, was baptized into the Church during the Nauvoo period in 1845. Reverend Lane died in Wilkes-Barre on May 6, 1859 (BYUS 9, no. 2 [spring]: 338–40).

Chester County

■ WEST NANTMEAL TOWNSHIP (NOW WALLACE TOWNSHIP)—**Edward Hunter's Stone House and Farm Called "Delight"**

Edward Hunter's three-story stone house and farm were called "Delight" by its original owner, William Farguson, and the name

was retained by Edward. The stone house still stands in what was then West Nantmeal Township (known today as Wallace Township) and lies just 10.2 miles NW of West Chester. The house is immediately east of Glen Moore (also Glenmoore), on State 282, on the north side of Marshall

Edward Hunter's Stone House, West Nantmeal (Wallace) Township. (1993)

Road .2 mile west of the three-way intersection of Marshall Road, Chalfont Road, and Little Conestoga Road. It is set back in .2 mile to the north from Marshall Road and is difficult to see because of the trees. The house is privately owned.

Edward Hunter was the seventh child and second son of Edward and Hannah Hunter. He was born in Newton Township, Delaware Co., PA, on June 22, 1793. He acquired the trade of tanner and currier, attended school and mastered the art of surveying, entered business with a Philadelphia merchant, and farmed for a number of years before moving to Chester County (ThC 6:242–43). He bought "Delight" in 1827. He continued to add to the property and by 1839 had amassed some 500

Edward Hunter (Courtesy of LDSCA)

acres (about 260 acres of the original farm have been retained by its present owner, Mr. Albert M. Greenfield Jr.).

The stone house, called "Delight," was built in three sections beginning in 1742 and extending over a succession of years by the

Farguson, Fisher, and Hunter families.[1] A tenant house, large barn
(the Edward Hunter barn burned about 1900), and spring-house
were also added to the farm. Edward took possession of the farm
in 1828 and brought with him his unmarried sister Hannah. He
soon went courting and, at age 37, married Ann Standly in Chester
on Sept. 30, 1830. Edward continued to add to the farm buildings
after his arrival, among them a 74' x 40' wagon shed with a granary
on the west end (EHFS 35–40; AMGJ, Dec. 17, 1993).

In 1839 Edward learned of a Mormon elder, Elijah H. Davis,
who was going to preach in nearby Locust Grove. Edward heard
that the elder "was liable to be badly treated." Edward attended the
meeting for the express purpose of "seeing that the stranger was
not imposed upon" by malcontents in the area. When Elder Davis
was rudely cut off by some opposers, Edward defended the elder's
right to complete his sermon, saying: "I resolved as I lived that Mr.
Davis should be protected, if I had to meet the rabble on their own
ground. I kept my eye on them and determined to stand by him at
the risk of person and property" (ThC 6:244). His actions gained
him the ire of some of his neighbors.

Upon reaching his home that night, he lay awake for a period
of time and reflected on what had taken place. "Why have I taken
such a decided stand for those strangers," Edward questioned, ". . .
and I asked the Lord: 'Are these Mormons thy servants?'" What
happened next greatly influenced the course of his life: "Instantly,
a light came in the room at the top of the door, so great that I
could not endure it. I covered my head with the bed-clothes and
turned over to the wall. I had exerted my mind and body much
that day and soon fell asleep" (ThC 6:244). From that time forth
his home was open to the elders passing through that locality.
Preaching success was such in that sector of the Brandywine Valley
that it was accorded the name of "Mormon Hollow."

Among Edward's Mormon visitors was the **Prophet Joseph
Smith,** who spent several days in his home in Jan. 1840. The
Prophet had gone to Washington, D.C., in Nov. 1839 to present the
Saints' petitions for redress for Missouri losses to President Martin
Van Buren and the United States Congress. In Jan. the Prophet

---

[1] Through the kind arrangement of Diane Bryant (LDS Public Affairs Specialist for the
Marshallton Ward, Downington, PA), Mr. Albert M. Greenfield Jr., owner of the Hunter
home for some 40 years, very graciously conducted the author through the house from
basement to attic and explained the various additions, Dec. 17, 1993.

preached in Philadelphia and also took time to visit the Saints in Chester County. While there, Joseph preached in the West Nantmeal Seminary (see below). When the Prophet left West Nantmeal, Edward accompanied him to the nearest railway station at Downington to take the train back to Philadelphia. From this initial acquaintance a strong friendship emerged between the two men.

In the spring of 1841 **Hyrum Smith** also paid Edward a visit. As the two of them walked along the east branch of Brandywine Creek they discussed the eternal condition of the Hunter children who had died, particularly that of little George Washington Hunter. Hyrum affirmed, "Your son will act as an angel to you; not your guardian angel, but an auxiliary angel, to assist you in extreme trials." Edward declared that his son appeared to him in a vision about a year and a half later to assure his father. Brother Hunter stated, "In appearance he was more perfect than in natural life—the same blue eyes, curly hair, fair complexion, and a most beautiful appearance. I felt disposed to keep him, and offered inducements for him to remain. He then said, in his own familiar voice: 'George has many friends in heaven'" (ThC 6:244–45).

After serious reflection and constant prayer, Edward finally concluded to unite himself with the Latter-day Saints. Elder Orson Hyde visited with the Hunters at West Nantmeal while on his way to Palestine in the Near East, and Edward expressed his great desire to be baptized at the hands of the Apostle. He was immersed in the McConchee Mill Race on his own property, Oct. 8, 1840 (ThC 6:245; EHFS 52–53).

■ WEST NANTMEAL SEMINARY. The West Nantmeal Seminary is located in the NE corner of the old Edward Hunter estate. From the three-way intersection of Marshall Road, Chalfont Road, and Little Conestoga Road proceed north on Little Conestoga Road .3 mile to the West Nantmeal Seminary on the left (west) side of the road. The seminary is set back 42 yards to the west of the Little Conestoga Road. There is a bell tower on the 26' x 30' stone building. Just under the front eave is a half-moon sign which reads, "Wallace Seminary 1830" (the seminary is in Wallace Township today but was originally in West Nantmeal Township). The Seminary is a private dwelling today and owned by Mr. Albert M. Greenfield Jr., who also owns the Edward Hunter home.

West Nantmeal Seminary, built by Edward Hunter in 1830 and preached in by the Prophet Joseph Smith in 1840. (1993)

Immediately north of the West Nantmeal Seminary is the junction of Little Conestoga Road and Seminary Road.

Originally, a log schoolhouse stood on the site of the existing seminary in the NW portion of Edward's property. When that log structure accidentally burned down, Edward's neighbors along Brandywine Creek requested that Edward rebuild it. He then constructed the stone meetinghouse known as the West Nantmeal Seminary in 1830[2] and leased the land for ninety-nine years to West Nantmeal Township. The building was to be for educational purposes and also for holding religious meetings. Edward insisted on one stipulation in the written agreement: that "they would allow all persons and persuasions to meet in it to worship God" (ThC 6:243).

In the spring of 1839, Edward heard of a strange sect called "Mormons," who were preaching in the region. The LDS missionaries had learned of the West Nantmeal Seminary and attempted to make arrangements to meet in the building. Certain of the leading citizens objected to their use of the building. When Edward

---

[2] The *West Chester Village Record*, published in West Chester, PA, Mar. 12, 1870, specified that the West Nantmeal Seminary was built in 1830, and the existing sign on the building reads 1830. However, William E. Hunter's *Edward Hunter, Faithful Steward*, 1970, p. 40, stipulated construction in 1833 (see EHFS 40).

Hunter learned of the missionaries' exclusion from the house, a sense of the injustice being done was aroused within him, and he reminded the people: "When I gave the lease for that land and helped to build that house, it was particularly agreed and stated in the lease that people of every religion should have the privilege of meeting there to worship God. Now, those Mormons are going to have their rights, or else the lease is out and I'll take the Seminary." The bigots were silenced and the missionaries had their preaching station (ThC 6:243–44).

Elder Lorenzo Barnes had been appointed presiding elder in Chester County on Sept. 10, 1839, and Elder Elijah H. Davis was called to assist him (T&S Dec. 1839 1:28). The Saints in Chester County were known as the Brandywine Branch. They gathered in "Mormon Hollow" at the seminary during Dec. 1839. The *West Chester Village Record* noted proceedings, "The Mormons are holding a protracted meeting at the Nantmeal Seminary, in this county.—We understand that about forty members have been baptized in all" (BJ Dec. 14, 1839; PENR 114). By Oct. of 1840 it was estimated that some 130 members were residing within Chester County (JH Oct. 31, 1840).

Joseph Smith Jr. was among those who used the building. During the Prophet's Jan. 1840 visit to the Hunter farm, a conference was held in the West Nantmeal Seminary and Joseph preached to the branch. "Great harmony" persisted and "much important instruction" was given during the gathering (PEN 142–45; ThC 6:244–45).

Edward Hunter moved his family to Nauvoo, IL, in June 1842. There he served on the Nauvoo City Council. A man of means, he was a major contributor in assisting the financially strapped Church in Illinois. After the death of the Prophet, he was called by Brigham Young as Bishop of the Nauvoo Fifth Ward, being ordained by Bishop Newel K. Whitney. During the exodus to the Rocky Mountains, he was appointed captain of 100 wagons, and his company arrived in the Salt Lake Valley on Sept. 29, 1847. Edward was called as bishop of the Salt Lake City Thirteenth Ward. When the Presiding Bishop of the Church, Newel K. Whitney, died, Edward Hunter was chosen to succeed him on Apr. 7, 1851. For the next 32 years he presided over the Aaronic Priesthood of the Church and carried out the other responsibilities of his office. Edward Hunter's death occurred on Oct. 16, 1883, in Salt Lake City (ThC 6:245–50).

Philadelphia County

■ **PHILADELPHIA**

Philadelphia, the largest city in Pennsylvania, is located in the SE sector of the state on the Delaware River. Arterial routes I-95 and I-76 provide ease of access.

EARLY MISSIONARY WORK IN PHILADELPHIA. Latter-day Saint missionary work in Philadelphia began very gradually. Orson Pratt visited the city in 1835, followed by Erastus Snow in 1836. Francis Gladden Bishop labored here in 1837. Elders Jedediah M. Grant, Joshua Grant, and Benjamin Winchester proselyted in the Philadelphia area in Sept. or Oct. 1837. However, a more sustained work was begun by Elders Samuel and Lewis James, who arrived in the city in June 1839. By Dec. 31, 1839, Elder Samuel James had baptized six persons (EMP 147; PEN 150).[3]

● **1. VISITORS CENTER, INDEPENDENCE NATIONAL HISTORICAL PARK.** The visitors center at 3rd and Chestnut Streets is a good place to begin a tour of Philadelphia. Here you can obtain maps, learn of daily park activities, and see exhibits.

● **2. FIRST BANK OF THE UNITED STATES.** First Bank, on 3rd St. between Walnut and Chestnut Streets, was established by Alexander Hamilton as the First Bank of the United States.

● **3. CARPENTERS' HALL.** Carpenters' Hall (320 Chestnut St.) was built in 1770 and was used by the first Continental Congress when they met in Sept. 1774. Today it houses a small display.

● **4. NEW HALL MILITARY MUSEUM.** The New Hall Military Museum, located on Chestnut St. between 3rd and 4th Sts., recounts the histories of the United States Army, Navy, and Marine Corps from 1775 to 1800.

---

[3] Through the hospitality of President Richard H. Morley of the Pennsylvania Philadelphia Mission, the author was introduced to John Shiffert (LDS public affairs specialist for the Jarrettown Ward, Philadelphia Pennsylvania Stake) and Sidney Witzman, a Jewish gentleman from Philadelphia, who outlined the LDS sites: the latter conducted the author to the places of significance to Mormonism, Sept. 25, 1993.

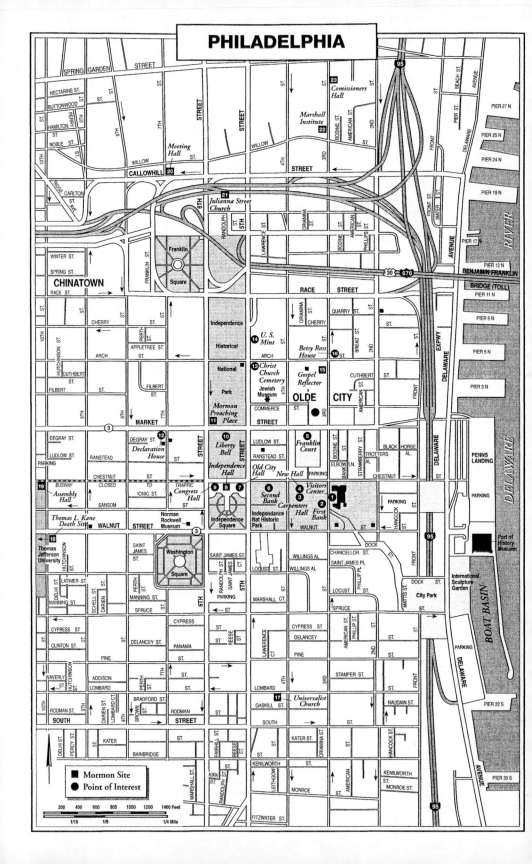

PHILADELPHIA

- **5. FRANKLIN COURT.** The remains of a home that Benjamin Franklin owned from 1763 to 1790 can be found at Franklin Court located between 3rd, 4th, Chestnut, and Market Sts. There is also a museum that displays examples of many of Franklin's inventions, shows a film on his life, and houses other exhibits.

- **6. SECOND BANK OF THE UNITED STATES.** The Second Bank of the United States was located at 420 Chestnut St. This once important financial institution has been restored and now houses the National Portrait Gallery.

The Second Bank of the United States, Philadelphia.

- **7. OLD CITY HALL.** Chief Justice John Jay presided over the Supreme Court from 1791 to 1800 at Old City Hall (5th and Chestnut Sts.). This restored building contains exhibits on early courts.

- **8. INDEPENDENCE HALL.** Independence Hall is located on the south side of Chestnut Street, between Fifth and Sixth Streets, and is at the heart of the **Independence National Historical Park.** Once the statehouse of Pennsylvania, the building was first opened in 1748. It served as the meeting place for the Second Continental Congress and saw the adoption of the **Declaration of Independence** as well as the drafting of the **United States Constitution.** Western and eastern wings were added to Independence Hall in 1789 and 1791, respectively. It also once housed the office of **Thomas L. Kane,** ardent friend of the Mormons.

    The signers of the Declaration of Independence appeared to President **Wilford Woodruff** in the St. George Temple in 1877. President Woodruff said:

> I am going to bear my testimony . . . that those men who laid the foundation of this American Government and signed

Independence Hall, Philadelphia.

the Declaration of Independence were the best spirits the God of Heaven could find on the face of the earth. They were choice spirits, not wicked men. General Washington and all the men that labored for the purpose were inspired of the Lord. Another thing I am going to say here, because I have a right to say it. Every one of those men that signed the Declaration of Independence with General Washington called upon me, as an Apostle of the Lord Jesus Christ, in the Temple at St. George two consecutive nights, and demanded at my hands that I should go forth and attend to the ordinances of the house of God for them. (TMH 87)

President Woodruff had J.D.T. McAllister baptize him for the signers of the Declaration of Independence and 50 other eminent men, including John Wesley and Christopher Columbus. President Woodruff then baptized J.D.T. McAllister for every president of the

Assembly Room of Independence Hall, Philadelphia.

United States except three: Martin Van Buren, James Buchanan, and Ulysses S. Grant. The baptisms took place on Aug. 21, 1877, and the endowment occurred the following day (JWW 7:369; TMH 87–88).

Five of these men were vicariously ordained as high priests following the completion of their temple work. Four are known: George Washington and John Wesley (Aug. 22); Benjamin Franklin (Aug. 23); and Christopher Columbus (Aug. 24). An unknown fifth person was ordained on Aug. 24 (JWW 7:369).

Thomas L. Kane, the great friend of the Mormon people (see Kane, PA), was appointed Clerk of the U.S. District Court for the Eastern District of Pennsylvania in 1847. He "occupied an office at the eastern end of the second floor of the building"—not far from the office of his father, Judge John Kintzing Kane, U.S. Judge for the District of Pennsylvania. (Site 32n). **Wilford Woodruff** visited with Thomas L. Kane in his office on Oct. 5 and 7, 1848 (JWW 3:374–75). In a letter to George A. Smith, Woodruff observed: "I have had two interviews with Col. Kane with-in a few day[s]. He manifested much kindness and friendship. The court room was filled with men. He left all business, came to me as soon as he saw me, grasped my hand for about 10 minutes, appeared more like being alone with me on a west-

Thomas L. Kane.
(Courtesy LDSCA)

ern prairie than in a court house filled [with] men waiting to do business" (JH Oct. 9, 1848). (See "Kane, Pennsylvania" herein for more information about Kane's role as a special friend to the Mormons.

● **9. CONGRESS HALL.** Congress Hall (6th and Chestnut Sts.) was the meeting place of Congress between 1790 and 1800. Both George Washington (in his second term) and John Adams took their presidential oaths of office here.

● **10. LIBERTY BELL PAVILION.** The Liberty Bell, one of America's most cherished symbols, is preserved in the **Liberty Bell Pavilion** (Market St. between 5th and 6th Sts.). The ringing of the bell called the town's citizens together for the first public reading of the

Liberty Bell, Philadelphia.

Declaration of Independence on July 8, 1776. The bell rang for the last time on George Washington's birthday in 1846. The Liberty Bell Pavilion was erected in commemoration of America's Bicentennial and opened on Jan. 1, 1976. The bell can be viewed 24 hours a day.

■ **11. MORMON PREACHING PLACE.** Preaching meetings were held by the Philadelphia Branch of the Church on the NE corner of Market and Sixth Streets (JoHi 11:367). This preaching station was slightly NW of the modern day Liberty Bell Pavilion, which now stands near the SE corner of that same intersection. President Samuel Bennett, Benjamin Winchester, and perhaps Sidney Rigdon, who stayed in Philadelphia until Mar. 5, 1840, were apparently among the preachers at this location (JoHi 11:366–67).

● **12. DECLARATION HOUSE.** Thomas Jefferson was staying in this house (7th and Market Sts.) when he wrote the Declaration of Independence. Today, the reconstructed house contains exhibits and a short film on the Declaration of Independence.

● **13. CHRIST CHURCH CEMETERY.** Five signers of the Declaration of Independence, including Benjamin Franklin, are buried in the Christ Church Cemetery (5th and Arch Sts.).

● **14. U.S. MINT.** Guided tours of the U.S. Mint are available. It is located just north of the Christ Church Cemetery.

■ **15. BROWN, BICKING, & GUILBERT PRINTING FIRM SITE.** The *Gospel Reflector* was published at the printing firm of Brown, Bicking & Guilbert. The site is located at 56 North Third Street between Arch and Market Streets.

    Elder Benjamin Winchester, recently returned from England, presided at a special conference of officers and members held at the Marshall Institute on Dec. 14, 1840. Elder Winchester stated that the purpose of the meeting was to adopt some measures "to spread the gospel more generally in this section of the country."

Elder Erastus Snow presented the prospectus of a periodical to be known as the *Gospel Reflector*, which had been proposed by Elder Winchester. The vote was unanimous in support of the project (EMP 155; JoHi 11:371).

The *Gospel Reflector* was edited by Benjamin Winchester. It ran for 12 numbers, semi-monthly, from Jan. 1, 1841, to June 15, 1841, and contained a total of 316 pages. Winchester quit publishing the periodical in June 1841 primarily because of a lack of funds. Elder Winchester had substantial literary talent, and the publication proved to be an excellent exponent of the tenets of the restored gospel (EMP 154; JoHi 11:371).

● **16. BETSY ROSS FLAG HOUSE.** The Betsy Ross Flag House at 239 Arch St. is traditionally thought to be the place where Betsy Ross sewed the first American flag.

■ **17. UNIVERSALIST CHURCH.** The First Independent Church of Christ at 412 Lombard St. belonged to the Universalist Society in Joseph Smith's day but is now an Orthodox Jewish synagogue occupied by Congregation Kesher Israel. An Orthodox Jewish congregation procured the building in 1888. The building is on the south side of the street. A new entrance has been added on the front at the east, while the original structure is to the west.

After petitioning in Washington, D.C., for redress for Mormon losses in real and personal properties in Missouri, the Prophet and his party visited the Saints in Philadelphia in Jan. 1840. Accompanied by **Sidney Rigdon, Joseph Smith** spoke to a large congregation gathered in the First Independent Church of Christ. The exact date of the Prophet's sermon is not known. However, through the research efforts of President Richard M. Morley, Dan Rolph, and Sidney Weitzman, the old ledger book of the Universalist Church was located at the Jewish synagogue. The rental agreement with the Mormons reads, "1840 January 14 For use of the Church from Rev. J[oseph]. Smith by G. H. McCully $13.63" (ENS 23 [May 1993]: 101). **Parley P. Pratt,** then on his way to the British Mission, was present for the Prophet's famous sermon and recorded his recollections:

> A very large church was opened for him to preach in, and about three thousand people assembled to hear him [perhaps

this is a cumulative figure as it exceeds the capacity of the building for a single congregation, which is about 600]. Brother
Rigdon spoke first, and dwelt on the Gospel, illustrating his
doctrine by the Bible. When he was through, brother Joseph
arose like a lion about to roar; and being full of the Holy
Ghost, spoke in great power, bearing testimony of the visions
he had seen, the ministering of angels which he had enjoyed;
and how he had found the plates of the Book of Mormon, and
translated them by the gift and power of God. He commenced
by saying: "If nobody else had the courage to testify of so glorious a message from Heaven, and of the finding of so glorious a
record, he felt to do it in justice to the people, and leave the
event with God." The entire congregation were astounded;
electrified, as it were, and overwhelmed with the sense of the
truth and power by which he spoke, and the wonders which he
related. A lasting impression was made; many souls were gathered into the fold. (APPP 298–99; see also T&S 1:104)

■ **18. GENERAL THOMAS L. KANE DEATH SITE.** Thomas L. Kane died of
pneumonia on Dec. 26, 1883. His death occurred at "1304 Walnut
Street, where he had been temporarily residing" (SIT 226–29). He
died from pneumonia said to have been "caught while caring for
his eldest son, who had been badly burned in a natural gas explosion" (ENS 1 [Oct. 1971]: 5; for the Mormon reaction to his passing and his place of burial, see Kane, PA).

■ **19. ASSEMBLY BUILDING.** This structure was located at the SW corner of Tenth and Chestnut Streets at the site of what is today the
Gibbon Building, which now houses the Thomas Jefferson
University Hospital. It was a four-story brick building erected in
1834, and "opened to the public in 1839 for the accommodation
of religious gatherings, lectures, debating societies, concerts, etc."
The building was destroyed by fire in Mar. 1851 (JoHi
12:111–12).

The first Latter-day Saint service held in the Assembly Building
convened Jan. 2, 1842, in the north room of the third story.
Preaching services were also continued at the Marshall Institute.
However, in the Apr. 6, 1842, conference a move from the Marshall
Institute to the Assembly Building was approved under the direc-
tion of **Elder Erastus Snow,** the presiding officer. Elders George J.

Adams and Benjamin Winchester entered into a public discussion with Reverend George Montgomery West, D.D., a celebrated theologian, at this location from Aug. 1–14, 1842. And on Oct. 15 of that same year **Presidents Hyrum Smith** and **William Law** were present for the installation of Peter Hess as president of the Philadelphia Branch (JoHi 12:111–14).

■ **20. MEETING HALL SITE.** This four-story brick building was located on the NE corner of Seventh and Callowhill Streets. It no longer exists but once stood on what is now a small v-shaped cement island in the middle of the street, framed by a short Callowhill Street on the north, an extended Callowhill Street on the south, and Seventh Street on the west.

Enjoying some success in proselyting, Elder Winchester procured a hall in the second story. It was opened to the public for a preaching service on Wed., Oct. 16, 1839, at 7 P.M. The **Prophet Joseph Smith** arrived in Philadelphia on Dec. 21, 1839, and preached to large audiences in this building, in the Universalist Church, and in other locations in the city (JoHi 11:362–63). On Dec. 23, 1839 (the Prophet's 34th birthday), Joseph Smith again presided at Seventh and Callowhill when the Philadelphia Branch was organized with Samuel Bennett as president. The Prophet presided once again on Jan. 13, 1840, in company with his "redress" delegation to the nation's capitol; Sidney Rigdon, Elias Higbee, Orrin Porter Rockwell, and Robert D. Foster were all part of the delegation. Elders Parley and Orson Pratt, who were then on their way to Great Britain, were also present. The mission of the committee seeking redress for the Saints' losses in Missouri at Washington, D.C., was presented and approved by the congregation. During the latter part of January the Prophet's delegation returned to Washington, D.C., leaving Sidney Rigdon with the Saints to recuperate from his illness (JoHi 11:365–68).

■ **21. JULIANNA STREET CHURCH SITE.** The Julianna Street Church was a brick chapel on the west side of Julianna Street (now Randolph Street), between Wood and Callowhill Streets. In 1919 it was at 328 Randolph Street. Today, however, Randolph Street has been blocked off by a brick patio, shrubbery, and trees just south of where the old Julianna Street Church once stood. Now I-676 goes right over the top of the site. The chapel was built in about 1835 or

1836 by the *Deutsche Evangelische Gemeinde* (German Lutheran Church).

The **initial Latter-day Saint service** in the building was held on Sun., Nov. 20, 1842. As 1842 came to a close the Philadelphia Branch counted 85 persons who had been baptized that year. Although many families had gathered to Nauvoo, the branch membership still numbered 300 (JoHi 12:114–16).

A "Special Message to the Saints in Philadelphia" was issued by Brigham Young and the Twelve dated May 20, 1843. The directive read: "All the members of that branch of the Church of Jesus Christ of Latter-day Saints which is located in Philadelphia, Pennsylvania, who are desirous of doing the will of heaven and of working out their own salvation by keeping the laws of the celestial kingdom, are hereby instructed and counseled to remove from thence without delay and locate themselves in the city of Nauvoo, where God has a work for them to accomplish" (HC 5:413). Many heeded this mandate, making personal arrangements for their removal to Nauvoo.

■ **22. MARSHALL INSTITUTE SITE.** The site of the Marshall Institute is on the west side of Third Street just north of the NW corner of the junction of Third Street and Willow Street in what is now the parking lot of the Social Security Administration Building or SSI. Erected early in the 19th century, it was a four-story brick building and "was one of the most popular public halls in the district of the Northern Liberties." In 1840 it was the third door north of Willow Street and in 1918 was at 444 and 446 North Third Street. The building was subsequently demolished and no longer exists (JoHi 11:367–68).

On Apr. 4, 1840, **Benjamin Winchester** announced that meetings of the Latter-day Saints would no longer be held at Seventh and Callowhill Streets, but that services were now to be conducted in the third story of the Marshall Institute. The first meeting was held on Sunday, Apr. 5, 1840.

Commencing on Oct. 17, 1840, **Elder Orson Hyde** presided at a conference of the Church in the Marshall Institute. Thirteen branches from the region were represented, showing a membership of 896 persons (JoHi 11:369–70). The next year President Hyrum Smith presided at the Apr. 6–7, 1841, conference. He read to the congregation the Jan. 19, 1841, revelation of the Prophet

(D&C 124), and instructed the Philadelphia Saints in regard to the gathering at Nauvoo and to the need of members' support of the building of the Nauvoo temple (JoHi 11:371–72).

After a time away from the Marshall Institute, Church services resumed there on Sept. 10, 1843. On July 8, 1884, news reached the Saints in Philadelphia of the assassination of the Prophet Joseph and his brother Hyrum Smith. On Sunday, July 14, resolutions were passed and "an appropriate badge of mourning [was] adopted to be worn for thirty days" (JoHi 13:509–10).

On May 13, 1846, **Elder Jesse C. Little,** president of the New England and Middle Atlantic States Mission, presided at a conference in the Marshall Institute. After the meetings he was introduced to Colonel Thomas L. Kane, a non-Mormon observer. This providential meeting led to Kane's close association with Little and to President James K. Polk's subsequent call of the Mormon Battalion for service in the U.S. Army during the Mexican War. Colonel Kane afterwards gave a lifetime of invaluable service to the Latter-day Saints at highly crucial times in their history (see Kane, PA).

■ **23. COMMISSIONERS HALL OF THE NORTHERN LIBERTIES.** The site of the Commissioners Hall is located on Third Street, between Willow Street and Spring Garden in a district known as the Northern Liberties. The building no longer stands, having been torn down in 1868. It was on the east side of the street, just south of the existing Fire Administration Building, and occupied what are now 515–519 Third Street (under the old numbering system it was 281 North Third Street). The Commissioners Hall was a three-story brick building and had served originally as the officers' quarters of the military barracks erected by the provincial government in 1757. During the Revolutionary War it housed troops of the Continental Army. The commissioners of the district of the Northern Liberties used the building as a town hall from 1815 to 1854 (JoHi 11:361–62).

Benjamin Winchester secured the use of the building and posted the first LDS service for Sept. 9, 1839, in the *Public Ledger and Daily Transcript:* "Notice: There will be a meeting of the Latter Day Saints, or Mormons, this evening at early candle light, at Commissioners Hall, N.L. The meeting will be addressed by the Reverend B. Winchester (JoHi 11:361)." The building was used through September, and Elder Winchester gave some 12 sermons during the period. He also entered into a debate with Dr. Bird, a Presbyterian clergyman, during the occupancy of these quarters. On Oct. 1, 1839, a number of new converts were baptized. William Small is reported to have been the first candidate baptized in Philadelphia (JoHi 1:70; 11:362). In Sept. 1840, George W. Elley gave a series of lectures against Mormonism. **Orson Hyde,** then on his way to Palestine, visited Philadelphia and joined with the elders in their defense of the faith against Elley (JoHi 11:369).

SIDNEY RIGDON IN PHILADELPHIA. In 1861 Sidney Rigdon received correspondence from a former adherent, Joseph Newton, who was a merchant in Philadelphia. Newton had gathered a small group together who subscribed to Joseph Smith's "Prophecy on War" (D&C 87) and felt that the Civil War was the final war before "the coming of the Son of Man." In response to Newton's entreaties, Sidney visited in Philadelphia in 1863 for a period of three weeks. While here he helped organize The Church of Jesus Christ of the Children of Zion. Numbers of the group later lost faith in their prophet, Sidney Rigdon, and some were proselyted to the Reorganized Church in 1867 (SR 405–7, 436).

Franklin County

■ **"ADVENTURE FARM"—Place of Gathering for Sidney Rigdon's Church of Christ**

Sidney Rigdon
(Courtesy of RLDSLA)

Greencastle is located in the Cumberland Valley, not far from the Maryland state border in south-central Pennsylvania. It is situated in Antrim Township, Franklin Co., at the junction of U.S. 11 and State 16. The site of nearby "Adventure Farm," so designated by the previous owner, was the place of gathering for Sidney Rigdon's The Church of Christ from 1845 to 1847. It is 1.2 miles west of Greencastle on State 16 where that highway intersects Conococheague Creek. The 390-acre farm lay on the north side of State 16 and

on the east side of Conococheague Creek. The large barn, which
once belonged to The Church of Christ and where many sermons
were preached by its elders, stood on the east side of the creek and
north of the road until a few years ago when it was destroyed by fire
(LC). In Rigdon's time a beautiful five-arch stone bridge crossed
Conococheague Creek at a point ½ to ¾ mile SW of the farm buildings.
The bridge no longer stands. A number of graves from the Rigdon
occupation were accidentally uncovered in the **"Mormon Graveyard"**
on the farm in July 1980 (KHS 18:64, 67).

Sidney Rigdon felt inspired to designate a place of gathering
for the Church of Christ where Zion could be established. He and
William E. McLellin visited Greencastle and vicinity in early Aug.
1845 and investigated the 390-acre "Adventure Farm" of Andrew G.
McLanahan west of that community. Sidney Rigdon is reported to
have declared to McLellin, "This is the place the Lord has shown
us in visions to be the site of the city of the new Jerusalem."
McLanahan valued his property at $14,700. Rigdon's brother-in-law,
Peter Boyer, placed a $1,500 deposit on the land and followed that
with an additional payment of $5,400. The remaining balance of
$8,700 was due in a lump sum on Apr. 1, 1847. The deed to the
farm was signed Apr. 1, 1846. The monies of Peter Boyer, Carvel
Rigdon, and others would later be forfeited for failure to meet the
legal requirements as specified (SR 379–80; KHS 18:63).

Rigdon and his family left Pittsburgh for Greencastle on May
13, 1846. Between 150 and 200 followers remained in the fold at
this time and numbers of them began working the farm. Ebenezer
Robinson, an experienced printer from the Kirtland and Nauvoo
days, joined with editors Sidney Rigdon and Samuel Bennett to
publish the *Messenger and Advocate* in Greencastle. Ebenezer said
that they "published a few numbers of the *Messenger and Advocate of
the Church of Christ,* Monthly, in the summer and fall of 1846, in the
borough of Greencastle" (FCSA 53). Both Sidney Rigdon and
Ebenezer Robinson chose to live in Greencastle rather than on the
farm. Ebenezer Robinson and Samuel James served as counselors
to Sidney Rigdon. Other leaders included William Richards, Dr.
George M. Hinkle, Jeremiah Hatch Jr., Edward B. Wingate, Joseph
H. Newton, Leonard Soby, and Amos B. Tomlinson. Each Sabbath
the faithful heard preaching from Sidney Rigdon and other
brethren during worship services held in the Church's large barn

(SR 382 n. 7, 388; SRM 143; KHS 18:64; FCSA Nov. 17–21, 1930, 53–54).

Rigdon's relationships with the inhabitants of Greencastle were often less than productive. At one juncture his hostile rhetoric towards them was pointedly designed to provoke a reaction. He informed the citizens that "the conflict would rage till the streets were drenched with blood" and that there was not enough religion in the town "to save a nest of woodpeckers" (SRM 143). These antagonisms, coupled with the congregation's financial woes and a combination of related matters, soon caused many of Rigdon's adherents to join the ranks of the disillusioned. John Wickliffe Rigdon stated that his father's "few followers became discouraged and did not believe their object would be accomplished and went away" (SR 90–91).

Unable to make the final payment to Andrew McLanahan, the property was seized on Apr. 7, 1847. In Oct. 1847 the farm was sold at a sheriff's sale, and Andrew McLanahan was the high bidder. The properties were listed at that time as consisting of "a two story log dwelling House, three tenant houses, and a big barn thereon erected" (KHS 18:64). Sidney Rigdon had earlier withdrawn to the home of his son-in-law George W. Robinson in Cuba, NY, to await the final outcome of the faith's financial difficulties in Pennsylvania. Ultimately there was no assessed need to return (SR 382 n. 7, 388; SRM 143; see also Friendship, NY).

Allegheny County

■ **PITTSBURGH**

Pittsburgh is located in SW Pennsylvania at the confluence of the Allegheny and Monongahela Rivers as they merge to form the Ohio River. Interstate Highways 76 and 79 are among the major arteries connecting with Pittsburgh.

■ **THE FIRST BAPTIST CHURCH OF PITTSBURGH.** The site of the First Baptist Church of Pittsburgh, where Sidney Rigdon was pastor from 1822–23, is located on the NE corner of the intersection of 3rd Avenue and Grant Street in downtown Pittsburgh. This one-story meetinghouse was replaced by a two-story brick structure in 1833.

The church house in which Sidney Rigdon preached no longer exists. A state charter was granted to "the First Baptist Church and congregation of the city of Pittsburgh" in 1822. That original charter is currently housed in the modern First Baptist Church of Pittsburgh at 159 North Bellefield Avenue (SW corner of Bellefield Ave. and Bayard Street). Heading the list of charter members is the signature of Sidney Rigdon. Rigdon's name is also carved in the wall of the vestibule of the existing church as one of the original pastors (DBS; HACP 367–68). There is a bronze plaque on a building across the street, on the SE corner of the intersection of 3rd Avenue and Grant Street, that specifies, "Near this site, the First Baptist Church of Pittsburgh organized in [Apr.] 1812, built its first sanctuary, and worshipped therein."

In Nov. 1821, while residing in Trumball Co., OH, Sidney Rigdon, an ordained Baptist minister, was requested by the First Baptist Church of Pittsburgh to take the "pastoral charge of said Church." He served as pastor from Jan. 28, 1822, to Oct. 11, 1823. Unable to uphold the doctrines taught in this congregation of the Redstone Baptist Association, Sidney said he withdrew as pastor. Baptist records simply state that he was excommunicated. They don't mention that the majority of the congregation accompanied Rigdon (SR 26–32).

DEVELOPMENT OF THE PITTSBURGH BRANCH. Zebedee Coltrin of Strongsville, OH, and his companion, Jesse Gause, started from Ohio on a mission to the East on Aug. 1, 1832. They visited a number of communities in NE Ohio and then crossed into Pennsylvania, arriving at Pittsburgh on Aug. 16, 1832. In summation of their mission, Zebedee stated that they had taken every opportunity to preach and also bear witness of the restoration and the Book of Mormon (PEN 104–6).

In Oct. 1832, eight families from the areas of Mendon Township, NY, and Columbia Township, PA, met at Olean Point, NY, the headwaters of the Allegheny River, to travel together to Zion, Jackson Co., MO, via the Allegheny and Ohio Rivers. They built two family boats and floated down to Pittsburgh. Here, two of the families, those of **Lorenzo D. Young** and **Phinehas H. Young,** elected to remain in Pittsburgh for a season and subsequently organized a branch of the Church in the community. They labored in Pittsburgh from Oct. 27, 1832, to July 3, 1833 (MHBY xxxii; PEN 89).

Pittsburgh became another geographical crossroads of the Church and was home to one of the most important of the eastern branches. An innumerable train of elders labored in and passed through this key city on their way to assignments.

While proselyting in Pittsburgh in 1842, **Apostle John E. Page** wrote of his experience: "I have sold a good quantity of the Books of Mormon, voice of Warning, Hymn books, Bro. Orson Pratt's 'Origin of the Book of Mormon' and 'Slander Refuted' of my own publication. Our books sell fast, no mistake, and all helps the work. The fact is the day of creeping is over, the cause is onward, thank God" (JH Jan. 30, 1842). Elder Page and others secured the use of the "old Cumberland Church" in Pittsburgh on a two-year lease for their meetings commencing in 1842 (T&S 3:843). The Cumberland Church was erected on "Sixth street, nearly opposite Trinity Protestant Episcopal Church" (HACP 323–24).

Brigham Young informs us of a visit of six of the Quorum of the Twelve to the Pittsburgh Branch. The Apostles present included Brigham Young, Heber C. Kimball, Orson Pratt, John E. Page, Wilford Woodruff, and George A. Smith, who preached in Pittsburgh Temperance Hall and at the homes of Jeremiah Cooper and Richard Savary in July 1843. At Brother Savary's, Brigham Young explained to the elders, "They should in the first place control themselves and bring their passions into subjection to the law of God, then preside over their wives and children in righteousness, which would qualify them to preside over Branches of the Church" (MHBY July 27–29, 1843, 137–39).

In June 1844, just nine days before the Prophet Joseph was martyred at Carthage, IL, Sidney Rigdon and his family left Nauvoo for Pittsburgh. Outwardly, it appeared that Sidney Rigdon and the Prophet were still closely aligned, and President Rigdon was merely going to Pittsburgh to regulate affairs. Behind the scenes, however, the two men had serious differences over the Prophet's stand on the matter of plural marriage (SRC 133).

As news of the death of the Prophet and Hyrum Smith reached Pittsburgh, Sidney Rigdon returned to Nauvoo, arriving on Aug. 3, 1844. At a gathering of the Saints on Aug. 8, 1844, the Twelve Apostles were sustained by the body of the Church as their spiritual leaders, and the proffered "guardianship" of Sidney Rigdon was rejected. Though he outwardly seemed to accept the direction of the Twelve, Sidney began to organize against the Twelve and was excommunicated on Sept. 8, 1844 (BE 1:34). He left Nauvoo onboard the *Osprey* on Sept. 10, 1844, for St. Louis. There he boarded the *Mayflower* on a return passage to Pittsburgh (SR 359).

In Pittsburgh, Sidney lost little time in rallying his supporters, organizing what he would later call the Church of Christ, and publishing the first issue of a newspaper borrowing its title from the Kirtland days, the *Latter Day Saint's Messenger and Advocate,* Oct. 15, 1844. The congregation met for worship at 201 Liberty Street. Among those attracted to Rigdon's organization were George W. Robinson, Ebenezer Robinson, Samuel James, William E. McLellin, Austin Cowles, Oliver F. Olney, George M. Hinkle, and Benjamin Winchester (JWEM 332–37; SRM 136–37). Sidney soon announced that the Lord had directed the Church to gather as a body in the Cumberland Valley, near Greencastle, PA. At their Apr. 1845 conference, he informed the membership that the next conference in October would convene at the newly designated site (SR 376–81, 388; see "Adventure Farm" near Greencastle, PA).

■ **ST. CLAIR TOWNSHIP**

The site of the William Rigdon home, where **Sidney Rigdon** was born, is located 1.3 miles NW of the small community of Library. (Library is 10.5 miles SW of the Civic Arena in downtown Pittsburgh.) According to the landowner's 1851 map, the Rigdon homestead was situated on the SE corner of the intersection of what

is now the junction of State 88 (Library Road) and Berryman Road in the borough of Bethel Park. That intersection is .4 mile north of the junction of State 88 (Library Road) and the Clifton Road on State 88. "The Rigdon house at that location was standing in 1900 and has been referred to locally as the Mormon Temple because Sidney Rigdon preached there after leaving Nauvoo in 1844. The property was purchased from the Rigdon family in about 1903 and the Rigdon house was torn down. The house that now

Sidney Rigdon, pastor
(Courtesy of RLDSLA)

stands there was built about 1905 by W. I. Berryman. Today's address of the Rigdon homestead is 6115 Library Road, Bethel Park, Pennsylvania" (SGB).

After the Revolutionary War, William Rigdon located in what was then St. Clair Township, Washington Co. Today the area is part of Bethel Park Borough and South Park Township, Allegheny Co. (SGB Dec. 31, 1996). William obtained 358⅝ acres situated along the Piney Fork Branch of Peters Creek (SR 4). Sidney Rigdon was born on Feb. 19, 1793, to William Rigdon and Nancy Gallaher in St. Clair Township (SR 4). At a young age, Sidney was baptized by Reverend David Philips as a member of the Peters Creek Baptist Church (HACP 368).

Luke S. Johnson related that in 1831 he accompanied Sidney Rigdon on a mission from Kirtland, OH, to Pennsylvania. Luke said, "We journeyed to Pittsburg, (in the vicinity where Sidney was born and raised), where we preached the Gospel to his relatives, and I baptized his mother [Nancy] and his older brother [Carvel Rigdon], also several others in that neighborhood, and we organized a Branch" (MS 26:835).

■ **PETERS CREEK BAPTIST CHURCH AND CEMETERY.** The Peters Creek Baptist Church is located ½ mile south on State 88 from the William Rigdon homesite and .1 mile west of State 88. A plaque on the exterior wall of the modern meetinghouse reads: "Peters Creek Baptist Church, Organized 1773, First Building 1780, Second Building 1856, Third Building 1884, Fourth Building 1958, An Historic Church Older Than the Nation" (SGB).

The Rigdons were members of this church. It was the first Baptist Church established in western Pennsylvania, and the particular society is still in existence today. William Rigdon, born in 1748, died on May 26, 1810, at age 62 when Sidney was only 17 years old. He is buried in the cemetery on the south side of the road, immediately west of the Peters Creek Baptist Church (SGB; SR 3–7, 11 n. 1).

■ **NEW ENGLAND HOLLOW**

Stephen G. Beus, LDS Church leader and local historian, informed the author of a body of Mormons who lived in New England Hollow, about eight miles SE of Pittsburgh in the 1880s. They were apparently a residue of the followers of Sidney Rigdon and lived in a valley called New England Hollow (SGB). These Saints requested rebaptism into the LDS faith in 1885. William Palmer, president of the Northwestern States Mission, held a conference here on May 16, 1886, and, according to a plaque on the modern ward house, organized a branch on May 17, 1886 (FTHV 4). They were formed into the New England Branch and were presided over by George Barnes. "The New England Branch evolved into the Wilson Branch in 1923, the Pleasant Hills Branch on June 27, 1965, and the Pittsburgh 2nd Ward on May 11, 1969, with the organization of the Pittsburgh Pennsylvania Stake. The chapel housing the Pittsburgh 2nd and 5th Wards is located about one mile to the west of New England Hollow" at 210 Old Clairton Road, Clairton, PA (SGB).

Washington County

■ MONONGAHELA—The Church of Christ

Monongahela is located 18 miles south of Pittsburgh, on the Monongahela River and at the junction of State 837 and State 481. The Church of Christ headquarters and meetinghouse is situated in that community on the SE corner of Lincoln and Sixth Streets. This general church building was dedicated on Oct. 19, 1930, by W. H. Cadman. It houses the Monongahela Branch of the Pennsylvania District.

William Bickerton was converted to Sidney Rigdon's Church of Christ in 1845 and was called to preside over a branch in West Elizabeth. When the Rigdonites faltered in 1847, William and others continued to meet and drew away many of the disassociated Saints in western Pennsylvania. William Bickerton wrote to the LDS Church at Council Bluffs, IA, requesting that elders be sent to assist them. Elders Murray and Ross were assigned to labor in West Elizabeth and there organized a branch of the Church on May 25, 1851. William Bickerton was sustained as presiding elder of the branch. However, he and others separated from President Young and the Twelve on Mar. 10, 1852, over the issue of plural marriage. Bickerton later organized the Church of Christ at Green Oak (now Greenock), PA, in 1862 (HCJC 1–9, 195–97; PENR 218; FTHV 57).

Since 1862 the doctrines of the Church of Christ have been

widely preached nationally and internationally with extensive missionary work being done in Canada, Ghana, India, Italy, Mexico,
Nigeria, South America, and throughout the United States (DPOR
90).

McKean County

■ KANE—Named in Honor of Thomas Leiper Kane

The borough of Kane, McKean Co., PA, is located at the junction of U.S. 6 and State 321 in the SW corner of this NW highlands
county.

Thomas Leiper Kane was born in Philadelphia on Jan. 27, 1822,
to the well-known jurist, Judge John Kintzing Kane and Jane Duval
Leiper Kane. After completing his college training in the United
States, Thomas lived in both England and France for a season. He
spent considerable time in Paris as an attaché of the American
Legation. After returning to America he became engaged in the
anti-slavery struggle and was heavily involved in the "Underground
Railroad." On Mar. 4, 1846, he was admitted to the bar in
Philadelphia. "He attained the position of clerk of the U.S. District
Court for the Eastern District of Pennsylvania, having his office
near his father in Independence Hall [second floor, eastern end]."
After the passage of the fugitive slave law, he found that his duties
conflicted with his conscience, and he resigned his appointment
(SIT 6–11, note on 32; BTLK 14–15; CWD 447).

The Borough of Kane, nestled in the Appalachian Mountain
plateau known as the Alleghenies, is named in honor of **Thomas
Leiper Kane.** In 1857, Thomas's father, Judge John K. Kane, organized what was called the McKean, Elk, Land and Improvement
Company. When the charter was drawn up it was necessary to find
someone who could map the area, estimate the value of timber and
minerals, survey roads, and identify sites for settlements. Thomas
Kane was offered the job. His industrious endeavors to develop the
natural resources in the area were curtailed by his arbitration in the
Utah War in 1858, and again interrupted by the advent of the Civil
War in Apr. 1861.

Thomas L. Kane was among the very first to volunteer for the
Civil War. He organized the famous 42nd Pennsylvania Regiment

known as "the bucktails." He gave the honor of colonelcy to Mexican War veteran Charles J. Biddle and served as Lt. Colonel. However, he succeeded Biddle on Nov. 25, 1861, and was promoted from Lt. Col. to Brigadier General on Sept. 7, 1862. General Kane and his men were celebrated for their bravery throughout the war. He fought in numerous battles and was wounded in five of these engagements. Kane was brevetted Major-General for his exceptional gallantry at the battle of Gettysburg. After the war General Kane returned to his project of founding a town. As president of the New York, Lake Erie & Western Coal Railroad Company, General Kane was responsible for building the great Kinzua Viaduct in 1882. At the time of its construction it was the highest railroad bridge in the world. It spans 2,053 feet across the Kinzua Creek Valley and stands 301 feet high. Rebuilt in 1900, it is still operative today through the auspices of the Knox, Kane, Kinzua Railroad, Marienville, PA. In 1977 the Kinzua Bridge was placed on the National Register of Historic Places and in 1982 was designated as a national historic civil engineering landmark (BTLK 21–25; CWD 447–48; PPN 220–21; SIT 204, 247–54; CN Oct. 17, 1970, 7).

In May 1846, **Jesse C. Little,** presiding elder of the New England and Middle Atlantic States Mission, was passing through Philadelphia on his way to Washington, D.C., to meet with the president of the United States, James K. Polk. At the instigation of Brigham Young and the Twelve, it was Elder Little's intent to offer the president any assistance that would be mutually beneficial to the government's expansion of American interests in the West and to the Mormons' exodus from Nauvoo. Little stayed in Philadelphia to preside at a Church conference on May 13, 1846. Seated in the congregation was observer Thomas L. Kane. At his request, Colonel Kane was introduced to Elder Little. Little stated that Colonel Kane expressed his interest in obtaining "information relative to our people going to California, having a desire to travel with them, in company with the Twelve. I made an appointment to meet him . . . at his father's" (SIT 3).

Elder Little met with Kane and explained the exodus of the Mormons from Nauvoo, the general gathering of the Saints from the eastern states, and his own intended meeting with President Polk. The ensuing friendship that developed between the two men led to Kane's writing a letter of introduction to George M. Dallas, vice president of the United States, and in making an offer to personally assist in getting appropriations for the Saints. Kane journeyed to Washington and personally called on the secretary of state, the secretary of war, and President Polk on behalf of his Mormon friends. The two men's calls on government officials included more than one visit with President James K. Polk (BYUS 21, no. 4 [fall]: 389–91).

Their joint efforts culminated in the enlistment of the Mormon Battalion in the Mexican War in July 1846. Kane and Little traveled to St. Louis, MO, together, Elder Little going on to Nauvoo, IL, while Colonel Kane continued on to Fort Leavenworth, KS, with orders for Colonel Stephen W. Kearny. Colonel Kane then traveled to Council Bluffs, IA, and was instrumental in the recruitment of the battalion. While there he became seriously ill from pulmonary tuberculosis. He was nursed back to health by the pioneers, endearing him further to the Saints. Assisting in Kane's recuperation was Church **Patriarch John Smith,** uncle of the Prophet Joseph. Although Thomas was not a member of the Church, he asked John to give him a patriarchal blessing. His request was honored on Sept. 7, 1846, at Cutler's Park, Omaha Nation. In the blessing he was assured with these words: "The Lord thy God is well pleased with thy exertions." Thomas next went to Nauvoo himself, and after returning to the East, lectured favorably on the merits of his Latter-day Saint friends. His best-known treatise on the subject was his Philadelphia address entitled *The Mormons, A discourse Delivered Before The Historical Society of Pennsylvania, March 26, 1850,* which he printed and distributed in pamphlet form at his own expense. It was later published both in English and several foreign languages for use by LDS missionaries (SIT 13–33, 42–49; CN Mar. 22, 1980, 12–13; EH 648).

When Mormon leaders in Salt Lake City decided to apply for territorial status in 1849, a delegation consisting of Wilford Woodruff and John M. Bernhisel visited Colonel Kane in Philadelphia. Kane urged them to seek statehood rather than territorial status. Thus, he argued, they could enjoy more local autonomy and be freed from certain governmental appointees by the Washington bureaucracy. The attempt to secure statehood was made through the U.S. Congress but was denied because of the Compromise of 1850. The Territory of Utah was created instead. Colonel Kane, nevertheless, had once again displayed his foresight in favor of the needs of the Mormon people (SIT 34–41).

In 1858 Thomas L. Kane traveled to Utah under the alias of "Dr. A. Osborne," supposedly "a botanist" from Philadelphia. He came as an unofficial envoy of President James Buchanan and was very influential in arranging a settlement in the Utah War of 1857–58. "Run-a-way officials" from Utah had reported a supposed insurrection in the territory. Without proper investigation of the actual circumstances, President Buchanan had dispatched 2,500 U.S. Army troops to the territory, which troops were held in abeyance by Utah Militia. Kane arrived in Salt Lake City on Feb. 25, 1858. During his meetings with Brigham Young, the discussion turned to the health of Kane, who was very ill. President Young consoled his confidant: "The Lord has sent you here, friend Thomas, and He will not let you die. No, you cannot die until your work is done. Your name will live with the saints in all eternity. You have done a great work, and you will do a greater work still" (CN Mar. 22, 1980, 13). Colonel Kane was successful in bringing together the leaders of the conflict. He instigated a meeting between Brigham Young and the replacement governor, Alfred Cumming, and made it possible for "peace commissioners" Lazarus W. Powell and Major Ben McCulloch to negotiate an equitable solution to a very volatile situation. President Buchanan hailed Colonel Kane as a peacemaker in his annual message to Congress in 1858 (ENS 1 [June 1971]: 26).

Thomas L. Kane was never baptized into the LDS Church. Brigham Young sent a letter to Thomas, dated May 8, 1858, in which he mentions to his friend that he had not taken occasion to speak with him except in a "casual" manner on the subject of religion. He now, however, wished permission to converse with or write him on the subject. However, President Young's efforts did not result in the "secret baptism" of Kane as some have speculated (LOL 94–95, 105–6 n. 14).

■ **THOMAS L. KANE MEMORIAL CHAPEL.** The Thomas L. Kane Memorial Chapel is at 30 Chestnut Street in Kane (SW corner of Chestnut and Edgar Streets). An LDS missionary couple are on duty at the site, living in a cottage on the chapel grounds. The chapel houses the Kane Branch of the Church (GR).

Thomas Lieper Kane provided the land for the Church building. Funds were primarily furnished by his aunt, Ann Gray Thomas. A large marble tablet in the sanctuary bears the inscription, "This Church is erected by Ann Gray Thomas in memory of her father

Thomas Leiper, her mother, Elizabeth Coultas Gray and of their children." This is followed by a listing of the ten Leiper children and concludes with the biblical passage from Joshua 24:15: "Choose ye this day whom ye will serve [. . .] as for me and my house, we will serve the Lord."

Thomas L. Kane Memorial Chapel and statue. (1992)

Work on the church began in 1876. The cornerstone was laid by Mrs. Ann Gray Thomas that summer. The construction phase was practically completed at the time of the Aug. 1877 dedicatory services. However, the first worship service did not occur until the building's final completion on Sept. 1, 1878.

The church was designed in the form of a cross using the liturgical pattern of the Anglican Church. The building was donated to the Presbyterians and was designated the first Presbyterian church of Kane, Pennsylvania. It was built upon lines not conforming to any street or thoroughfare in the town, and so laid out that the head of the Cross, the Chancel area, is facing east and is geographically oriented toward Jerusalem, the angle being exactly South 70 degrees East (ATTC 18–25).

Thomas L. Kane, a special friend of the Mormons.

The building walls are of tan-, buff-, and pink-tinted sandstone quarried in the vicinity of Kane. The roof, originally made of slate, has been restored. The inside of the chapel has likewise been restored to its 1878 status. Its ceiling is of heartwood black cherry harvested in the area. Beautiful stained glass windows adorn the church. A pipe organ was added in 1910, a gift from the Andrew Carnegie Foundation. Surrounding the interior of the chapel today are showcases displaying an array of Kane family documents and memorabilia.

Latter-day Saint leaders had long sought for appropriate opportunities to memorialize Thomas L. Kane for his unique friendship and substantial aid to the Mormon people. The Saints had previously honored Colonel Kane in 1848 by naming their settlement at Miller's Hollow, Council Bluffs, IA, **"Kanesville."** When it was created in 1860, south-central Utah's Kane County was named in his honor. Also, the small community of Kanesville, Davis Co., UT, was named in his honor Apr. 27, 1886. On Jan. 14, 1959, a heroic bronze statue of Thomas L. Kane was unveiled in the rotunda of the Utah State Capitol Building in Salt Lake City. Ortho R. Fairbanks was the sculptor of this exceptional work (CN Jan. 17, 1959, 2–3, 15; SIT xiii–xv).

When the Presbyterian Church, who had owned the building for many years, put the chapel up for sale in 1970, the Brethren eagerly purchased the building. The **Kane Memorial Chapel** was formally opened to the public with a series of open house meetings and organ recitals June 2–6, 1970, with **Elder Marion D. Hanks** representing the General Authorities (CN May 29, 1971, 5). On July 1, 1972, a heroic-size bronze statue of General Kane was unveiled by Elder Marion D. Hanks near the west entrance to the chapel. It was placed on a base of native sandstone bearing a bronze plaque with the inscription, "General Thomas L. Kane, courageous Civil War hero and friend of the Mormon People." Among the speakers at the ceremonies were **J. Willard Marriott** and **E. Kent Kane,** a grandson of Kane (CN June 17, 1972, 4). On June 21, 1992, the 114-year-old chapel was rededicated after a year of renovation and careful restoration. President Lowell R. Tingey of the Pennsylvania Pittsburgh Mission presided (CN July 4, 1992, 11).

The remains of "the Little Colonel" (one source specified that he stood 5' 4" and weighed 95 pounds, see CWD 447–48; however, another listed him at 5' 6" and a "frail 130 pounds," [see BYUS 21, no. 4 (fall): 390] are interred in a recess situated between the two front entrances to the chapel on the west side. The granite slab covering the site simply reads, "Thomas Leiper Kane, Bvt. Major General U.S. Vols., Born Jan. 27, 1822, Died Dec. 26, 1883." Kane died in Philadelphia at "1304 Walnut Street, where he had been temporarily residing" (SIT 228; see also Philadelphia, site no. 18).

He "died from a siege of pneumonia, caught while caring for his eldest son, who had been badly burned in a natural gas explosion" (ENS 11 [Oct. 1971]: 5).

Thomas's wife, Elizabeth Dennistoun Wood Kane, notified President George Q. Cannon of the death that same day by telegraph. This was followed by a letter on the 30th, again to President Cannon, describing the circumstances of his death. She wrote: "Your friend suffered intensely until a few hours of his release, and his mind was wandering from the outset of the attack. Yet in the intervals of consciousness he was fully persuaded of the approach of death, and made efforts to give us counsel and to bid us farewell. In one of these lucid moments, he said: 'My mind is too heavy, but do send the sweetest message you can make up to my Mormon friends—*to all my dear Mormon friends.*' Nothing I could 'make up,' I am persuaded could be sweeter to you than this evidence that you were in his latest thoughts" (SIT 228–29; ENS 11 [Oct. 1971]: 5).

■ **ANOUTOK, OR KANE MANOR.** Anoutok is located on the east side of Kane as you enter the community on U.S. 6. At the junction of U.S. 6 and Clay Street proceed north to 230 Clay Street, on the right-hand (east) side of the street. Today the house, a bed-and-breakfast establishment, is called the Kane Manor Country Inn.

Following the death of Thomas L. Kane, his widow, Elizabeth Dennistoun Wood Kane, built Anoutok, which she named after an Eskimo word meaning "wind loved spot." Jean Du Val Kane, a great-grandson of General Kane, informed the author:

> According to my Mother Ruth Wade Kane, Col. Kane may have been aware of the plans to build Anoutok. My lst. cousin who was born and raised in Anoutok and is the son of one of the Elisha Kent Kanes, tells me that he knows Col. Thomas Leiper Kane never lived in Anoutok. . . . Another of Col. Kane's sons, Dr. Evan O'Neil Kane, my grandfather, inherited Anoutok from his mother Dr. Elizabeth Denniston Wood Kane. My grand father had a son named Elisha Kent Kane, that the family called Sashy. Sashy's son Thomas L. Kane, my first cousin grew up in Anoutok and inherited it when his mother Gladys Kane died. The place became too much of a burden for him

and he sold it about ten years ago. Anoutok is now operated as a bed and breakfast inn.[4] (JDK Aug. 4, 1996)

Elizabeth Dennistoun Wood Kane, born on May 12, 1836, died in Kane, PA, on May 29, 1909. She is buried in the Kane family crypt set in the side of a hill on the north edge of the Forest Lawn Cemetery ¼ mile south of Kane on State 66. A granite slab identifies nine other members of the Kane Family who are also buried in the crypt (ELB Oct. 10, 1996).

Erie County

Erie County is located in the NW corner of Pennsylvania, bounded on the north by Lake Erie, on the east by the state of New York, and on the west by the state of Ohio.

Due to its unique "peninsular" location between Ohio (just 60 miles east of Kirtland) and New York, Erie Co. received an unusual amount of attention from Mormon missionaries going to and coming from New York, New England, and Canada. Missionaries could travel along either the Lake Road, close to Lake Erie, or along the Ridge Road, which was 1½ to 2 miles south of the lake. The Ridge Road took the elders through the villages of West Springfield, Springfield, Fairview, Swanville, Erie, and North East Township (PEN 22–25).

■ **SPRINGFIELD TOWNSHIP**

Springfield Township is 24 miles SW of Erie, PA, the county seat, and is in the NW corner of the county. The community of West Springfield is located on U.S. 20 and was one of the early preaching stations for the missionaries.

On Sept. 22, 1831, **Jared Carter** and **Ebenezer Page** left Kirtland, OH, on a mission to the East. They passed through Erie Co., preaching and relieving pain through their administrations to the infirm. They later split their efforts, Ebenezer Page going to the

---

[4] Jean Du Val Kane and his wife, Judith Flatter Kane, have been members of the LDS Church since 1962. The author cannot help but think that Thomas L. Kane would be very pleased that such family alliances have since been formed with his "dear Mormon friends."

town of Chenango, NY, and Jared going on to Benson, VT. Jared started his return west on Jan. 15, 1832. In the town of Springfield, PA, he encountered **Samuel Smith** and **Orson Hyde** on Feb. 25, 1832. The missionaries held a number of meetings in the area (JCJ 1, 6–8; MNE 20–21). Elders Hyde and Smith baptized five or six converts in Springfield Township. Before going on to the "eastern countries" they ordained Brother Simmons an elder (probably Horace T. Simmons) and organized a small branch. Elders John F. Boynton and Evan M. Greene followed, arriving in Springfield on Jan. 17, 1833. Their labors resulted in the baptism of 13 converts (PEN 30–31, 37; MECP 66).

■ **ELK CREEK TOWNSHIP**

Elk Creek Township is 16 miles SW of Erie, PA, the county seat. The community of Cranesville, located on State 18 1½ miles north of the intersection of U.S. 6N and State 18, is on the western border of Elk Creek Township.

Elders John F. Boynton and Evan M. Greene proselyted in Erie Co. from Jan. to Apr. of 1833, working in the communities of Elk Creek, Springfield, Taylor Settlement, Girard, Jackson's Settlement, and Sherman's Corners. A total of 90 persons were baptized. Twenty-nine of this number were in Elk Creek, where they organized a branch of the Church. **Stephen Winchester,** who later marched with Zion's Camp in 1834 under the name of Lupton Winchester, was ordained a teacher by Elders Boynton and Greene at the organization of the branch and told to "watch over the Church at Elk Creek" (MECP 76; PEN 37).

Benjamin Winchester, another future marcher in Zion's Camp, a great missionary, and a pamphleteer, was baptized by Elders Boynton and Greene at Elk Creek on Jan. 27, 1833. Moses Martin, who also marched with Zion's Camp, joined the Church at Elk Creek on Feb. 19, 1833. **Jedediah M. Grant,** another member of Zion's Camp, and later Second Counselor to President Brigham Young in 1854, was baptized by John Boynton at Elk Creek on Mar. 2, 1833. Among other future Zion's Camp marchers who joined the Church in Erie Co. during this same general time period were William H. H. Sagers (Harrison Sagers), Samuel T. Winegar, and Joseph Hartshorn (PEN 38–41; MECP 54, 64, 77).

ABOUT THE GENERAL EDITOR

Dr. LaMar C. Berrett, the general editor of the six-volume work *Sacred Places* and an author in volume two, is a professor emeritus of Church History and Doctrine at Brigham Young University. He was born and reared in Riverton, UT, and served as a rifleman and platoon runner in the Second Infantry Division of the United States Army during World War II. While serving, Dr. Berrett spent 110 "combat days" in Belgium, Germany, and Czechoslovakia during the famous Battle of the Bulge. He later served a mission in the Southern states where he served as a counselor to the mission president, and has since served in many positions in the Church including stake clerk, high councilor, bishop's counselor, and bishop. He was a member of the Church Historical Arts and Sites subcommittee for three years, and was the president of his family genealogical organization for 25 years.

Dr. Berrett received a bachelor's degree in business from the University of Utah. He went on to earn a master's degree in Church history and philosophy and a doctorate in educational administration from BYU. Following nine years as a seminary teacher, Dr. Berrett joined the BYU faculty, teaching at the university for 29 years and serving as the chair of the Church History Department for nine years before his retirement in 1991.

Dr. Berrett has researched, written, and directed many TV and video productions for use in the classroom. He is the author of several books, including the much acclaimed *Discovering the World of the Bible*. He conducted a comprehensive aerial photography project in 1978, which involved infrared photography of significant Church history sites from New Hampshire to Salt Lake City. Dr. Berrett has also conducted numerous Church history travel tours and has hosted over 150 tours worldwide.

Over 50 percent of the text of *Sacred Places* was written by Dr. Berrett, and with the help of the authors, he produced all of the maps included in the series and took all photographs unless otherwise noted.

A lifetime of researching the history of The Church of Jesus Christ of Latter-day Saints has been to Dr. Berrett a "soul-satisfying labor of love."

Dr. Berrett and his wife, the former Darlene Hamilton, reside in Orem, UT. The couple has nine children.

ABOUT THE AUTHOR

Dr. Larry C. Porter is a professor of Church History and Doctrine at Brigham Young University. He received his B.A. degree in history from Utah State University. His M.A. and Ph.D. degrees are from BYU in history of religion with an emphasis on LDS Church history. After 11 years in the LDS Seminary program, Dr. Porter joined Brigham Young University full-time in 1970. For seven years he served as chair of the Department of Church History and Doctrine and six years as director of the Church history area of the BYU Religious Studies Center. Dr. Porter is presently on the *BYU Studies* Board of Editors. Since 1998 he has been designated the Richard L. Evans Professor of Religious Understanding. He is an accomplished author of books and articles on LDS Church history. Dr. Porter has served as a missionary in the Northern States Mission and as a bishop and high councilman. For 11 years he was a member/chair of the Correlation Review Committee of the Church and served for three years with the Melchizedek Priesthood and Relief Society Curriculum Writing Committee of the Church. He is currently a high priest group leader in his ward. Dr. Porter was born in Logan, Utah. He is married to the former LaDawn Thain of Benson Ward, Utah, and they are the parents of nine children.

Abbreviations Used in Photo Captions

LDSCA   Archives Division, Church Historical Department, The Church of Jesus Christ of Latter-day Saints, Salt Lake City, UT

RLDSLA   Library-Archives and Museum, Reorganized Church of Jesus Christ of Latter Day Saints, World Headquarters, Independence, MO

USHS   Utah State Historical Society, Salt Lake City, UT

Bibliography

ABCHP   Bean, Willard. *A.B.C. History of Palmyra and the Beginning of "Mormonism."* Palmyra, NY: Palmyra Courier Co., 1938.

ABM   Van Wagoner, Richard S., and Steven C. Walker. *A Book of Mormons.* Salt Lake City: Signature Books, 1982.

AHB   Barben, Arnold H. "Notes on 'The Kingdom.'" Seneca Fall Historical Society, n.d.

AMB   Flake, Chad J., ed. *A Mormon Bibliography 1830–1930.* Salt Lake City: University of Utah Press, 1978.

AMGJ   Greenfield, Albert M., Jr. Interview by Larry C. Porter. Glen Moore, PA.

AOJ   Greeley, Horace. *An Overland Journey.* New York: C.M. Saxton, Barker, and Co., 1860.

APH   Rogers, David White. In *A Proud Heritage.* Vol. 2. Comp.

Carolyn B. Strong. N.p., n.d. Copy in possession of Patricia Hoffman, Orem, UT.

APPP   Pratt, Parley P. *Autobiography of Parley P. Pratt.* 4th ed. Salt Lake City: Deseret Book Co., 1938; see also 1985 Classics in Mormon Literature edition.

APT   Matthews, Robert J. *"A Plainer Translation": Joseph Smith's Translation of the Bible; History and Commentary.* Provo, UT: Brigham Young University Press, 1975.

ASG   Bangerter, Geraldine Hamblin, and Susan Easton Black. *My Servant Algernon Sidney Gilbert: Provide for My Saints (D&C 57:10).* N.p.: Rollins, Bangerter, and Hamblin families, 1989.

ATTC   Bodine, Charles W., and others. *A Tale of Three Churches.* Kane, PA: Centennial Observance Committee, The First United Church of Kane, United Presbyterian, 1974.

AWB   Bean, Willard Washington. "Autobiography of Willard Washington Bean." Typescript. Copy in possession of Larry C. Porter, Department of Church History and Doctrine, Brigham Young University, Provo, UT.

AYP   Dunshee, Kenneth H. *As You Pass By.* New York: Hastings House Publishers, 1952.

BE   Jenson, Andrew, comp. *Latter-day Saint Biographical Encyclopedia.* 4 vols. Salt Lake City: Andrew Jenson Memorial Association, 1901–36; Salt Lake City: Deseret News Press, 1971.

BGC   Fink, Daniel. *Barns of the Genesee Country, 1790–1915.* Geneseo, NY: James Brunner, 1988.

BHR   Madsen, Truman G. *Defender of the Faith: The B. H. Roberts Story.* Salt Lake City: Bookcraft, 1980.

BJ   *Brother Jonathan.* (Published weekly) Wilson and Co., New York, December 14, 1839. Vol. 1, no. 23.

BTLK   Kane, Sybil Kent. "Biography of General Thomas L. Kane." Typescript. In possession of Larry C. Porter, Department of Church History and Doctrine, Brigham Young University, Provo, UT.

BWM   Mace, Wandle. *The Biography of Wandle Mace as Told to Rebecca E. H. Mace, His Second Wife.* Salt Lake City: William M. Mace, n.d.

BY   Youngreen, Buddy. Interview by Larry C. Porter, Provo, UT.

BYAH   Spencer, Clarissa Young, with Mabel Harmen. *Brigham Young at Home.* Salt Lake City: Deseret Book Co., 1947.

BYAM   Arrington, Leonard J. *Brigham Young: American Moses.* New York: Alfred A. Knopf, 1985.

BYNY   Palmer, Richard F., and Karl D. Butler. *Brigham Young: The New York Years.* Provo, UT: Charles Redd Center for Western Studies, Brigham Young University, 1982; distributed by Signature Books, Midvale, UT.

BYUS   *Brigham Young University Studies.* Published quarterly at Brigham Young University, Provo, UT.

CD   Decker, Charles. Interview by Larry C. Porter. Afton, NY.

CEZ   Zefla, Elizabeth (Mrs. Clarence). Interview by Larry C. Porter. Morris, PA.

CHC   Roberts, Brigham H. *A Comprehensive History of the Church of Jesus Christ of Latter-day Saints.* 6 vols. Salt Lake City: The Church of Jesus Christ of Latter-day Saints, 1930.

ChCh   Jenson, Andrew, comp. *Church Chronology.* Salt Lake City: Deseret News Press, 1914.

CHFT   *Church History in the Fullness of Times* [Church Educational System Manual]. Salt Lake City: The Church of Jesus Christ of Latter-day Saints, 1989.

CHST   Willers, Diedrich. *Centennial Historical Sketch of the Town of Fayette, Seneca County, New York.* Geneva, NY: W. F. Humphrey, 1900.

CLNY   Shelgren, Olaf William Jr. and others. *Cobblestone Landmarks of New York State.* Syracuse: Syracuse University Press, 1978.

CM   Schmidt, Carl F. *Cobblestone Masonry.* Scottsville, NY: N.p., 1966.

CN   *LDS Church News.* Salt Lake City: The Church of Jesus Christ of Latter-day Saints, 1936–.

COLC   Copyright Office, Library of Congress, Washington, D.C.

CRB   Baker, Charles R. [Friends (Quaker) Church]. Interview by Larry C. Porter. Farmington, NY.

CS   *Deseret News,* Church Section. Salt Lake City, UT.

CTA   Baugh, Alexander L. "A Call to Arms: The 1838 Mormon Defense of Northern Missouri." Ph.D. diss., Brigham Young University, 1996.

CWD   Boatner, Mark Mayo, III. *The Civil War Dictionary*. Rev. ed. New York: McKay Books, 1988.

DA   Monson, Samuel C. "The Deseret Alphabet." Master's thesis, Columbia University, 1948.

DBS   Skoubye, Dan B. Interview by Larry C. Porter. Pittsburgh, PA.

DEN   *Deseret Evening News*. Salt Lake City, UT, 1867–1920.

DFB   Boone, David F. Interview by Larry C. Porter. Provo, UT.

DHW   Hinckley, Bryant S. *Daniel Hanmer Wells and Events of His Time*. Salt Lake City: Deseret News Press, 1942.

DIA   *Dialogue: A Journal of Mormon Thought*. Dialogue Foundation, Salt Lake City, UT.

DIH   Haight, Isaac. Diary. Typescript. In possession of Larry C. Porter, Department of Church History and Doctrine, Brigham Young University, Provo, UT.

DJT   Tanner, Maurice. *Descendents of John Tanner*. Salt Lake City: Tanner Family Association, 1923.

DLC   Cook, David L. Letter to Larry C. Porter, Rochester, NY, Sept. 8, 1999.

DLE   Enders, Donald L. Interview by Larry C. Porter. Salt Lake City, UT.

DLP   Sudweeks, Joseph. *Discontinued L.D.S. Periodicals*. Provo, UT: Brigham Young University, 1955.

DN   *Deseret News*, 1850–.

DNCA   *Deseret News Church Almanac*. Published biannually in Salt Lake City by the *Deseret News* in cooperation with the LDS Church Historical Department, 1974–.

DPOR   Shields, Steven L. *Divergent Paths of the Restoration*, 4th ed. Los Angeles: Restoration Research, 1990.

DWI   *David Whitmer Interviews: A Restoration Witness*. Ed. Lyndon W. Cook. Orem, UT: Grandin Book Co., 1991.

EBB   Beavers, Edward B. Interview by Larry C. Porter. Manchester, NY.

EC   Wyld, Lionel D., ed. *40'x 28' x 4': The Erie Canal— 150 Years*. Rome, NY: Oneida County Erie Canal Commemoration Commission, 1967.

EEL   Lupold, Earl E. Interview by Larry C. Porter. Manchester, NY.

EH   Jenson, Andrew. *Encyclopedic History of the Church of Jesus Christ of Latter-day Saints.* Salt Lake City: Deseret News Publishing Co., 1941.

EHFS   Hunter, William E. *Edward Hunter, Faithful Steward.* Ed. Janath Russell Cannon. Salt Lake City: Mrs.William E. Hunter, Lithographed in U.S.A. by Publishers Press, 1970.

EJ   *Elder's Journal of the Church of Latter Day Saints.* Kirtland, Ohio, October 1837–December 1837. Far West, Missouri, July–August 1838.

EL   Peterson, Janet, and LaRene Gaunt. *Elect Ladies.* Salt Lake City: Deseret Book Co., 1990.

ELB   Baxter, Edward L. Interview by Larry C. Porter. Kane, PA.

EMP   Whittaker, David J. "Early Mormon Pamphleteering." Ph.D. diss., Brigham Young University, 1982.

EMS   *Evening & Morning Star.* Published in Independence, MO, June 1832–July 1833; Kirtland, OH, December 1833–September 1834.

EM   Ludlow, Daniel H., ed. *Encyclopedia of Mormonism.* 5 vols. New York: Macmillan Publishing Co., 1992.

ENS   *Ensign.* Published monthly by The Church of Jesus Christ of Latter-day Saints, Salt Lake City, UT. 1971–.

EPPP   Pratt, Parley P. *The Essential Parley P. Pratt.* Salt Lake City: Signature Books, 1990.

ERA   *Improvement Era.* Salt Lake City: The Church of Jesus Christ of Latter-day Saints, 1897–1970.

ES   Larson, Andrew Karl. *Erastus Snow: The Life of a Missionary and Pioneer for the Early Mormon Church.* Salt Lake City: University of Utah Press, 1971.

ETB   Dew, Sheri L. *Ezra Taft Benson, A Biography.* Salt Lake City: Deseret Book Co., 1987.

EvM   *New York City Evening Mirror.*

EWW   Shaw, Ronald E. *Erie Water West: A History of the Erie Canal, 1792–1854.* Lexington: University of Kentucky Press, 1966.

EXWM   Mace, Wandle. *Excerpts from the Life Story of Wandle Mace, 1809–1890.* Dugway, UT: Pioneer Press, 1970.

FCSA   Franklin County School Annual. Chambersburg, PA.
            Nov. 17–21, 1930.

FNYWR   *Friendship (New York) Weekly Register.*

FTHV   Aston, Ralph R., Matilda Lux Aston, and Duane R.
            Aston. *From These Hills and Valleys: A Brief History of The
            Church of Jesus Christ of Latter-day Saints in Southwestern
            Pennsylvania.* Ed. David Brent and Lynn Matthews
            Anderson.Wilkinsburg, PA: Hoechstetter Printing,
            1986.

FWR   *Far West Record: Minutes of The Church of Jesus Christ of
            Latter-day Saints, 1830–1844.* Ed. Donald Q. Cannon
            and Lyndon W. Cook. Salt Lake City: Deseret Book
            Co., 1983.

GAS   Jarvis, Zora Smith, comp. *Ancestry, Biography and Family
            of George A. Smith.* Provo, UT: Brigham Young
            University Press, 1962.

GBTW   Clark, John A. *Gleanings by the Way.* Philadelphia: W. J.
            and J. K. Simon, 1842.

GHSW   Welch, E. L. *"Grip's" Historical Souvenir of Waterloo, N. Y.*
            No. 16 of the Historical Souvenir Series. Waterloo, NY:
            N.p., 1903.

GLR   Rhodes, Gary L. Interview by Larry C. Porter.
            Belleville, NY.

GNY   Spafford, Horatio Gates. *A Gazetteer of the State of New-
            York.* Albany: B. D. Packard, 1824.

GNYS   French, J. H. *Gazetteer of the State of New York.* Syracuse:
            R. P. Smith, 1860.

GR   Ricks, Gordon. Letter to Larry C. Porter. Kane, PA.

GSNY   *A Gazetteer of the State of New-York.* Albany: J. Disturnell,
            1842.

HAC   Minard, John S. *History of Allegany County and Its People.*
            Ed. Georgia Drew Merrill. Alfred, NY: W.A. Fergusson
            & Co., 1896.

HACP   Cushing, Thomas B., ed. *History of Allegheny County,
            Pennsylvania.* Chicago: A. Warner and Co., 1889.

HC   Smith, Joseph, Jr. *History of the Church of Jesus Christ of
            Latter-day Saints.* 7 vols. Edited by B. H. Roberts. 4th ed.
            Salt Lake City: Deseret Book Co., 1965.

HCJ   Jacob, R. Leone. *A History of Colesville 1785–1985.*
            Published by the Town of Colesville, 1978.

HCJC   Cadman, W. H. *A History of the Church of Jesus Christ* [Bickertonites]. Monongahela, PA: The Church of Jesus Christ, 1945.

HCKM   Kimball, Stanley B. *Heber C. Kimball: Mormon Patriarch and Pioneer.* Urbana: University of Illinois Press, 1981.

HFT   *Honeoye Falls (New York) Times.*

HHC   Christensen, Horace H. Interview by Larry C. Porter. Endwell, NY.

HIB   Young, S. Dilworth. *"Here Is Brigham . . ."* Salt Lake City: Bookcraft, 1964.

HiR   *The Historical Record.* (Periodical published monthly in Salt Lake City by Andrew Jenson, assistant Church historian, 1882–90.) Vols. 5–8 published in *Church Encyclopedia.* Book 1. Salt Lake City: Andrew Jenson, 1889.

HJS   Smith, Lucy Mack. *History of Joseph Smith by His Mother, Lucy Mack Smith.* Salt Lake City: Bookcraft, 1958.

HOC   McIntosh, W. H. *History of Ontario County, New York.* Philadelphia: Everts, Ensign and Everts, 1876.

HONY   Milliken, Charles F. *A History of Ontario County, New York, and Its People.* New York: Lewis Historical Publishing Co., 1911.

HPGP   Turner, Orasmus. *History of the Pioneer Settlement of Phelps and Gorham's Purchase.* Rochester: William Alling, 1851.

HSP   Corbett, Pearson H. *Hyrum Smith, Patriarch.* Salt Lake City: Deseret Book Co., 1963.

HVNY   Van Denbergh, John Wyman. *History of Victor, New York, from 1669 to 1900.* Extracts from the *Victor Herald,* Jan. 5, to July 20, 1900. Victor, NY: N.p., 1900.

HVW   Becker, John E. *A History of the Village of Waterloo, New York.* Waterloo: Waterloo Library and Historical Society, 1949.

IAD   Dillman, Allie W. Interview with Larry C. Porter. Victor, NY.

IBMW   Anderson, Richard Lloyd. *Investigating the Book of Mormon Witnesses.* Salt Lake City: Deseret Book Co., 1981.

IBS   Barlow, Ora H. *The Israel Barlow Story and Mormon Mores.* Salt Lake City: Publishers Press, 1968.

IGA   Anderson, Gary. Interview by LaMar C. Berrett. Provo, UT, Apr. 7, 1988.

IJWW   Welch, John W. Interview. Brigham Young University, Provo, UT.

IOM   Stokes, I. N. Phelps. *The Iconography of Manhattan Island, 1498–1909*. Vol. 3. New York: Arno Press, 1967.

IWP   Index of Wills and Proceedings. Surrogate's Office, St. Lawrence County, Canton, NY.

JCJ   Carter, Jared. Journal. Special Collections, Harold B. Lee Library, Brigham Young University, Provo, UT.

JD   *Journal of Discourses*. 26 Vols. Liverpool: Latter-day Saints' Book Depot, 1853–86.

JDK   Kane, Jean Du Val. Letter to Larry C. Porter. Richmond, VA.

JEdS   Stevenson, Edward. Journal. Holograph. LDS Church Archives, Salt Lake City, UT.

JH   Journal History of The Church of Jesus Christ of Latter-day Saints. Manuscript. LDS Church Archives, Salt Lake City, UT.

JI   *Juvenile Instructor.* Variation of title of *The Instructor.* See ThI.

JJET   Talmage, James E. Journal. Special Collections, Harold B. Lee Library, Brigham Young University, Provo, UT.

JJNS   Smith, Jesse Nathaniel. *The Journal of Jesse Nathaniel Smith.* 3d ed. Ed. Oliver R. Smith. Provo, UT: Jesse N. Smith Family Association, 1970.

JOBH   Huntington, Oliver B. Journal. Utah State Historical Society, Salt Lake City, Utah.

JoHi   *Journal of History.* 18 vols. Lamoni, IA, and Independence, MO: Board of Publication, Reorganized Church of Jesus Christ of Latter Day Saints, 1908–25.

JMG   Judd, Mary G. *Jedediah M. Grant, Pioneer-Statesman.* Salt Lake City: Deseret News Press, 1959.

JRC   Fox, Frank W. *J. Reuben Clark, the Public Years.* Provo, UT: Brigham Young University Press; Salt Lake City: Deseret Book Co., 1980.

JSF   Fisher, J. Sheldon. Interview by Larry C. Porter. Fisher, NY.

JSFV   Backman, Milton V., Jr. *Joseph Smith's First Vision.* 2d ed. Salt Lake City: Bookcraft, 1980.

JSGe   Genung, John S. Interview by Larry C. Porter. Waterloo, NY.

JS—H   Joseph Smith—History. The Pearl of Great Price. Salt Lake City: The Church of Jesus Christ of Latter-day Saints, 1981.

JSN   Anderson, Richard L. *Joseph Smith's New England Heritage.* Salt Lake City: Deseret Book Co., 1971.

JSPM   Black, Susan Easton, and Charles D. Tate Jr., eds. *Joseph Smith: The Prophet, The Man.* Provo, UT: Religious Studies Center, Brigham Young University, 1993.

JSR   Barrett, Ivan J. *Joseph Smith and the Restoration.* 2d ed. Provo, UT: Brigham Young University Press, 1973.

JTHF   Tanner, George S. *John Tanner and His Family.* Salt Lake City: John Tanner Family Association, 1974.

JWEM   McLellin, William E. *The Journals of William E. McLellin 1831–1836.* Ed. Jan Shipps and John W. Welch. Provo, UT: Brigham Young University Studies: Brigham Young University; Urbana: University of Illinois Press, 1994.

JWHy   Hyde, William. Journal. Typescript in possession of Larry C. Porter, Department of Church History and Doctrine, Brigham Young University, Provo, UT.

JWMa   Mace, Wandle. Journal. Special Collections, Harold B. Lee Library, Brigham Young University, Provo, UT. Typescript.

JWW   Woodruff, Willford. *Wilford Woodruff's Journal, 1833–1898.* 9 vols. Ed. Scott G. Kenney. Midvale, UT: Signature Books, 1983.

KCJ   *Kansas City [MO] Journal.*

KCDJ   *Kansas City [MO] Daily Journal.*

KHS   Wright, Kenneth D. "Mormons on the Conococheague." *The Kittochtinny Historical Society: Papers Read Before the Society, September 1981 to May 1984.* Vol. 18. Waynesboro, PA: The Caslon Press, 1984.

LAE   Everrett, Addison. Letter to Joseph F. Smith. St. George, UT, Jan. 16, 1882.

LAS   Skabelund, Lynn A. Interview by Larry C. Porter. Logan, Utah.

LBF   Weems, M. L. *The Life of Benjamin Franklin.*
          Philadelphia: Uriah Hunt and Sons, 1845.

LC   Colletta, Lil [Kittochtinny Historical Society]. Inter-
          view by Larry C. Porter. Chambersburg, PA.

LCD   Longwith, David. *Longwith's City Directory* (New York
          City). Published annually by New York State Historical
          Society, New York, NY.

LHCK   Whitney, Orson F. *Life of Heber C. Kimball.* 5th ed. Salt
          Lake City: Kimball Family, 1888.

LJT   Roberts, Brigham H. *The Life of John Taylor, Third
          President of The Church of Jesus Christ of Latter-day Saints.*
          Salt Lake City: Bookcraft, 1963.

LJTC   Townsend, Jesse. Letter to Elisha Camp. Palmyra, N.Y.,
          Aug. 16, 1834. Cornell University, Ithaca, New York.

LNY   Packer, Rand Hugh. "History of Four Mormon
          Landmarks in Western New York: The Joseph Smith
          Farm, Hill Cumorah, the Martin Harris Farm, and the
          Peter Whitmer, Sr., Farm." Master's thesis, Brigham
          Young University, 1975.

LOL   Black, Susan Easton and Larry C. Porter, eds. *Lion of
          the Lord: Essays on the Life and Service of Brigham Young.*
          Salt Lake City: Deseret Book Co., 1995.

LOP   England, Breck. *The Life and Thought of Orson Pratt.* Salt
          Lake City: University of Utah Press, 1985.

LS   Smith, Lucy Mack. Manuscript. LDS Church Archives,
          Salt Lake City, UT.

LTGP   Peck, Reverend George. *The Life and Times of Reverend
          George Peck,* D.D. New York: Nelson and Phillips, 1874.

LWCNY   Cowles, George W. *Landmarks of Wayne County, New
          York.* Syracuse: D. Mason and Co., 1895.

LZC   Stephens, Calvin R. "The Life and Contributions of
          Zebedee Coltrin." Master's thesis, Brigham Young
          University, 1974.

M&A   *Messenger and Advocate.* Kirtland, OH: The Church of
          Jesus Christ of Latter-day Saints, 1834–37.

MCSC   *Manual of the Churches of Seneca County with Sketches of
          Their Pastors.* Seneca Falls, NY: Courier Printing Co.,
          1896.

ME   Newell, Linda King, and Valeen Tippetts Avery.

Mormon Enigma: Emma Hale Smith. Garden City, NY: Doubleday and Co., 1984.

MECP Bean, Cheryl Harmon, and Pamela Call Johnson, comps. *Rediscovering History: Mormons in Erie County, Pennsylvania, 1832–1833.* St. Anthony, ID: Cheryl's Creations and Publications, 1996.

MED Brown, Charles W. "Manchester in the Early Days." Typescript located in "Newspaper Clippings and Histories, 1883–1911." Special Collections, Harold B. Lee Library, Brigham Young University, Provo, UT.

MH Gunnell, Wayne Cutler. "Martin Harris—Witness and Benefactor to the Book of Mormon." Master's thesis, Brigham Young University, 1955.

MHBY Young, Brigham. *Manuscript History of Brigham Young.* Ed. Elden Jay Watson. Vol. *1801–1844,* Salt Lake City: Smith Secretarial Services, 1968. Vol. *1846–1847,* Salt Lake City: E. J. Watson, 1971.

MHPF Martin Harris Pension Files. War of 1812, National Archives, Washington, D.C.

MHS Tuckett, Madge Harris, and Belle Harris Wilson. *The Martin Harris Story.* Pleasant Grove, UT: Vintage Books, 1983; Provo, UT: Press Publishing, 1983.

MHT Tuckett, Madge Harris. Interview by Larry C. Porter. American Fork, UT.

MHWC Clark, Lewis H. *Military History of Wayne County, N.Y.* Sodus, NY: Lewis H. Clark, Hulett and Gaylord, 1883.

MLR Johnson, Benjamin F. *My Life's Review.* 1979 ed. Independence, MO: Zion's Printing and Publishing Co., 1947.

MNE Williams, Richard Shelton. "The Missionary Movements of the LDS Church in New England, 1830–1850." Master's thesis, Brigham Young University, 1969.

MS *Millennial Star.* Liverpool: The Church of Jesus Christ of Latter-day Saints, 1840–1970.

MT Sessions, Gene A. *Mormon Thunder: A Documentary History of Jedediah Morgan Grant.* Urbana: University of Illinois Press, 1982.

MTPa Patton, Minor T. Unpublished paper on the role of Christina Graves Grainger in the settlement of the

Martin Harris and E.B. Grandin mortgage agreement pertaining to the publication of the Book of Mormon. LDS Church Archives, Salt Lake City, UT.

MUV Howe, Eber D. *Mormonism Unvailed.* Painesville, OH: Published by the author, 1834.

MW Wentworth, Marjorie. Interview by Larry C. Porter. Friendship, NY.

MWN *Manhattan [New York] Ward Newsletter.*

NEW Porter, Larry C. "A Study of the Origins of the Church of Jesus Christ of Latter-day Saints in the States of New York and Pennsylvania, 1816–1831." Ph.D. diss., Brigham Young University, 1971.

NTAM *Naked Truths About Mormonism.* Oakland, CA: Deming & Co., Jan. and Apr. 1888.

NYCA *New York Commercial Advertiser.*

NYD Taylor, John, ed. *Trows' New York City Directory, 1856.* New York: n.p., 1856.

NYDH New York State Department of Health. Verified transcript from the Register of Deaths. Albany, NY.

NYH *New York [City] Herald.*

NYHi *New York History.* Cooperstown, NY: New York State Historical Association, n.d.

NYP *New York Post.*

NYT *New York Times.* New York: W. Holland, E. Sanford, E.W. Davis, Pub.

NYTC *New York Times and Commercial Intelligencer.* New York: N.T. Eldridge and Donald Macleod, Editors and Proprietors.

NYTCA *New York Times and Commercial Advertiser.* New York: Francis Hall and Co.

NYTr *New York Tribune.*

OCAR Ontario County, NY. Assessment Rolls. Office of the Ontario County historian, Ontario County Office Building, Canandaigua, NY.

OMP Holzapfel, Richard, and T. Jeffery Cottle. *Old Mormon Palmyra and New England.* Santa Ana, CA: Fieldbrook Productions, 1991.

OPH Carter, Kate B. comp. *Our Pioneer Heritage.* 20 vols. Salt Lake City: Daughters of the Utah Pioneers, 1958–77.

ORH Barron, Howard H. *Orson Hyde: Missionary, Apostle, Colonizer.* Bountiful, UT: Horizon Publishers, 1977.

ORPM Tucker, Pomeroy. *Origin, Rise, and Progress of Mormonism.* New York: D. Appleton and Co., 1867.

ORS Smith, Oliver R. Interview by Larry C. Porter. Provo, UT.

PAD Smith, Joseph F. *Proceedings at the Dedication of the Joseph Smith Memorial Monument.* Salt Lake City: The Church of Jesus Christ of Latter-day Saints, 1906.

PB Brown, Peggy. Interview by Larry C. Porter. Friendship, NY.

PBC Troskosky, Betty, ed. *Palmyra—A Bicentennial Celebration, 1789–1989.* Interlaken, NY: Heart of the Lakes Publishing, 1989.

PBP Packer, Palmyra Bean. Interview by Larry C. Porter. Provo, UT.

PCIR Palmyra Cemetery Interment Records. Palmyra City Cemetery Superintendent's Office, Palmyra, N. Y.

PEM Perris, William. *Maps of the City of New York, 1852.* New York: New York Historical Society Library, n.d.

PEN Curtis, V. Alan. "Missionary Activities and Church Organizations in Pennsylvania, 1830–1840." Master's thesis, Brigham Young University, Provo, UT, 1976.

PENR Rosenbaum, Paul Zilch. "The Church of Jesus Christ of Latter-day Saints in Pennsylvania (1830–1854)." Master's thesis, East Stroudsburg State College, 1982.

PJE Porter, Larry C., and Susan Easton Black, eds. *The Prophet Joseph: Essays on the Life and Mission of Joseph Smith.* Salt Lake City: Deseret Book Co., 1988.

PJS Smith, Joseph. *The Papers of Joseph Smith.* Ed. Dean C. Jessee. 2 vols. Salt Lake City: Deseret Book Co., 1989.

PNY *Palmyra, New York, 1789–1964, 175th Year.* Palmyra, NY: n.p., 1964.

POU Bagg, M. M. *The Pioneers of Utica.* Utica, NY: Curtiss and Childs, 1877.

PP Gregg, Thomas. *The Prophet of Palmyra.* New York: John B. Alden, 1890.

PPM Esshom, Frank. Pioneers and Prominent Men of Utah. Salt Lake City: Utah Pioneers Book Publishing Co., 1913.

PPN   Espenshade, A. Howry. *Pennsylvania Place Names.*
          Harrisburg: Evangelical Press, 1925.

PR   Dewey, Richard Lloyd. *Porter Rockwell: A Biography.* New
          York: Paramount Books, 1986.

PS   Steele, Pat. Interview by Larry C. Porter, Bolton
          Landing, NY.

PV   Cook, Thomas L. *Palmyra and Vicinity.* Palmyra:
          Palmyra Courier-Journal, 1930.

PWC   *Palmyra, Wayne County, New York.* Comp. Woman's
          Society of the Western Presbyterian Church. Rochester:
          Herald Press, 1907.

PWJS   Smith, Joseph. *The Personal Writings of Joseph Smith.* Ed.
          Dean C. Jessee. Salt Lake City: Deseret Book Co., 1984.

REF   *Reflector.* Palmyra, NY.

RFF   Robinson Family File. King's Daughters' Library.
          Palmyra, NY.

ROL   Lowe, Robert O. Interview by Larry C. Porter. Palmyra,
          NY.

RPJS   Cook, Lyndon W. *The Revelations of the Prophet Joseph
          Smith: A Historical and Biographical Commentary of the
          Doctrine and Covenants.* Provo, UT: Seventy's Mission
          Bookstore, 1981.

RSNY   Porter, Larry C., Milton V. Backman Jr., and Susan
          Easton Black, eds. *Regional Studies in Latter-day Saint
          Church History, New York.* Provo, UT: Department of
          Church History and Doctrine, Brigham Young
          University, 1992.

RSOH   Backman, Milton V., ed. *Regional Studies in Latter-day
          Saint Church History, Ohio.* Provo: Department of
          Church History and Doctrine, Brigham Young
          University, 1990.

SA   *Scientific American.* New York: Scientific American, Inc.

SCL   *Shipping and Commercial List and N.Y. Price Current.* New
          York: New York Historical Society, W. Burritt and E.H.
          Clayton.

SDN   *South Dayton [NY] News.*

SFR   *Seneca Falls [NY] Reveille.*

SFT   Long, Margaret. *The Santa Fe Trail: Following the Old
          Historic Pioneer Trails on the Modern Highways.* Denver:
          M. Long, W. H. Kistler Stationery Co., 1954.

SGAC   Gilbert, Algernon Sidney. "Articles and Covenants of the Church of Christ." Typescript. LDS Church Archives, Salt Lake City, UT.

SGB   Beus, Stephen G. Interview by Larry C. Porter. Pittsburgh, PA.

SH   *The Saints' Herald.* Reorganized Church of Jesus Christ of Latter Day Saints, Lamoni, IA, Independence, MO, Jan. 1860–.

SIS   Millet, Robert L., and Kent Jackson, eds. *Studies in Scripture: Vol. 1, The Doctrine and Covenants.* Sandy, UT: Randall Book Co., 1984.

SIT   Zobell, Albert L., Jr. *Sentinel in the East: A Biography of Thomas L. Kane.* Salt Lake City: Nicholas G. Morgan, 1965.

SLCI   Salt Lake City Cemetery Index.

SLIR   Salt Lake City Interment Record.

SmS   *Smart Set: The Young Women's Magazine.*

SOC   Davis, Inez Smith. *The Story of the Church.* Independence, MO: Herald Publishing House, 1964.

SP   Berrett, LaMar C., ed. *Sacred Places.* Salt Lake City: Bookcraft, 1999–.

SPR   *The Susquehanna [Montrose, PA] Register, and Northern Pennsylvanian.*

SR   Van Wagoner, Richard S. *Sidney Ridgon: A Portrait of Religious Excess.* Salt Lake City: Signature Books, 1994.

SRC   Chase, Daryl. "Sidney Rigdon—Early Mormon." Master's thesis, University of Chicago, 1931.

SRM   McKiernan, F. Mark. *The Voice of One Crying in the Wilderness: Sidney Rigdon, Religious Reformer: 1793–1876.* Lawrence, KS: Coronado Press, 1971.

SSS   *Silas Sanford Smith: Pioneer, Statesman, Colonizer, 1847–1910.* Comp. Albert E. Smith. Salt Lake City: n.p., 1963.

T&S   *Nauvoo Times and Seasons.* Published Monthly, 1839–46.

TAMF   Hartley, William G. *They Are My Friends: A History of the Joseph Knight Family. 1825–1850.* Provo, Utah: Grandin Book Co., 1986.

TCR   "Transcript of Conference Record, Rochester Conference, Eastern States Mission, 1923." LDS Church Archives, Salt Lake City, UT.

TCTC   Cowan, Richard O. *The Church in the Twentieth Century.*
        Salt Lake City: Bookcraft, 1985.
TF   Holmes, Reed M. *The Forerunners.* Independence, MO:
        Herald Publishing House, 1981.
ThC   *The Contributor.* 17 vols. Published monthly in Salt Lake
        City: Deseret News Press, 1879–96.
ThI   *The Instructor.* Published biweekly, monthly in Salt Lake
        City: Deseret Sunday School Union, Jan. 1, 1866–1929.
ThM   *The Mormon.* Published weekly in New York City, Feb.
        17, 1855–Sept. 19, 1857.
ThP   *The Prophet.* New York City, Society for the diffusion of
        Truth, May 18, 1844–May 24, 1845.
TMB   Wilkins, Lois Nickerson. *The Mormon Barn at Lakeville:
        A Haven for the Wanderer.* New York: Lois Nickerson
        Wilkins, 1978.
TMH   Lundwall, N. B. *Temples of the Most High.* 5th ed. Salt
        Lake City: Bookcraft, 1952.
TMS   Smith, T. Michael. Interview by Larry C. Porter. Salt
        Lake City, Utah.
TWOA   Leckie, Robert. *The Wars of America.* 2d ed., rev. and
        updated. New York: Harper Collins Publishers, 1992.
TWP   Bloxham, V. Ben, James R. Moss, and Larry C. Porter,
        eds. *Truth Will Prevail: The Rise of the Church of Jesus
        Christ of Latter-day Saints in the British Isles, 1837–1987.*
        Cambridge: The Church of Jesus Christ of Latter-day
        Saints, 1987.
UGHM   *Utah Genealogical and Historical Magazine.* Salt Lake City:
        Utah Genealogical and Historical Society, Jan.
        1910–Oct. 1940.
UTRP   Alexander, Thomas G. *Utah: The Right Place.* Salt Lake
        City: Gibbs-Smith, 1995.
VOB   Hansen, Lorin K. "Voyage of the Brooklyn." *Dialogue:
        A Journal of Mormon Thought.* 21, n. 3 (Autumn 1988).
WBFP   Zimmerman, Vicki Bean. "Willard Bean, 'The Fighting
        Parson.'" Utah: n.p., 1984.
WBFR   Bean, Willard W. "Willard Washington Bean Family
        Record." Copy in possession of Larry C. Porter,
        Department of Church History and Doctrine, Brigham
        Young University, Provo, UT.

WBM Nibley, Preston, comp. *The Witnesses of the Book of Mormon.* Salt Lake City: Stevens and Wallis, 1946.

WCJ *Wayne County [Palmyra, NY] Journal.*

WCLD Wayne County, NY, Land Deeds. Wayne County Office Building, Lyons, NY.

WM Tullidge, Edward W. *The Women of Mormondom.* New York: Tullidge and Crandall, 1877.

WSM Smith, William. *William Smith on Mormonism.* Lamoni, IA: Herald Steam Book and Job Office, 1883.

WSP *Wayne [Palmyra, NY] Sentinel*

WTSL Anderson, Karl R., and Keith W. Perkins. *A Walk Through the Sacred Land of "The Ohio": A Personal Guidebook Through the Land.* Provo, UT: n.p., 1995.

WW Woodruff, Wilford. *Wilford Woodruff, History of His Life and Labors.* Ed. Matthias F. Cowley. Salt Lake City: Bookcraft, 1964.

YR Yarn, David H., Jr. *Young Reuben; The Early Life of J. Reuben Clark.* Provo, UT: Brigham Young University Press, 1973.

ZCB Bradley, James L. *Zion's Camp, 1834: Prelude to the Civil War.* Salt Lake City: Publishers Press, 1990.

INDEX

Note: Italicized page numbers indicate photographs or illustrations; bold-faced page numbers indicate maps.